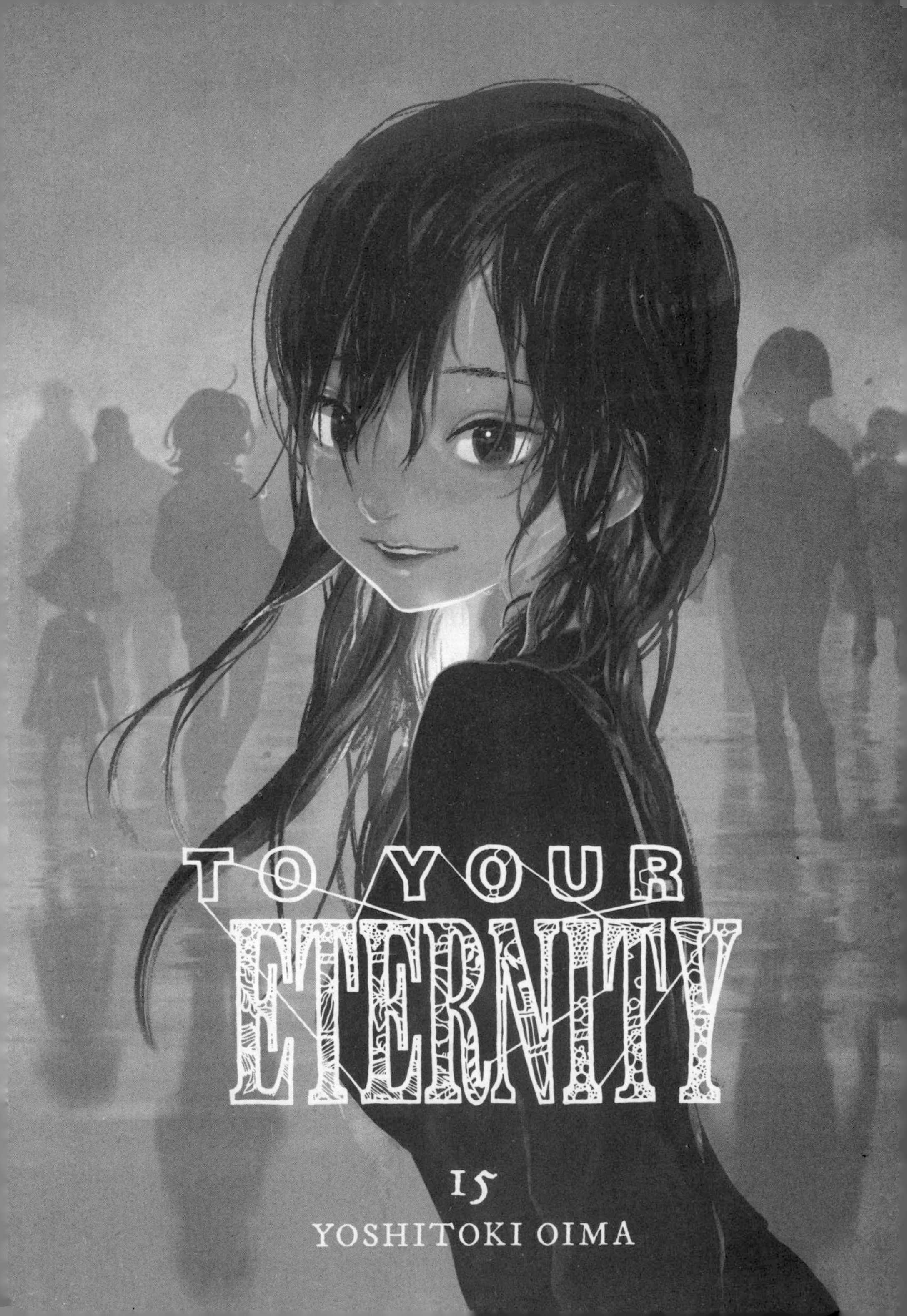
TO YOUR
ETERNITY
15
YOSHITOKI OIMA

CONTENTS

WARNING

This volume depicts instances of self-injury and suicide.
If you are experiencing suicidal thoughts or feelings,
you are not alone, and there is help.
Call the National Suicide Prevention Lifeline at
1-800-273-TALK (8255) or go to
SuicidePreventionLifeline.org.

#133 Record: Hirotoshi

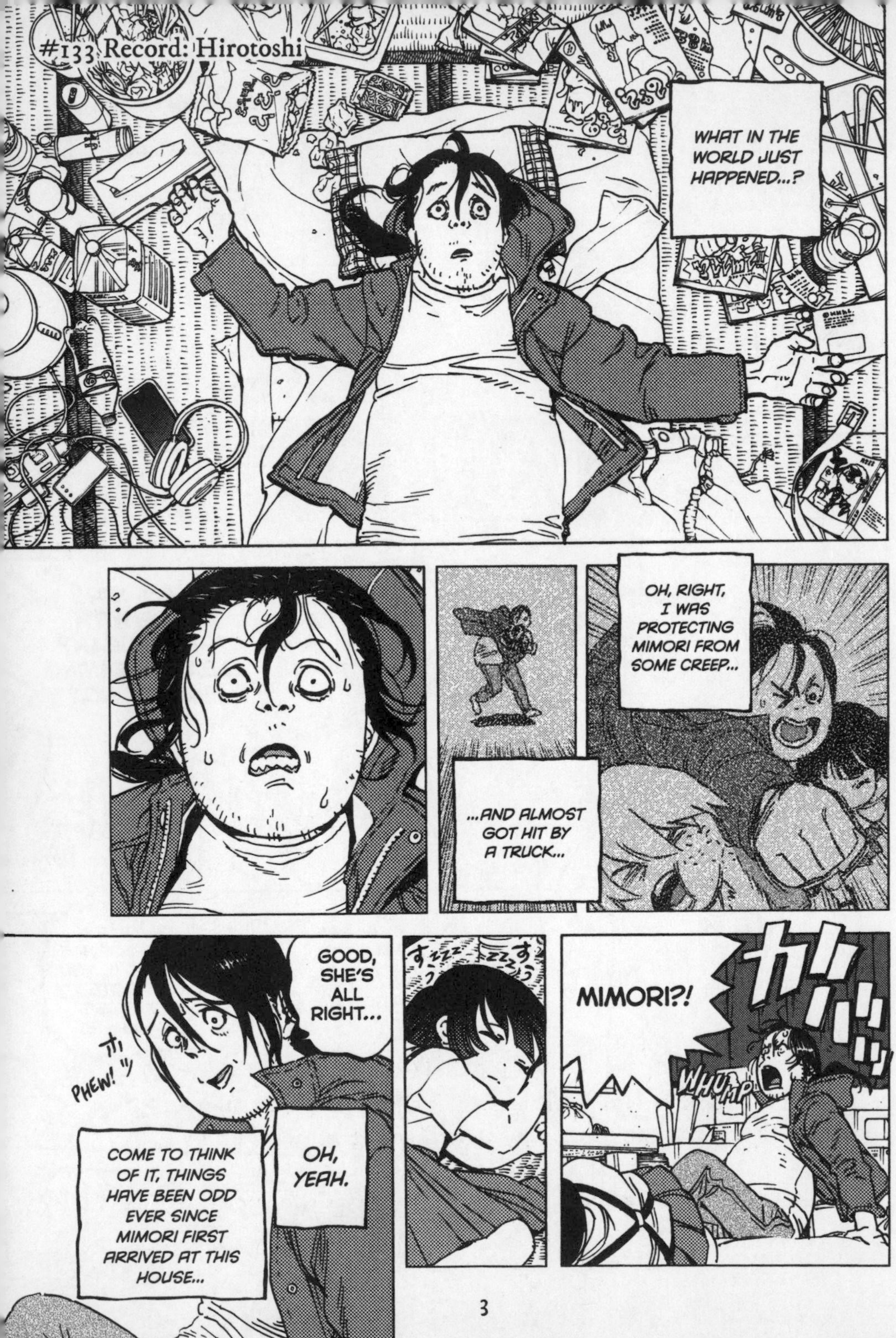
WHAT IN THE WORLD JUST HAPPENED...?
OH, RIGHT, I WAS PROTECTING MIMORI FROM SOME CREEP...
...AND ALMOST GOT HIT BY A TRUCK...
MIMORI?!
WHUMP
zzz
zzz
GOOD, SHE'S ALL RIGHT...
PHEW!
OH, YEAH.
COME TO THINK OF IT, THINGS HAVE BEEN ODD EVER SINCE MIMORI FIRST ARRIVED AT THIS HOUSE...

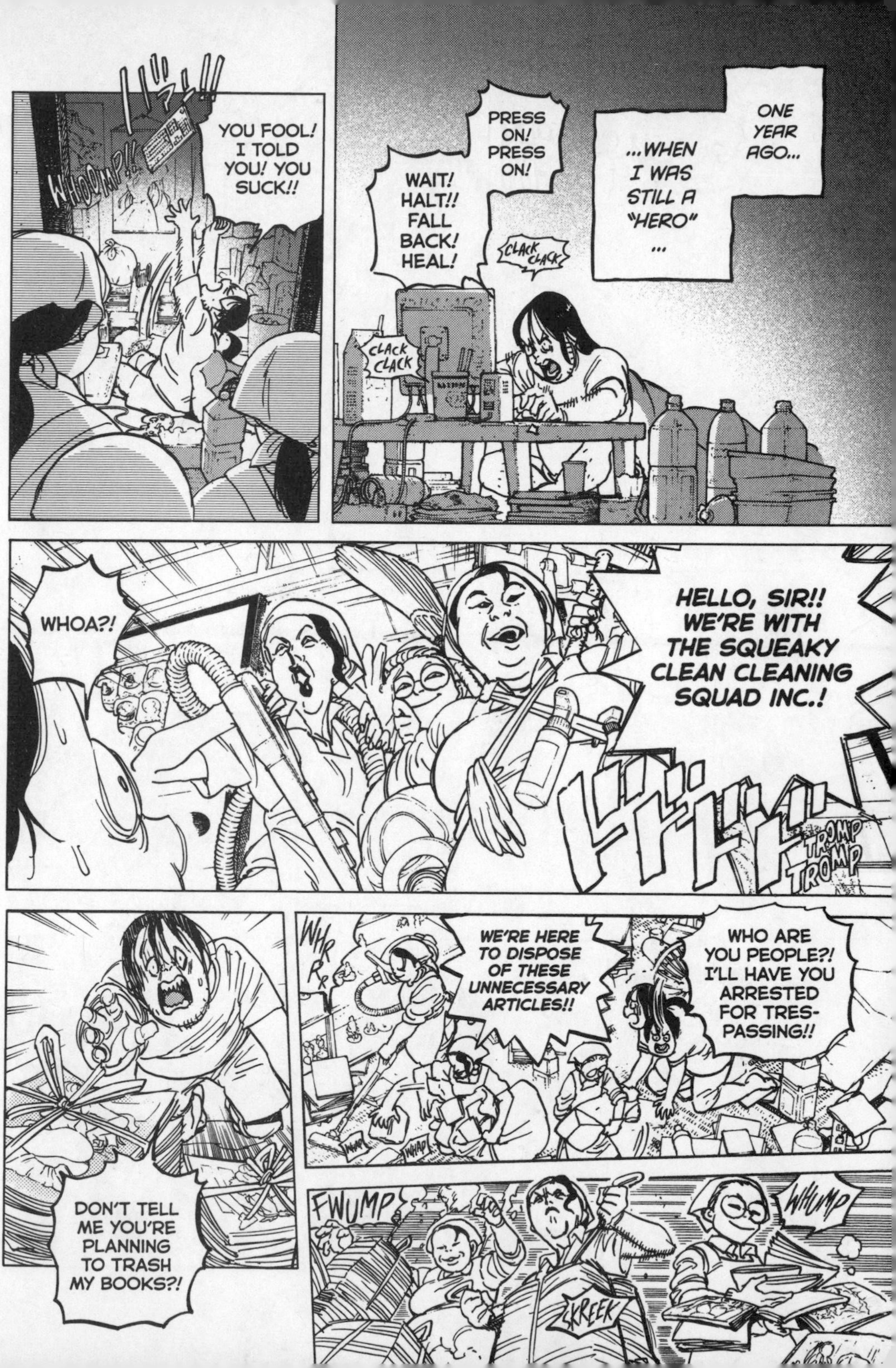
ONE YEAR AGO...
...WHEN I WAS STILL A "HERO" ...
PRESS ON! PRESS ON!
CLACK CLACK
WAIT! HALT!! FALL BACK! HEAL!
CLACK CLACK
YOU FOOL! I TOLD YOU! YOU SUCK!!
WHOOMP!!
HELLO, SIR!! WE'RE WITH THE SQUEAKY CLEAN CLEANING SQUAD INC.!
TROMP TROMP TROMP
WHOA?!
WHO ARE YOU PEOPLE?! I'LL HAVE YOU ARRESTED FOR TRES-PASSING!!
WE'RE HERE TO DISPOSE OF THESE UNNECESSARY ARTICLES!!
WHRR
WHAP
WHAP
WHUMP
SKREEK
FWUMP
DON'T TELL ME YOU'RE PLANNING TO TRASH MY BOOKS?!

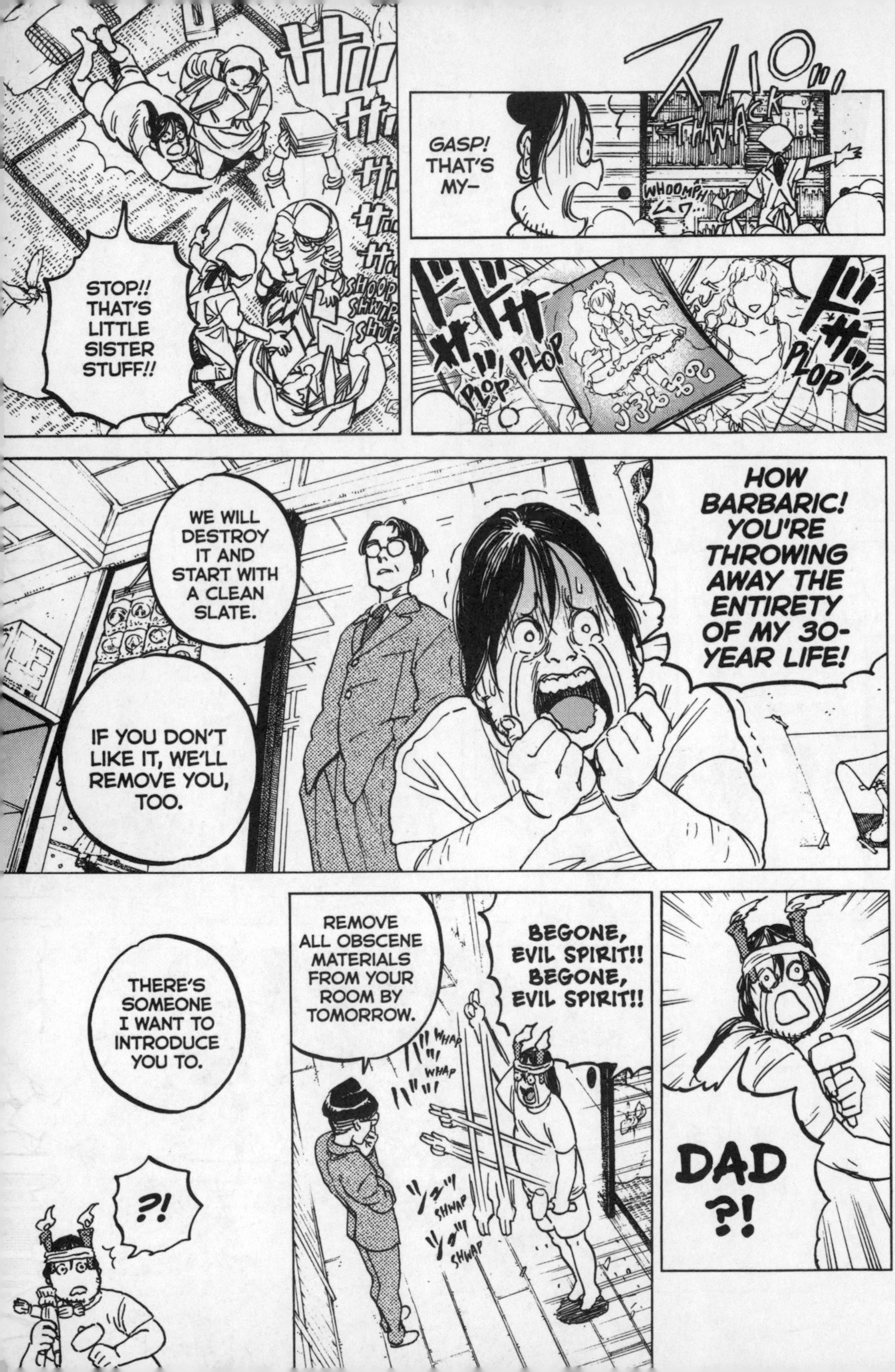
THWACK
GASP! THAT'S MY–
WHOOMPH
PLOP
PLOP
PLOP
STOP!! THAT'S LITTLE SISTER STUFF!!
SHOOP
SHWP
SHUP
HOW BARBARIC! YOU'RE THROWING AWAY THE ENTIRETY OF MY 30-YEAR LIFE!
WE WILL DESTROY IT AND START WITH A CLEAN SLATE.
IF YOU DON'T LIKE IT, WE'LL REMOVE YOU, TOO.
DAD ?!
BEGONE, EVIL SPIRIT!! BEGONE, EVIL SPIRIT!!
REMOVE ALL OBSCENE MATERIALS FROM YOUR ROOM BY TOMORROW.
WHAP
WHAP
SHWAP
SHWAP
THERE'S SOMEONE I WANT TO INTRODUCE YOU TO.
?!

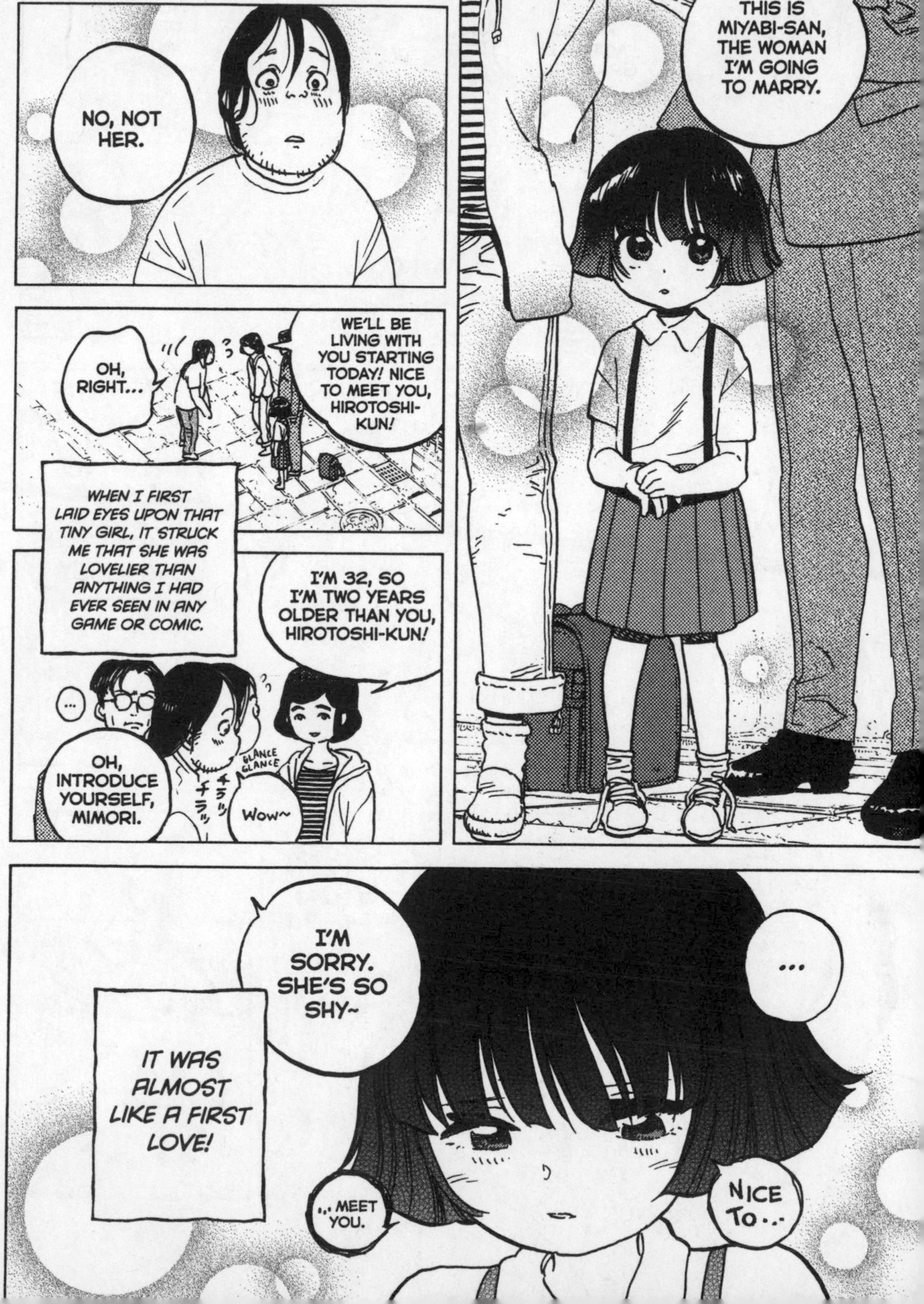
THIS IS MIYABI-SAN, THE WOMAN I'M GOING TO MARRY.
NO, NOT HER.
WE'LL BE LIVING WITH YOU STARTING TODAY! NICE TO MEET YOU, HIROTOSHI-KUN!
OH, RIGHT...
WHEN I FIRST LAID EYES UPON THAT TINY GIRL, IT STRUCK ME THAT SHE WAS LOVELIER THAN ANYTHING I HAD EVER SEEN IN ANY GAME OR COMIC.
I'M 32, SO I'M TWO YEARS OLDER THAN YOU, HIROTOSHI-KUN!
...
GLANCE GLANCE
チラッ チラッ
Wow~
OH, INTRODUCE YOURSELF, MIMORI.
...
I'M SORRY. SHE'S SO SHY~
NICE TO...
...MEET YOU.
IT WAS ALMOST LIKE A FIRST LOVE!

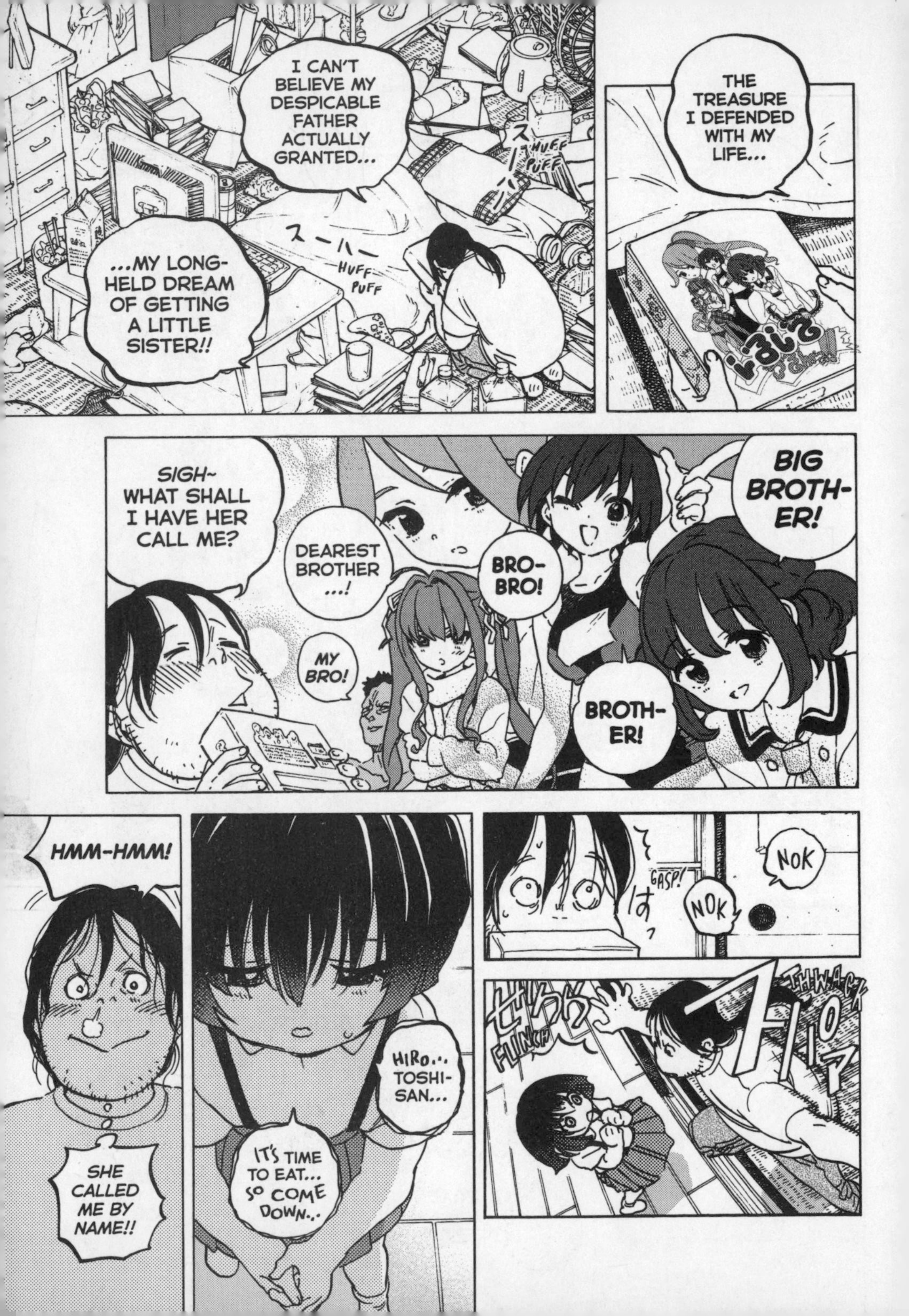
THE TREASURE I DEFENDED WITH MY LIFE...
I CAN'T BELIEVE MY DESPICABLE FATHER ACTUALLY GRANTED...
スーハー HUFF PUFF
...MY LONG-HELD DREAM OF GETTING A LITTLE SISTER!!
スーハー HUFF PUFF
BIG BROTHER!
SIGH~ WHAT SHALL I HAVE HER CALL ME?
DEAREST BROTHER ...!
BRO-BRO!
MY BRO!
BROTHER!
NOK
NOK
GASP!
THWACK
FLINCH
HIRO... TOSHI-SAN...
IT'S TIME TO EAT... SO COME DOWN..
HMM-HMM!
SHE CALLED ME BY NAME!!

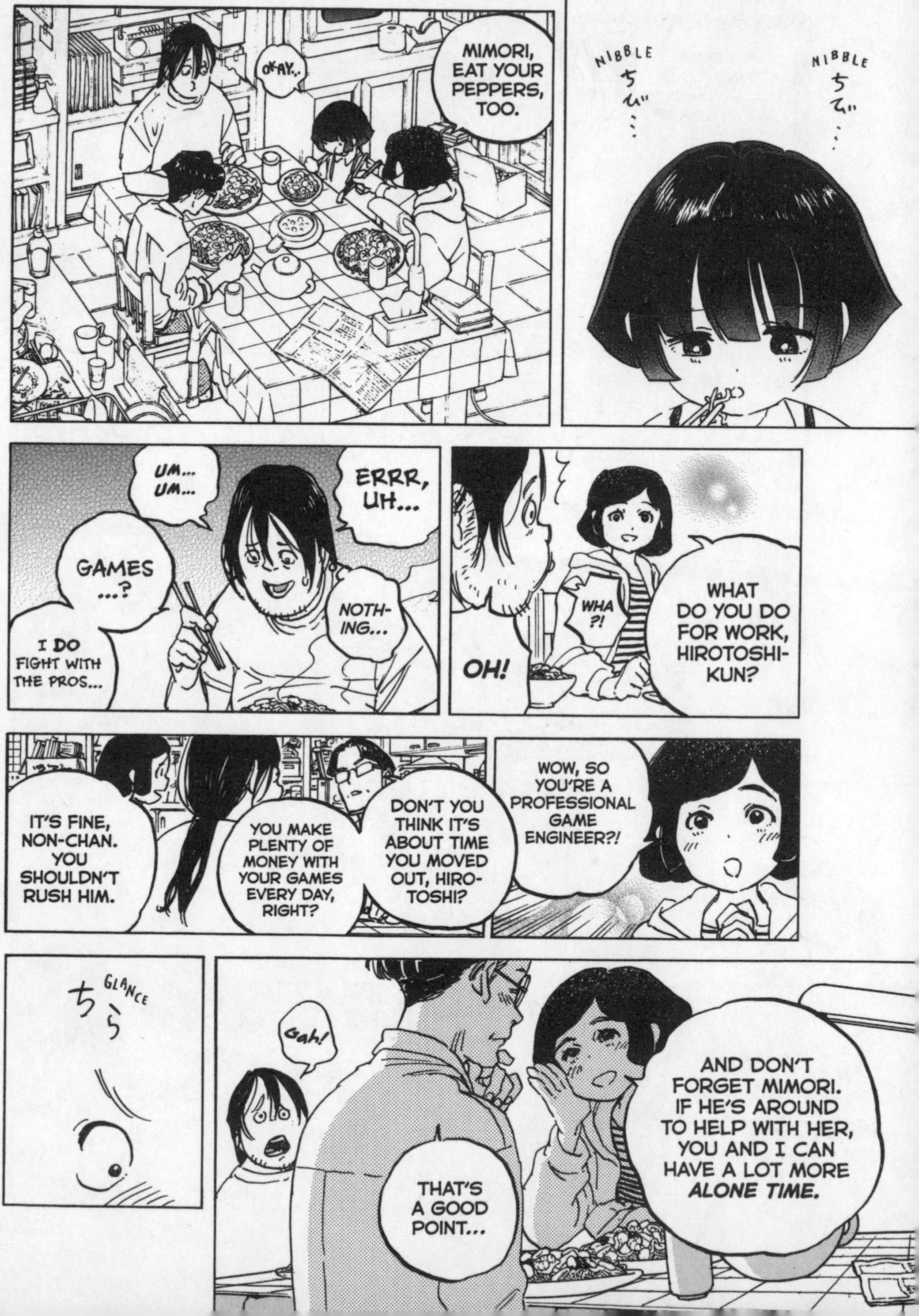
NIBBLE
NIBBLE
MIMORI, EAT YOUR PEPPERS, TOO.
OKAY...
WHAT DO YOU DO FOR WORK, HIROTOSHI-KUN?
WHA?!
OH!
ERRR, UH...
UM... UM...
NOTHING...
GAMES...?
I DO FIGHT WITH THE PROS...
WOW, SO YOU'RE A PROFESSIONAL GAME ENGINEER?!
DON'T YOU THINK IT'S ABOUT TIME YOU MOVED OUT, HIROTOSHI?
YOU MAKE PLENTY OF MONEY WITH YOUR GAMES EVERY DAY, RIGHT?
IT'S FINE, NON-CHAN. YOU SHOULDN'T RUSH HIM.
AND DON'T FORGET MIMORI. IF HE'S AROUND TO HELP WITH HER, YOU AND I CAN HAVE A LOT MORE *ALONE TIME.*
THAT'S A GOOD POINT...
Gah!
GLANCE

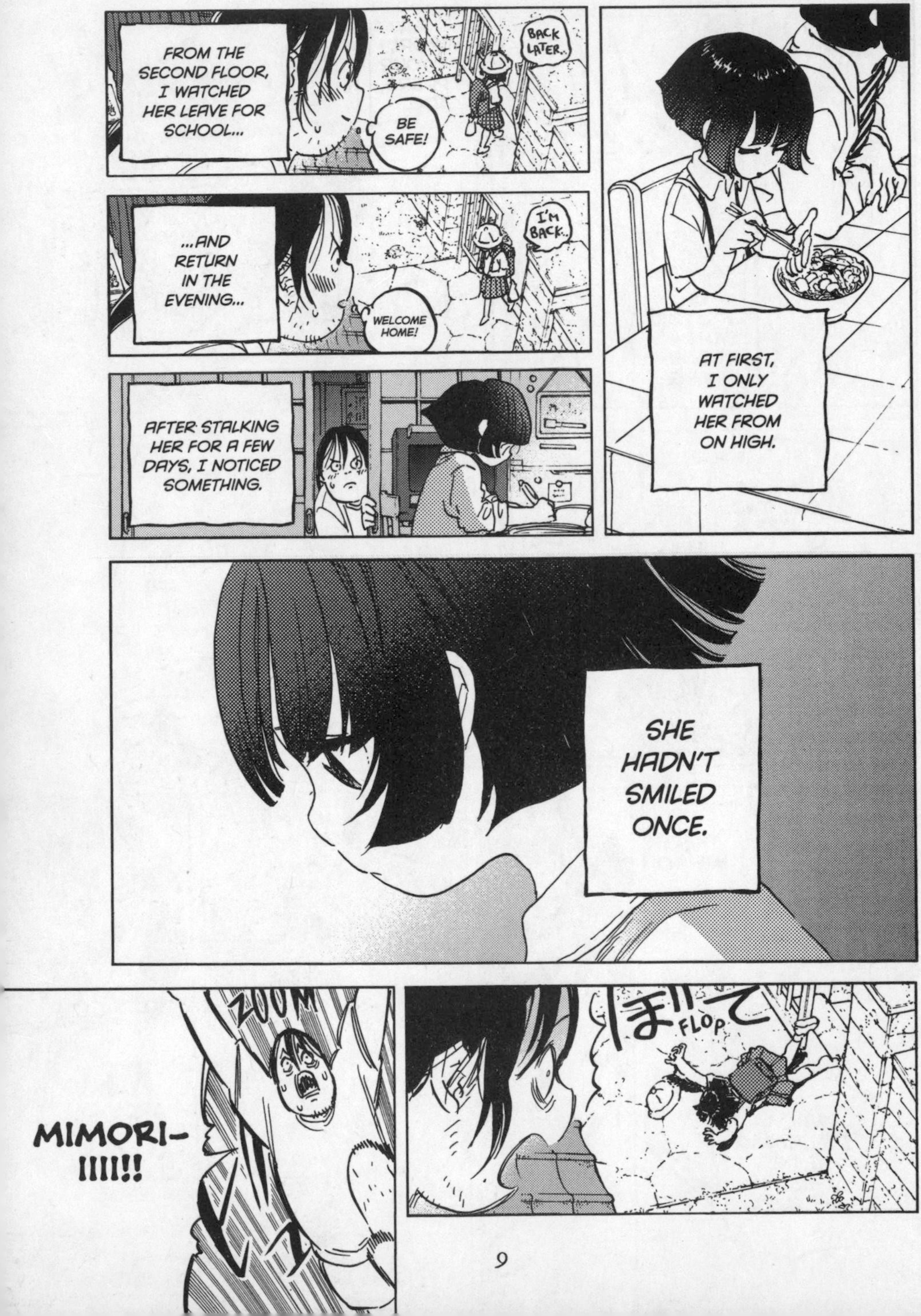

AT FIRST, I ONLY WATCHED HER FROM ON HIGH.
FROM THE SECOND FLOOR, I WATCHED HER LEAVE FOR SCHOOL...
BACK LATER..
BE SAFE!
...AND RETURN IN THE EVENING...
I'M BACK..
WELCOME HOME!
AFTER STALKING HER FOR A FEW DAYS, I NOTICED SOMETHING.
SHE HADN'T SMILED ONCE.
FLOP
ZOOM
MIMORI-IIIII!!

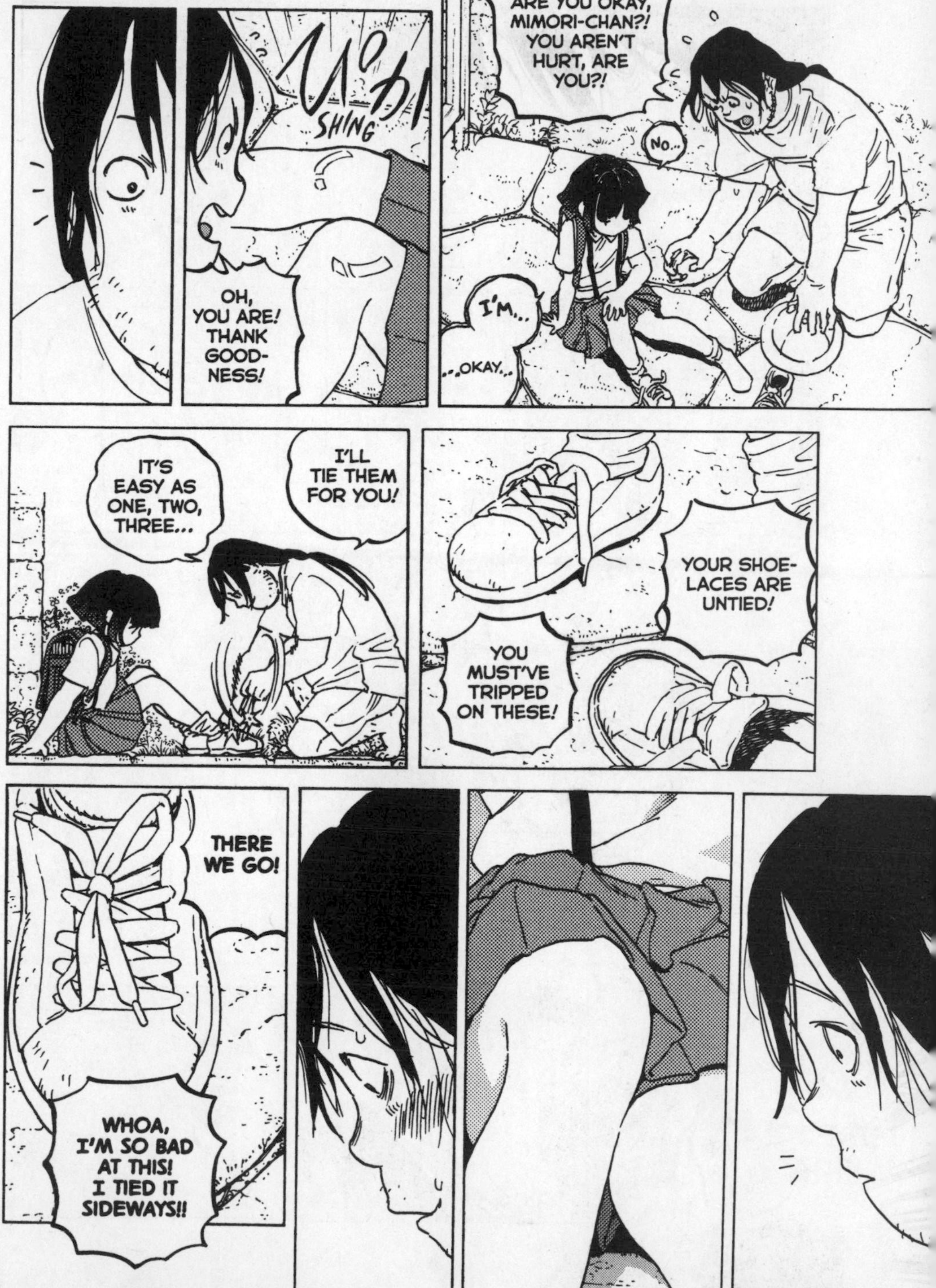
ARE YOU OKAY, MIMORI-CHAN?! YOU AREN'T HURT, ARE YOU?!
NO...
I'M...
...OKAY...
SHING
OH, YOU ARE! THANK GOOD-NESS!
YOUR SHOE-LACES ARE UNTIED!
YOU MUST'VE TRIPPED ON THESE!
I'LL TIE THEM FOR YOU!
IT'S EASY AS ONE, TWO, THREE...
THERE WE GO!
WHOA, I'M SO BAD AT THIS! I TIED IT SIDEWAYS!!

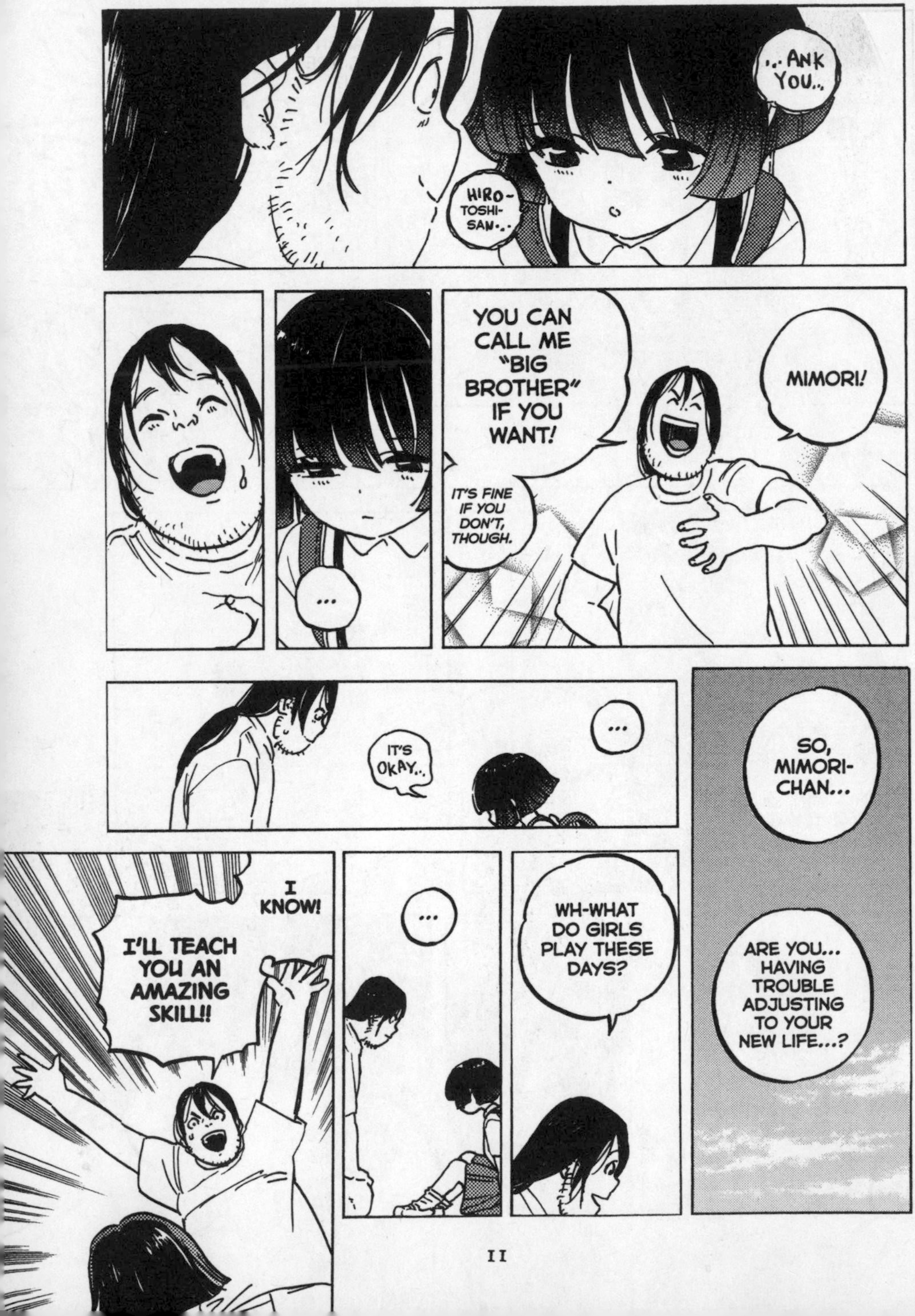
...ANK YOU...
HIRO-TOSHI-SAN...
MIMORI!
YOU CAN CALL ME "BIG BROTHER" IF YOU WANT!
IT'S FINE IF YOU DON'T, THOUGH.
...
SO, MIMORI-CHAN...
ARE YOU... HAVING TROUBLE ADJUSTING TO YOUR NEW LIFE...?
...
IT'S OKAY...
WH-WHAT DO GIRLS PLAY THESE DAYS?
...
I KNOW!
I'LL TEACH YOU AN AMAZING SKILL!!

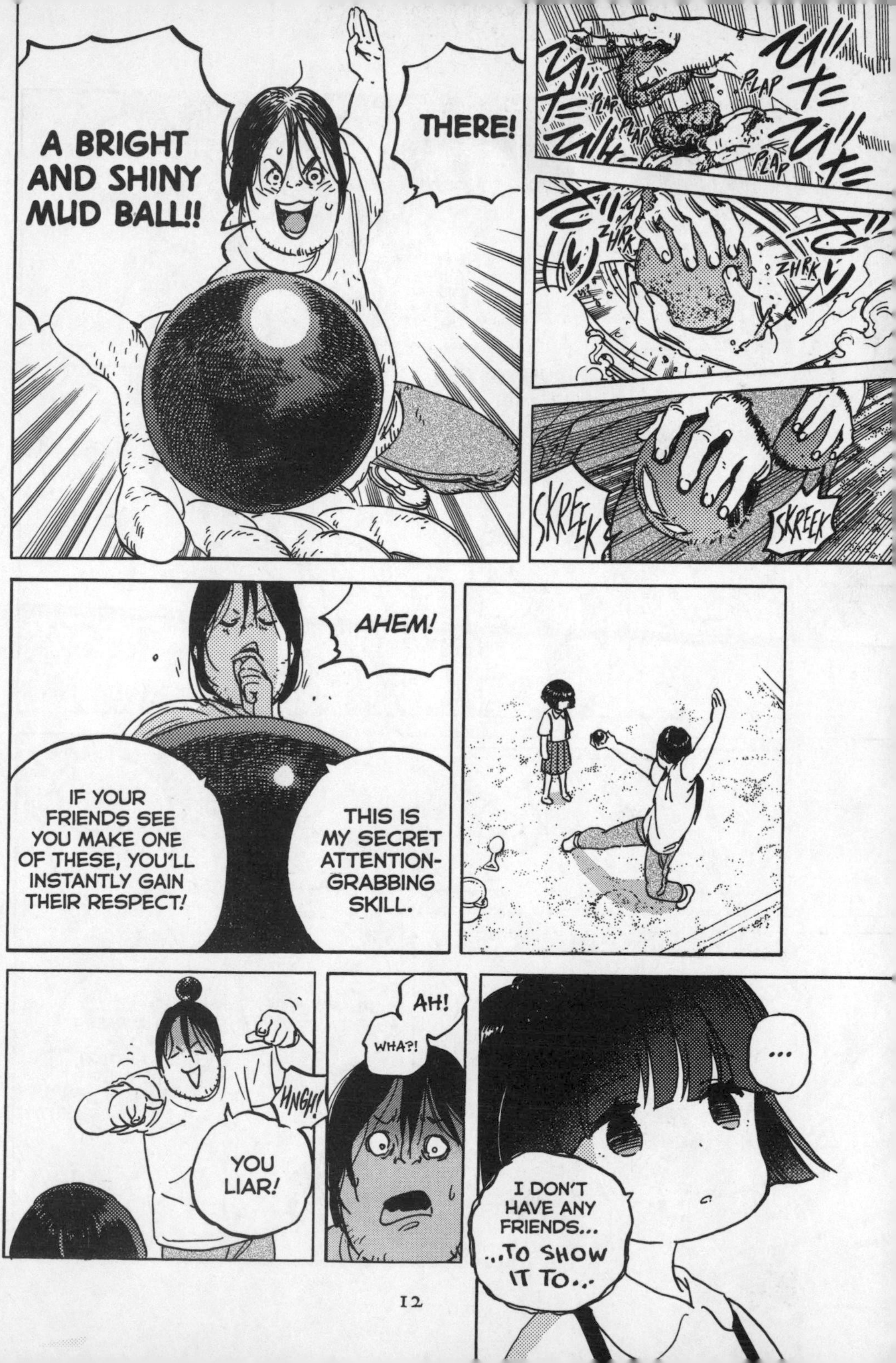

PLAP
PLAP
PLAP
PLAP
PLAP
ZHRK
ZHRK
SKREEK
SKREEK
THERE!
A BRIGHT AND SHINY MUD BALL!!
AHEM!
THIS IS MY SECRET ATTENTION-GRABBING SKILL.
IF YOUR FRIENDS SEE YOU MAKE ONE OF THESE, YOU'LL INSTANTLY GAIN THEIR RESPECT!
...
I DON'T HAVE ANY FRIENDS...
...TO SHOW IT TO...
AH!
WHA?!
HNGH!
YOU LIAR!

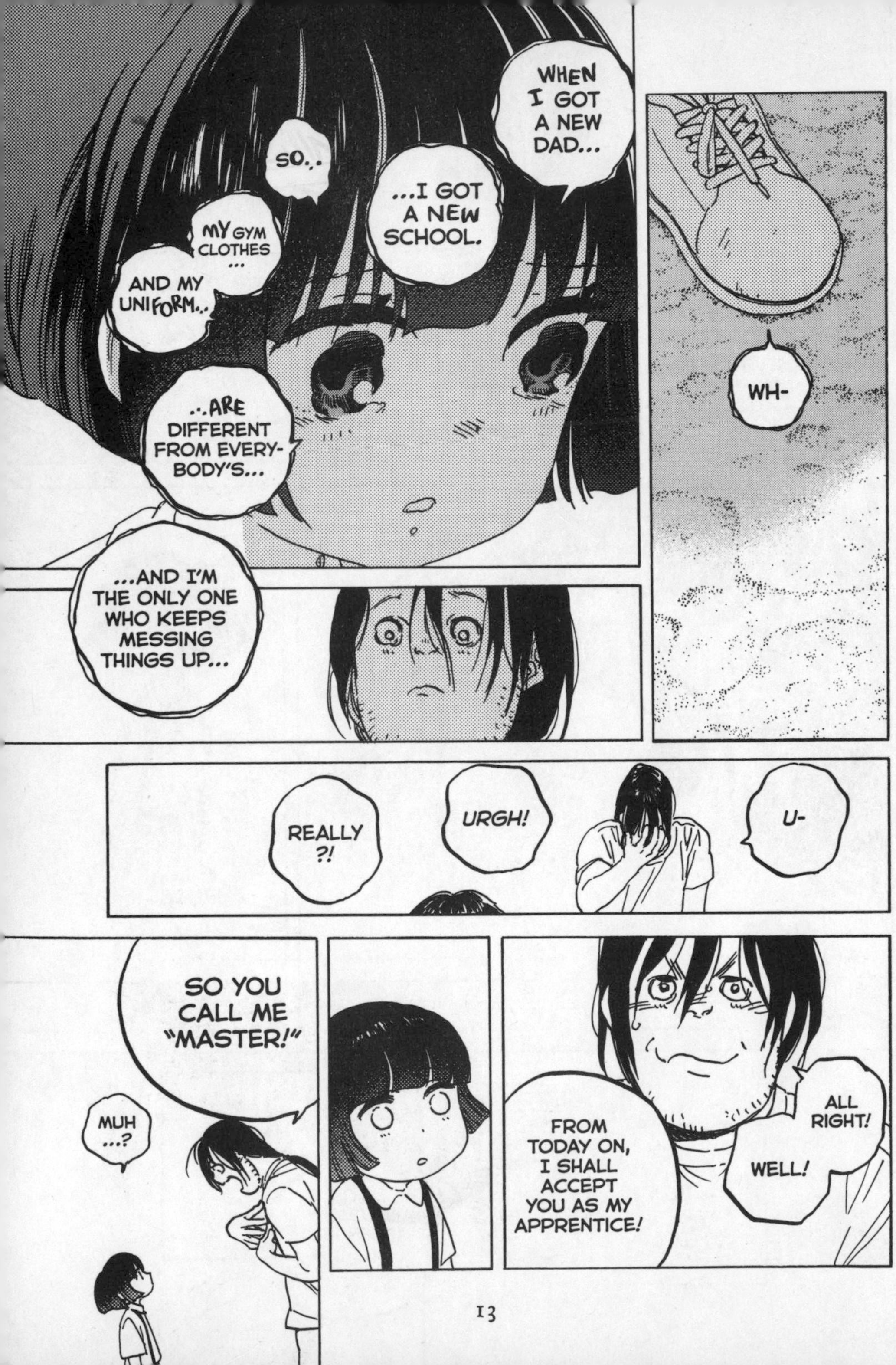
WH-
WHEN I GOT A NEW DAD...
...I GOT A NEW SCHOOL.
SO...
MY GYM CLOTHES ...
AND MY UNIFORM...
...ARE DIFFERENT FROM EVERYBODY'S...
...AND I'M THE ONLY ONE WHO KEEPS MESSING THINGS UP...
U-
URGH!
REALLY ?!
ALL RIGHT!
WELL!
FROM TODAY ON, I SHALL ACCEPT YOU AS MY APPRENTICE!
SO YOU CALL ME "MASTER!"
MUH ...?

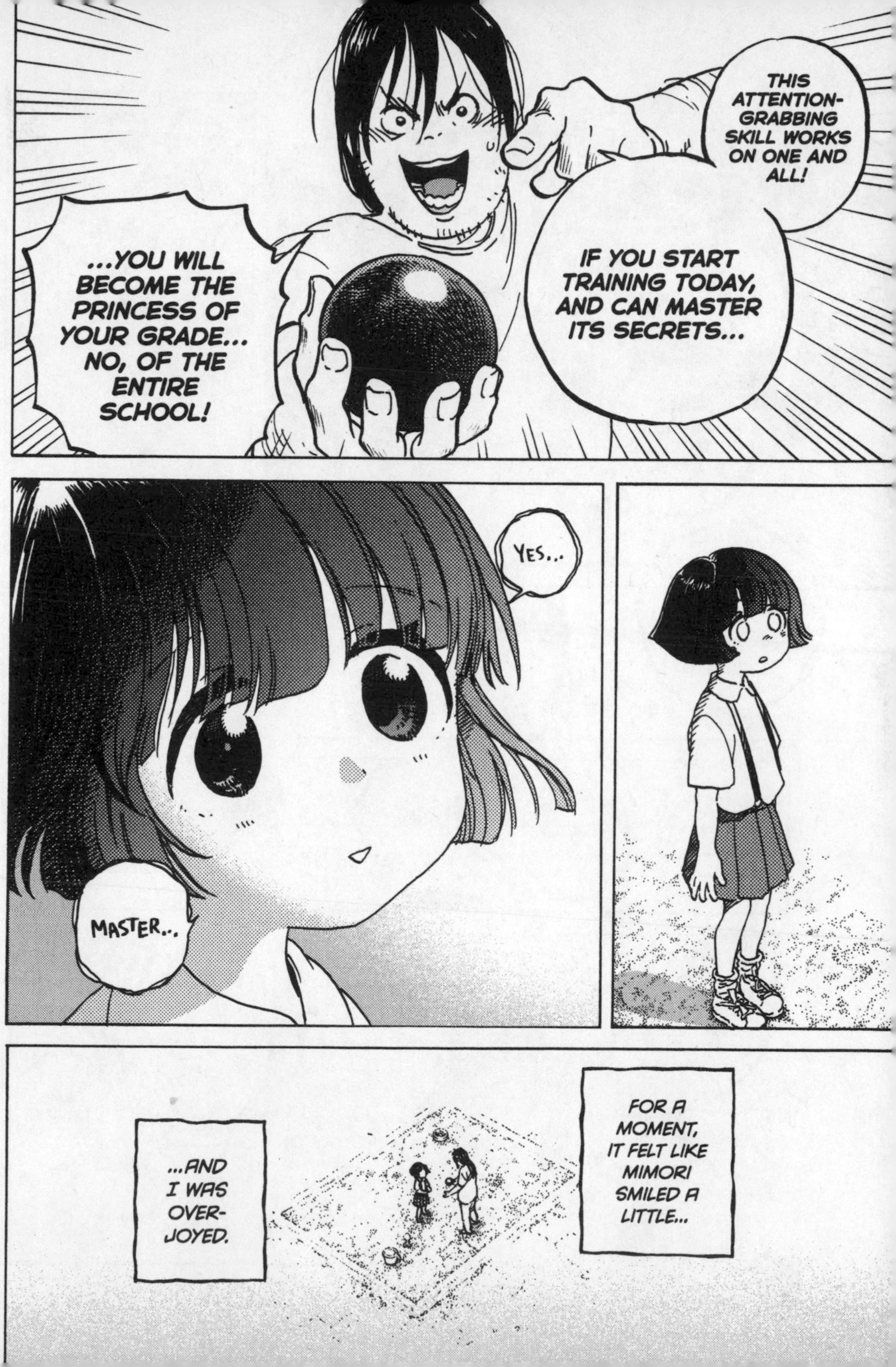
THIS ATTENTION-GRABBING SKILL WORKS ON ONE AND ALL!
IF YOU START TRAINING TODAY, AND CAN MASTER ITS SECRETS...
...YOU WILL BECOME THE PRINCESS OF YOUR GRADE... NO, OF THE ENTIRE SCHOOL!
YES...
MASTER...
FOR A MOMENT, IT FELT LIKE MIMORI SMILED A LITTLE...
...AND I WAS OVERJOYED.

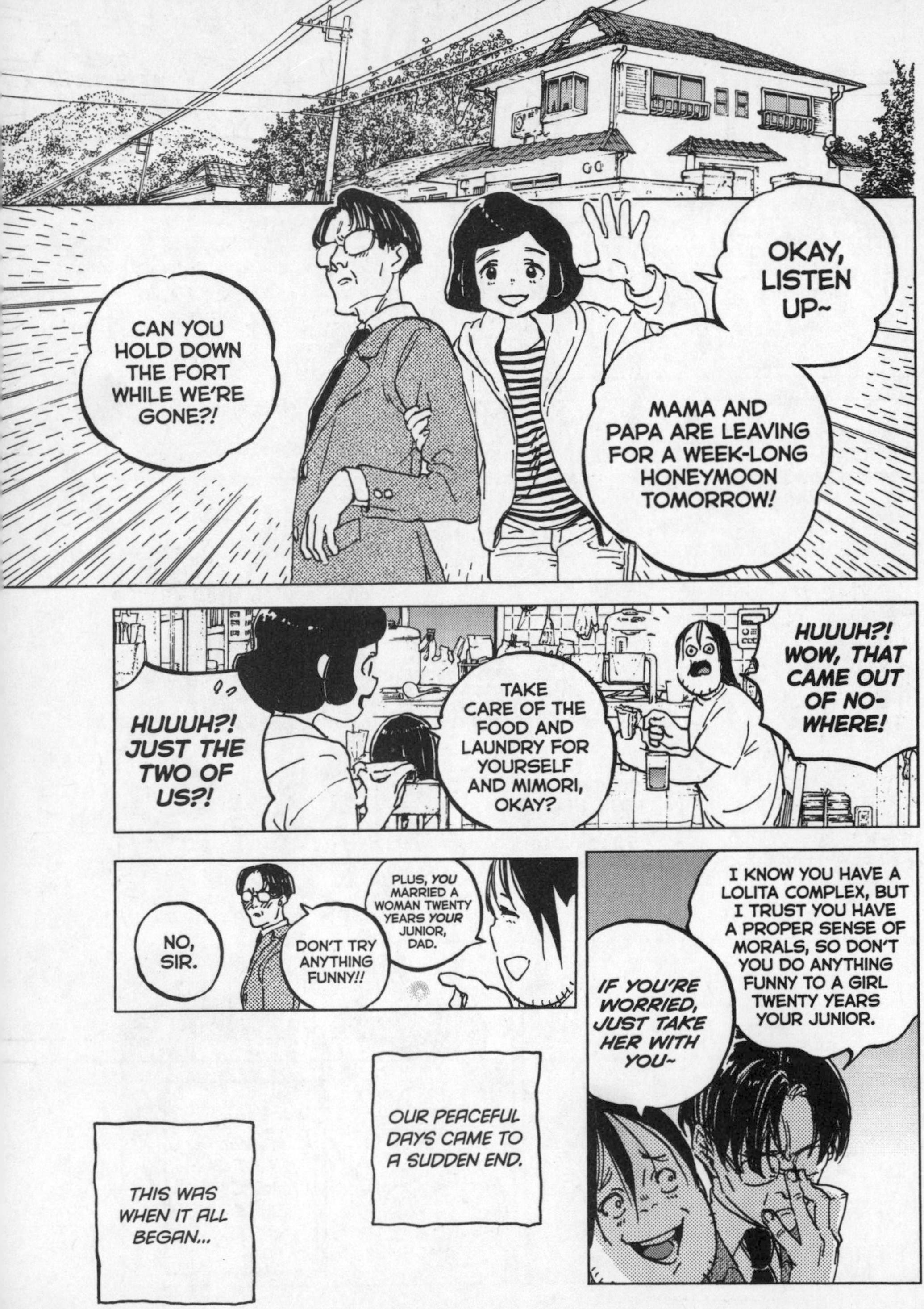
OKAY, LISTEN UP~
MAMA AND PAPA ARE LEAVING FOR A WEEK-LONG HONEYMOON TOMORROW!
CAN YOU HOLD DOWN THE FORT WHILE WE'RE GONE?!
HUUUH?! WOW, THAT CAME OUT OF NO-WHERE!
TAKE CARE OF THE FOOD AND LAUNDRY FOR YOURSELF AND MIMORI, OKAY?
HUUUH?! JUST THE TWO OF US?!
I KNOW YOU HAVE A LOLITA COMPLEX, BUT I TRUST YOU HAVE A PROPER SENSE OF MORALS, SO DON'T YOU DO ANYTHING FUNNY TO A GIRL TWENTY YEARS YOUR JUNIOR.
IF YOU'RE WORRIED, JUST TAKE HER WITH YOU~
PLUS, YOU MARRIED A WOMAN TWENTY YEARS YOUR JUNIOR, DAD.
DON'T TRY ANYTHING FUNNY!!
NO, SIR.
OUR PEACEFUL DAYS CAME TO A SUDDEN END.
THIS WAS WHEN IT ALL BEGAN...

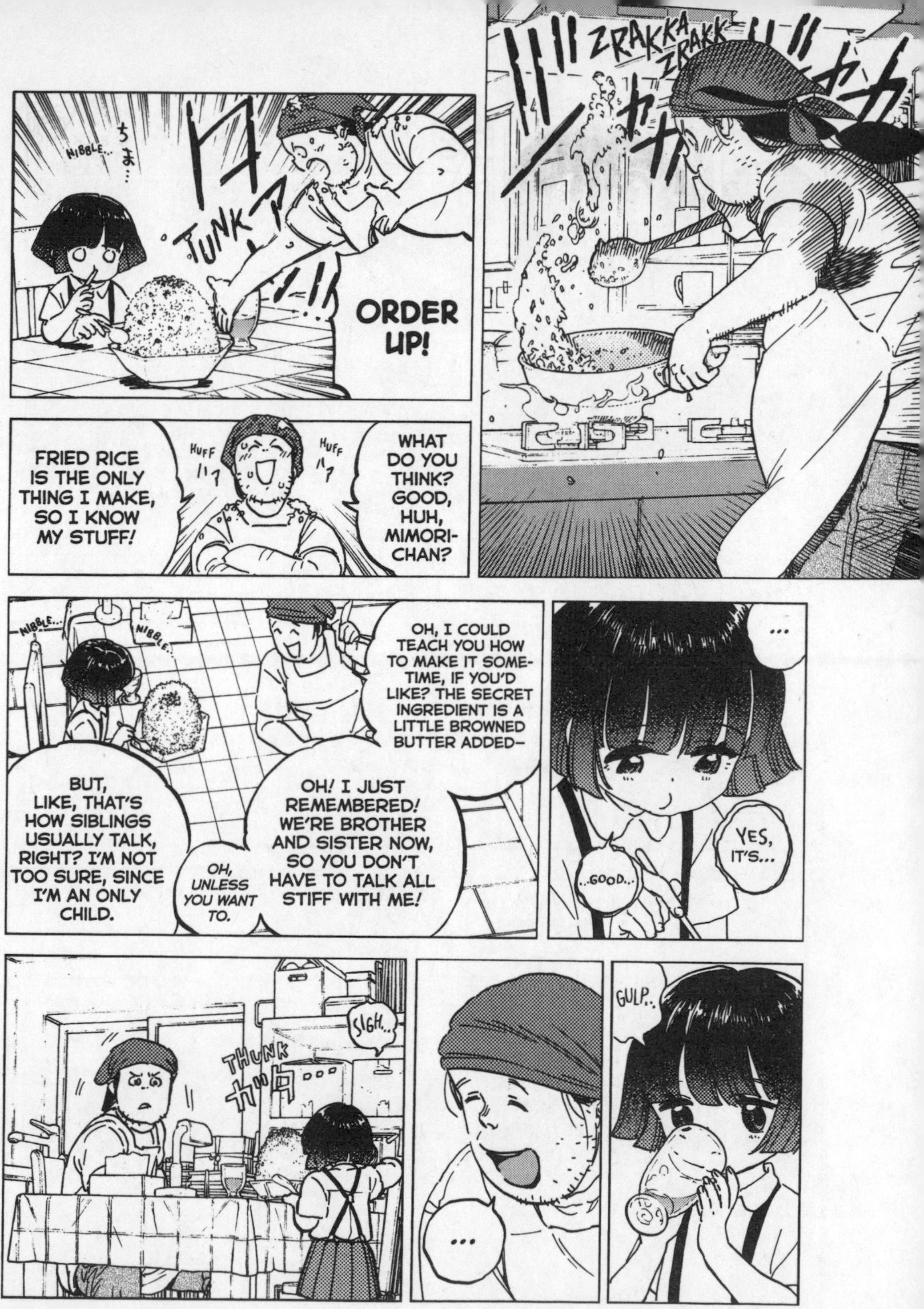
ZRAKKA
ZRAKK
TUNK
NIBBLE...
ORDER UP!
HUFF
HUFF
WHAT DO YOU THINK? GOOD, HUH, MIMORI-CHAN?
FRIED RICE IS THE ONLY THING I MAKE, SO I KNOW MY STUFF!
...
YES, IT'S...
..GOOD..
OH, I COULD TEACH YOU HOW TO MAKE IT SOME-TIME, IF YOU'D LIKE? THE SECRET INGREDIENT IS A LITTLE BROWNED BUTTER ADDED–
NIBBLE...
NIBBLE...
OH! I JUST REMEMBERED! WE'RE BROTHER AND SISTER NOW, SO YOU DON'T HAVE TO TALK ALL STIFF WITH ME!
OH, UNLESS YOU WANT TO.
BUT, LIKE, THAT'S HOW SIBLINGS USUALLY TALK, RIGHT? I'M NOT TOO SURE, SINCE I'M AN ONLY CHILD.
GULP...
...
SIGH...
THUNK

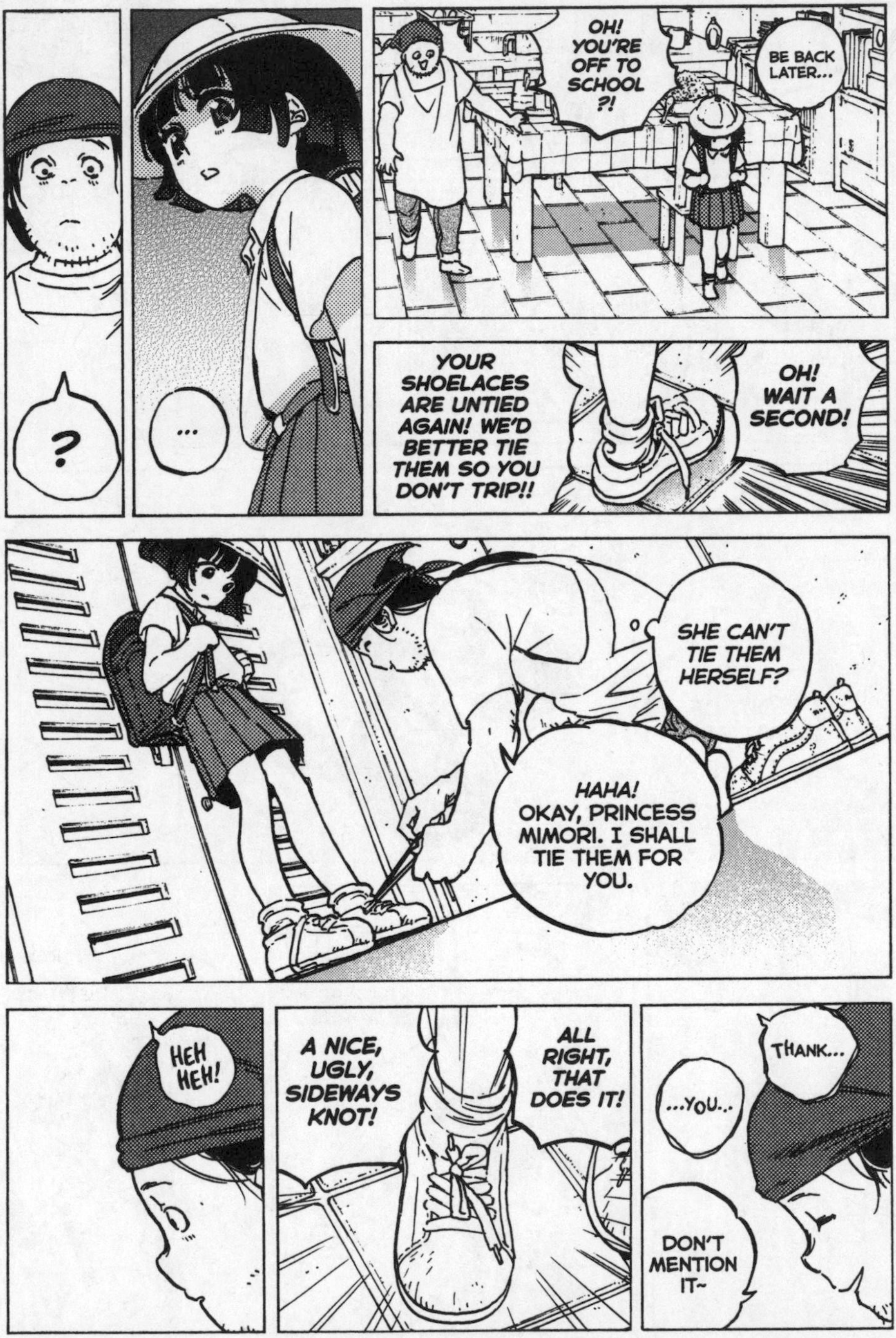
BE BACK LATER...
OH! YOU'RE OFF TO SCHOOL?!
OH! WAIT A SECOND!
YOUR SHOELACES ARE UNTIED AGAIN! WE'D BETTER TIE THEM SO YOU DON'T TRIP!!
...
?
SHE CAN'T TIE THEM HERSELF?
HAHA! OKAY, PRINCESS MIMORI. I SHALL TIE THEM FOR YOU.
THANK...
...YOU...
DON'T MENTION IT~
ALL RIGHT, THAT DOES IT!
A NICE, UGLY, SIDEWAYS KNOT!
HEH HEH!

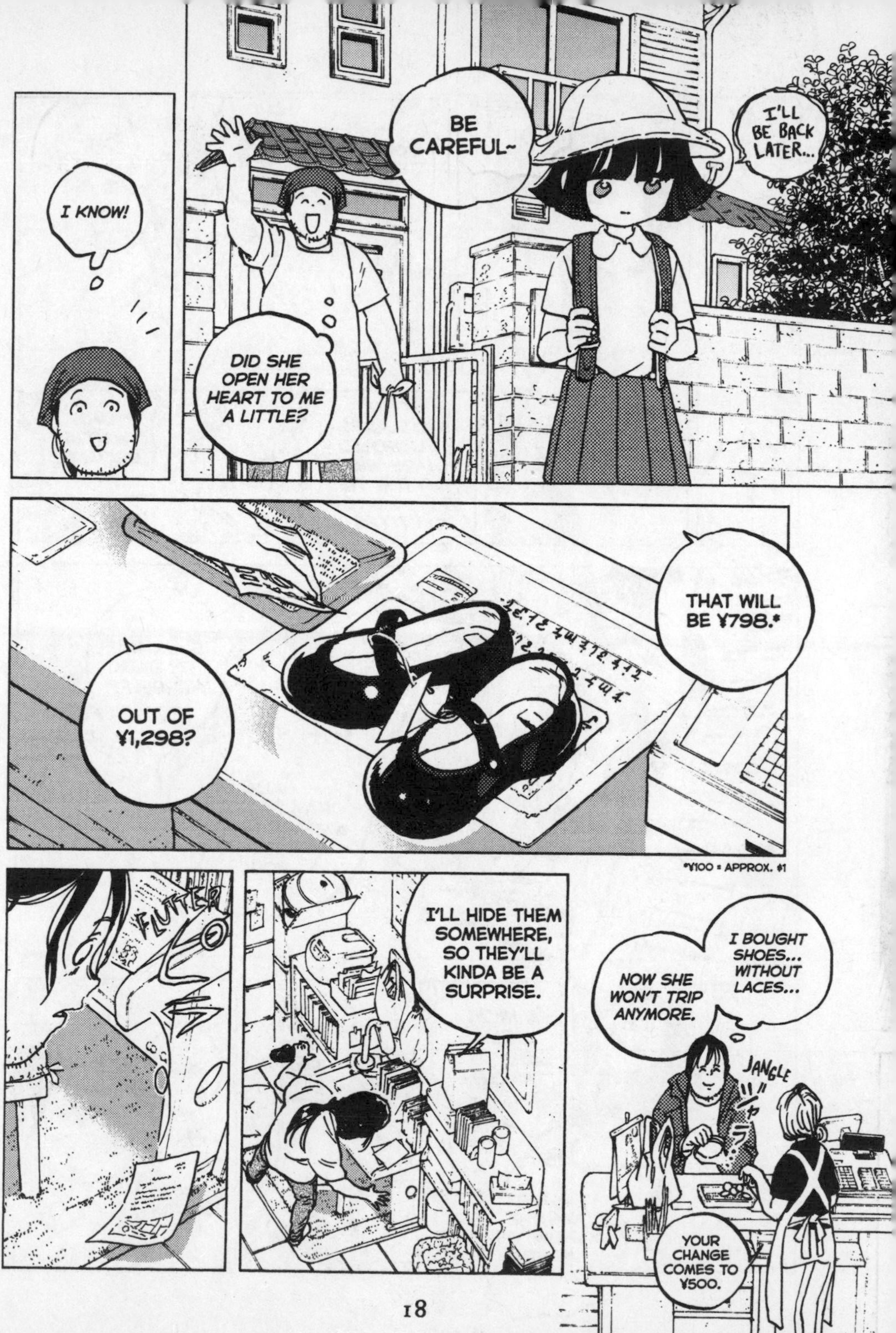

I'LL BE BACK LATER...
BE CAREFUL~
DID SHE OPEN HER HEART TO ME A LITTLE?
I KNOW!
THAT WILL BE ¥798.*
OUT OF ¥1,298?
I BOUGHT SHOES... WITHOUT LACES...
NOW SHE WON'T TRIP ANYMORE.
JANGLE
YOUR CHANGE COMES TO ¥500.
I'LL HIDE THEM SOMEWHERE, SO THEY'LL KINDA BE A SURPRISE.
FLUTTER

*¥100 = APPROX. $1

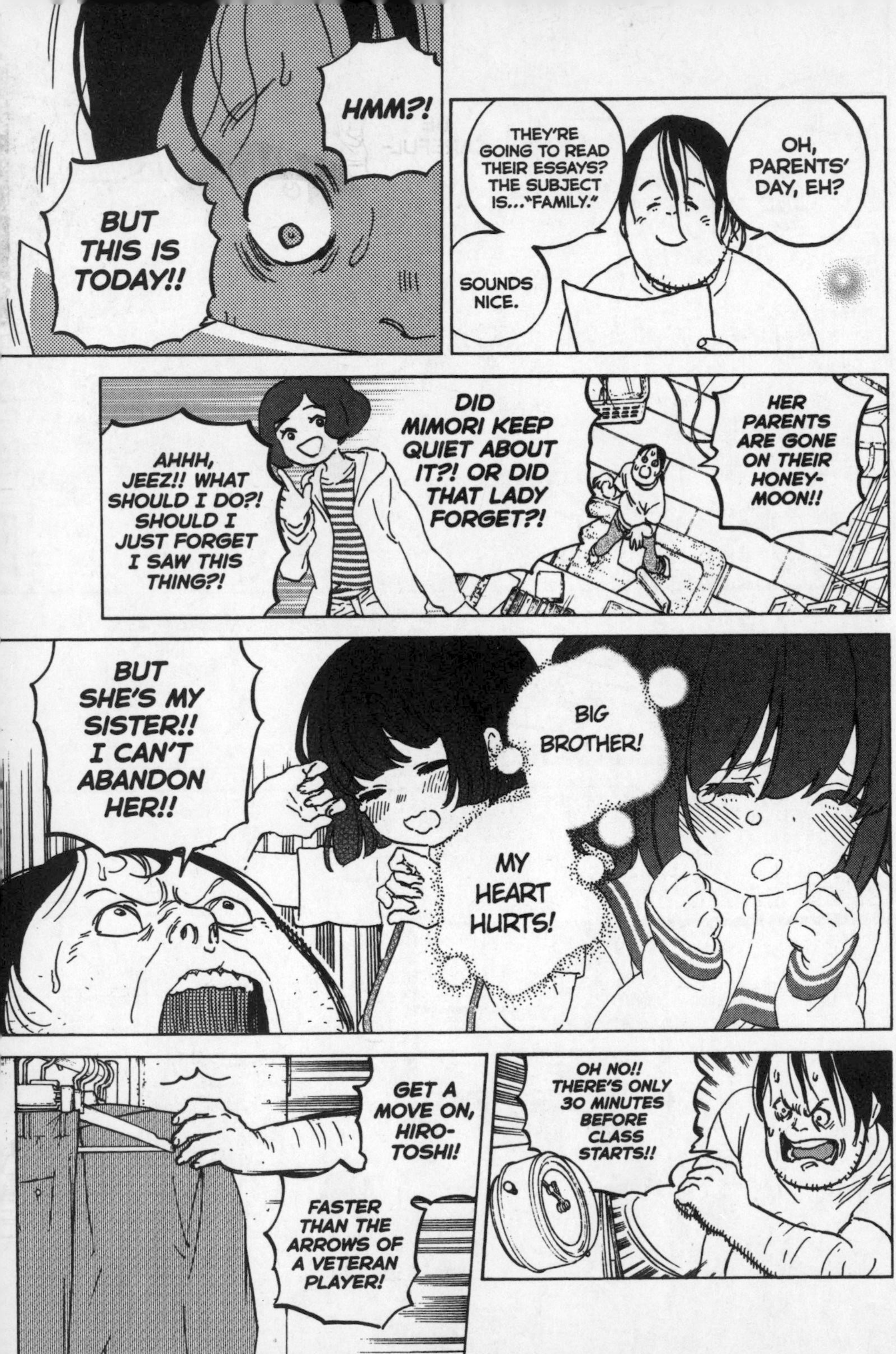
OH, PARENTS' DAY, EH?
THEY'RE GOING TO READ THEIR ESSAYS? THE SUBJECT IS..."FAMILY."
SOUNDS NICE.
HMM?!
BUT THIS IS TODAY!!
HER PARENTS ARE GONE ON THEIR HONEYMOON!!
DID MIMORI KEEP QUIET ABOUT IT?! OR DID THAT LADY FORGET?!
AHHH, JEEZ!! WHAT SHOULD I DO?! SHOULD I JUST FORGET I SAW THIS THING?!
BIG BROTHER!
MY HEART HURTS!
BUT SHE'S MY SISTER!! I CAN'T ABANDON HER!!
OH NO!! THERE'S ONLY 30 MINUTES BEFORE CLASS STARTS!!
GET A MOVE ON, HIRO-TOSHI!
FASTER THAN THE ARROWS OF A VETERAN PLAYER!

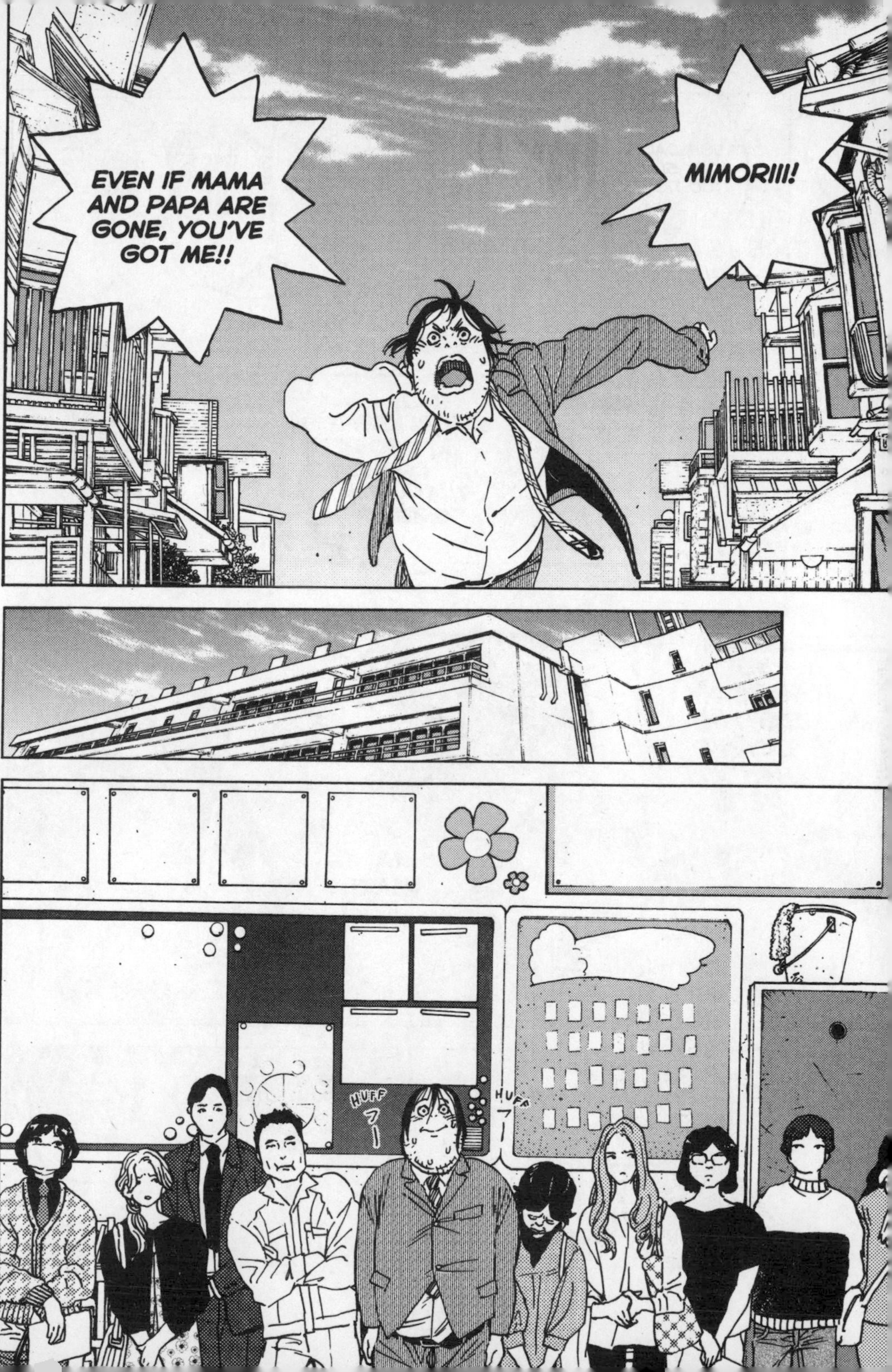
MIMORIII!
EVEN IF MAMA AND PAPA ARE GONE, YOU'VE GOT ME!!
HUFF
HUFF

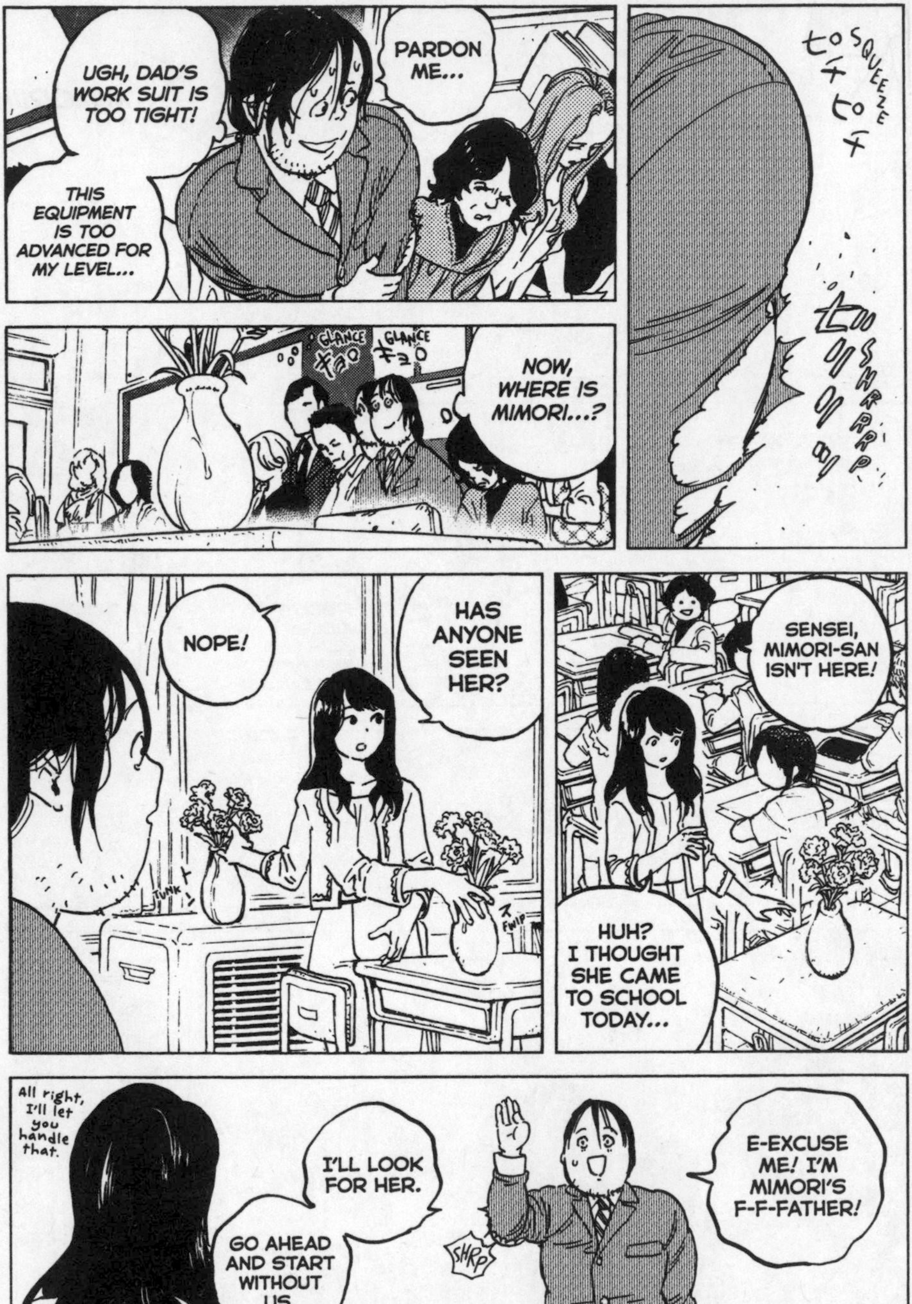
SQUEEZE
SHRRRP
PARDON ME...
UGH, DAD'S WORK SUIT IS TOO TIGHT!
THIS EQUIPMENT IS TOO ADVANCED FOR MY LEVEL...
NOW, WHERE IS MIMORI...?
GLANCE
GLANCE
SENSEI, MIMORI-SAN ISN'T HERE!
HUH? I THOUGHT SHE CAME TO SCHOOL TODAY...
HAS ANYONE SEEN HER?
NOPE!
FWIP
TUNK
E-EXCUSE ME! I'M MIMORI'S F-F-FATHER!
SHRP
I'LL LOOK FOR HER.
GO AHEAD AND START WITHOUT US.
All right, I'll let you handle that.

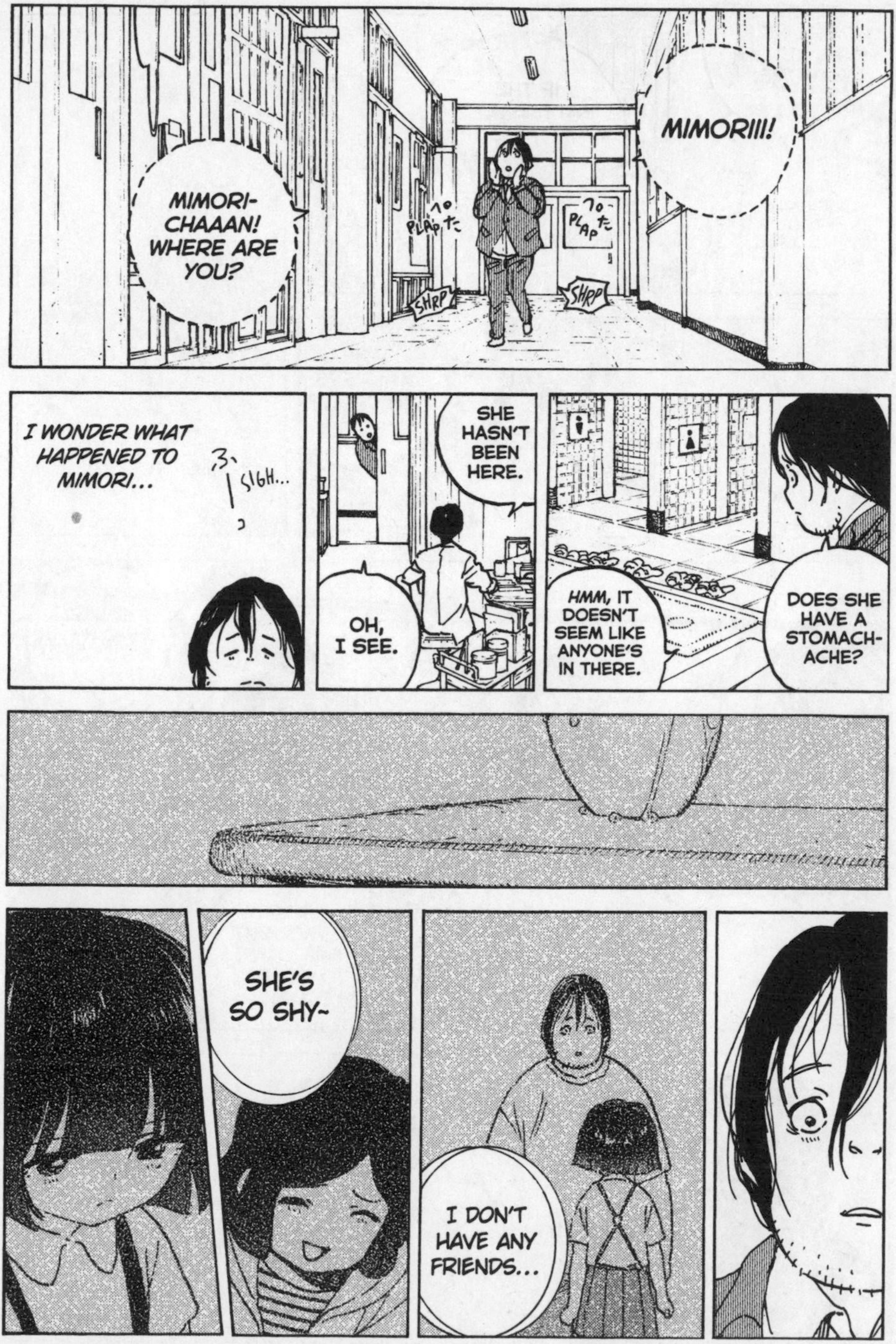
MIMORIII!
MIMORI-CHAAAN! WHERE ARE YOU?
PLAP
PLAP
SHRP
SHRP
DOES SHE HAVE A STOMACH-ACHE?
HMM, IT DOESN'T SEEM LIKE ANYONE'S IN THERE.
SHE HASN'T BEEN HERE.
OH, I SEE.
I WONDER WHAT HAPPENED TO MIMORI...
SIGH...
I DON'T HAVE ANY FRIENDS...
SHE'S SO SHY~

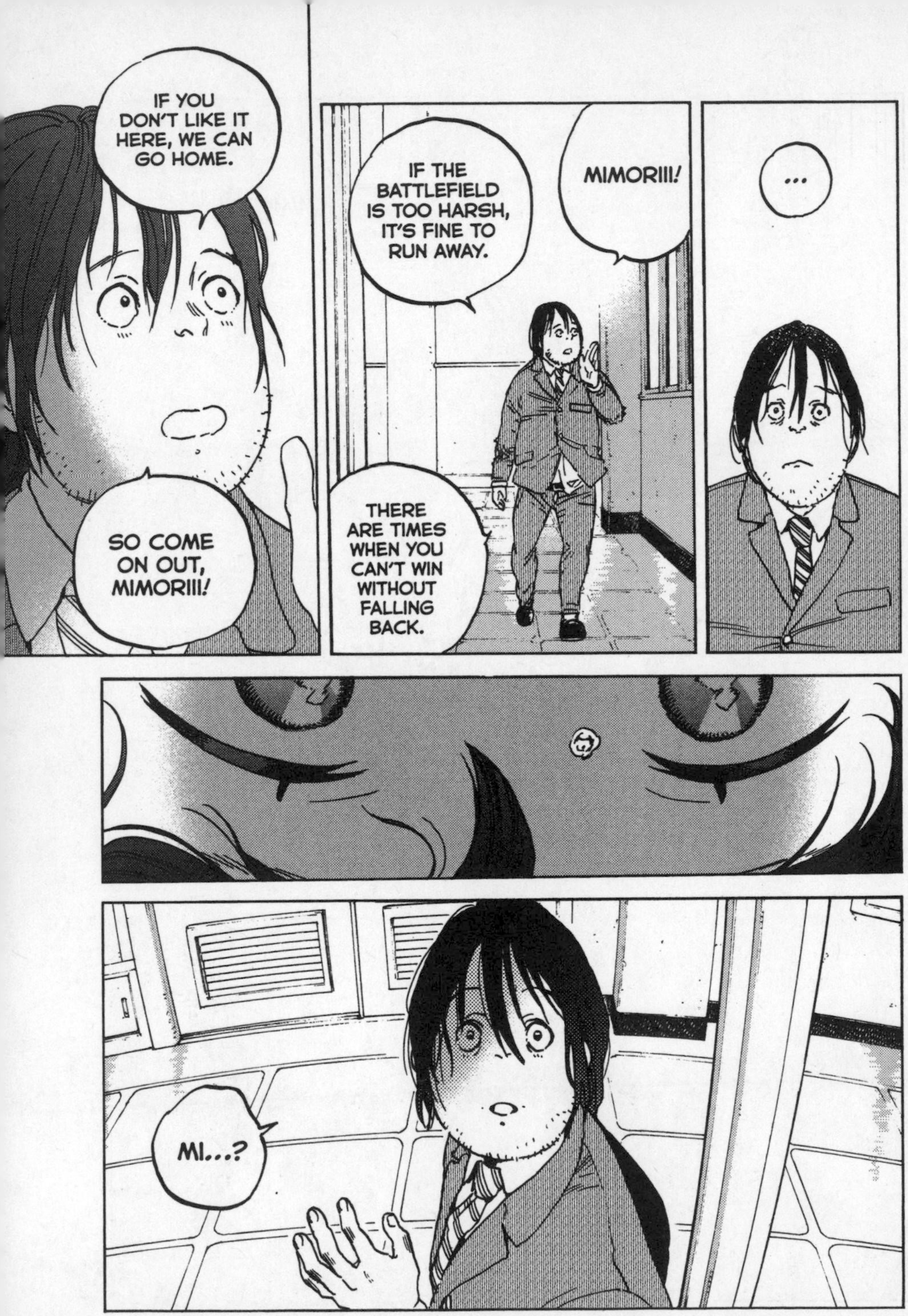
...
MIMORIII!
IF THE BATTLEFIELD IS TOO HARSH, IT'S FINE TO RUN AWAY.
THERE ARE TIMES WHEN YOU CAN'T WIN WITHOUT FALLING BACK.
IF YOU DON'T LIKE IT HERE, WE CAN GO HOME.
SO COME ON OUT, MIMORIII!
MI...?

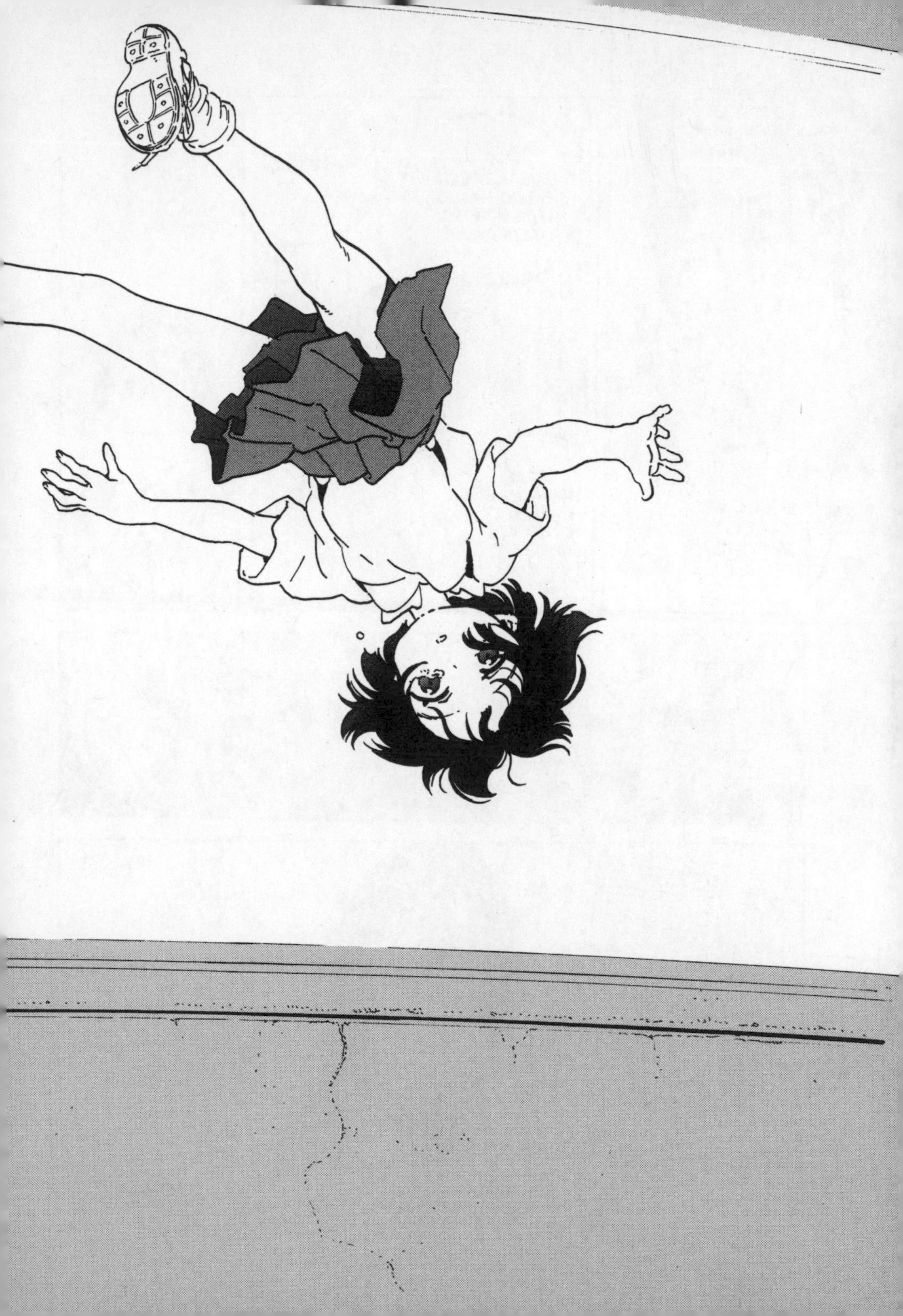

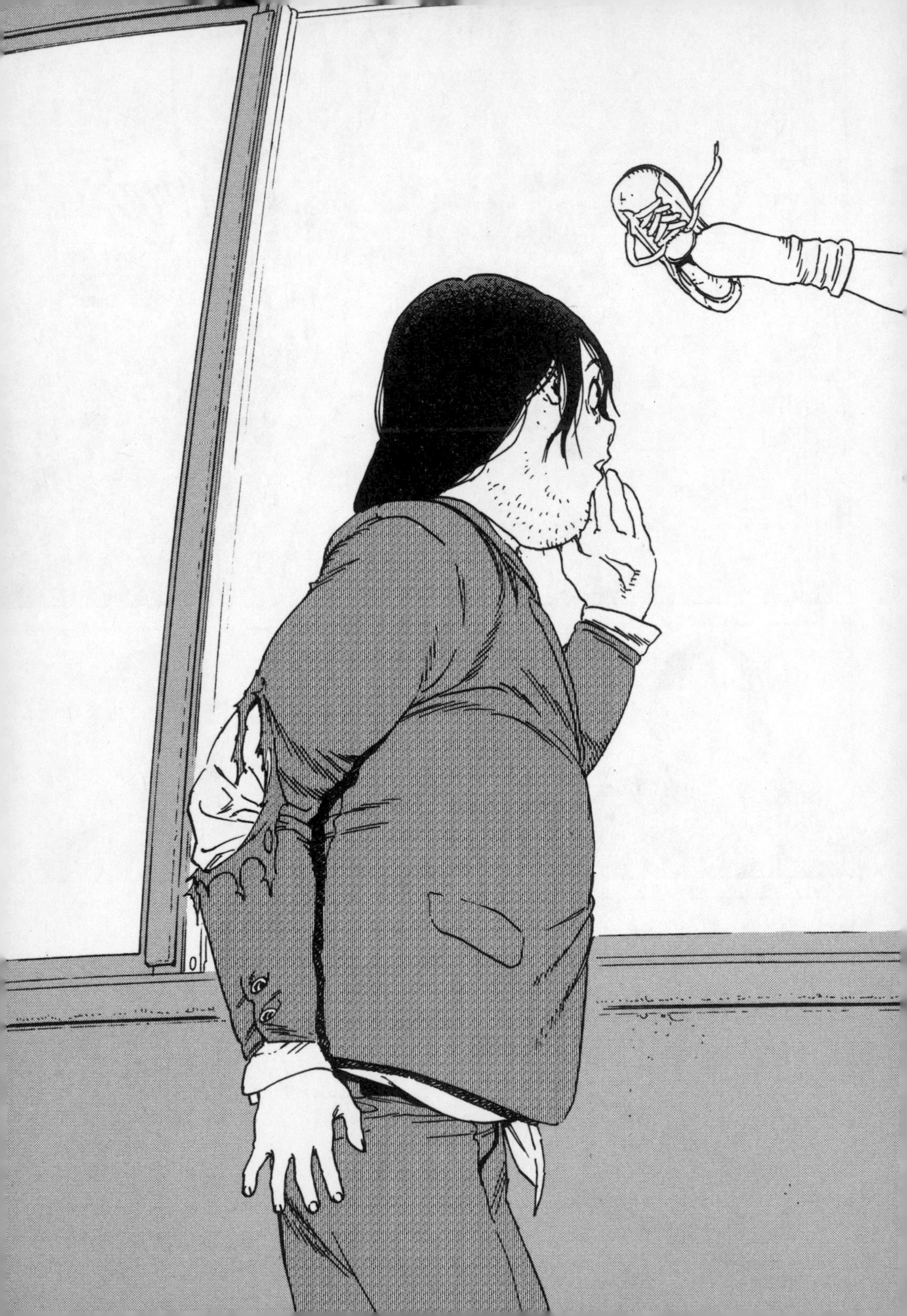

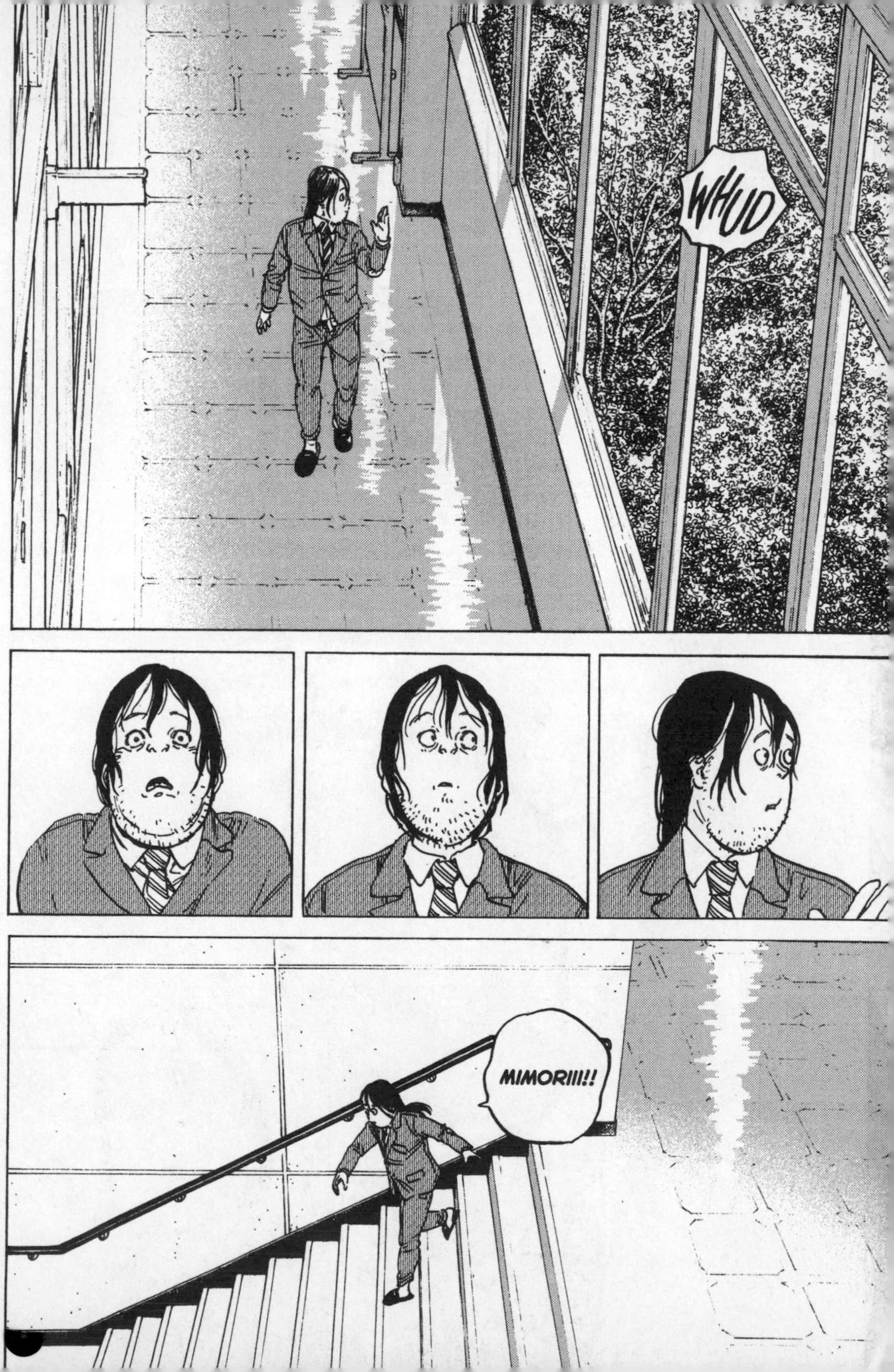
WHUD
MIMORIII!!

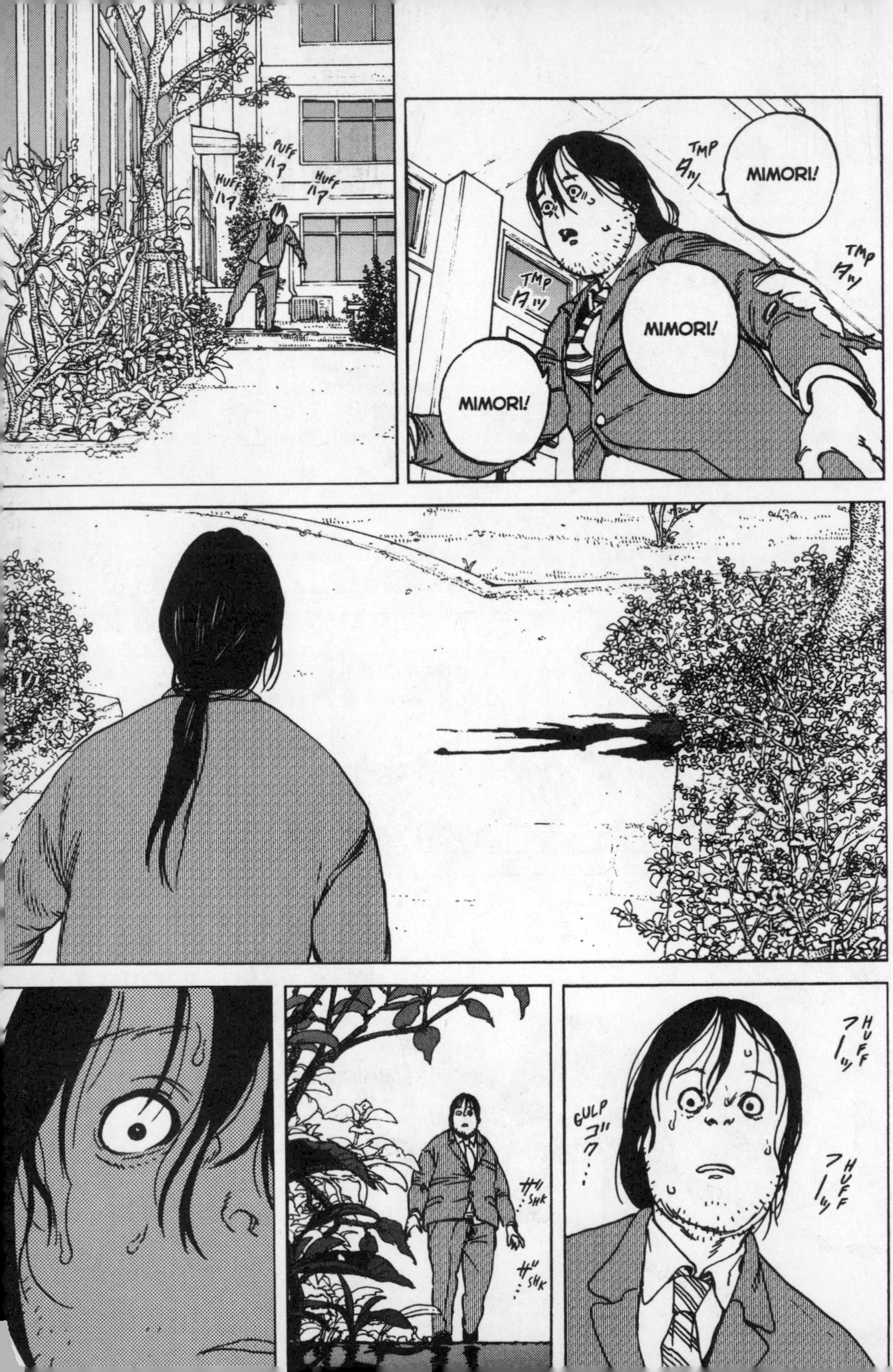
TMP
ダッ
MIMORI!
TMP
ダッ
TMP
ダッ
MIMORI!
MIMORI!
PUFF
ハア
HUFF
ハア
HUFF
フーッ
GULP
ゴク…
HUFF
フーッ
ザッ
SHK
ザッ
SHK

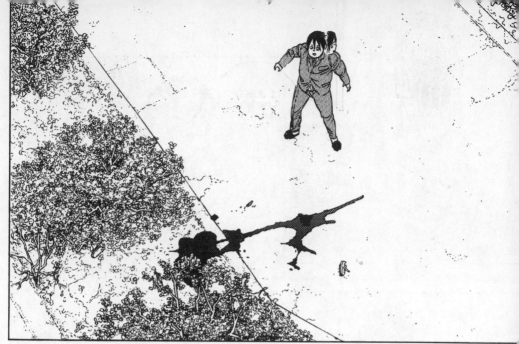

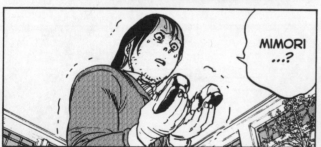

MIMORI
....?

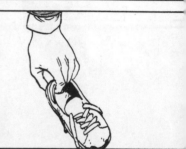

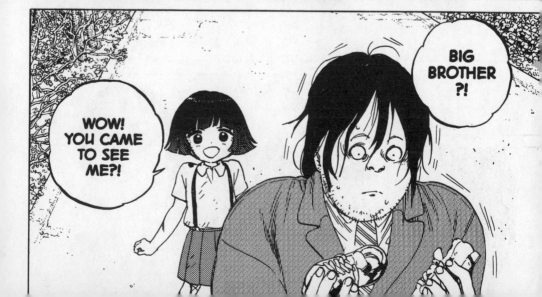

WOW! YOU CAME TO SEE ME?!

BIG BROTHER ?!

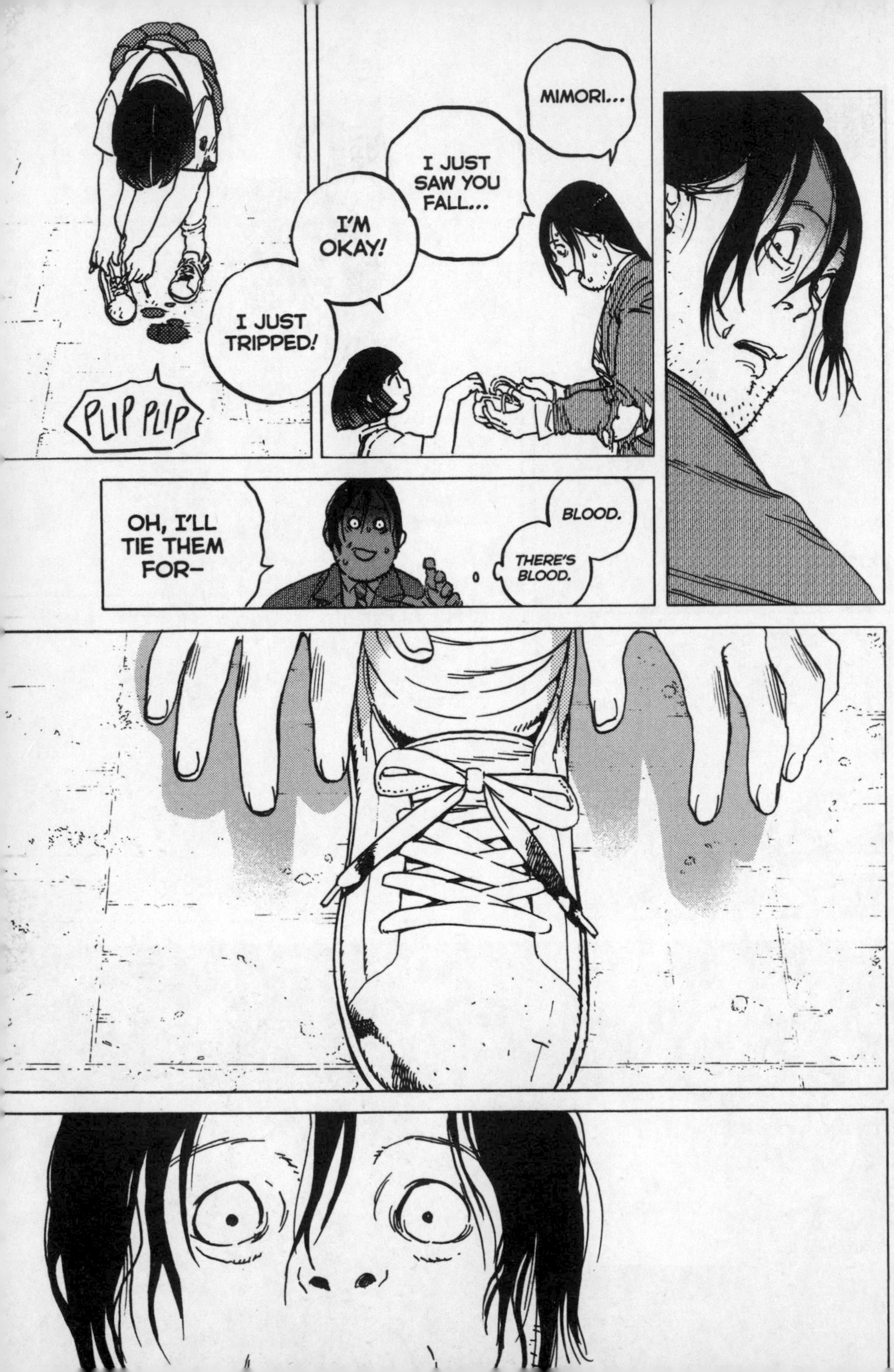
MIMORI...
I JUST SAW YOU FALL...
I'M OKAY!
I JUST TRIPPED!
PLIP PLIP
BLOOD.
THERE'S BLOOD.
OH, I'LL TIE THEM FOR–

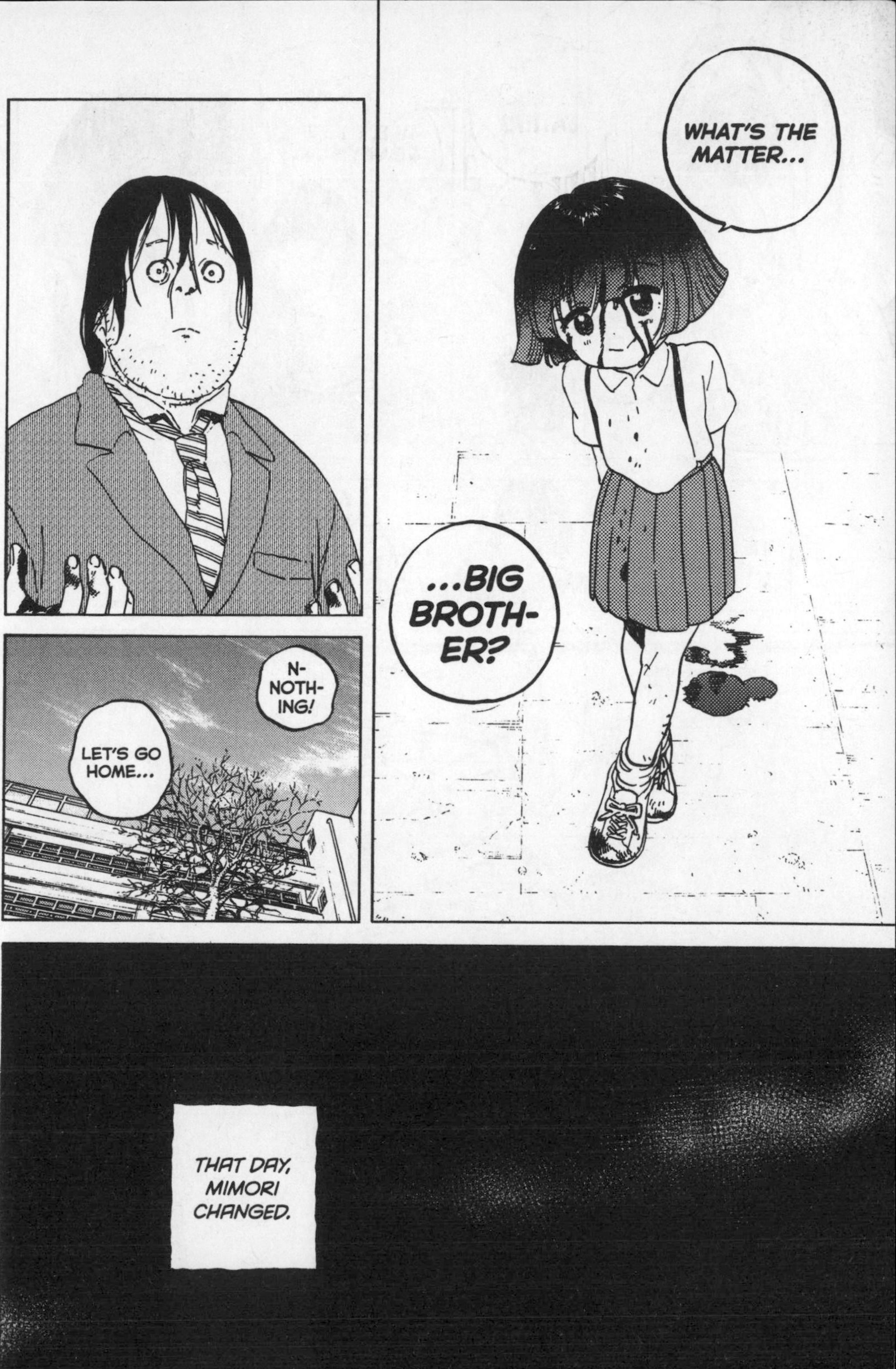
WHAT'S THE MATTER...
...BIG BROTH-ER?
N-NOTH-ING!
LET'S GO HOME...
THAT DAY, MIMORI CHANGED.

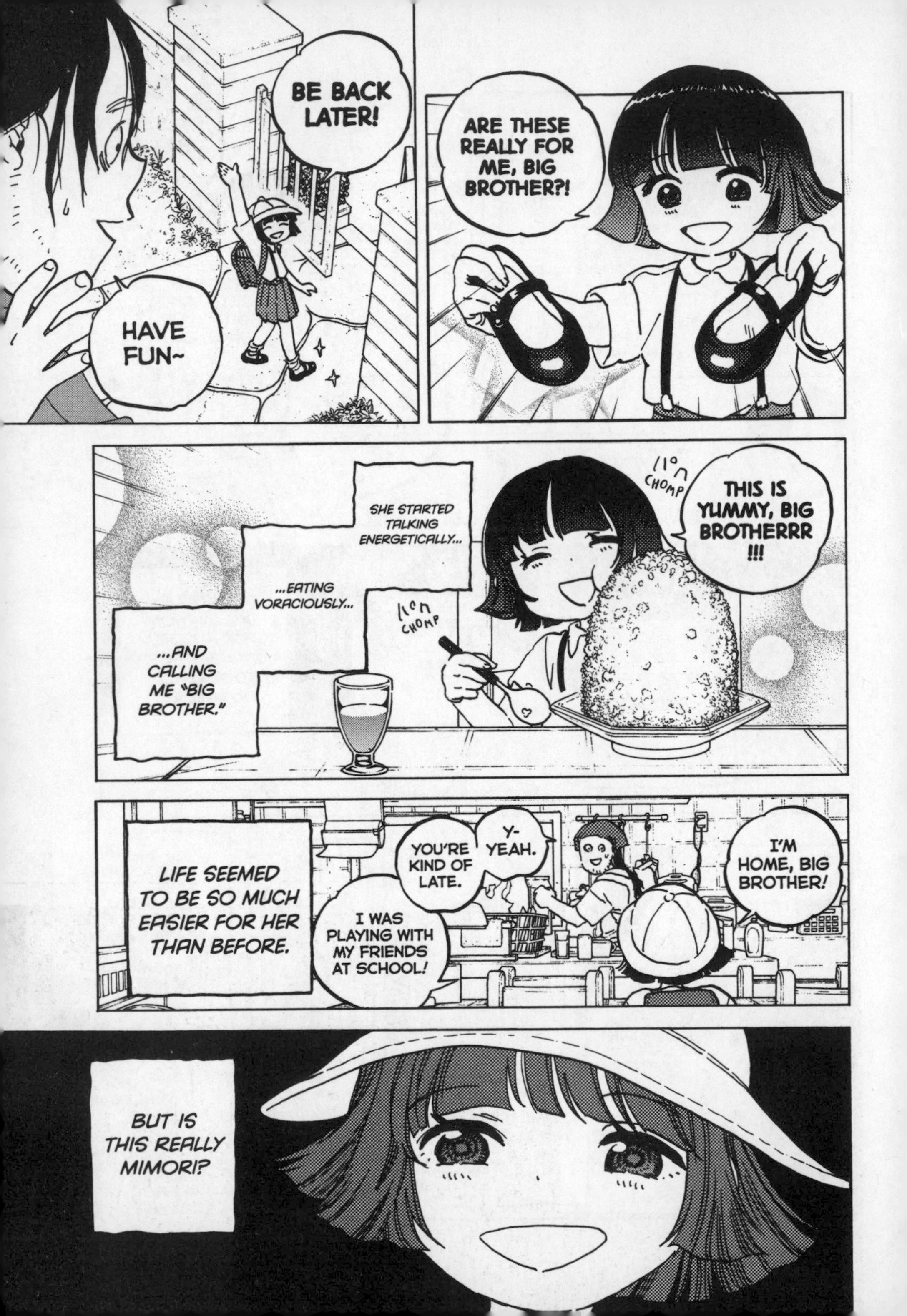
ARE THESE REALLY FOR ME, BIG BROTHER?!
BE BACK LATER!
HAVE FUN~
パク CHOMP
THIS IS YUMMY, BIG BROTHERRR !!!
SHE STARTED TALKING ENERGETICALLY...
...EATING VORACIOUSLY...
パク CHOMP
...AND CALLING ME "BIG BROTHER."
I'M HOME, BIG BROTHER!
Y-YEAH.
YOU'RE KIND OF LATE.
I WAS PLAYING WITH MY FRIENDS AT SCHOOL!
LIFE SEEMED TO BE SO MUCH EASIER FOR HER THAN BEFORE.
BUT IS THIS REALLY MIMORI?

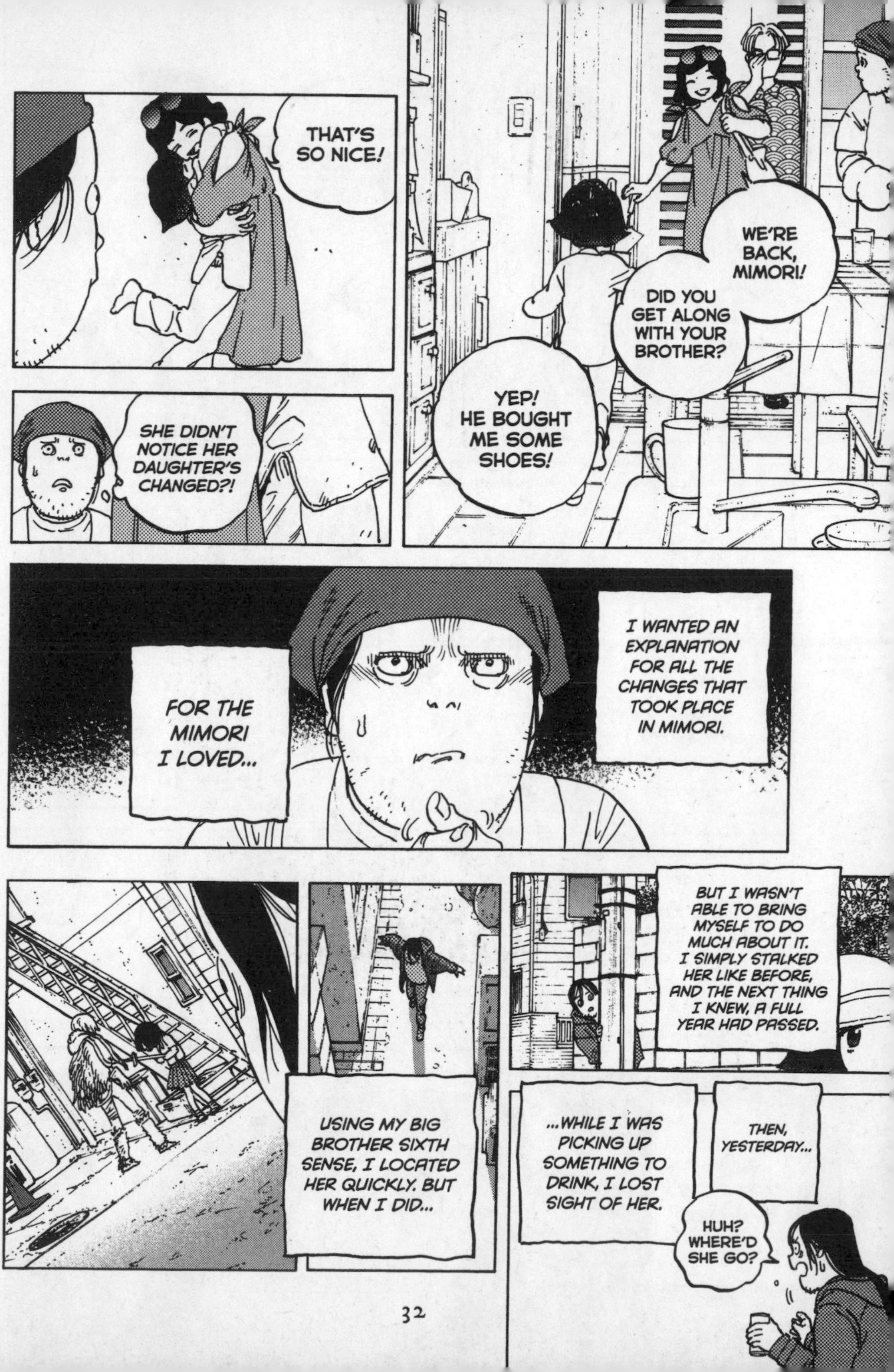
WE'RE BACK, MIMORI!
DID YOU GET ALONG WITH YOUR BROTHER?
YEP! HE BOUGHT ME SOME SHOES!
THAT'S SO NICE!
SHE DIDN'T NOTICE HER DAUGHTER'S CHANGED?!
I WANTED AN EXPLANATION FOR ALL THE CHANGES THAT TOOK PLACE IN MIMORI.
FOR THE MIMORI I LOVED...
BUT I WASN'T ABLE TO BRING MYSELF TO DO MUCH ABOUT IT. I SIMPLY STALKED HER LIKE BEFORE, AND THE NEXT THING I KNEW, A FULL YEAR HAD PASSED.
THEN, YESTERDAY...
...WHILE I WAS PICKING UP SOMETHING TO DRINK, I LOST SIGHT OF HER.
HUH? WHERE'D SHE GO?
USING MY BIG BROTHER SIXTH SENSE, I LOCATED HER QUICKLY. BUT WHEN I DID...

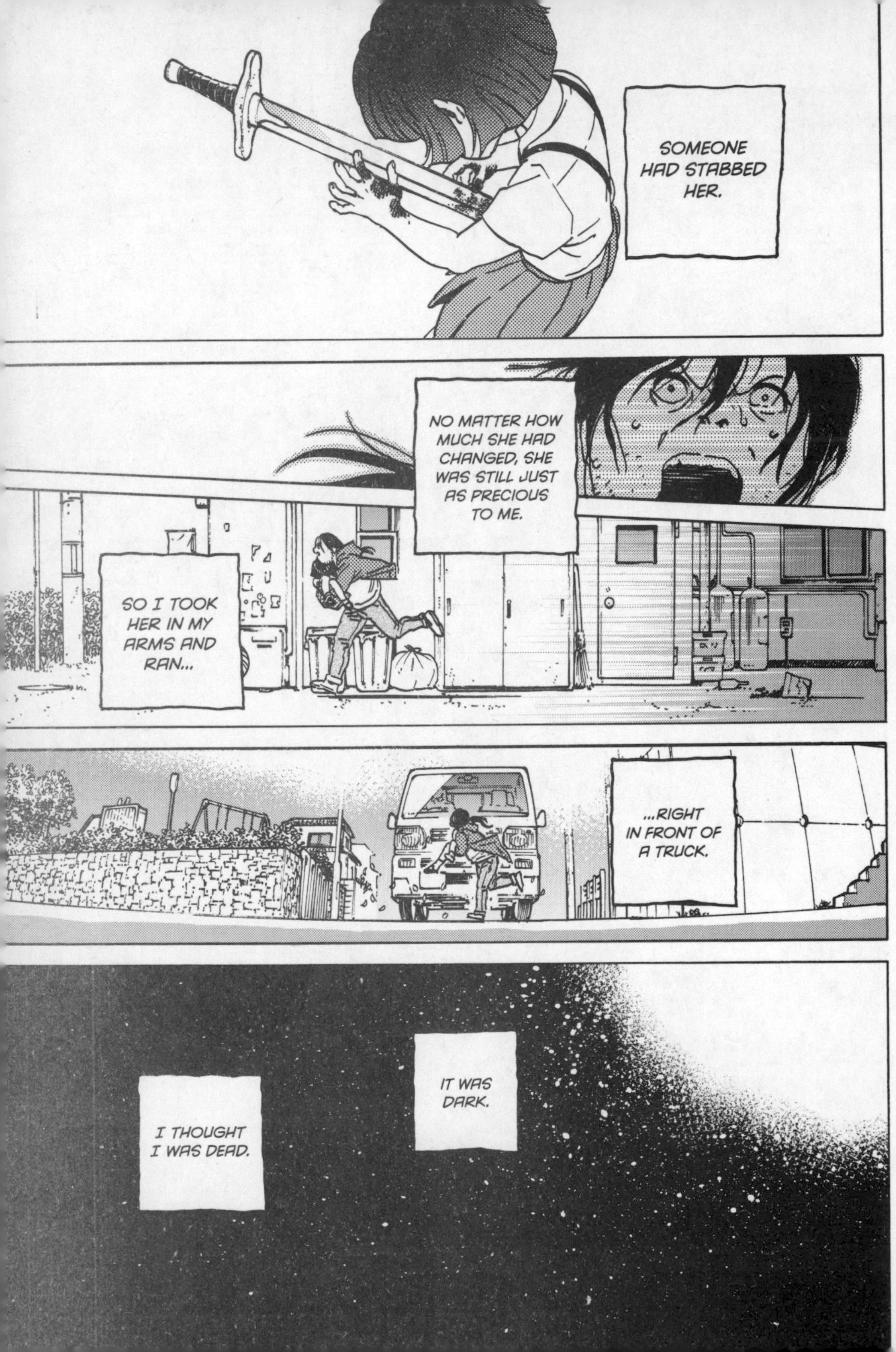
SOMEONE HAD STABBED HER.
NO MATTER HOW MUCH SHE HAD CHANGED, SHE WAS STILL JUST AS PRECIOUS TO ME.
SO I TOOK HER IN MY ARMS AND RAN...
...RIGHT IN FRONT OF A TRUCK.
IT WAS DARK.
I THOUGHT I WAS DEAD.

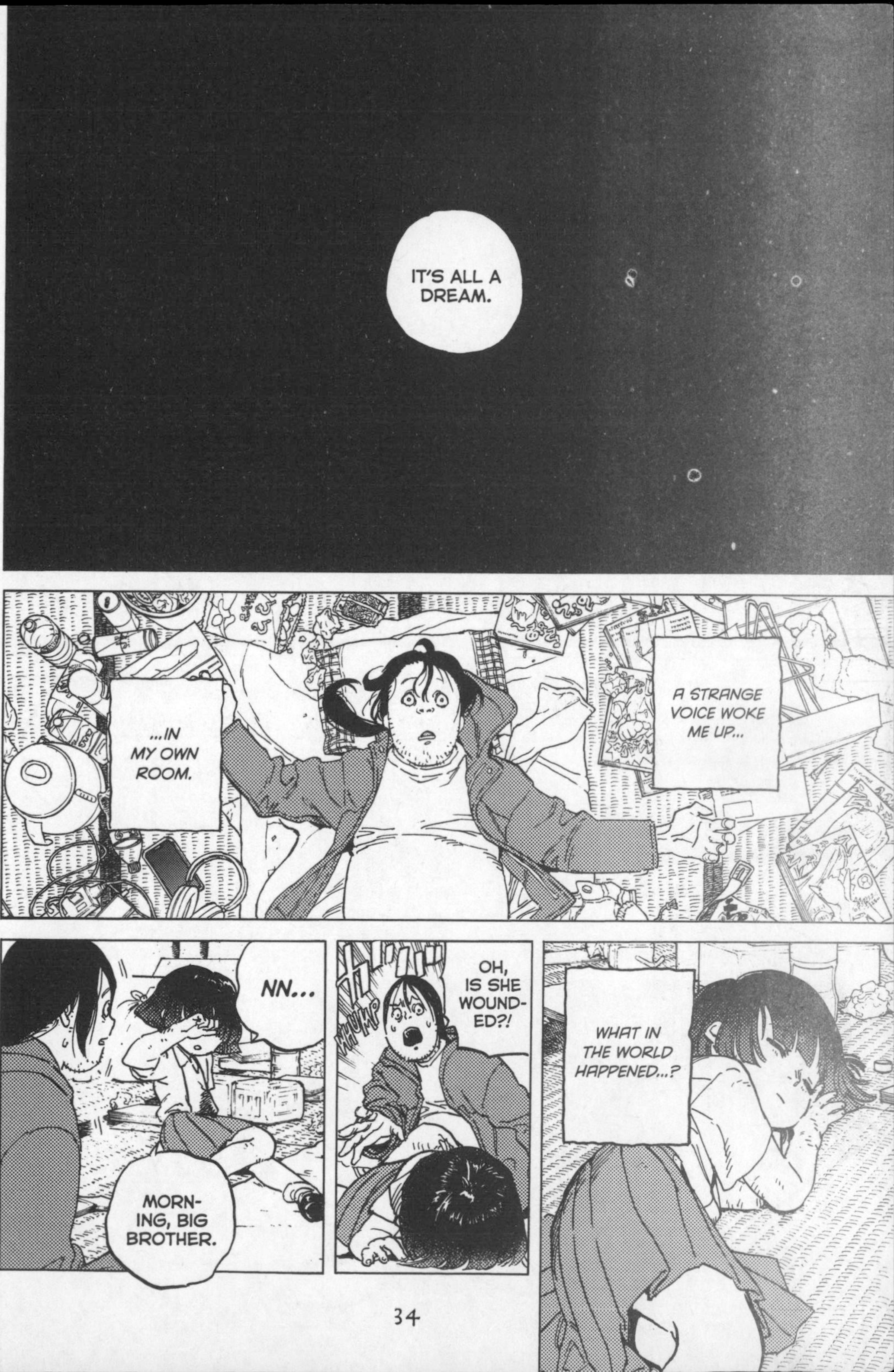
IT'S ALL A DREAM.
A STRANGE VOICE WOKE ME UP...
...IN MY OWN ROOM.
WHAT IN THE WORLD HAPPENED...?
OH, IS SHE WOUND-ED?!
NN...
MORN-ING, BIG BROTHER.

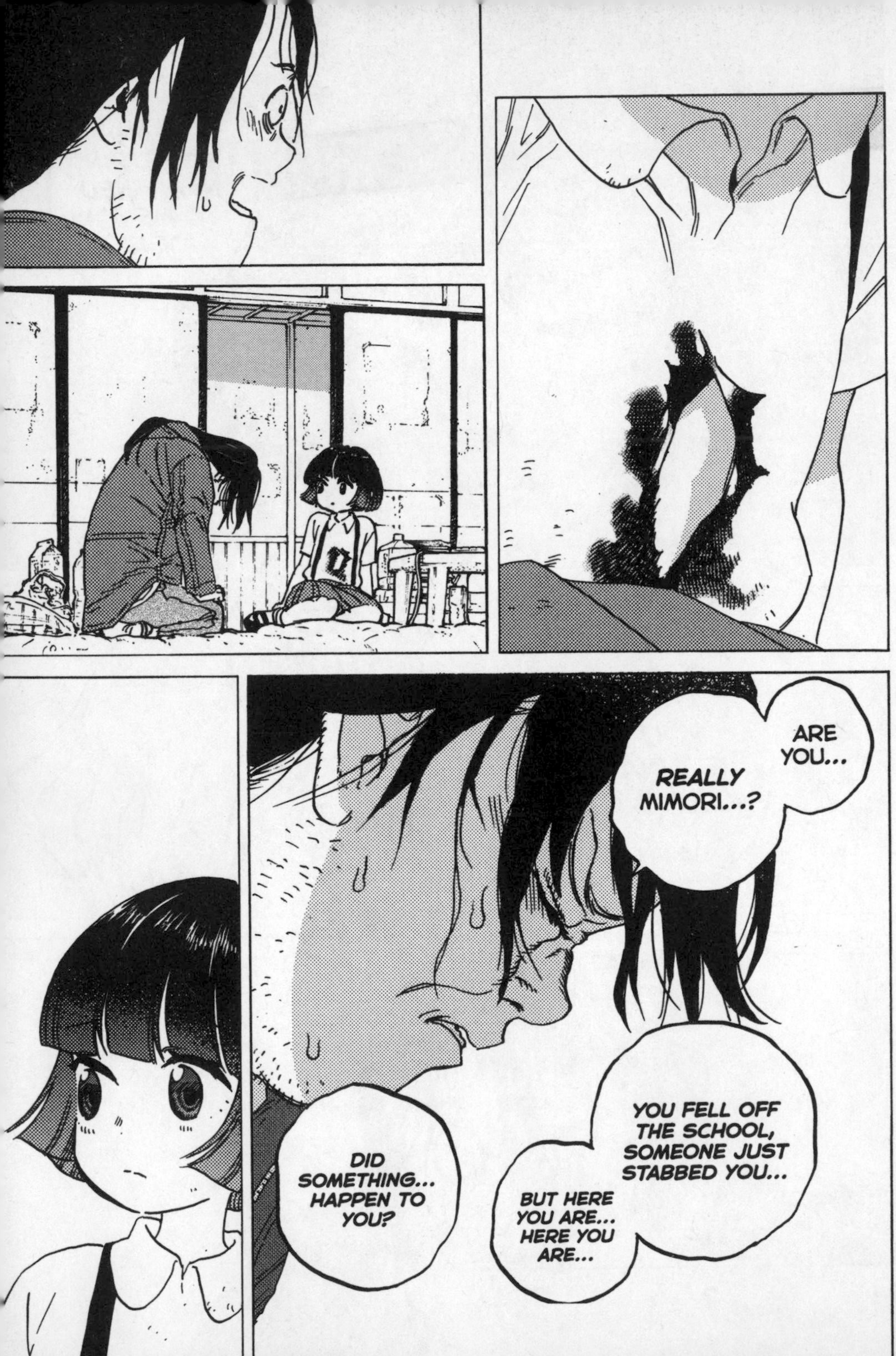
ARE YOU... REALLY MIMORI...?
YOU FELL OFF THE SCHOOL, SOMEONE JUST STABBED YOU...
BUT HERE YOU ARE... HERE YOU ARE...
DID SOMETHING... HAPPEN TO YOU?

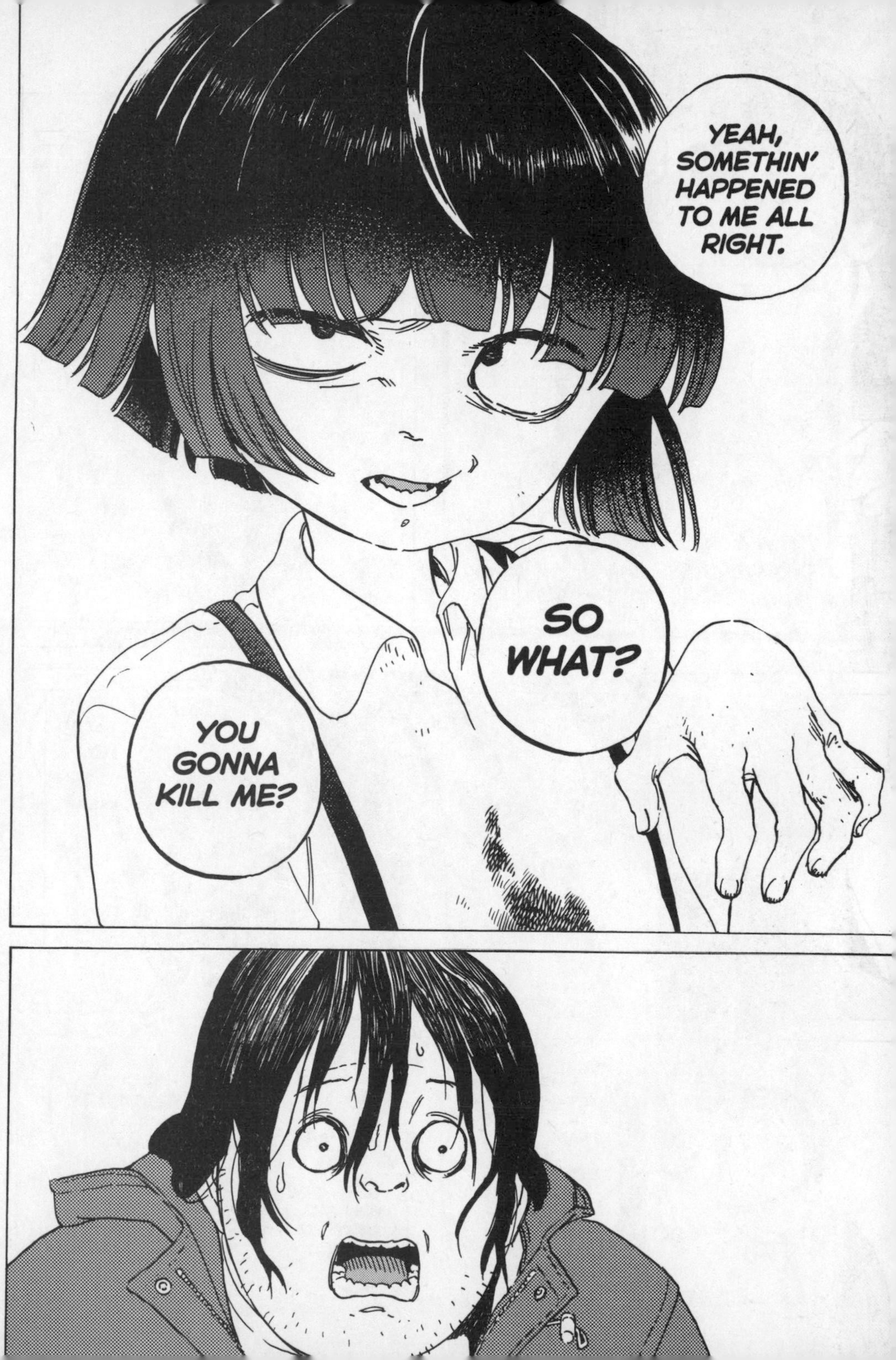
YEAH, SOMETHIN' HAPPENED TO ME ALL RIGHT.
SO WHAT?
YOU GONNA KILL ME?

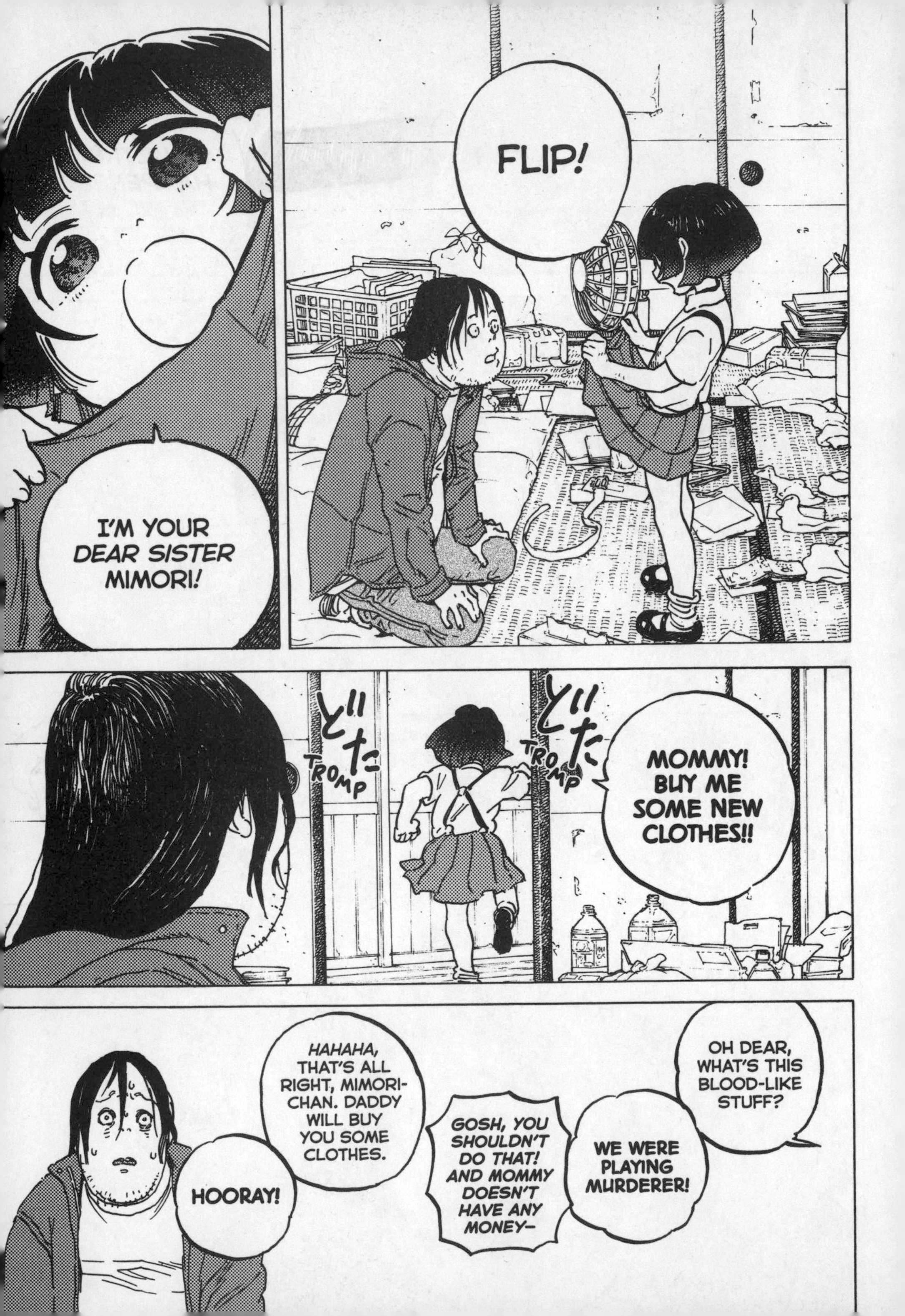
FLIP!
I'M YOUR DEAR SISTER MIMORI!
どた
TROMP
MOMMY! BUY ME SOME NEW CLOTHES!!
どた
TROMP
OH DEAR, WHAT'S THIS BLOOD-LIKE STUFF?
WE WERE PLAYING MURDERER!
GOSH, YOU SHOULDN'T DO THAT! AND MOMMY DOESN'T HAVE ANY MONEY–
HAHAHA, THAT'S ALL RIGHT, MIMORI-CHAN. DADDY WILL BUY YOU SOME CLOTHES.
HOORAY!

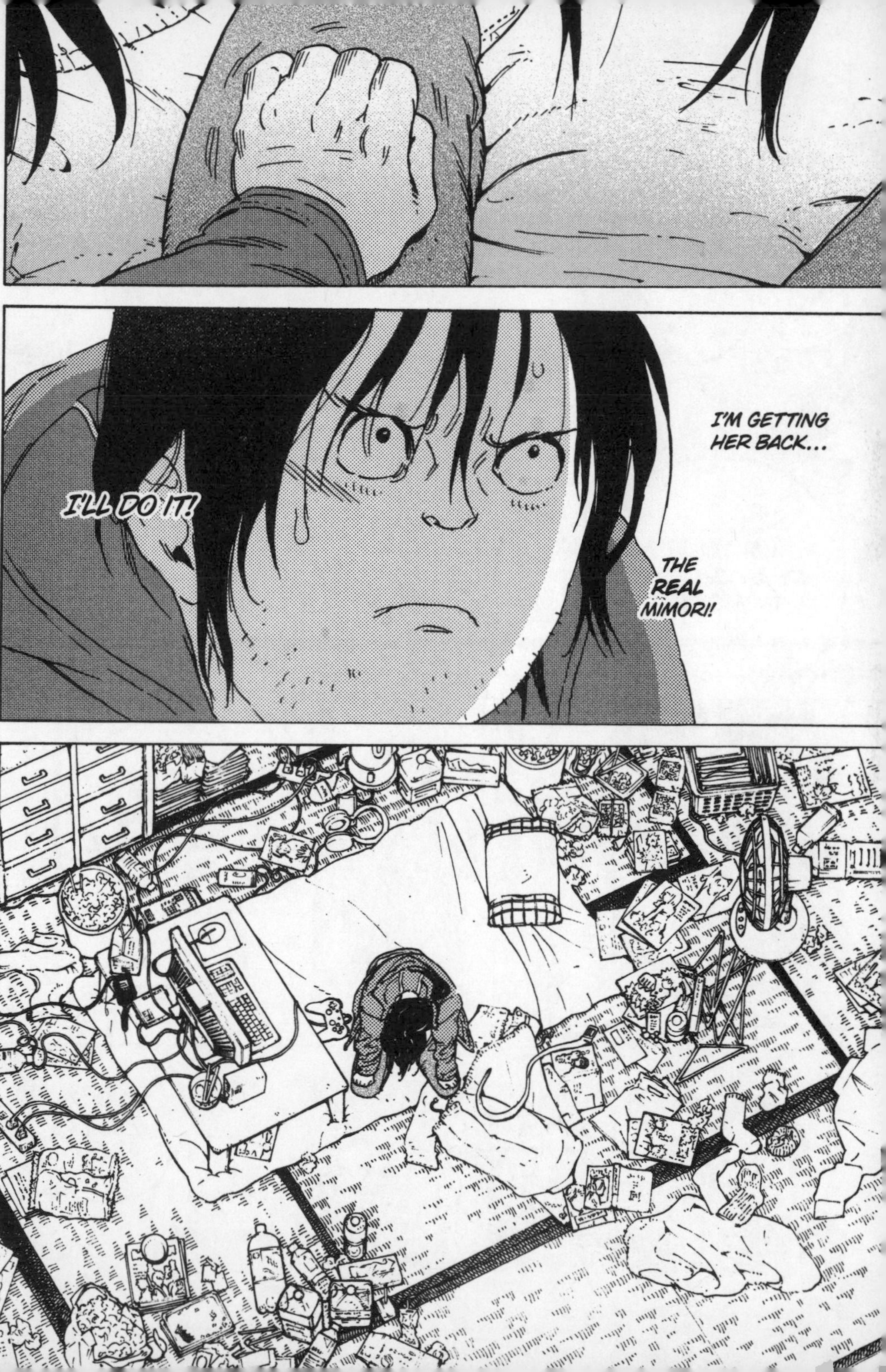
I'M GETTING HER BACK...
THE REAL MIMORI!
I'LL DO IT!

TO YOUR ETERNITY

TO YOUR ETERNITY

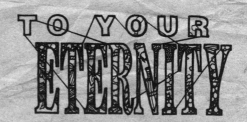

#134 Attack

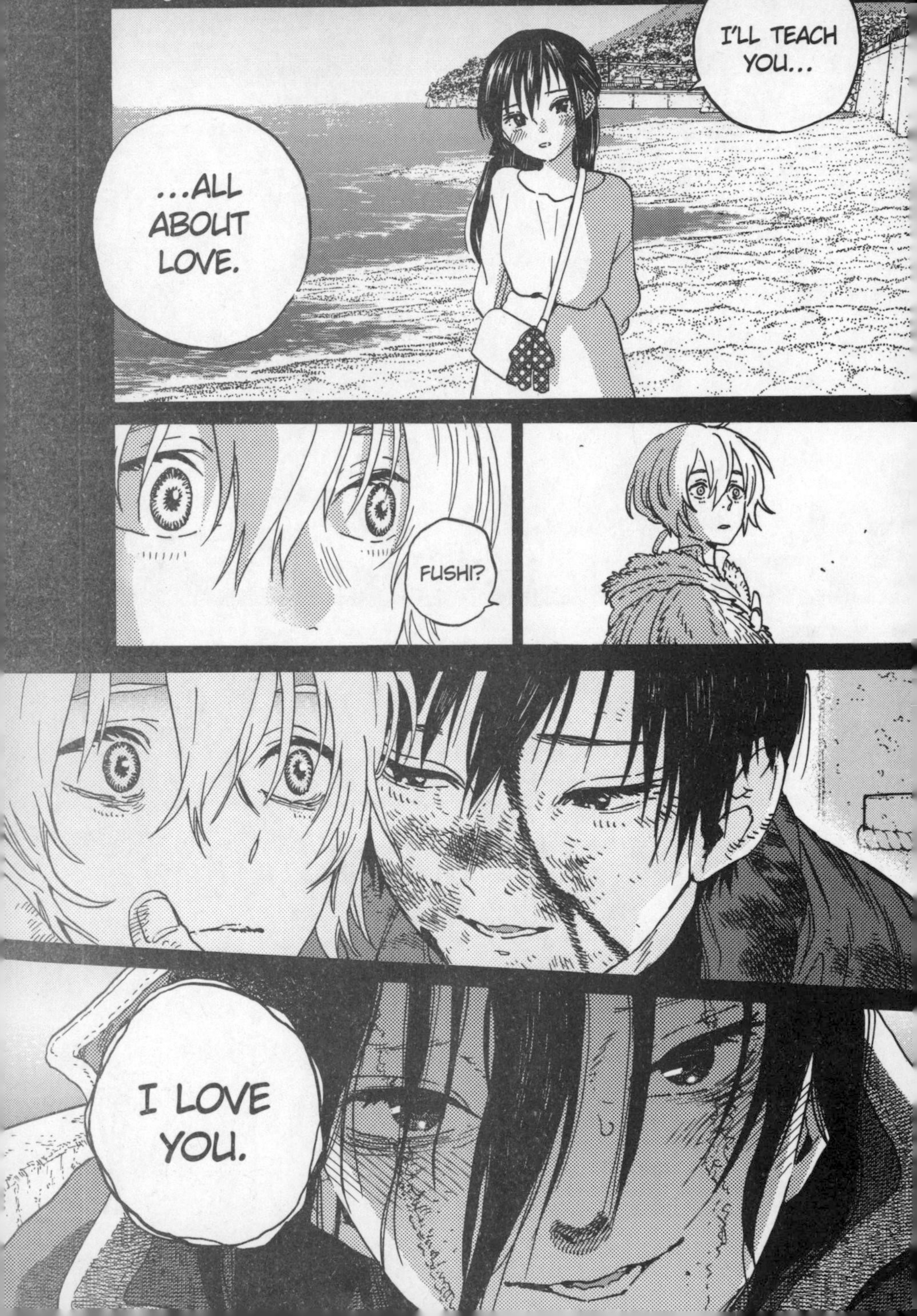

I'LL TEACH YOU...
...ALL ABOUT LOVE.
FUSHI?
I LOVE YOU.

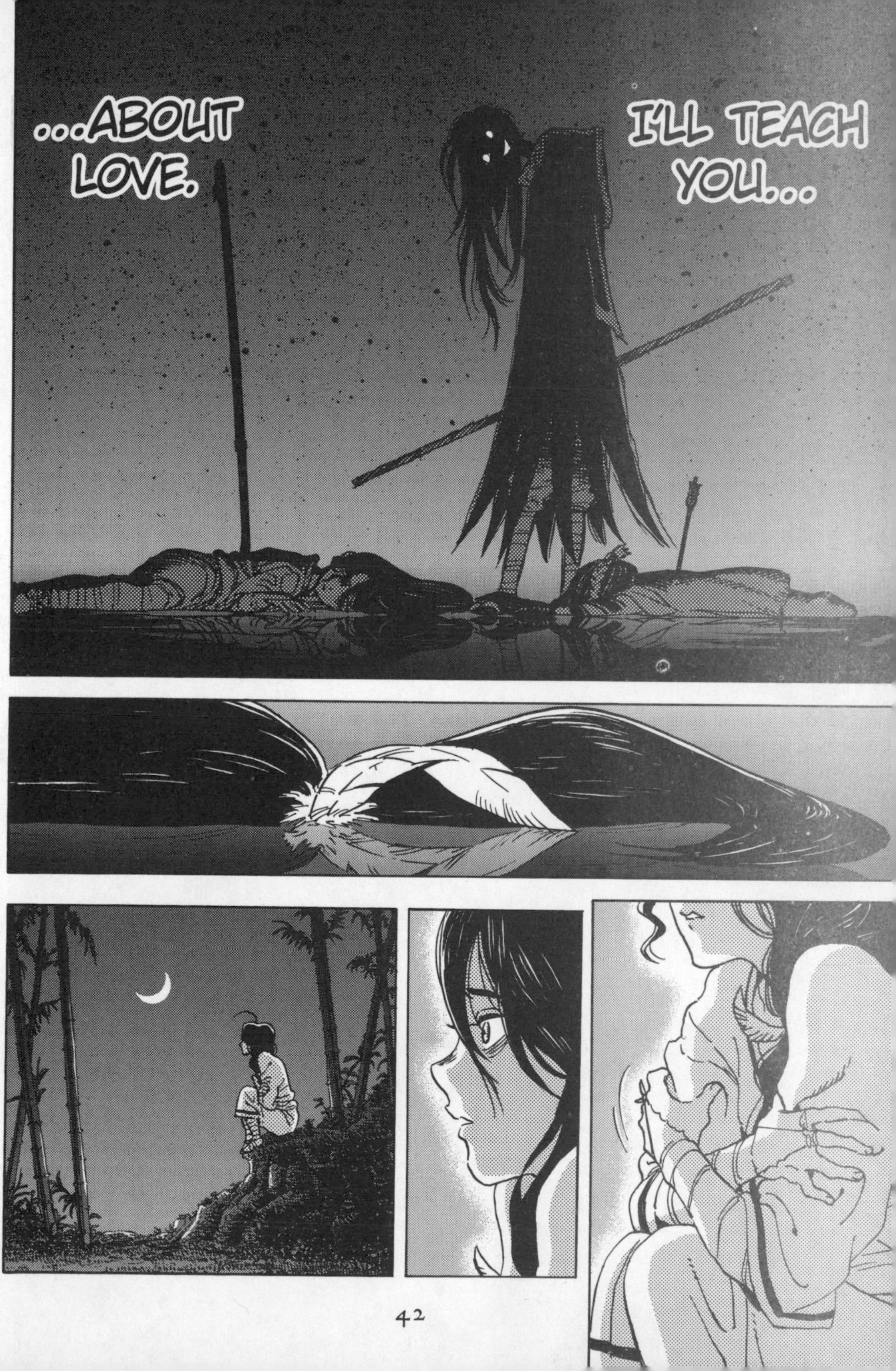
I'LL TEACH YOU...
...ABOUT LOVE.

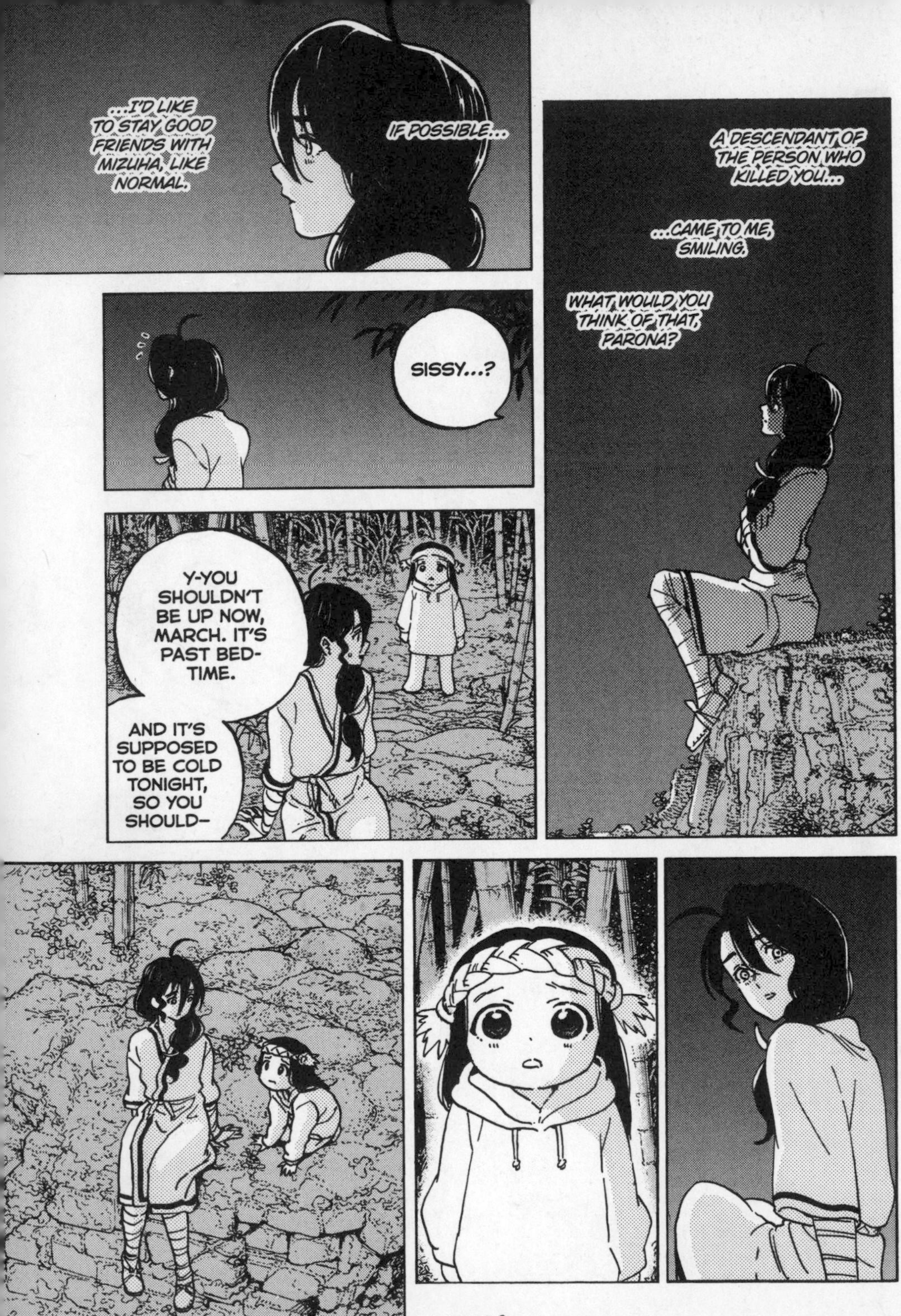
IF POSSIBLE...
...I'D LIKE TO STAY GOOD FRIENDS WITH MIZUHA, LIKE NORMAL.
A DESCENDANT OF THE PERSON WHO KILLED YOU...
...CAME TO ME, SMILING.
WHAT WOULD YOU THINK OF THAT, PARONA?
SISSY...?
Y-YOU SHOULDN'T BE UP NOW, MARCH. IT'S PAST BED-TIME.
AND IT'S SUPPOSED TO BE COLD TONIGHT, SO YOU SHOULD–

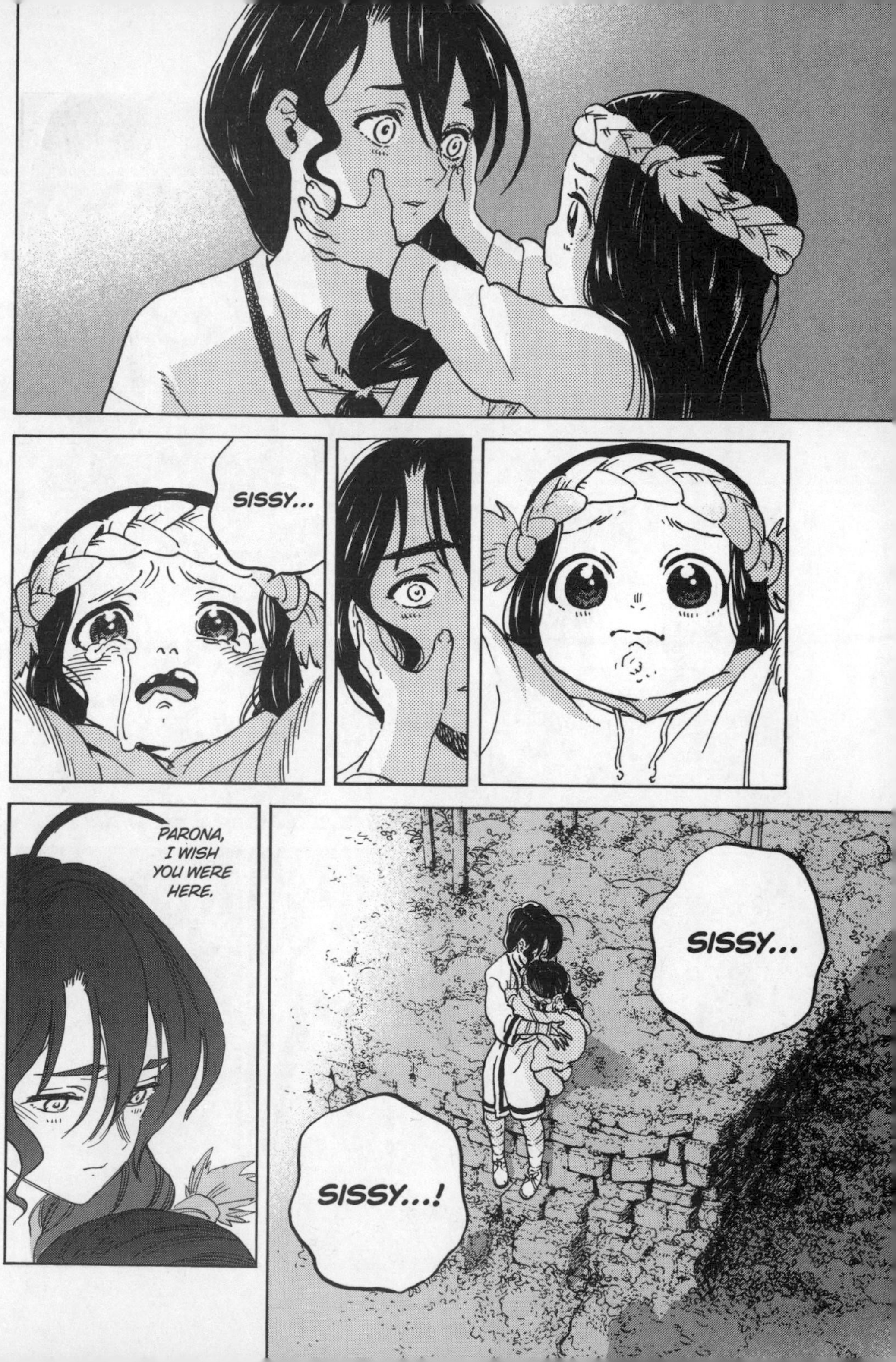
SISSY...
SISSY...
SISSY...!
PARONA, I WISH YOU WERE HERE.

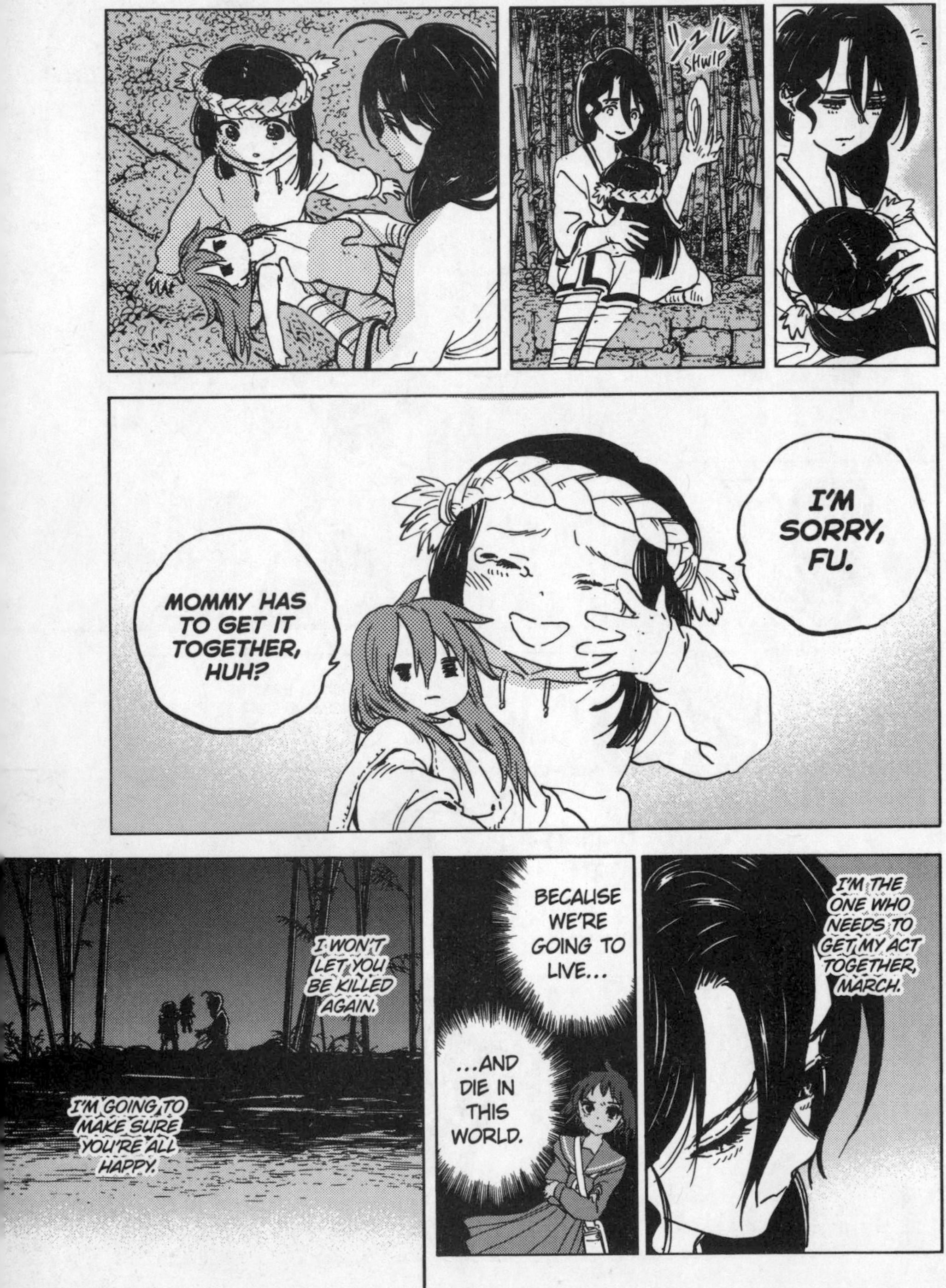
SHWIP
I'M SORRY, FU.
MOMMY HAS TO GET IT TOGETHER, HUH?
I'M THE ONE WHO NEEDS TO GET MY ACT TOGETHER, MARCH.
BECAUSE WE'RE GOING TO LIVE...
...AND DIE IN THIS WORLD.
I WON'T LET YOU BE KILLED AGAIN.
I'M GOING TO MAKE SURE YOU'RE ALL HAPPY.

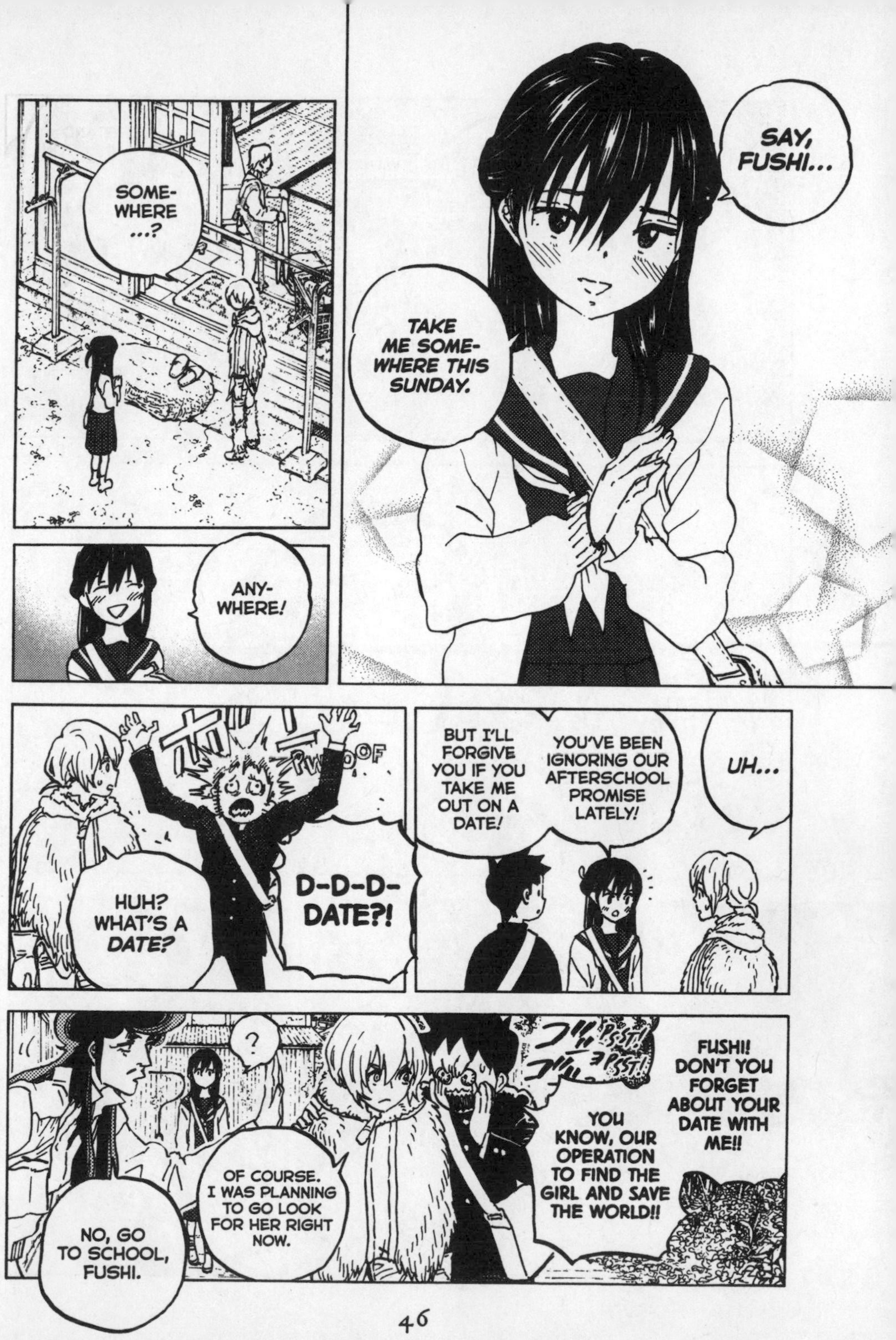

SAY, FUSHI...
TAKE ME SOMEWHERE THIS SUNDAY.
SOME-WHERE ...?
ANY-WHERE!
UH...
YOU'VE BEEN IGNORING OUR AFTERSCHOOL PROMISE LATELY!
BUT I'LL FORGIVE YOU IF YOU TAKE ME OUT ON A DATE!
D-D-D-DATE?!
HUH? WHAT'S A *DATE?*
FUSHI! DON'T YOU FORGET ABOUT YOUR DATE WITH ME!!
PSST! PSST!
YOU KNOW, OUR OPERATION TO FIND THE GIRL AND SAVE THE WORLD!!
?
OF COURSE. I WAS PLANNING TO GO LOOK FOR HER RIGHT NOW.
NO, GO TO SCHOOL, FUSHI.

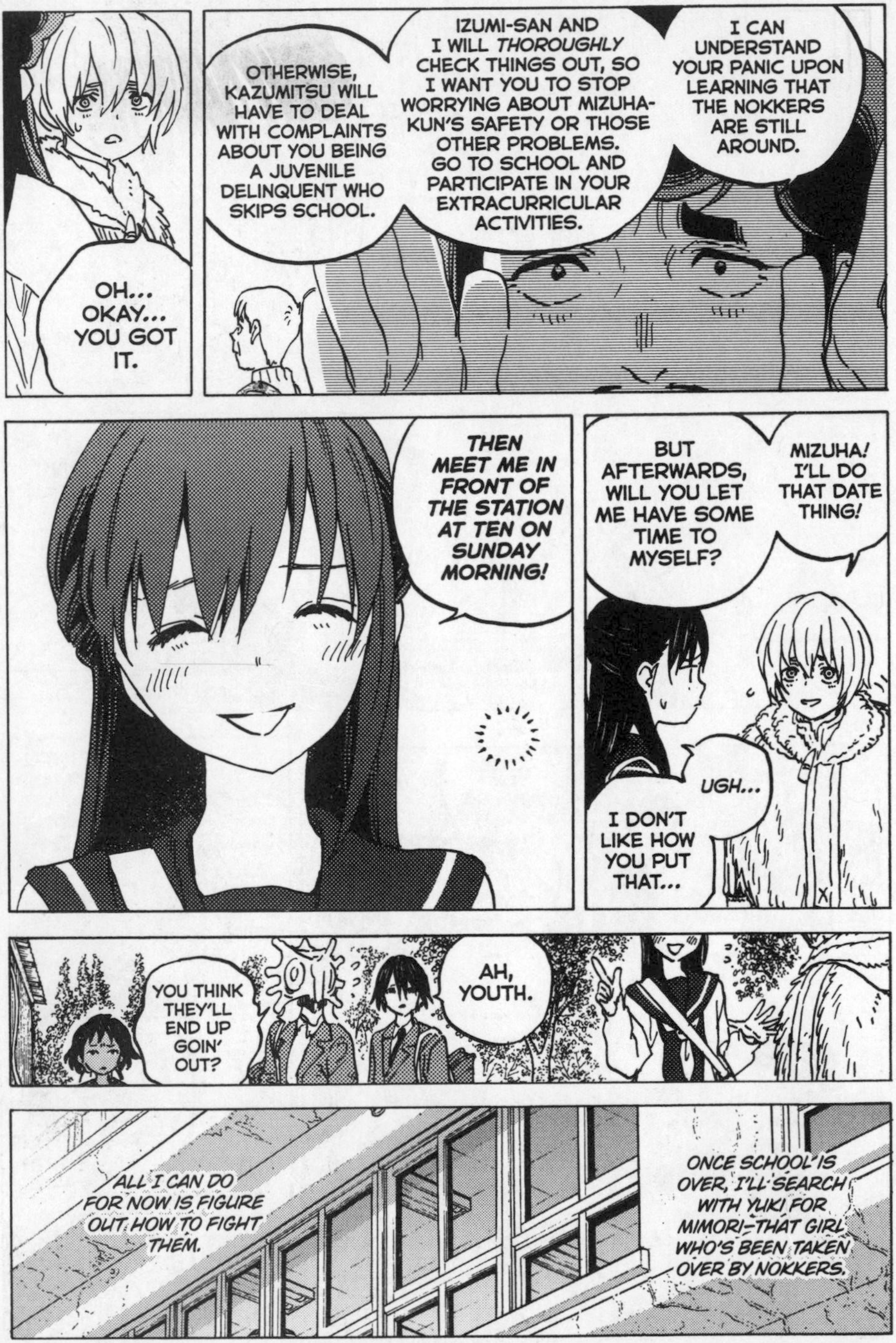
I CAN UNDERSTAND YOUR PANIC UPON LEARNING THAT THE NOKKERS ARE STILL AROUND.
IZUMI-SAN AND I WILL *THOROUGHLY* CHECK THINGS OUT, SO I WANT YOU TO STOP WORRYING ABOUT MIZUHA-KUN'S SAFETY OR THOSE OTHER PROBLEMS. GO TO SCHOOL AND PARTICIPATE IN YOUR EXTRACURRICULAR ACTIVITIES.
OTHERWISE, KAZUMITSU WILL HAVE TO DEAL WITH COMPLAINTS ABOUT YOU BEING A JUVENILE DELINQUENT WHO SKIPS SCHOOL.
OH... OKAY... YOU GOT IT.
MIZUHA! I'LL DO THAT DATE THING!
BUT AFTERWARDS, WILL YOU LET ME HAVE SOME TIME TO MYSELF?
UGH...
I DON'T LIKE HOW YOU PUT THAT...
THEN MEET ME IN FRONT OF THE STATION AT TEN ON SUNDAY MORNING!
AH, YOUTH.
YOU THINK THEY'LL END UP GOIN' OUT?
ONCE SCHOOL IS OVER, I'LL SEARCH WITH YUKI FOR MIMORI—THAT GIRL WHO'S BEEN TAKEN OVER BY NOKKERS.
ALL I CAN DO FOR NOW IS FIGURE OUT HOW TO FIGHT THEM.

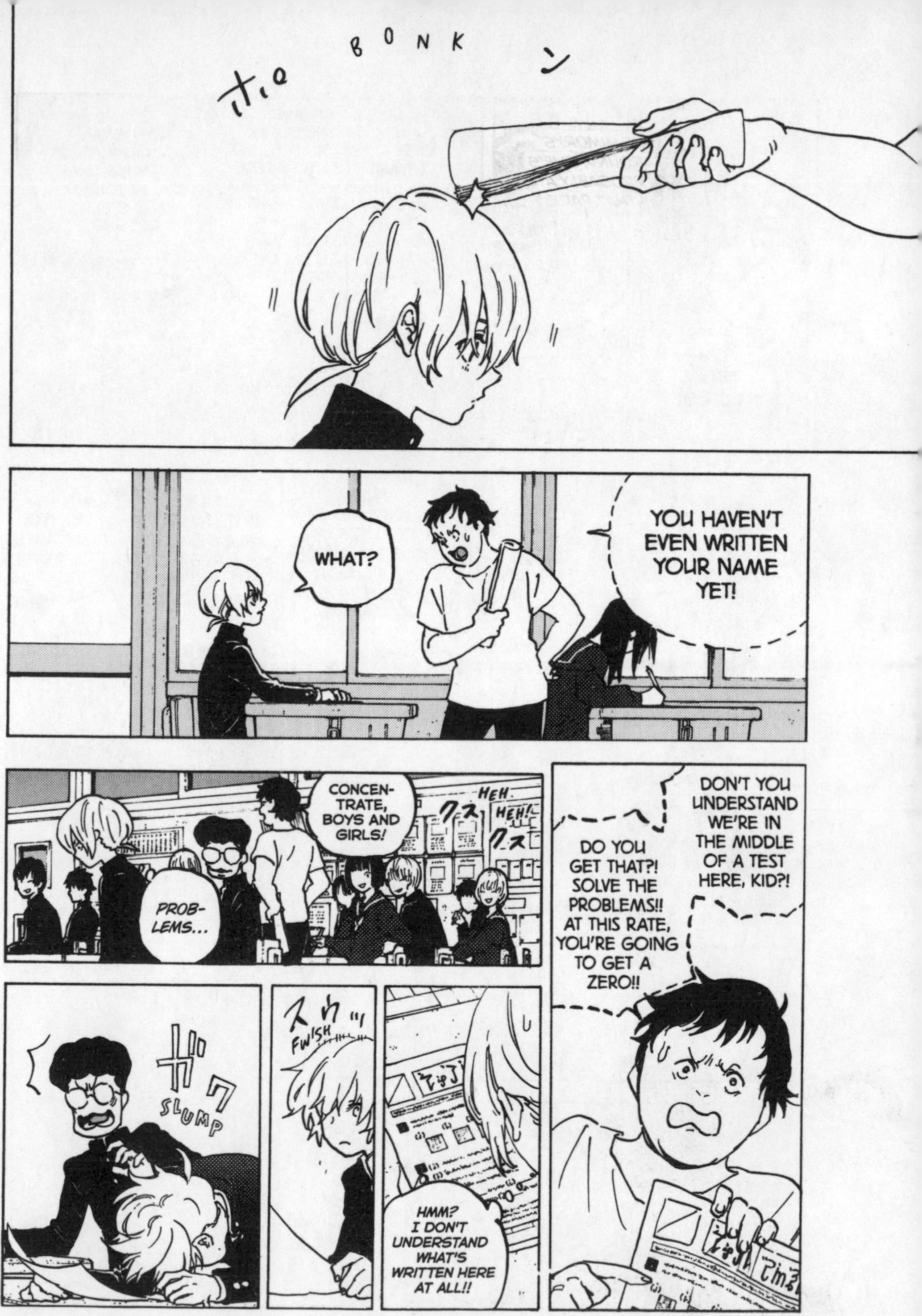
BONK
YOU HAVEN'T EVEN WRITTEN YOUR NAME YET!
WHAT?
DON'T YOU UNDERSTAND WE'RE IN THE MIDDLE OF A TEST HERE, KID?!
DO YOU GET THAT?! SOLVE THE PROBLEMS!! AT THIS RATE, YOU'RE GOING TO GET A ZERO!!
HEH HEH!
CONCEN-TRATE, BOYS AND GIRLS!
PROB-LEMS...
HMM? I DON'T UNDERSTAND WHAT'S WRITTEN HERE AT ALL!!
FWISH
SLUMP

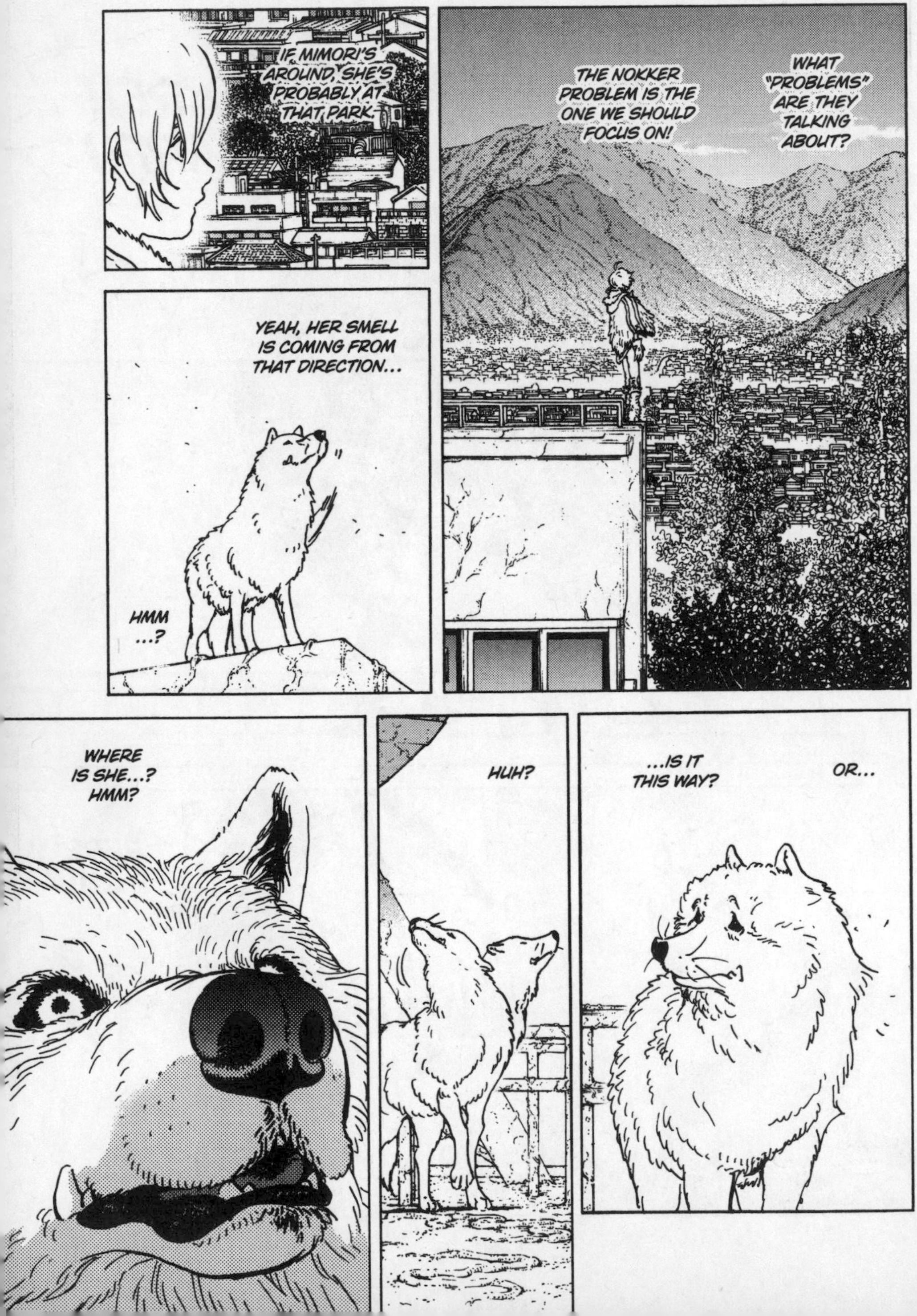
WHAT "PROBLEMS" ARE THEY TALKING ABOUT?
THE NOKKER PROBLEM IS THE ONE WE SHOULD FOCUS ON!
IF MIMORI'S AROUND, SHE'S PROBABLY AT THAT PARK.
YEAH, HER SMELL IS COMING FROM THAT DIRECTION...
HMM ...?
...IS IT THIS WAY?
OR...
HUH?
WHERE IS SHE...? HMM?

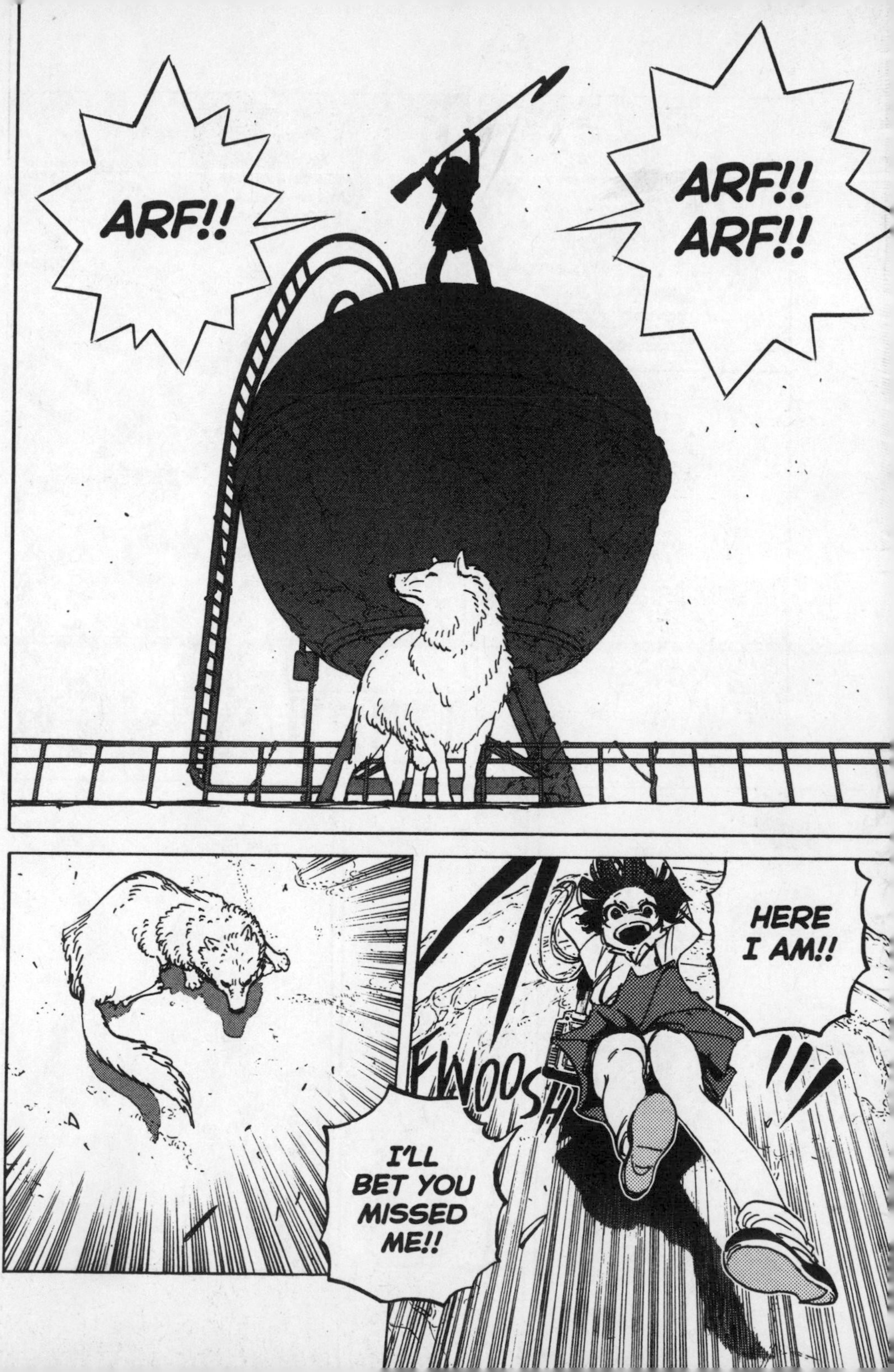

ARF!! ARF!!
ARF!!
HERE I AM!!
!!
FWOOSH
I'LL BET YOU MISSED ME!!

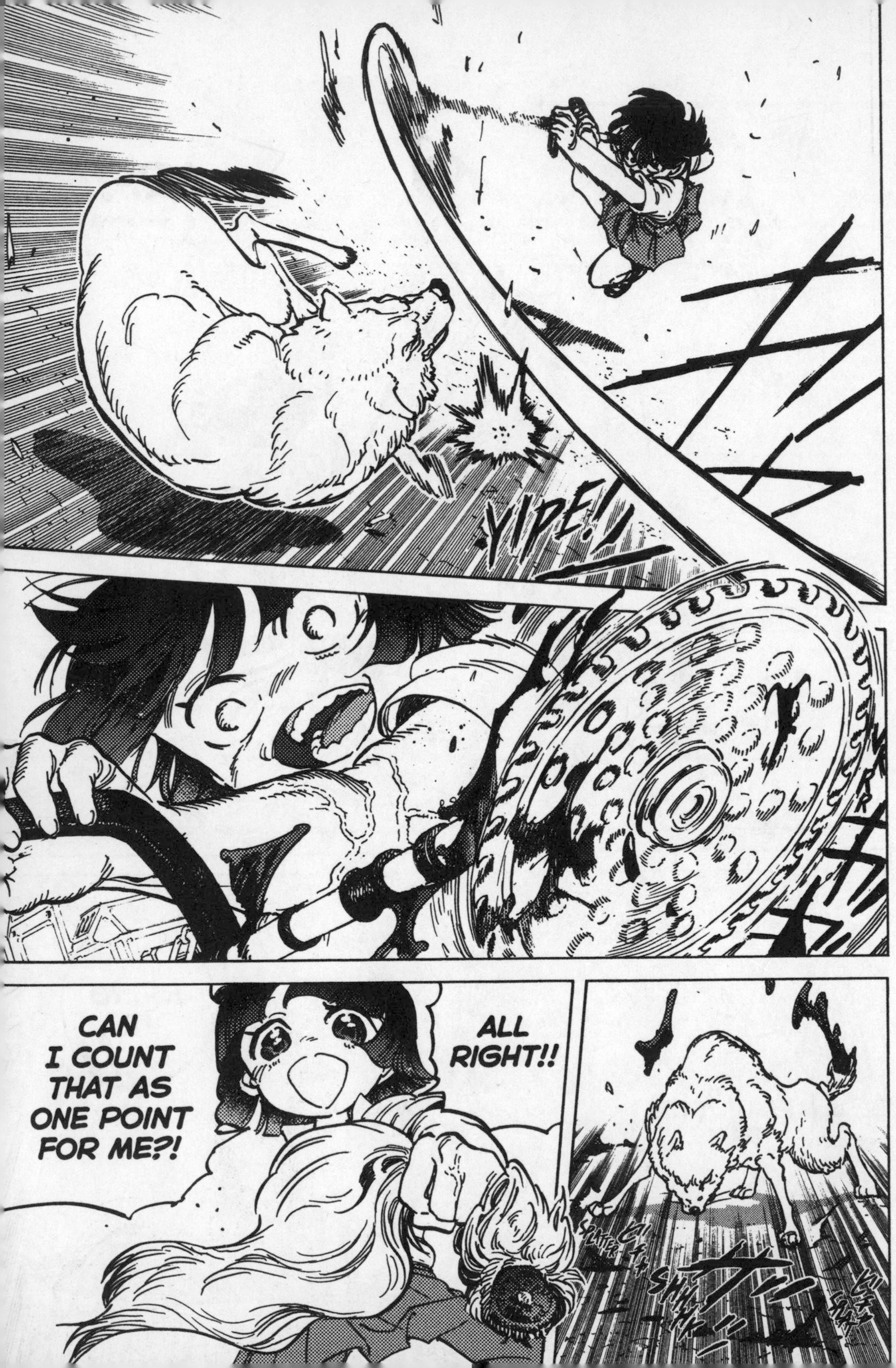
YIPE!!
SPLATTER
ALL RIGHT!!
CAN I COUNT THAT AS ONE POINT FOR ME?!

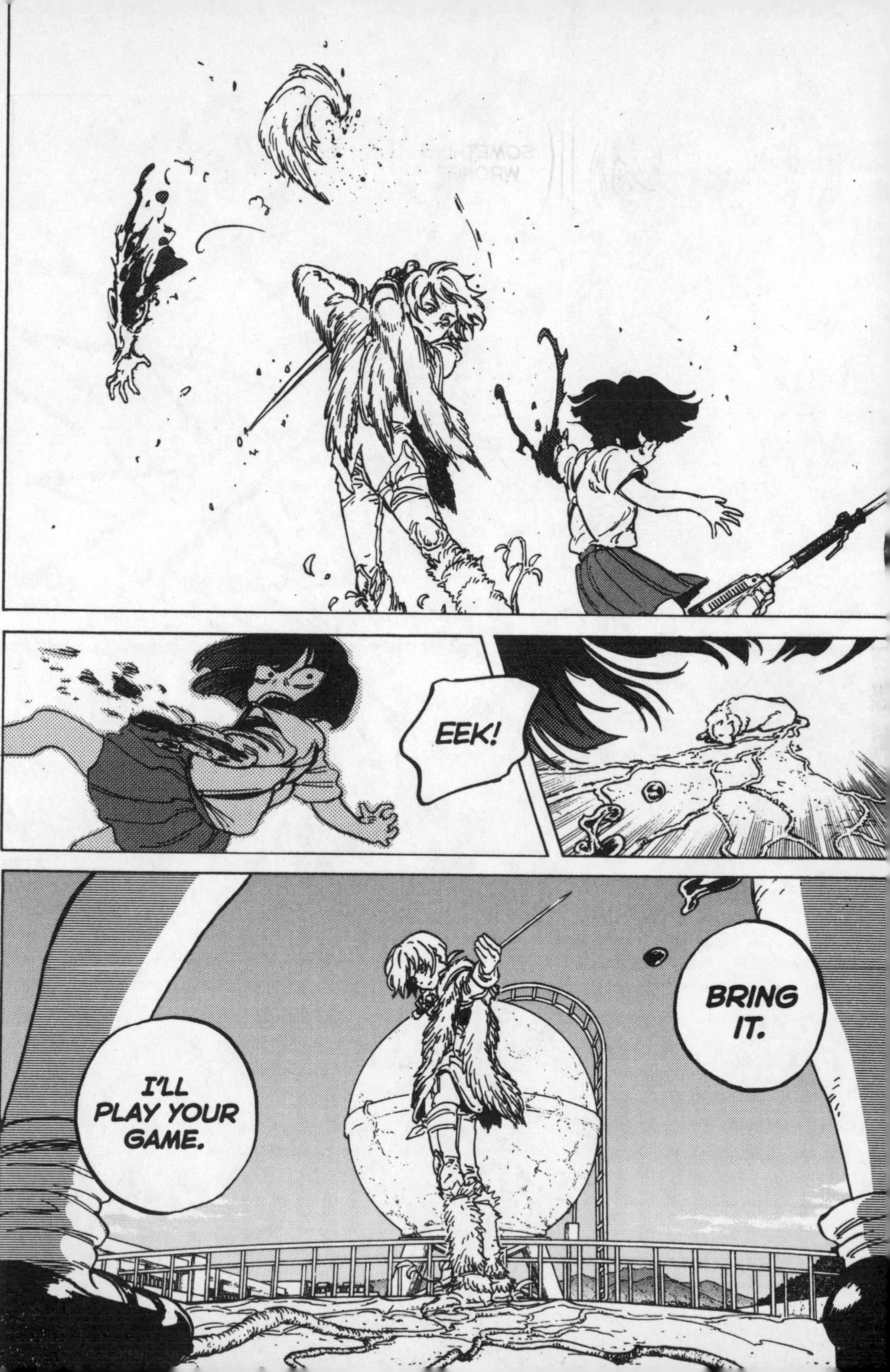
EEK!
BRING IT.
I'LL PLAY YOUR GAME.

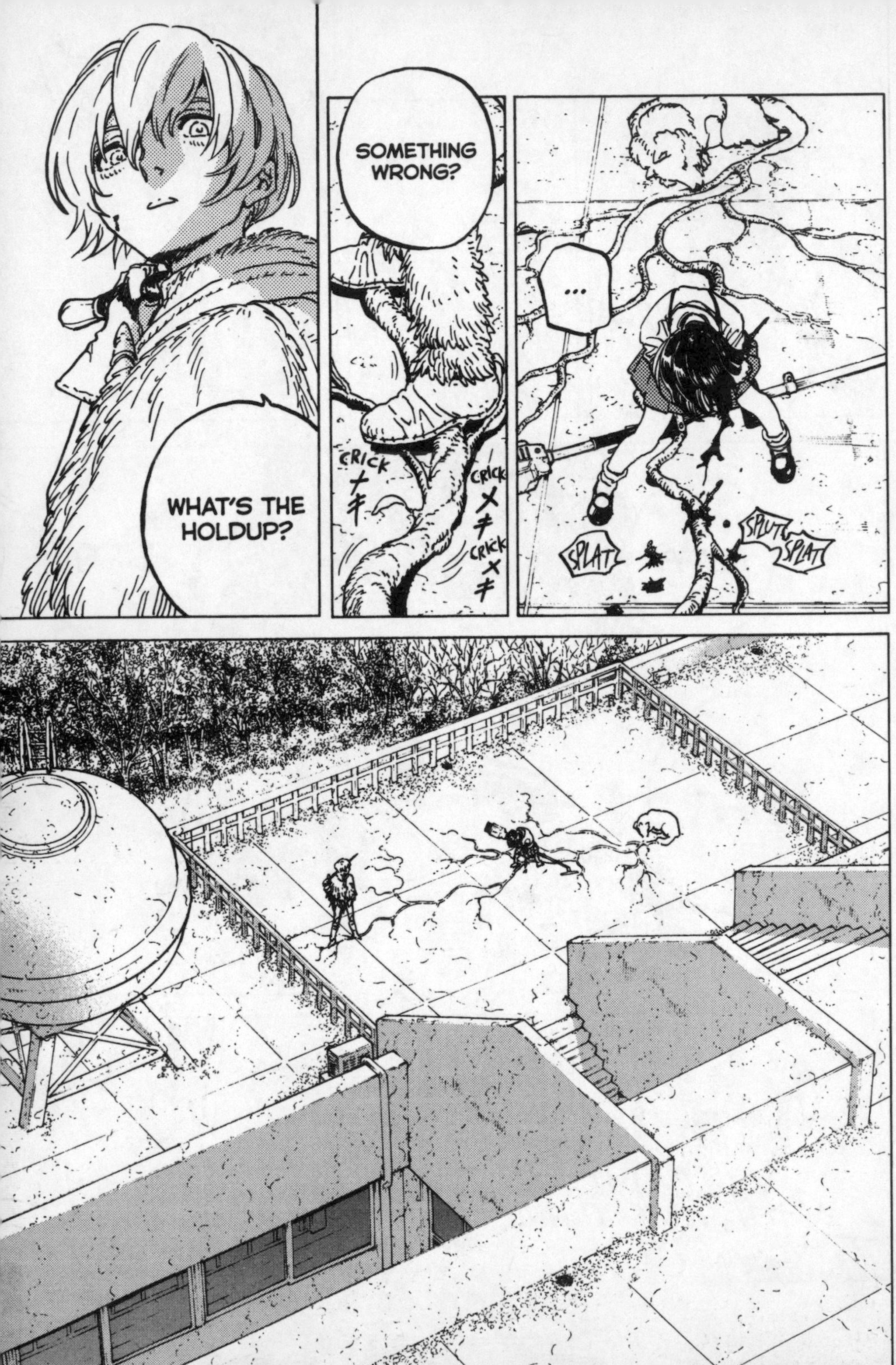
...
SPLAT
SPLUT
SPLAT
SOMETHING WRONG?
CRICK
CRICK
CRICK
WHAT'S THE HOLDUP?

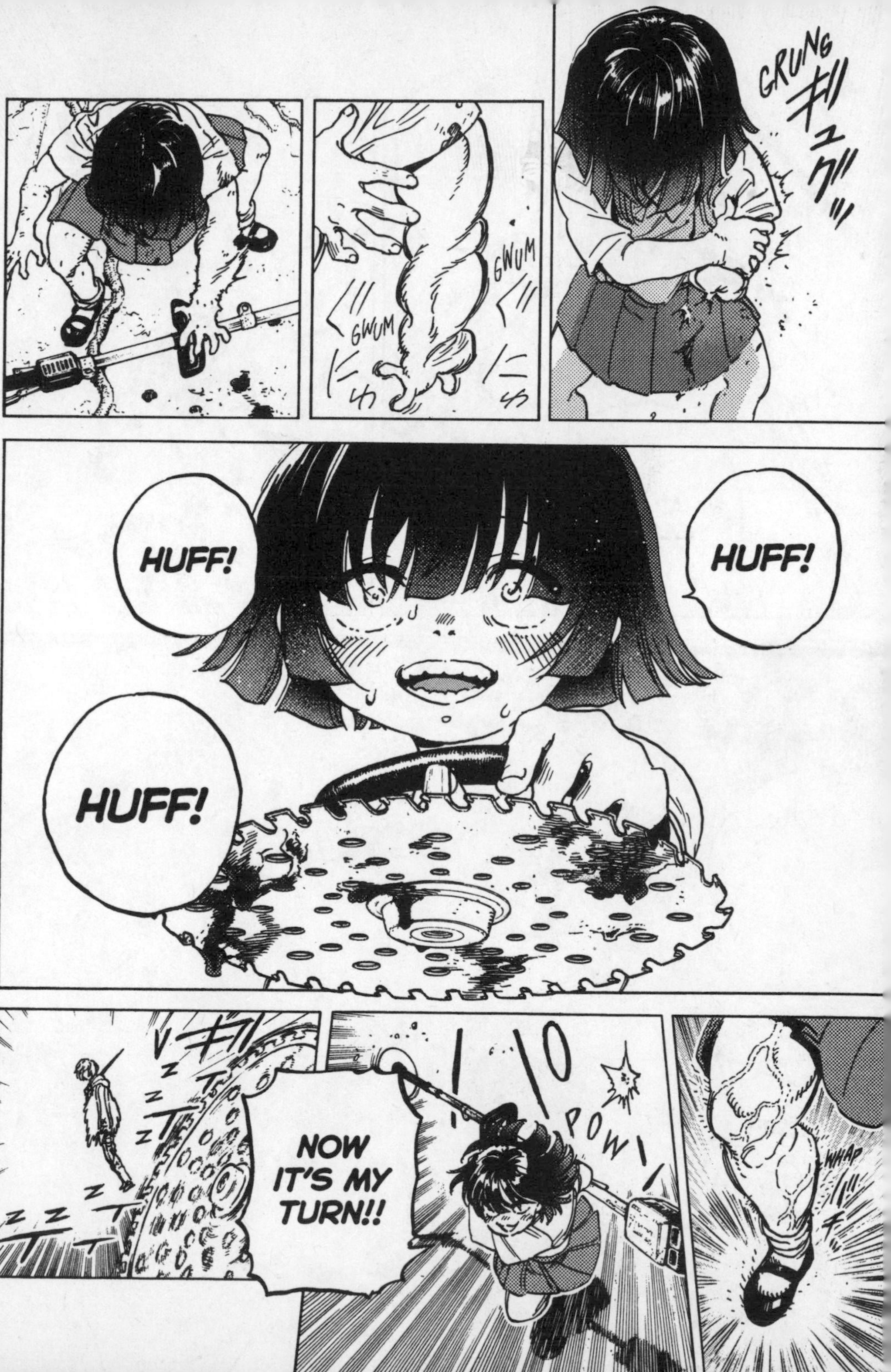
GRUNG
GWUM
GWUM
HUFF!
HUFF!
HUFF!
WHAP
POW
NOW IT'S MY TURN!!

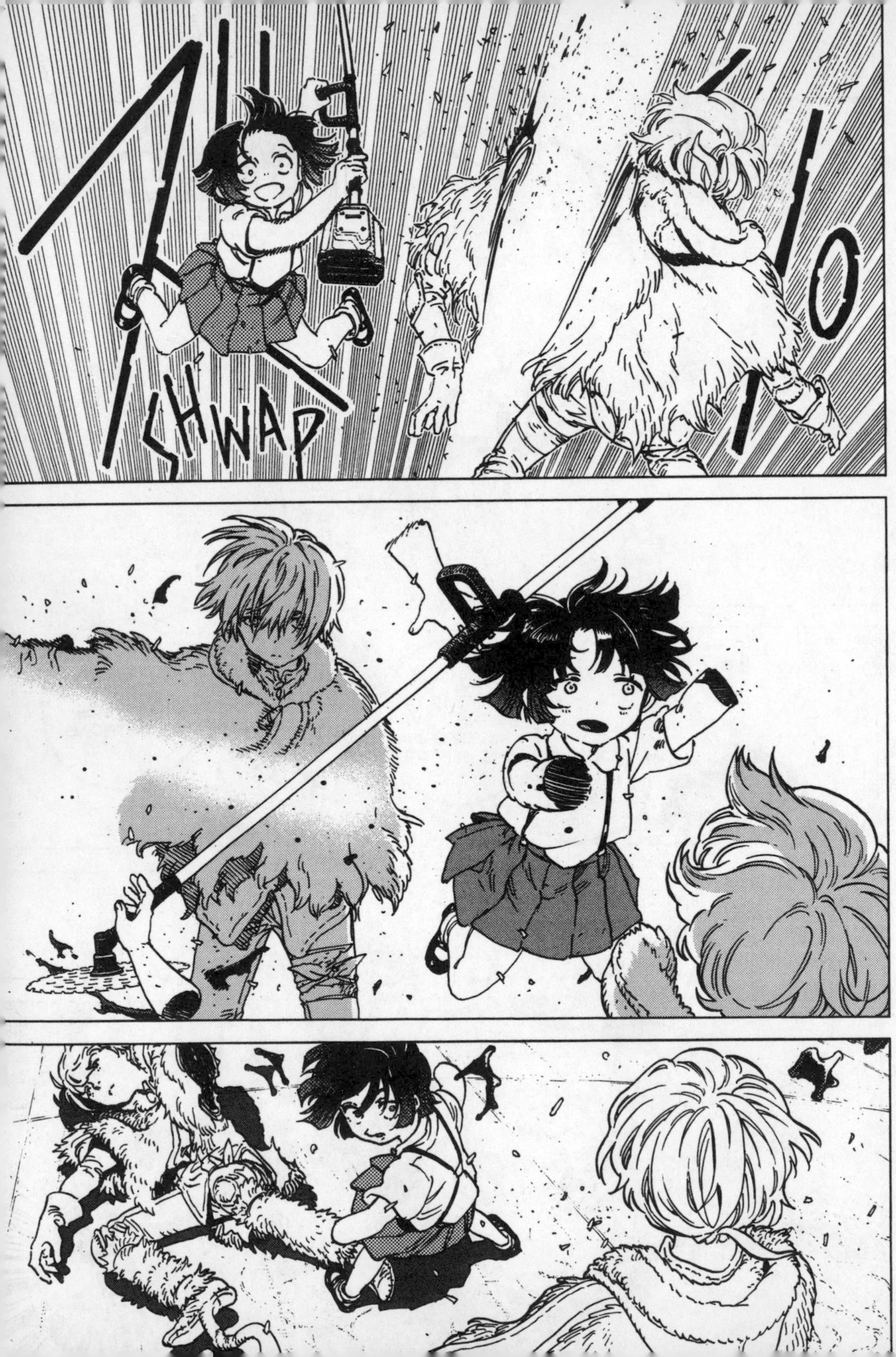
SHWAP

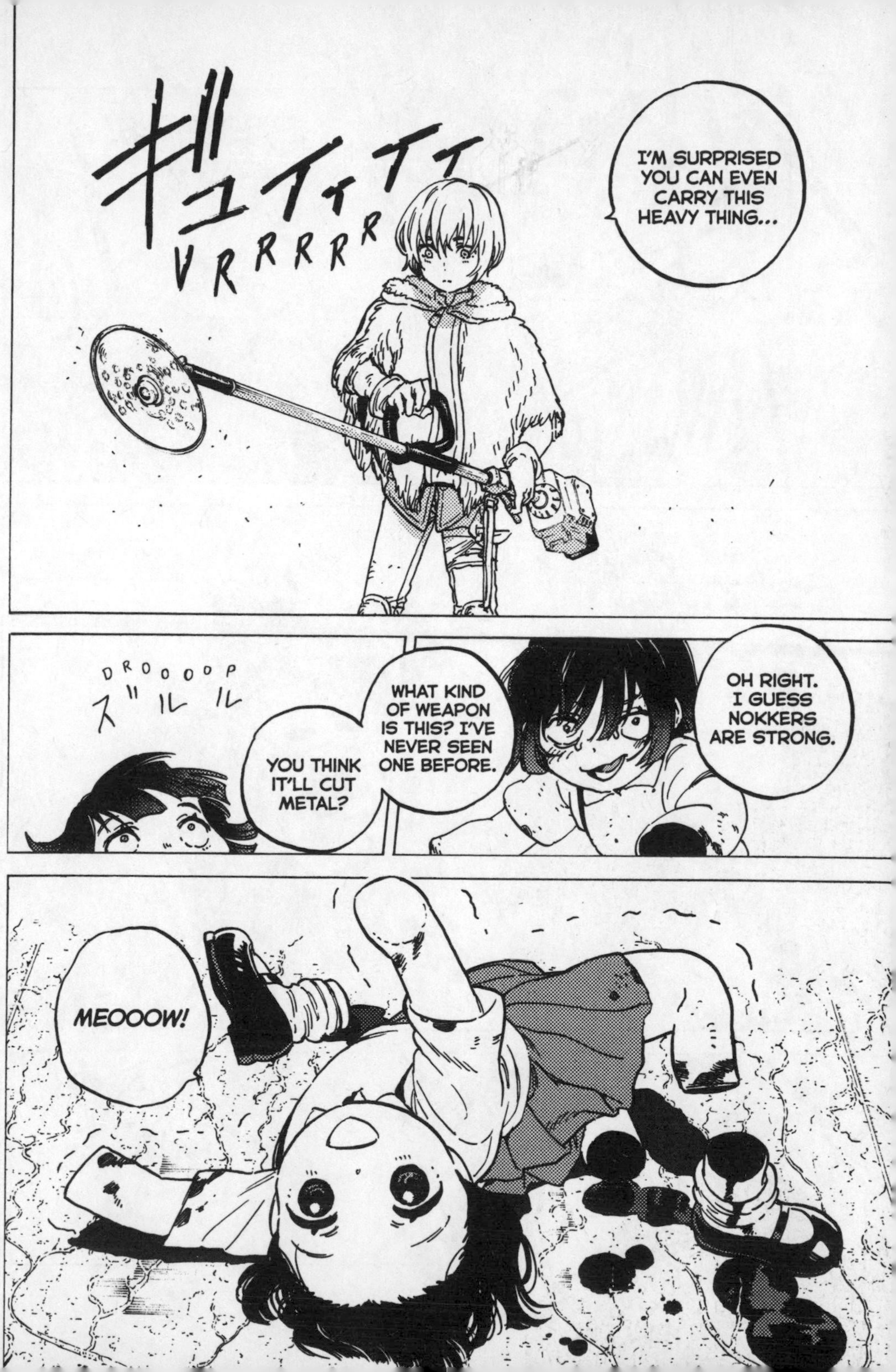
I'M SURPRISED YOU CAN EVEN CARRY THIS HEAVY THING...
ギュイィィィ
VRRRRR
OH RIGHT. I GUESS NOKKERS ARE STRONG.
WHAT KIND OF WEAPON IS THIS? I'VE NEVER SEEN ONE BEFORE.
DROOOOOP
ズルル
YOU THINK IT'LL CUT METAL?
MEOOOW!

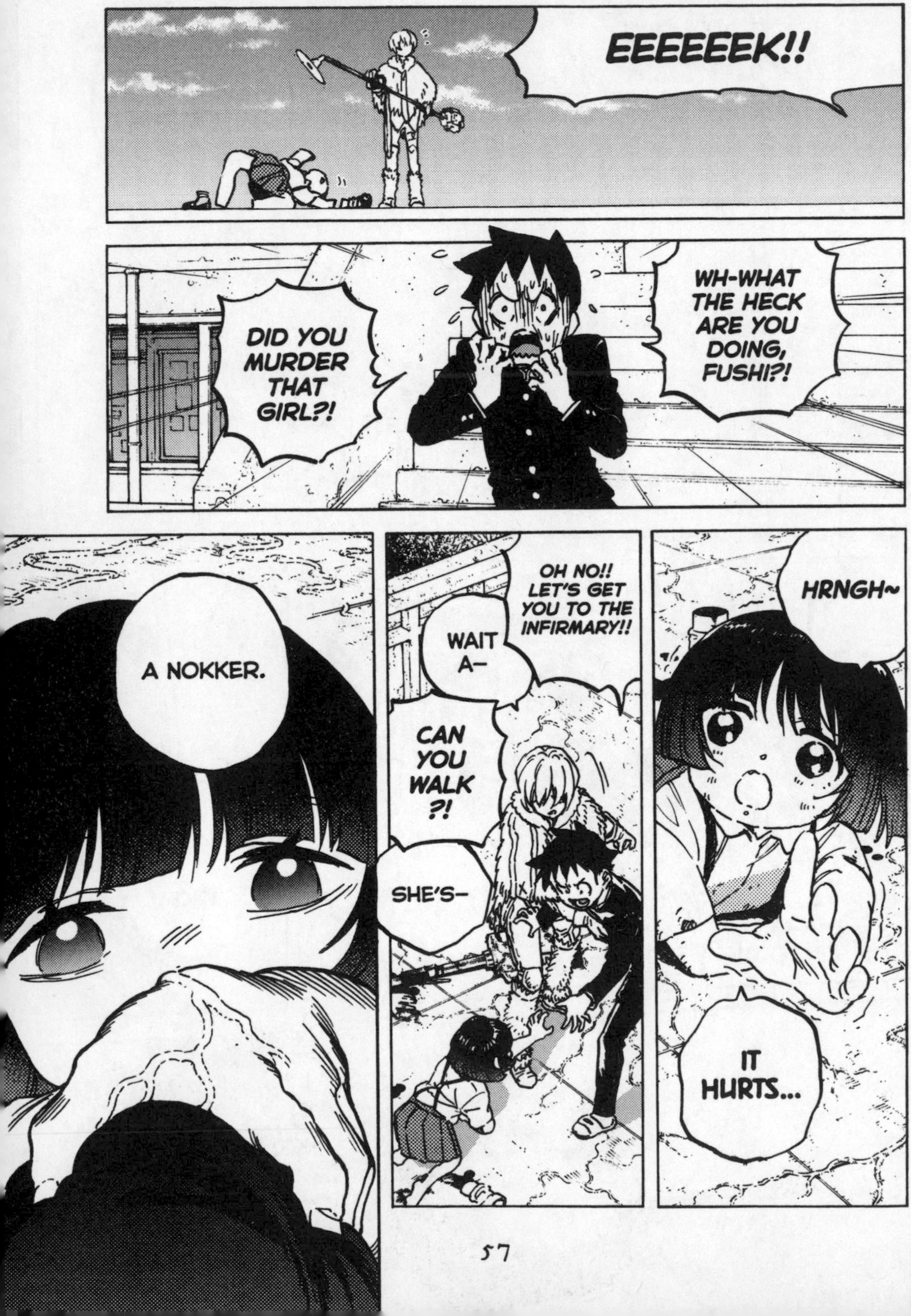
EEEEEEK!!
WH-WHAT THE HECK ARE YOU DOING, FUSHI?!
DID YOU MURDER THAT GIRL?!
HRNGH~
IT HURTS...
OH NO!! LET'S GET YOU TO THE INFIRMARY!!
WAIT A–
CAN YOU WALK ?!
SHE'S–
A NOKKER.

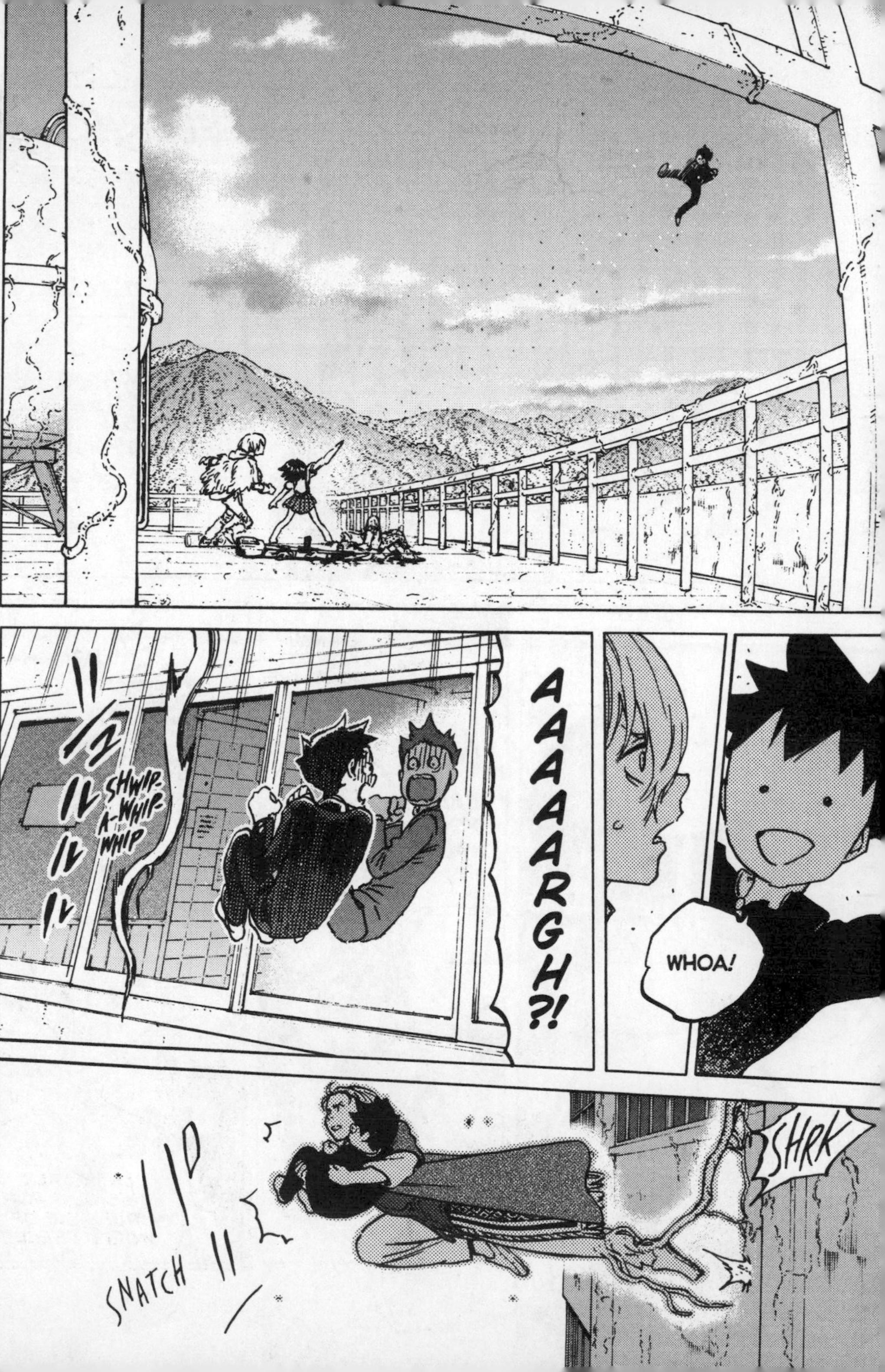
WHOA!
AAAAAARGH?!
SHWIP-A-WHIP-WHIP
SHRK
SNATCH

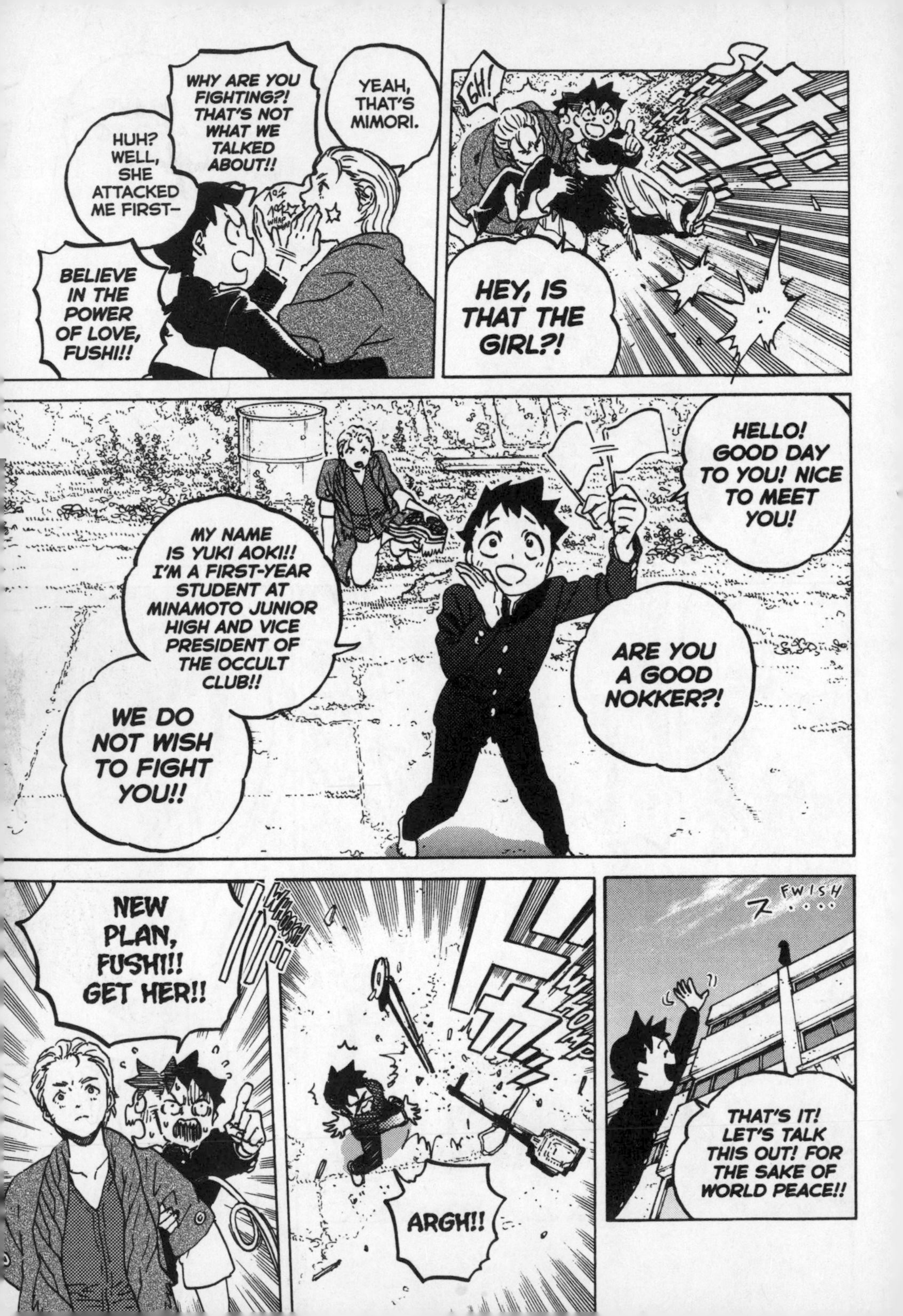
GH!
HEY, IS THAT THE GIRL?!
YEAH, THAT'S MIMORI.
WHY ARE YOU FIGHTING?! THAT'S NOT WHAT WE TALKED ABOUT!!
HUH? WELL, SHE ATTACKED ME FIRST–
BELIEVE IN THE POWER OF LOVE, FUSHI!!
HELLO! GOOD DAY TO YOU! NICE TO MEET YOU!
ARE YOU A GOOD NOKKER?!
MY NAME IS YUKI AOKI!! I'M A FIRST-YEAR STUDENT AT MINAMOTO JUNIOR HIGH AND VICE PRESIDENT OF THE OCCULT CLUB!!
WE DO NOT WISH TO FIGHT YOU!!
FWISH . . .
THAT'S IT! LET'S TALK THIS OUT! FOR THE SAKE OF WORLD PEACE!!
WHOMP
WHOOSH
ARGH!!
NEW PLAN, FUSHI!!! GET HER!!

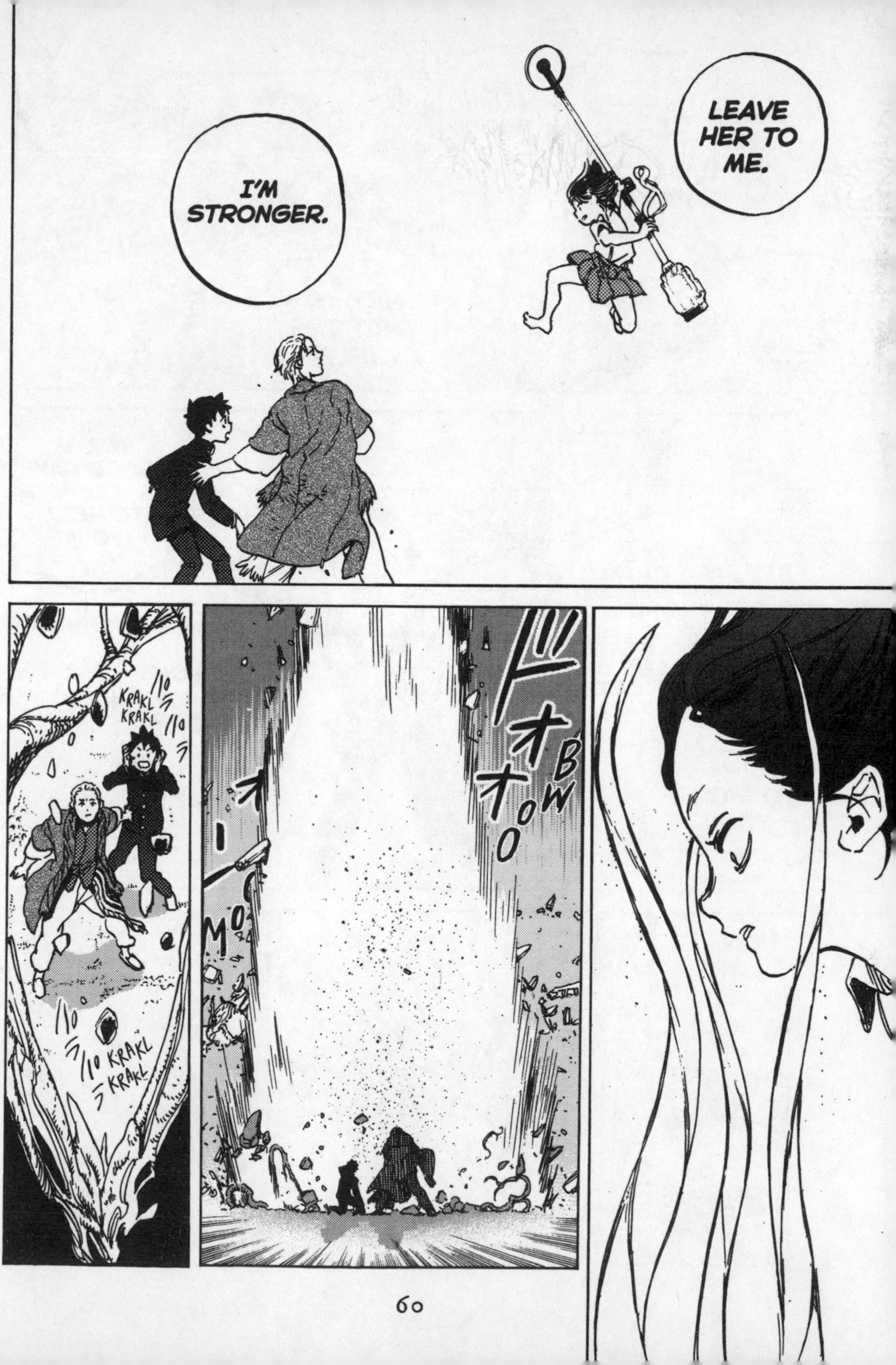
LEAVE HER TO ME.
I'M STRONGER.
BWOOO
KRAKL KRAKL
KRAKL KRAKL

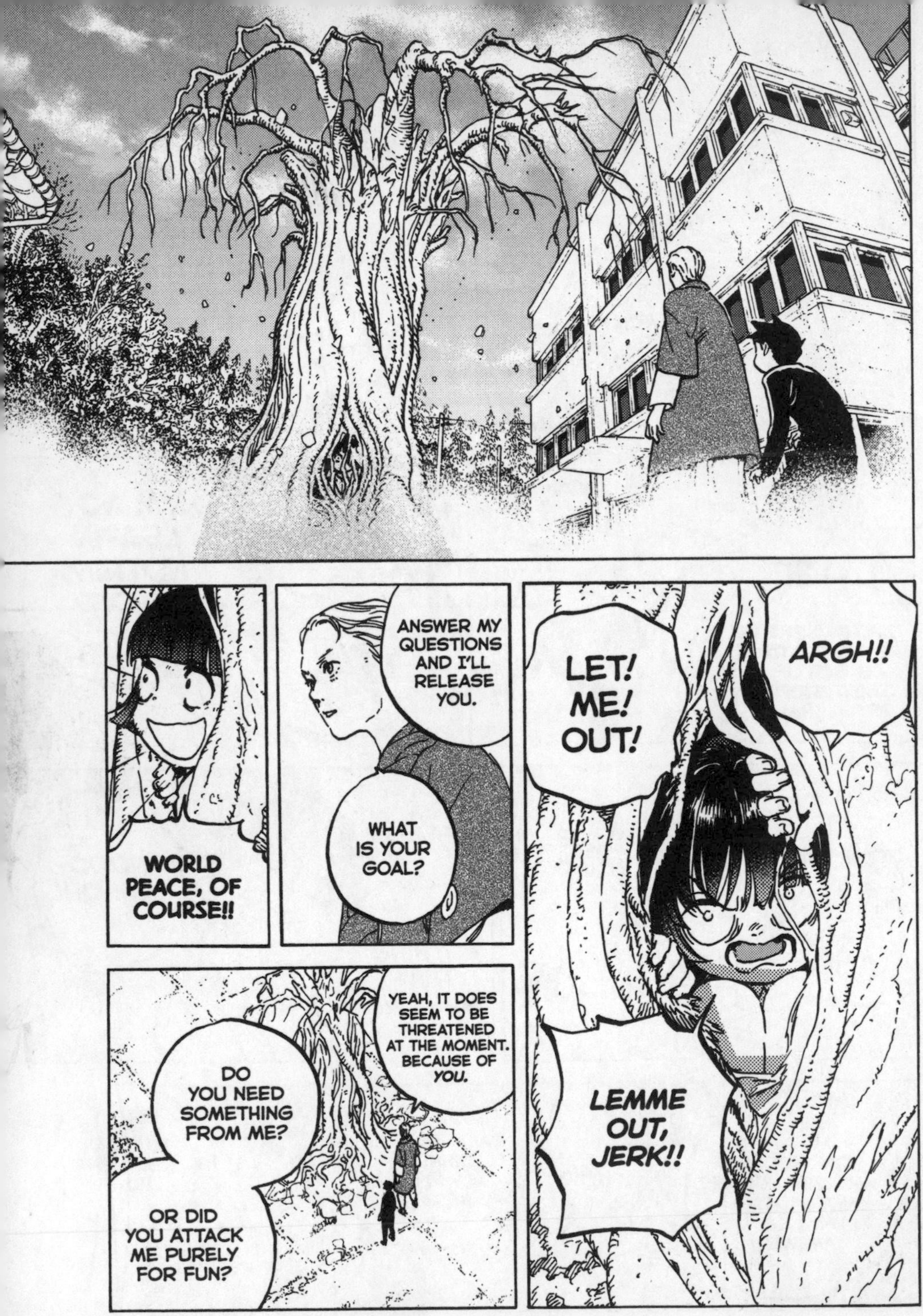
ARGH!!
LET! ME! OUT!
LEMME OUT, JERK!!
ANSWER MY QUESTIONS AND I'LL RELEASE YOU.
WHAT IS YOUR GOAL?
WORLD PEACE, OF COURSE!!
YEAH, IT DOES SEEM TO BE THREATENED AT THE MOMENT. BECAUSE OF *YOU.*
DO YOU NEED SOMETHING FROM ME?
OR DID YOU ATTACK ME PURELY FOR FUN?

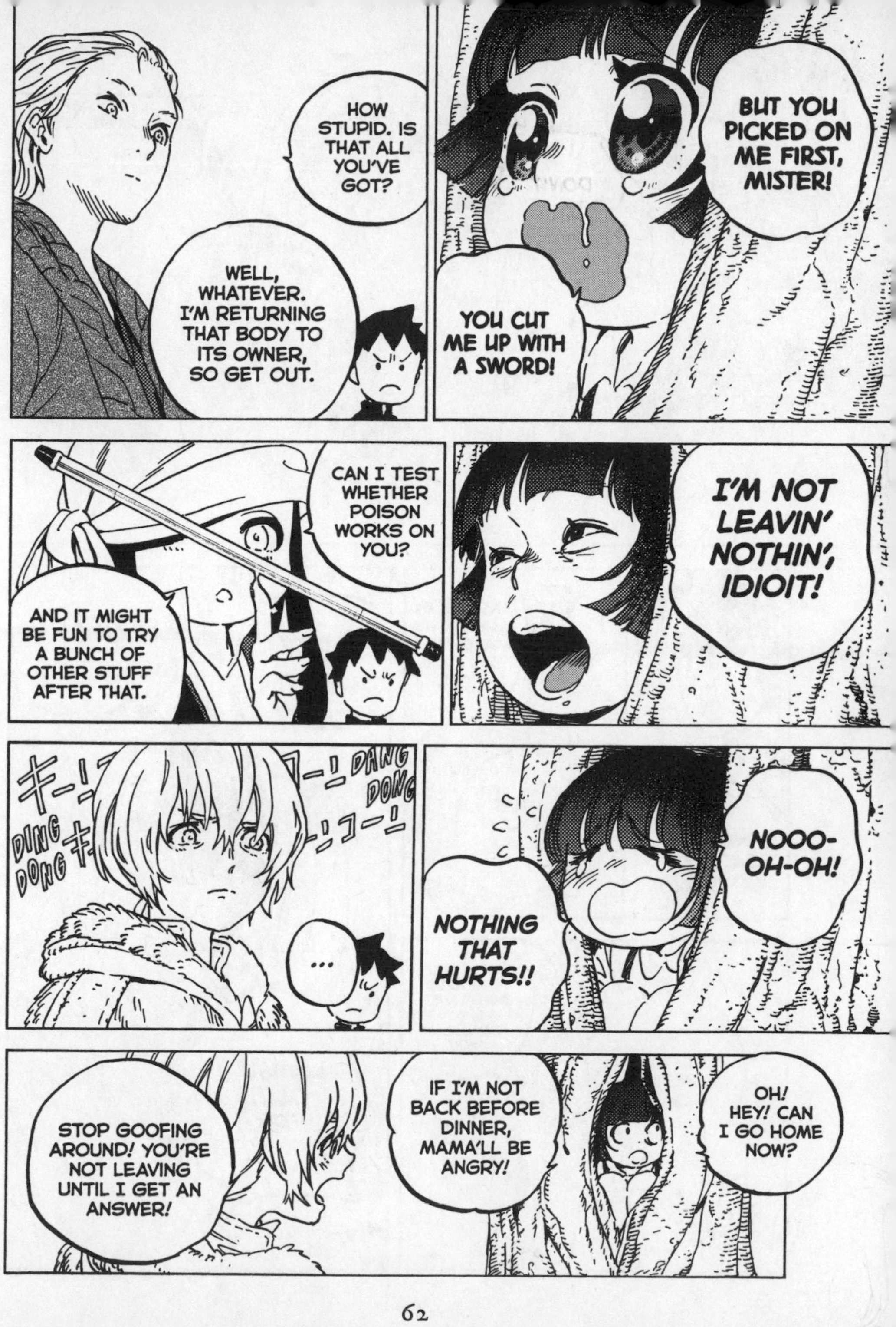
BUT YOU PICKED ON ME FIRST, MISTER!
YOU CUT ME UP WITH A SWORD!
HOW STUPID. IS THAT ALL YOU'VE GOT?
WELL, WHATEVER. I'M RETURNING THAT BODY TO ITS OWNER, SO GET OUT.
I'M NOT LEAVIN' NOTHIN', IDIOIT!
CAN I TEST WHETHER POISON WORKS ON YOU?
AND IT MIGHT BE FUN TO TRY A BUNCH OF OTHER STUFF AFTER THAT.
NOOO-OH-OH!
NOTHING THAT HURTS!!
DANG DONG
DING DONG
...
OH! HEY! CAN I GO HOME NOW?
IF I'M NOT BACK BEFORE DINNER, MAMA'LL BE ANGRY!
STOP GOOFING AROUND! YOU'RE NOT LEAVING UNTIL I GET AN ANSWER!

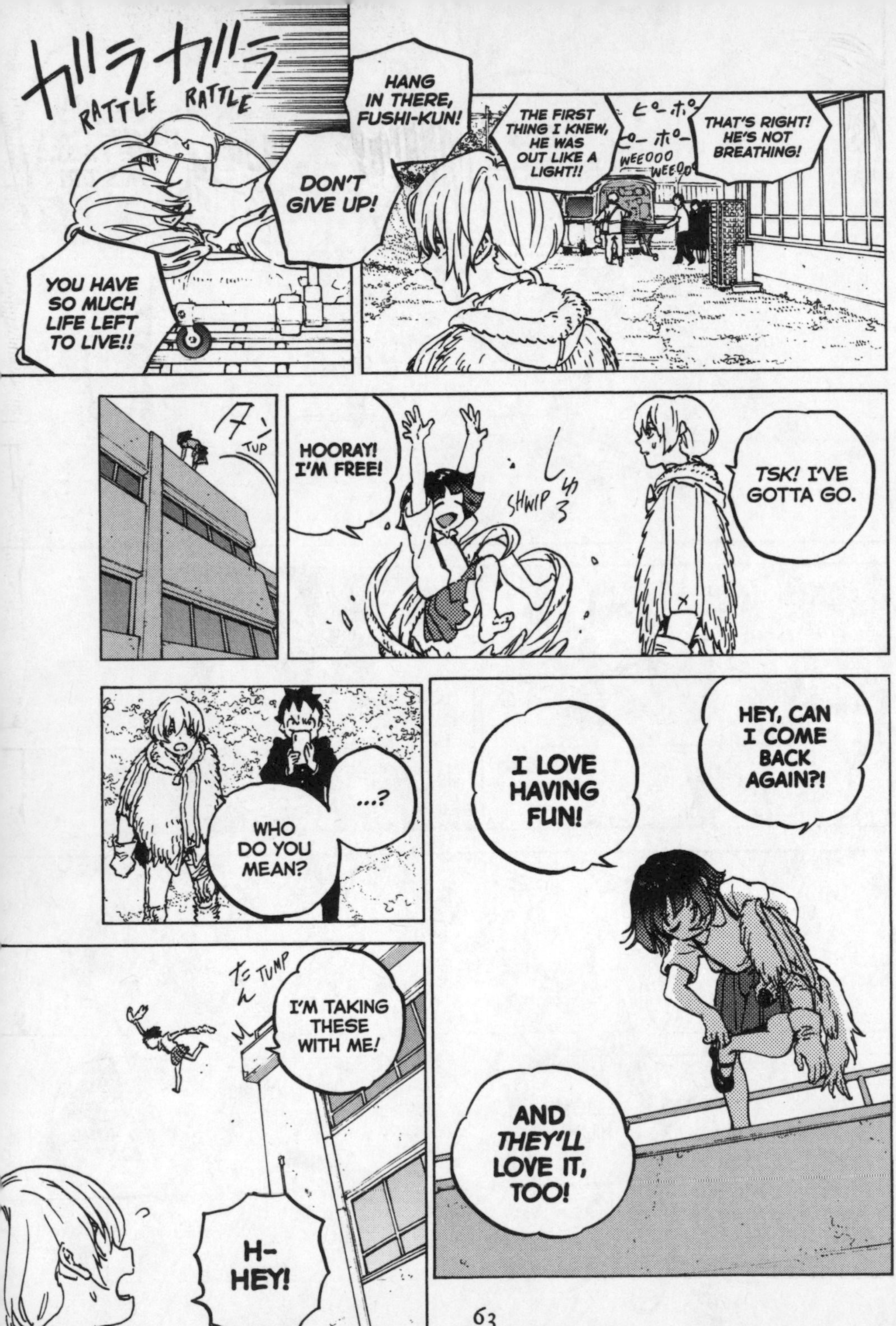
ピーポーピーポー
WEEOOO WEEOOO
THAT'S RIGHT! HE'S NOT BREATHING!
THE FIRST THING I KNEW, HE WAS OUT LIKE A LIGHT!!
ガラガラ
RATTLE RATTLE
HANG IN THERE, FUSHI-KUN!
DON'T GIVE UP!
YOU HAVE SO MUCH LIFE LEFT TO LIVE!!
TSK! I'VE GOTTA GO.
SHWIP
HOORAY! I'M FREE!
TUP
HEY, CAN I COME BACK AGAIN?!
I LOVE HAVING FUN!
AND THEY'LL LOVE IT, TOO!
...?
WHO DO YOU MEAN?
I'M TAKING THESE WITH ME!
TUMP
H-HEY!

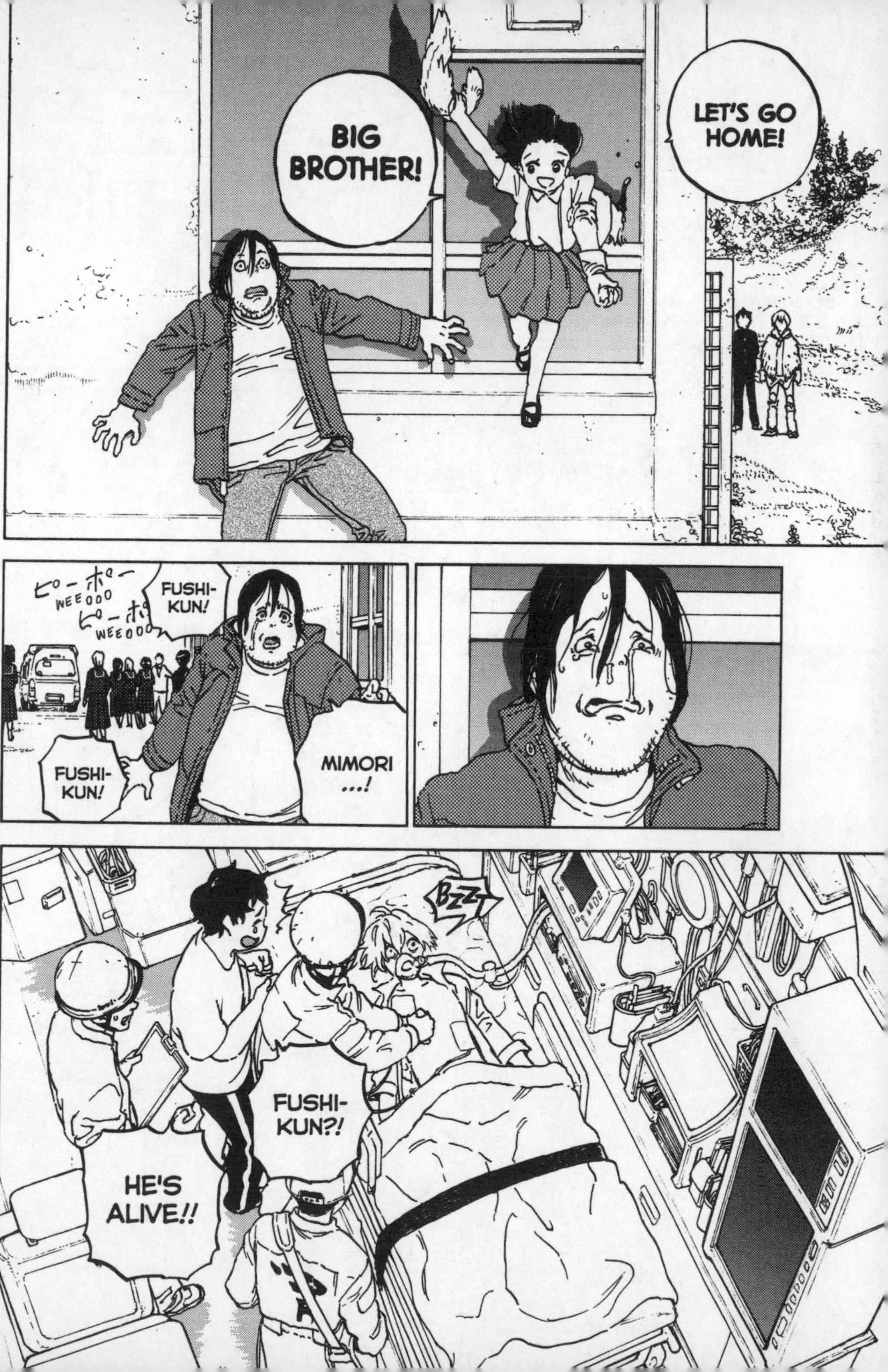
LET'S GO HOME!
BIG BROTHER!
FUSHI-KUN!
ピーポー
WEEOOO
ピーポ
WEEOOO
MIMORI ...!
FUSHI-KUN!
BZZT
FUSHI-KUN?!
HE'S ALIVE!!

TO YOUR
ETERNITY

Hirotoshi's Little Sister Game

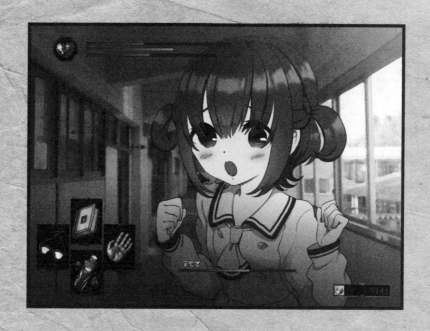

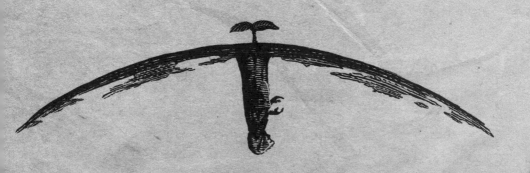

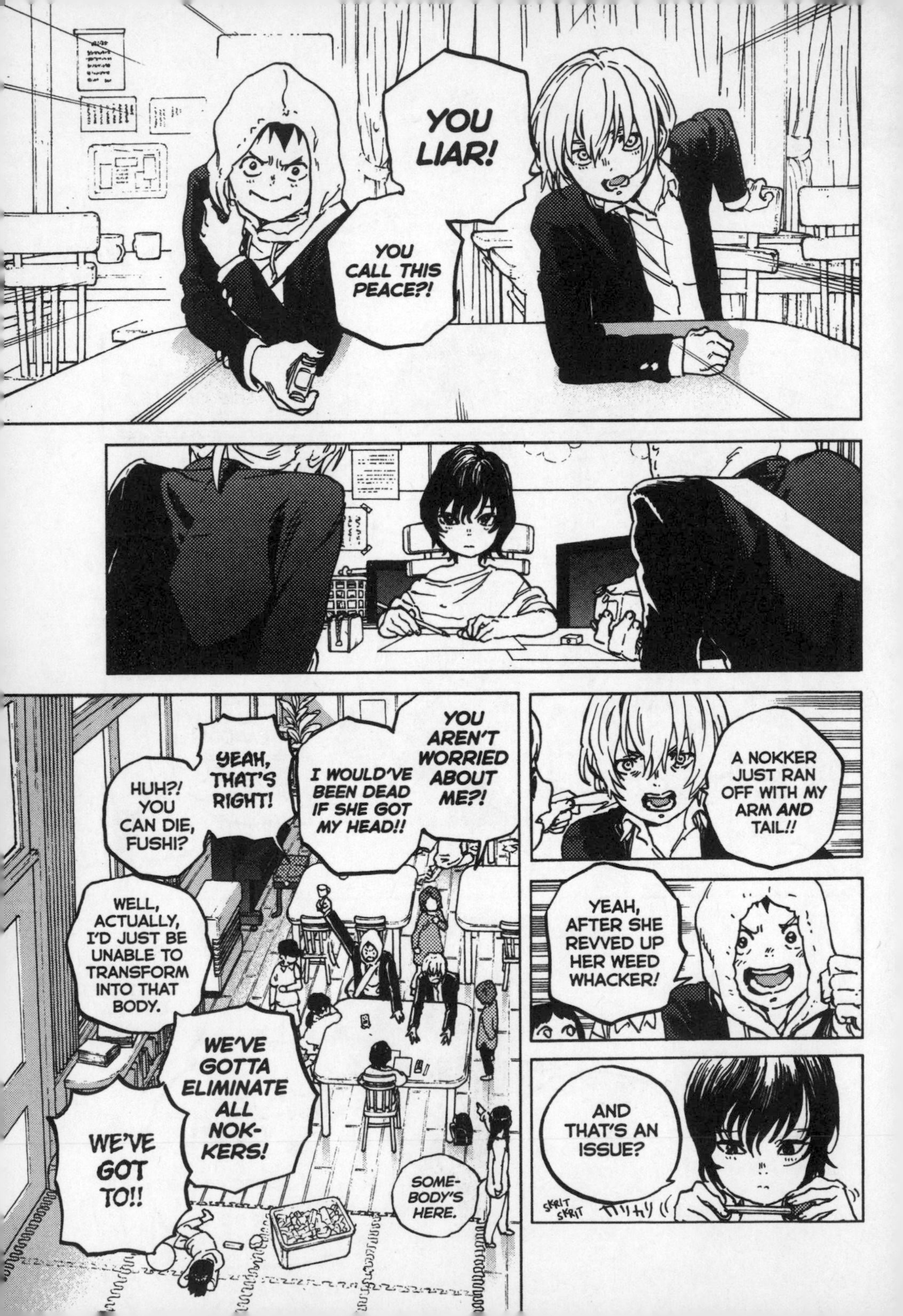
YOU LIAR!
YOU CALL THIS PEACE?!
A NOKKER JUST RAN OFF WITH MY ARM AND TAIL!!
YEAH, AFTER SHE REVVED UP HER WEED WHACKER!
AND THAT'S AN ISSUE?
SKRIT SKRIT
カリカリ
YOU AREN'T WORRIED ABOUT ME?!
I WOULD'VE BEEN DEAD IF SHE GOT MY HEAD!!
YEAH, THAT'S RIGHT!
HUH?! YOU CAN DIE, FUSHI?
WELL, ACTUALLY, I'D JUST BE UNABLE TO TRANSFORM INTO THAT BODY.
WE'VE GOTTA ELIMINATE ALL NOK-KERS!
SOME-BODY'S HERE.
WE'VE GOT TO!!

#135 Trouble

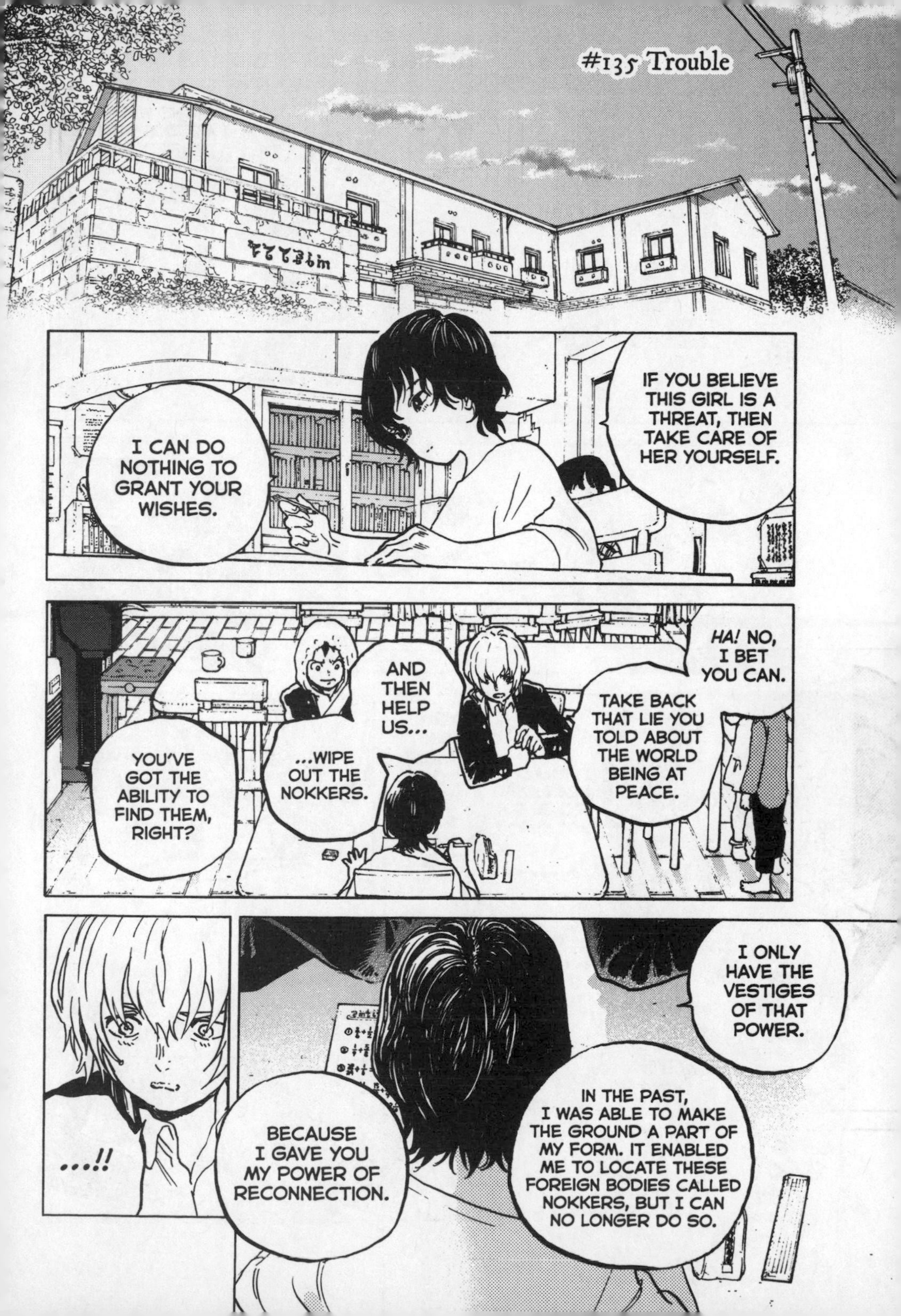
IF YOU BELIEVE THIS GIRL IS A THREAT, THEN TAKE CARE OF HER YOURSELF.
I CAN DO NOTHING TO GRANT YOUR WISHES.
HA! NO, I BET YOU CAN.
TAKE BACK THAT LIE YOU TOLD ABOUT THE WORLD BEING AT PEACE.
YOU'VE GOT THE ABILITY TO FIND THEM, RIGHT?
AND THEN HELP US...
...WIPE OUT THE NOKKERS.
I ONLY HAVE THE VESTIGES OF THAT POWER.
IN THE PAST, I WAS ABLE TO MAKE THE GROUND A PART OF MY FORM. IT ENABLED ME TO LOCATE THESE FOREIGN BODIES CALLED NOKKERS, BUT I CAN NO LONGER DO SO.
BECAUSE I GAVE YOU MY POWER OF RECONNECTION.
...!!

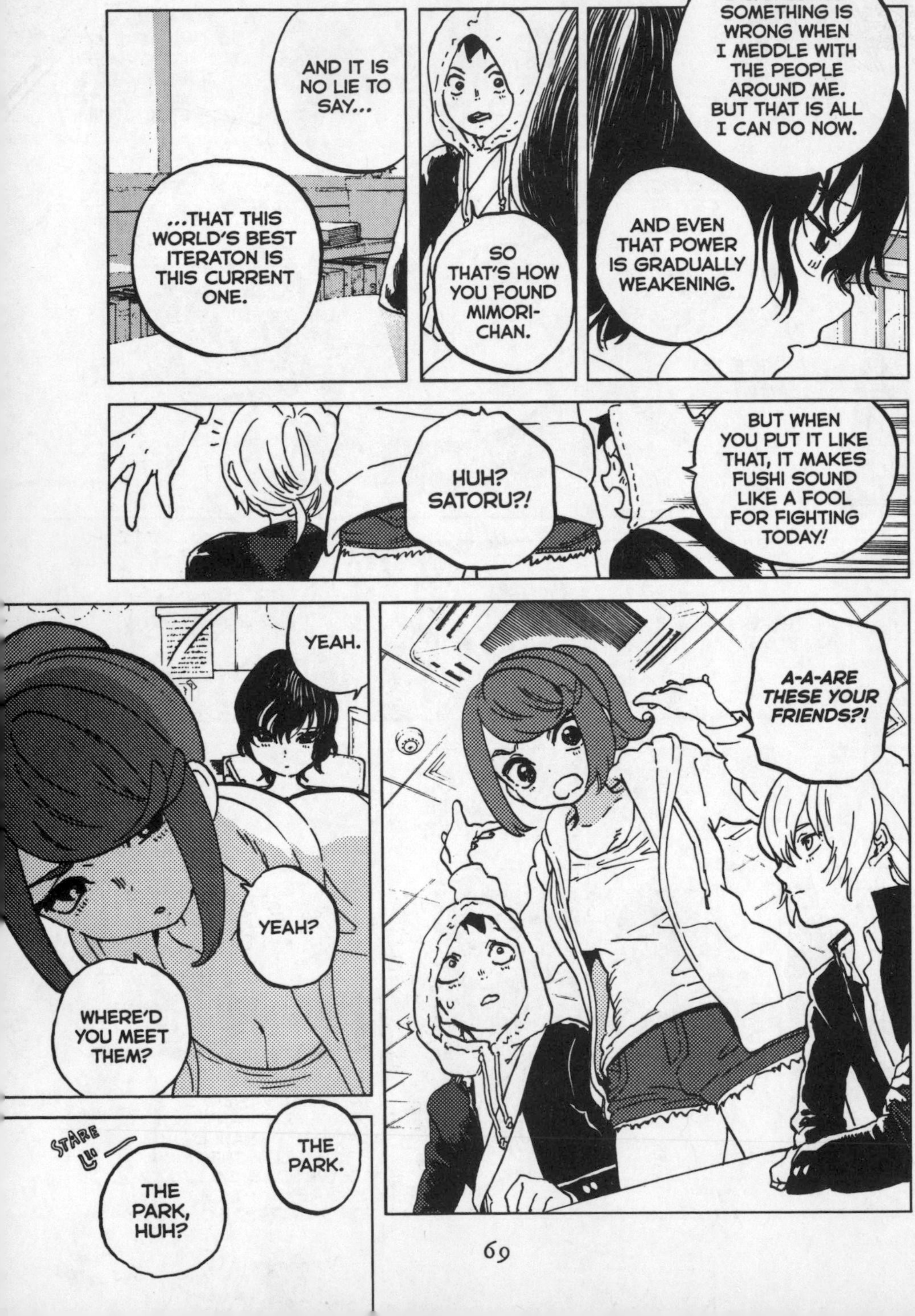
I CAN SENSE SOMETHING IS WRONG WHEN I MEDDLE WITH THE PEOPLE AROUND ME. BUT THAT IS ALL I CAN DO NOW.
AND EVEN THAT POWER IS GRADUALLY WEAKENING.
SO THAT'S HOW YOU FOUND MIMORI-CHAN.
AND IT IS NO LIE TO SAY...
...THAT THIS WORLD'S BEST ITERATON IS THIS CURRENT ONE.
BUT WHEN YOU PUT IT LIKE THAT, IT MAKES FUSHI SOUND LIKE A FOOL FOR FIGHTING TODAY!
HUH? SATORU?!
A-A-ARE THESE YOUR FRIENDS?!
YEAH.
YEAH?
WHERE'D YOU MEET THEM?
THE PARK.
STARE
THE PARK, HUH?

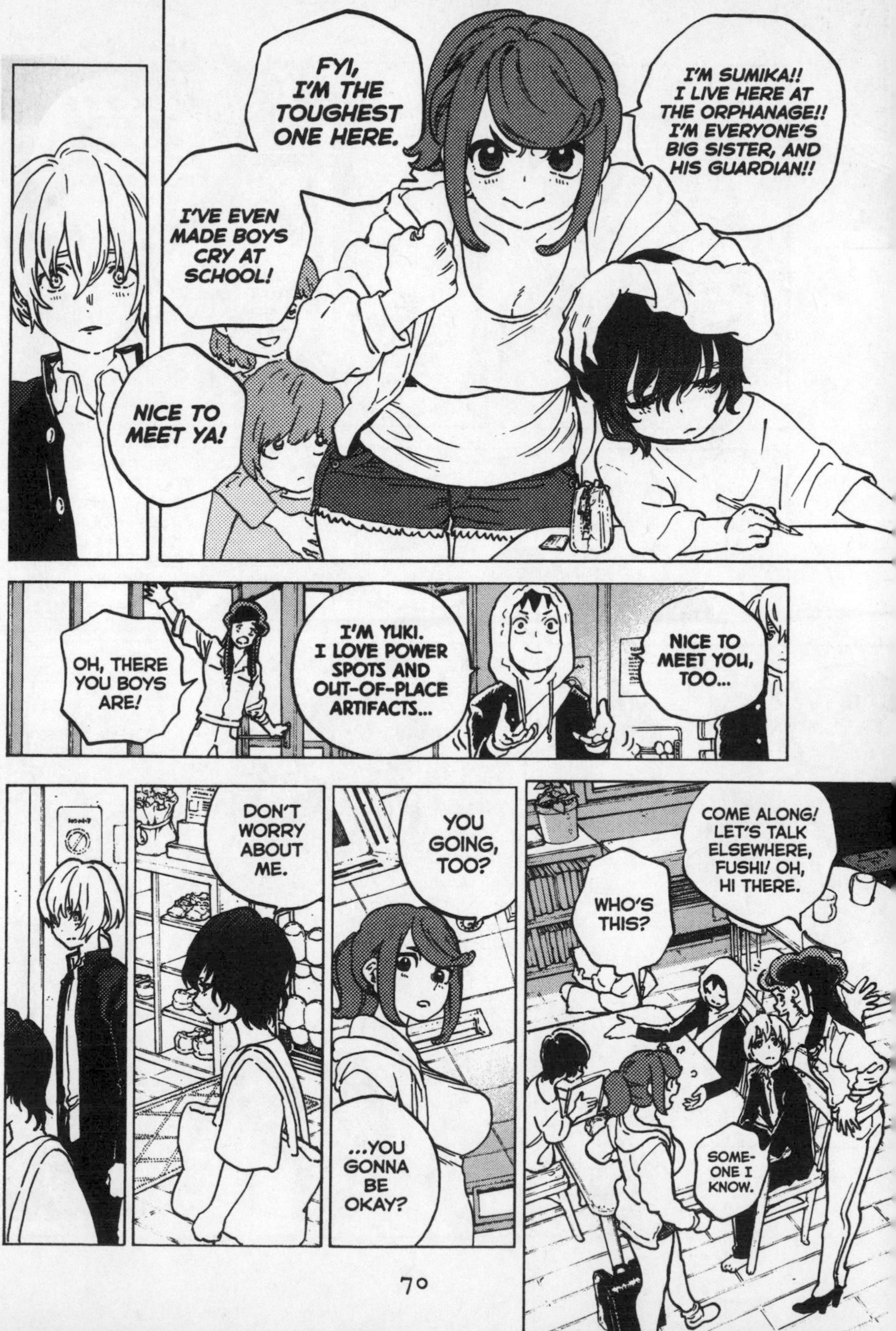
I'M SUMIKA!! I LIVE HERE AT THE ORPHANAGE!! I'M EVERYONE'S BIG SISTER, AND HIS GUARDIAN!!
FYI, I'M THE TOUGHEST ONE HERE.
I'VE EVEN MADE BOYS CRY AT SCHOOL!
NICE TO MEET YA!
NICE TO MEET YOU, TOO...
I'M YUKI. I LOVE POWER SPOTS AND OUT-OF-PLACE ARTIFACTS...
OH, THERE YOU BOYS ARE!
COME ALONG! LET'S TALK ELSEWHERE, FUSHI! OH, HI THERE.
WHO'S THIS?
SOME-ONE I KNOW.
YOU GOING, TOO?
...YOU GONNA BE OKAY?
DON'T WORRY ABOUT ME.

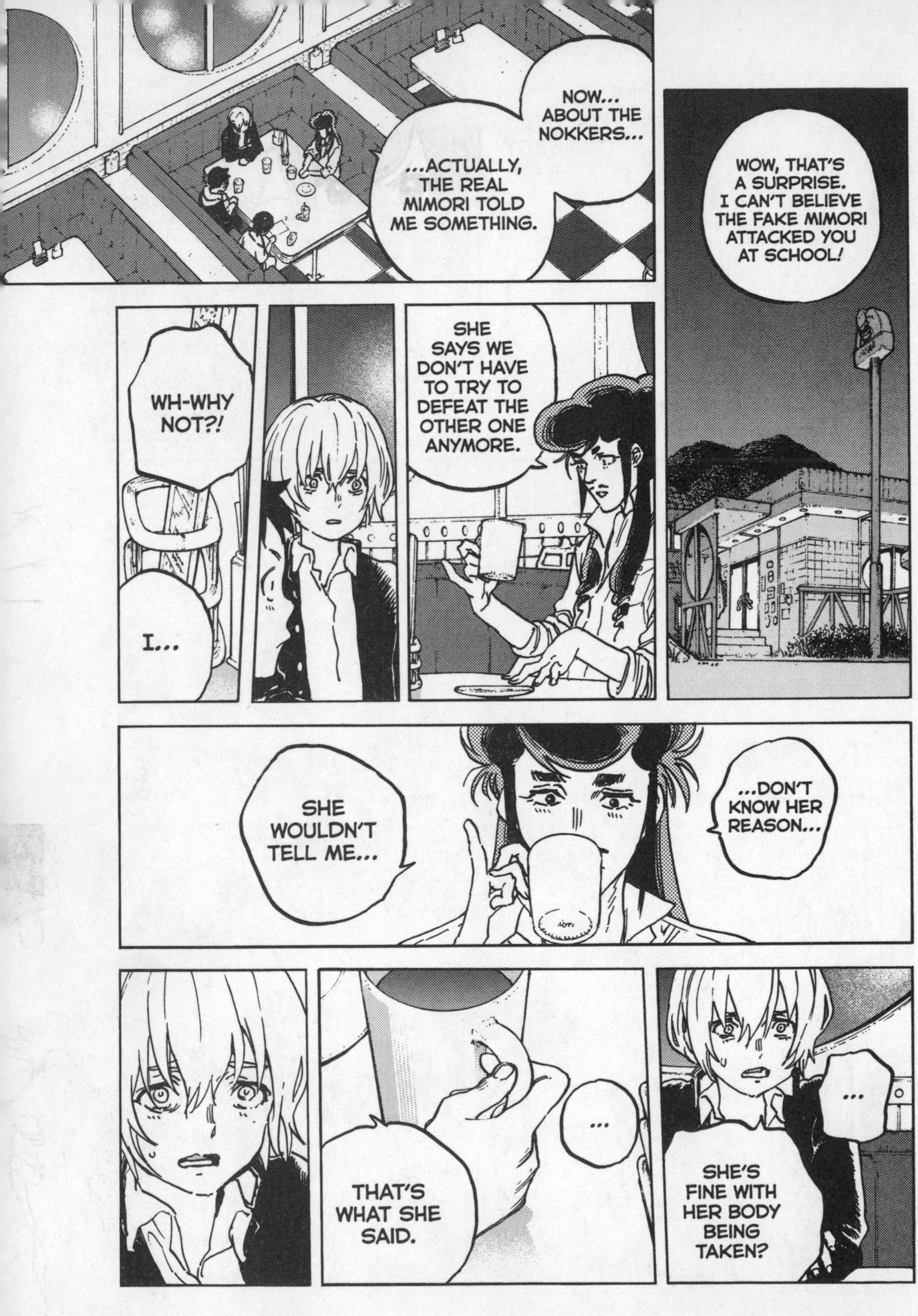
WOW, THAT'S A SURPRISE. I CAN'T BELIEVE THE FAKE MIMORI ATTACKED YOU AT SCHOOL!
NOW... ABOUT THE NOKKERS...
...ACTUALLY, THE REAL MIMORI TOLD ME SOMETHING.
SHE SAYS WE DON'T HAVE TO TRY TO DEFEAT THE OTHER ONE ANYMORE.
WH-WHY NOT?!
I...
...DON'T KNOW HER REASON...
SHE WOULDN'T TELL ME...
...
SHE'S FINE WITH HER BODY BEING TAKEN?
...
THAT'S WHAT SHE SAID.

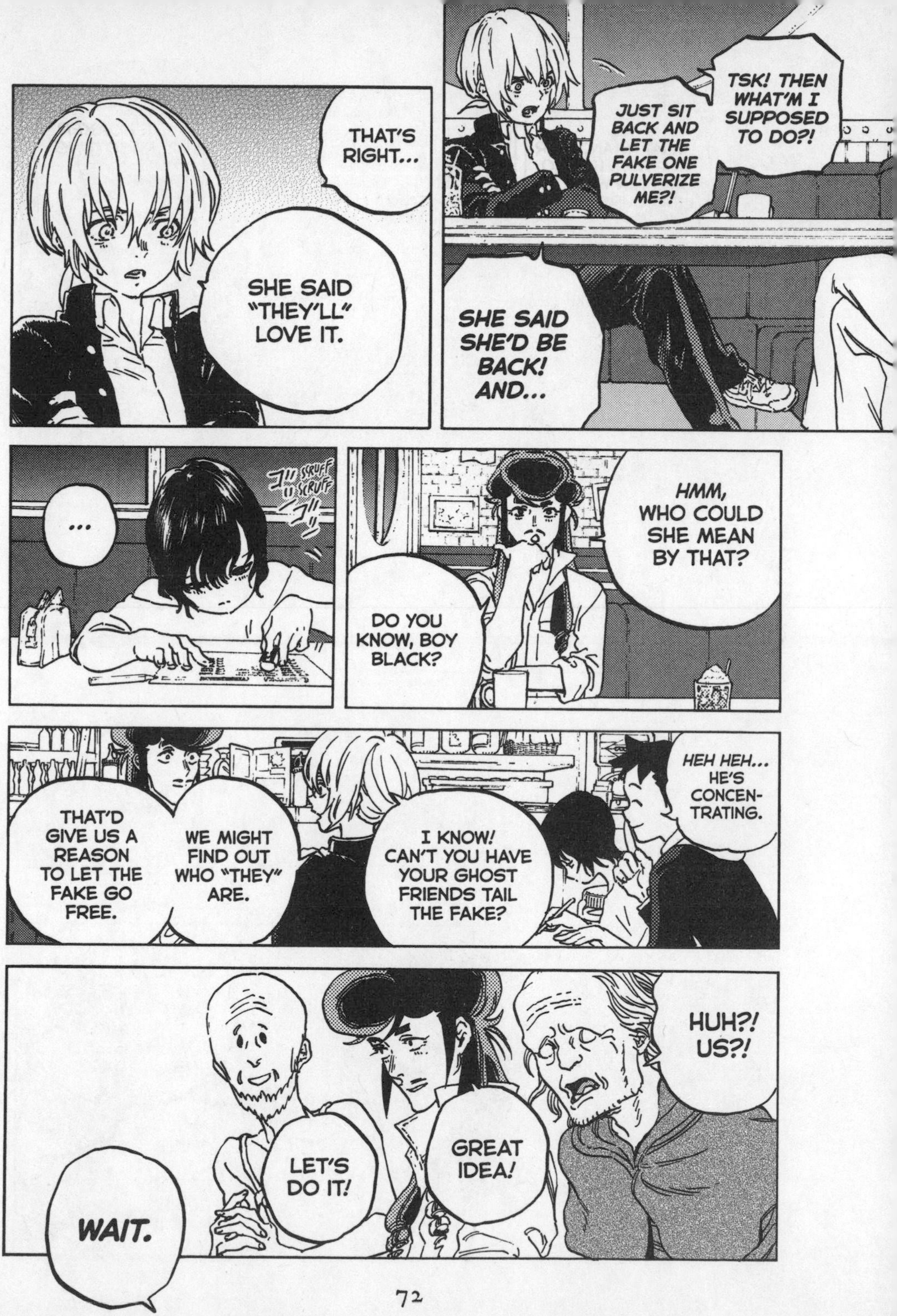
TSK! THEN WHAT'M I SUPPOSED TO DO?!
JUST SIT BACK AND LET THE FAKE ONE PULVERIZE ME?!
SHE SAID SHE'D BE BACK! AND...
THAT'S RIGHT...
SHE SAID "THEY'LL" LOVE IT.
HMM, WHO COULD SHE MEAN BY THAT?
DO YOU KNOW, BOY BLACK?
SCRUFF SCRUFF
...
HEH HEH... HE'S CONCEN-TRATING.
I KNOW! CAN'T YOU HAVE YOUR GHOST FRIENDS TAIL THE FAKE?
WE MIGHT FIND OUT WHO "THEY" ARE.
THAT'D GIVE US A REASON TO LET THE FAKE GO FREE.
HUH?! US?!
GREAT IDEA!
LET'S DO IT!
WAIT.

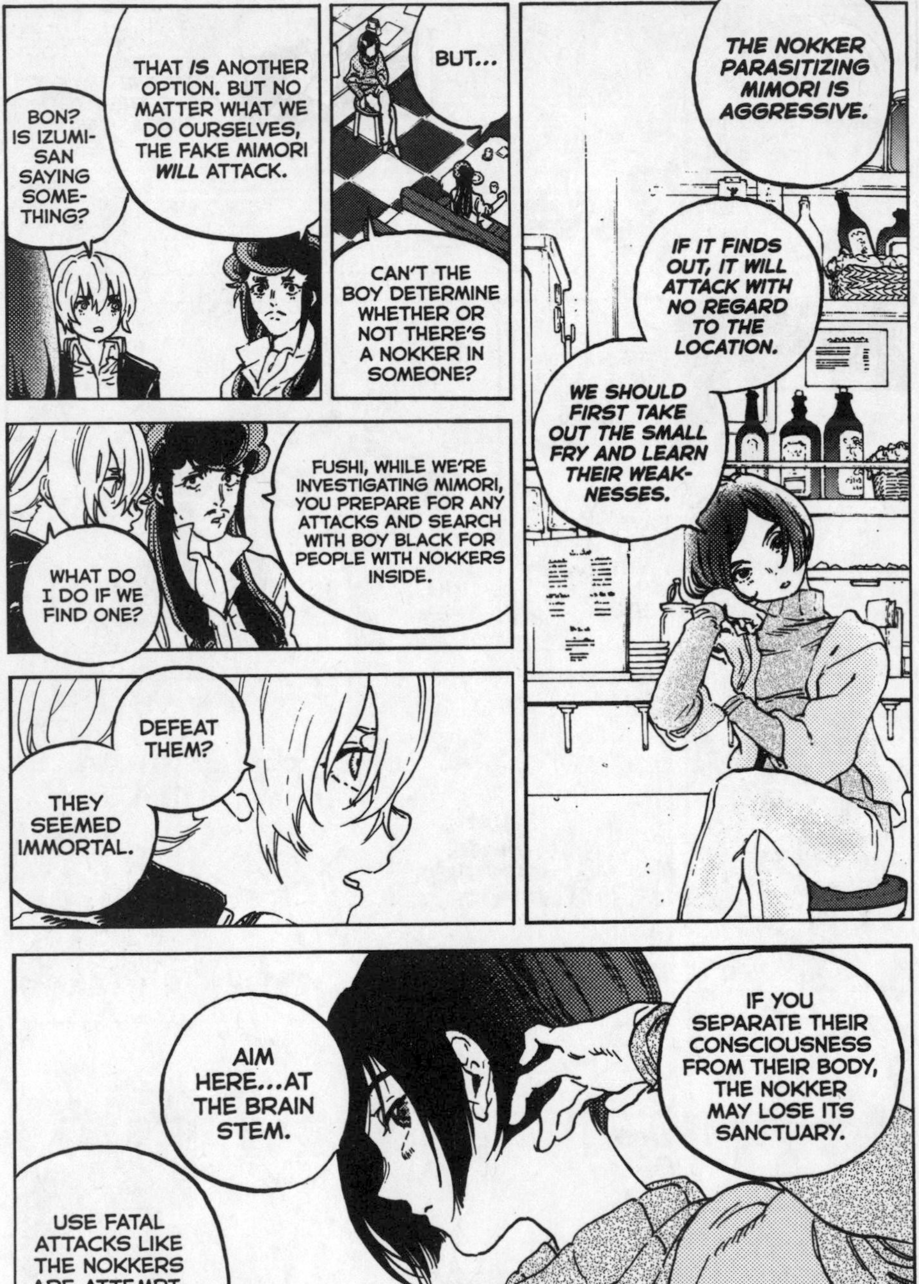
THE NOKKER PARASITIZING MIMORI IS AGGRESSIVE.
IF IT FINDS OUT, IT WILL ATTACK WITH NO REGARD TO THE LOCATION.
WE SHOULD FIRST TAKE OUT THE SMALL FRY AND LEARN THEIR WEAKNESSES.
BUT...
CAN'T THE BOY DETERMINE WHETHER OR NOT THERE'S A NOKKER IN SOMEONE?
THAT *IS* ANOTHER OPTION. BUT NO MATTER WHAT WE DO OURSELVES, THE FAKE MIMORI *WILL* ATTACK.
BON? IS IZUMI-SAN SAYING SOMETHING?
FUSHI, WHILE WE'RE INVESTIGATING MIMORI, YOU PREPARE FOR ANY ATTACKS AND SEARCH WITH BOY BLACK FOR PEOPLE WITH NOKKERS INSIDE.
WHAT DO I DO IF WE FIND ONE?
DEFEAT THEM?
THEY SEEMED IMMORTAL.
IF YOU SEPARATE THEIR CONSCIOUSNESS FROM THEIR BODY, THE NOKKER MAY LOSE ITS SANCTUARY.
AIM HERE...AT THE BRAIN STEM.
USE FATAL ATTACKS LIKE THE NOKKERS ARE ATTEMPTING ON YOU.

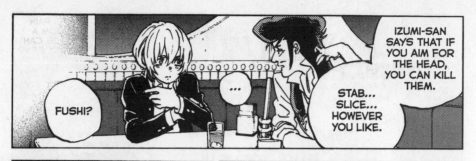

IZUMI-SAN SAYS THAT IF YOU AIM FOR THE HEAD, YOU CAN KILL THEM.
STAB... SLICE... HOWEVER YOU LIKE.
...
FUSHI?
R-RIGHT! I CAN KILL THEM.
I CAN KILL THEM.
WHAT'S THE MATTER? HAVEN'T YOU BEEN KILLING NOKKERS FOR AGES?
YOU MAY NOT HAVE KILLED THAT ONE TODAY, BUT YOU CERTAINLY FOUGHT IT OFF.
THAT ONE...
...FEELS PAIN...
THAT'S NEVER HAPPENED BEFORE...
...BUT I DEFI-NITELY...
...FELT IT THIS TIME.
SHE FELT THE SAME PAIN AS US.

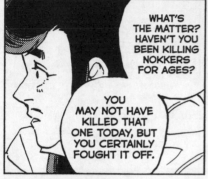

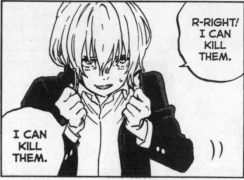

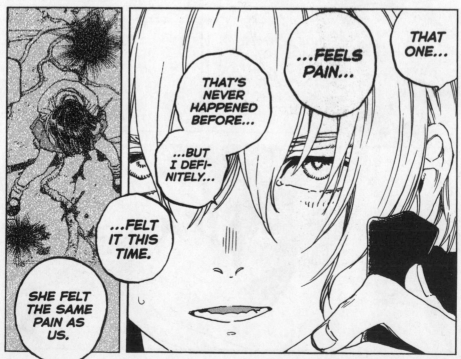

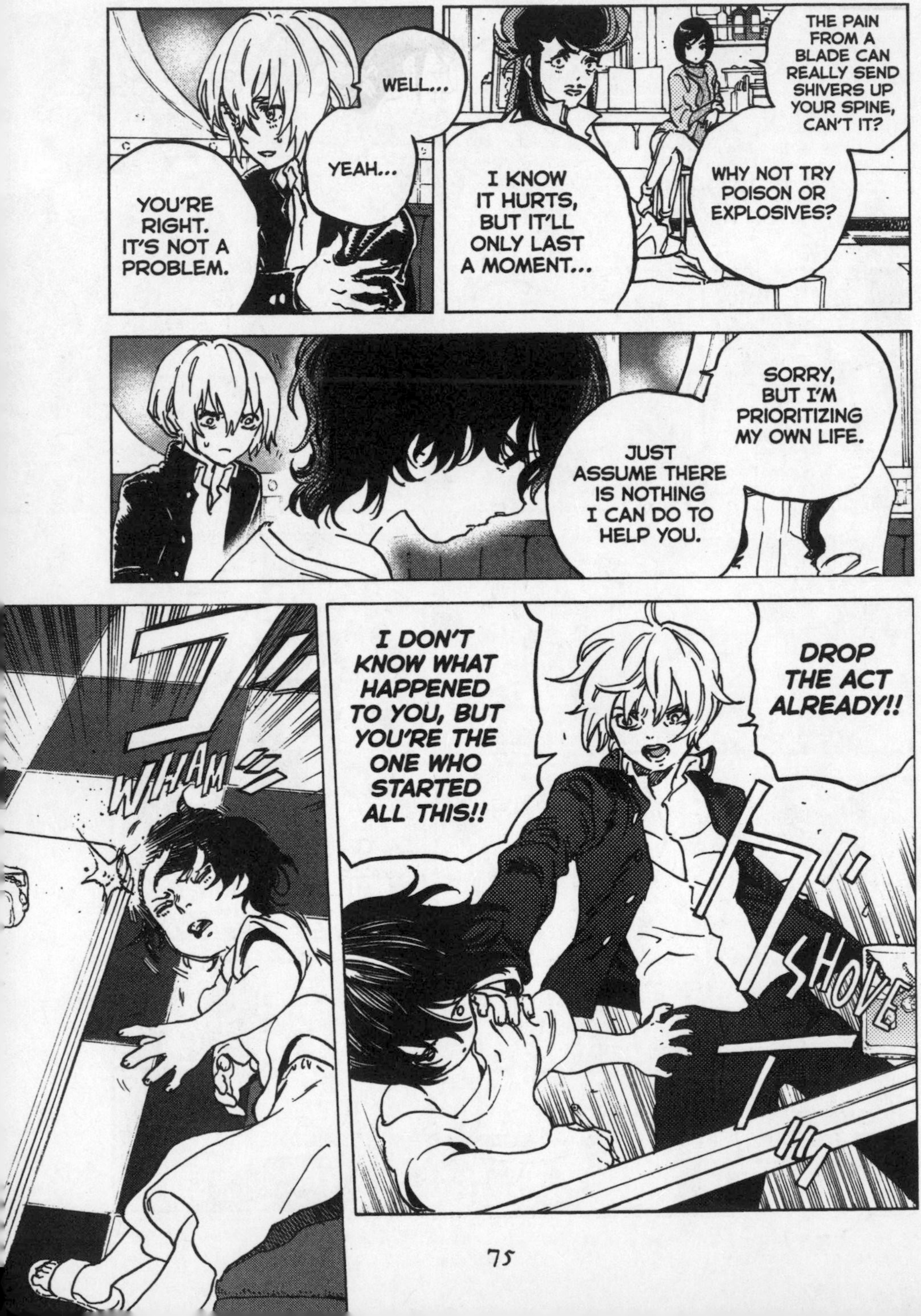
THE PAIN FROM A BLADE CAN REALLY SEND SHIVERS UP YOUR SPINE, CAN'T IT?
WHY NOT TRY POISON OR EXPLOSIVES?
I KNOW IT HURTS, BUT IT'LL ONLY LAST A MOMENT...
WELL...
YEAH...
YOU'RE RIGHT. IT'S NOT A PROBLEM.
SORRY, BUT I'M PRIORITIZING MY OWN LIFE.
JUST ASSUME THERE IS NOTHING I CAN DO TO HELP YOU.
DROP THE ACT ALREADY!!
I DON'T KNOW WHAT HAPPENED TO YOU, BUT YOU'RE THE ONE WHO STARTED ALL THIS!!
SHOVE
WHAM

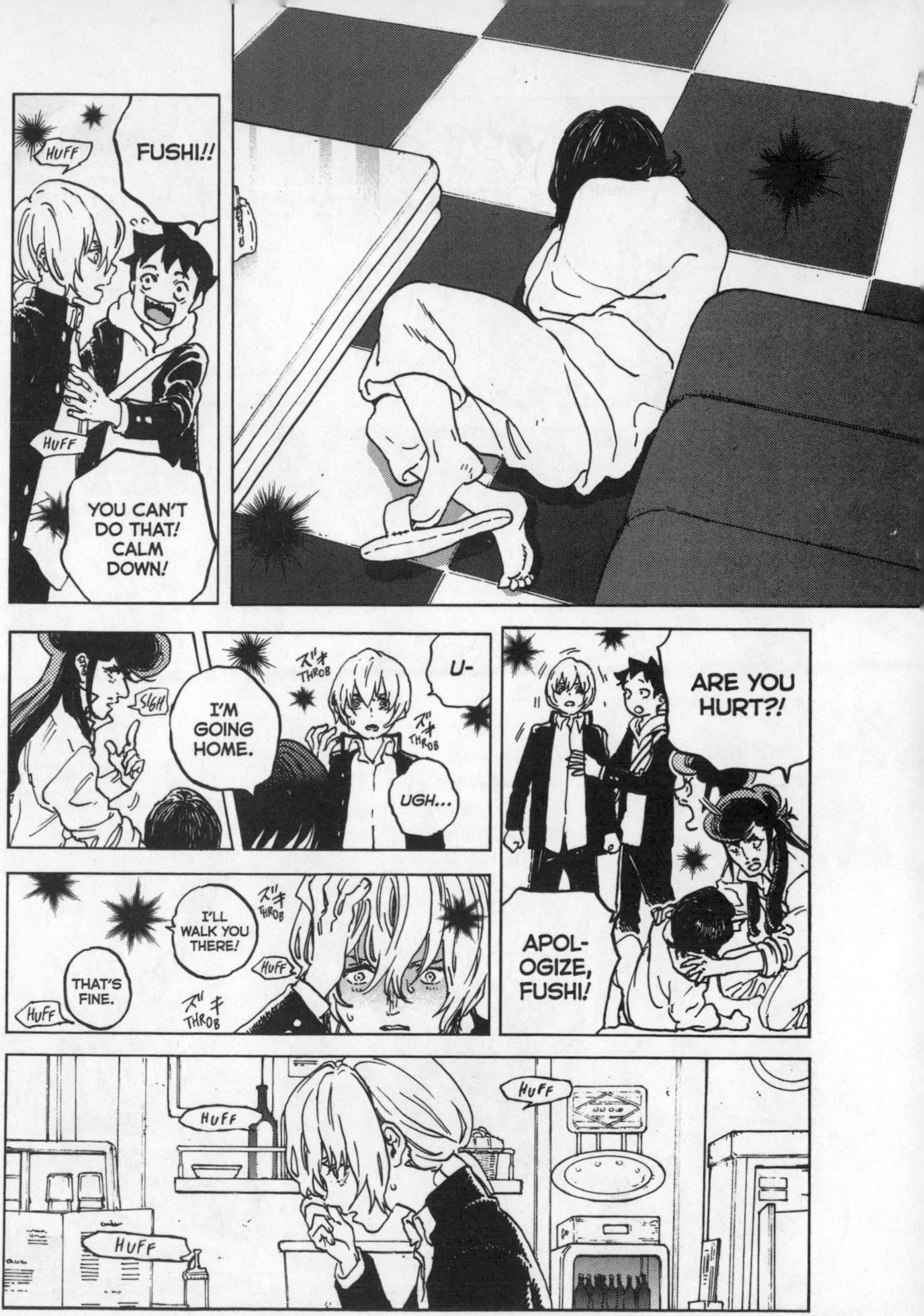
FUSHI!!
HUFF
HUFF
YOU CAN'T DO THAT! CALM DOWN!
ARE YOU HURT?!
APOL-OGIZE, FUSHI!
U-
ズキ THROB
ズキ THROB
I'M GOING HOME.
UGH...
SIGH
ズキ THROB
I'LL WALK YOU THERE!
HUFF
ズキ THROB
THAT'S FINE.
HUFF
HUFF
HUFF
HUFF

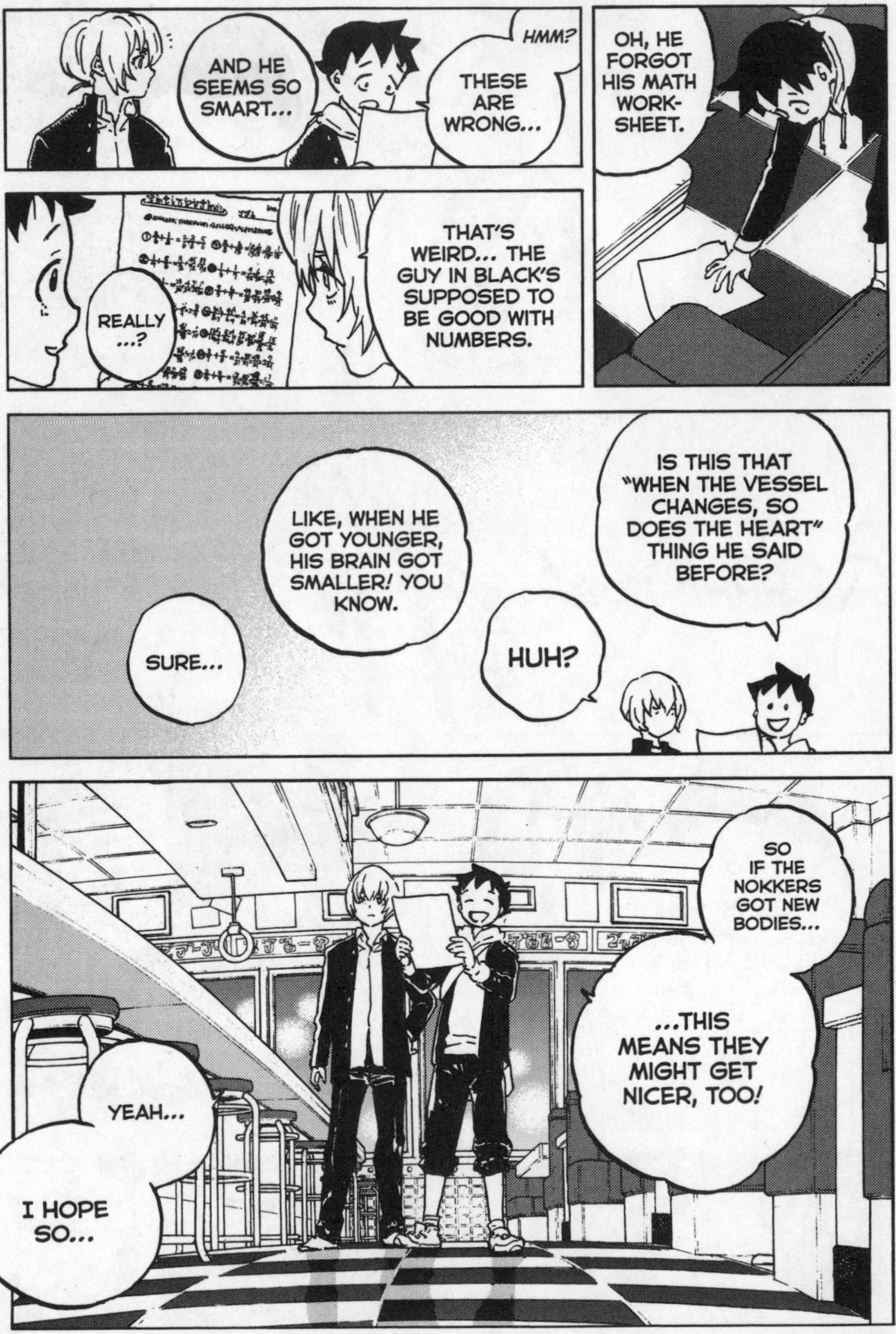
OH, HE FORGOT HIS MATH WORK-SHEET.
HMM?
THESE ARE WRONG...
AND HE SEEMS SO SMART...
THAT'S WEIRD... THE GUY IN BLACK'S SUPPOSED TO BE GOOD WITH NUMBERS.
REALLY ...?
IS THIS THAT "WHEN THE VESSEL CHANGES, SO DOES THE HEART" THING HE SAID BEFORE?
LIKE, WHEN HE GOT YOUNGER, HIS BRAIN GOT SMALLER! YOU KNOW.
HUH?
SURE...
SO IF THE NOKKERS GOT NEW BODIES...
...THIS MEANS THEY MIGHT GET NICER, TOO!
YEAH...
I HOPE SO...

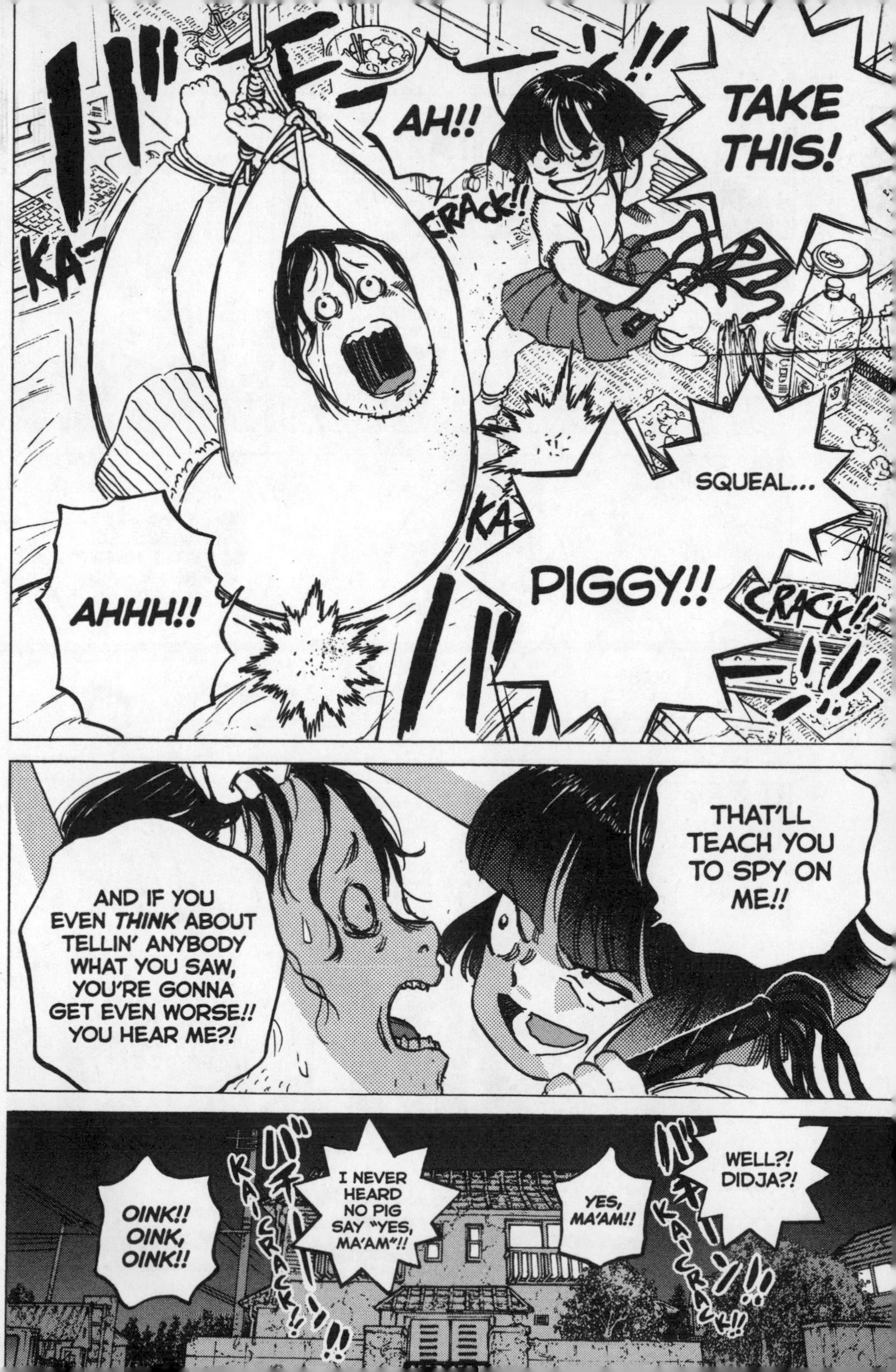
TAKE THIS!
AH!!
CRACK!!
KA-
SQUEAL...
PIGGY!!
CRACK!!
KA-
AHHH!!
THAT'LL TEACH YOU TO SPY ON ME!!
AND IF YOU EVEN *THINK* ABOUT TELLIN' ANYBODY WHAT YOU SAW, YOU'RE GONNA GET EVEN WORSE!! YOU HEAR ME?!
WELL?! DIDJA?!
KA-CRACK!!
YES, MA'AM!!
I NEVER HEARD NO PIG SAY "YES, MA'AM"!!
KA-CRACK!!
OINK!! OINK, OINK!!

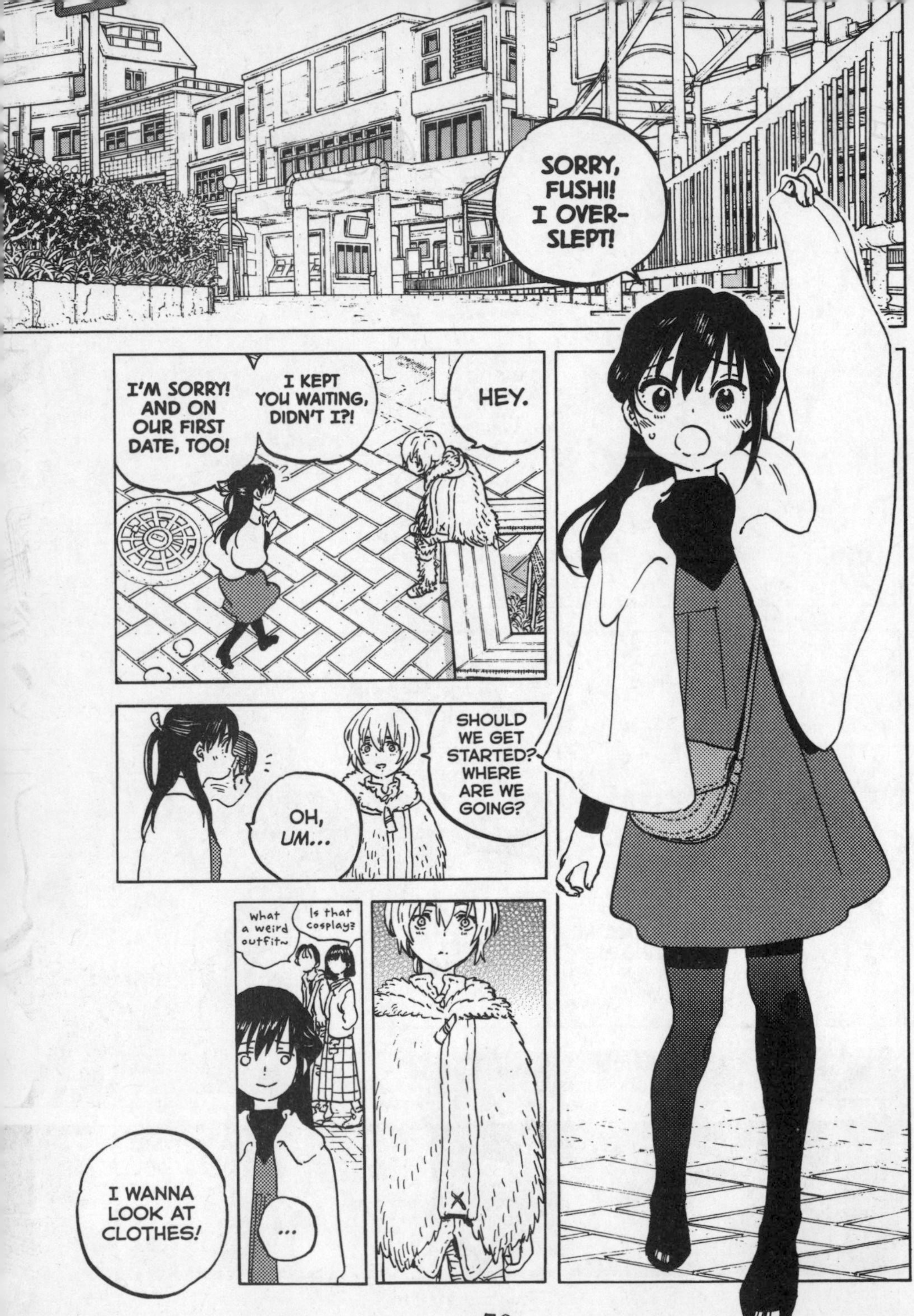
SORRY, FUSHI! I OVER-SLEPT!
HEY.
I KEPT YOU WAITING, DIDN'T I?!
I'M SORRY! AND ON OUR FIRST DATE, TOO!
SHOULD WE GET STARTED? WHERE ARE WE GOING?
OH, *UM*...
Is that cosplay?
What a weird outfit~
...
I WANNA LOOK AT CLOTHES!

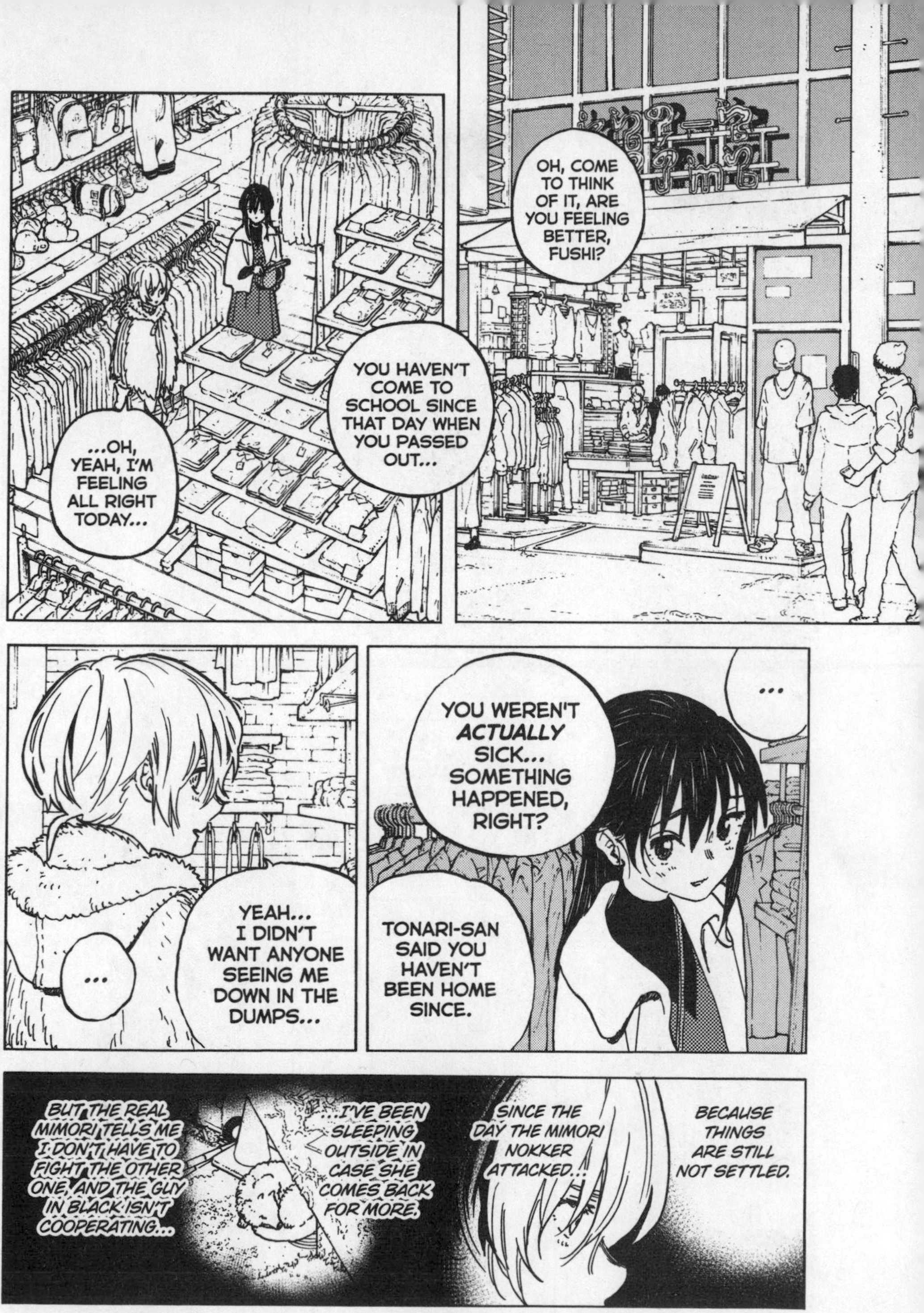
OH, COME TO THINK OF IT, ARE YOU FEELING BETTER, FUSHI?
YOU HAVEN'T COME TO SCHOOL SINCE THAT DAY WHEN YOU PASSED OUT...
...OH, YEAH, I'M FEELING ALL RIGHT TODAY...
...
YOU WEREN'T *ACTUALLY* SICK... SOMETHING HAPPENED, RIGHT?
TONARI-SAN SAID YOU HAVEN'T BEEN HOME SINCE.
YEAH... I DIDN'T WANT ANYONE SEEING ME DOWN IN THE DUMPS...
...
BECAUSE THINGS ARE STILL NOT SETTLED.
SINCE THE DAY THE MIMORI NOKKER ATTACKED...
...I'VE BEEN SLEEPING OUTSIDE IN CASE SHE COMES BACK FOR MORE.
BUT THE REAL MIMORI TELLS ME I DON'T HAVE TO FIGHT THE OTHER ONE, AND THE GUY IN BLACK ISN'T COOPERATING...

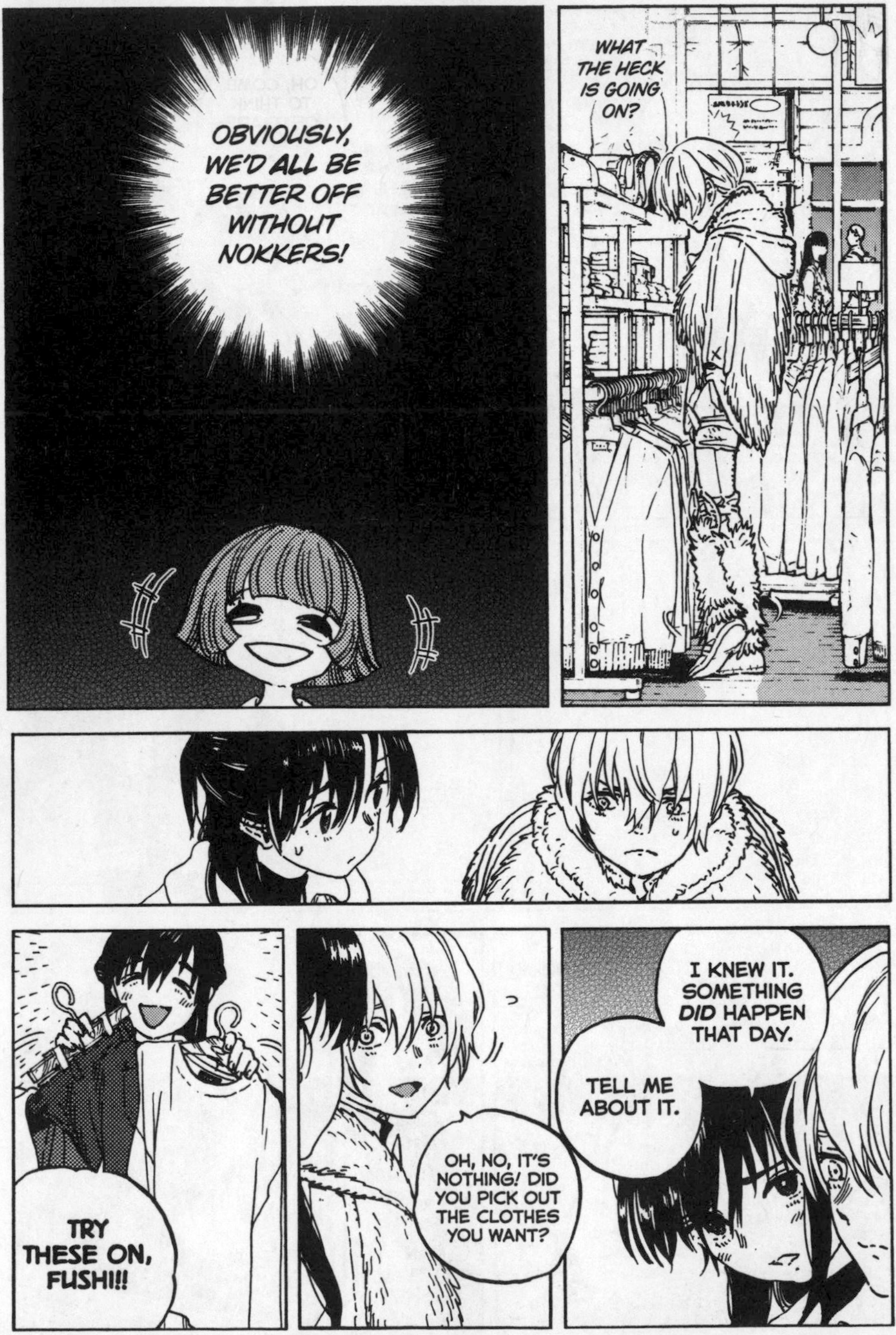
WHAT THE HECK IS GOING ON?
OBVIOUSLY, WE'D ALL BE BETTER OFF WITHOUT NOKKERS!
I KNEW IT. SOMETHING DID HAPPEN THAT DAY.
TELL ME ABOUT IT.
OH, NO, IT'S NOTHING! DID YOU PICK OUT THE CLOTHES YOU WANT?
TRY THESE ON, FUSHI!!!

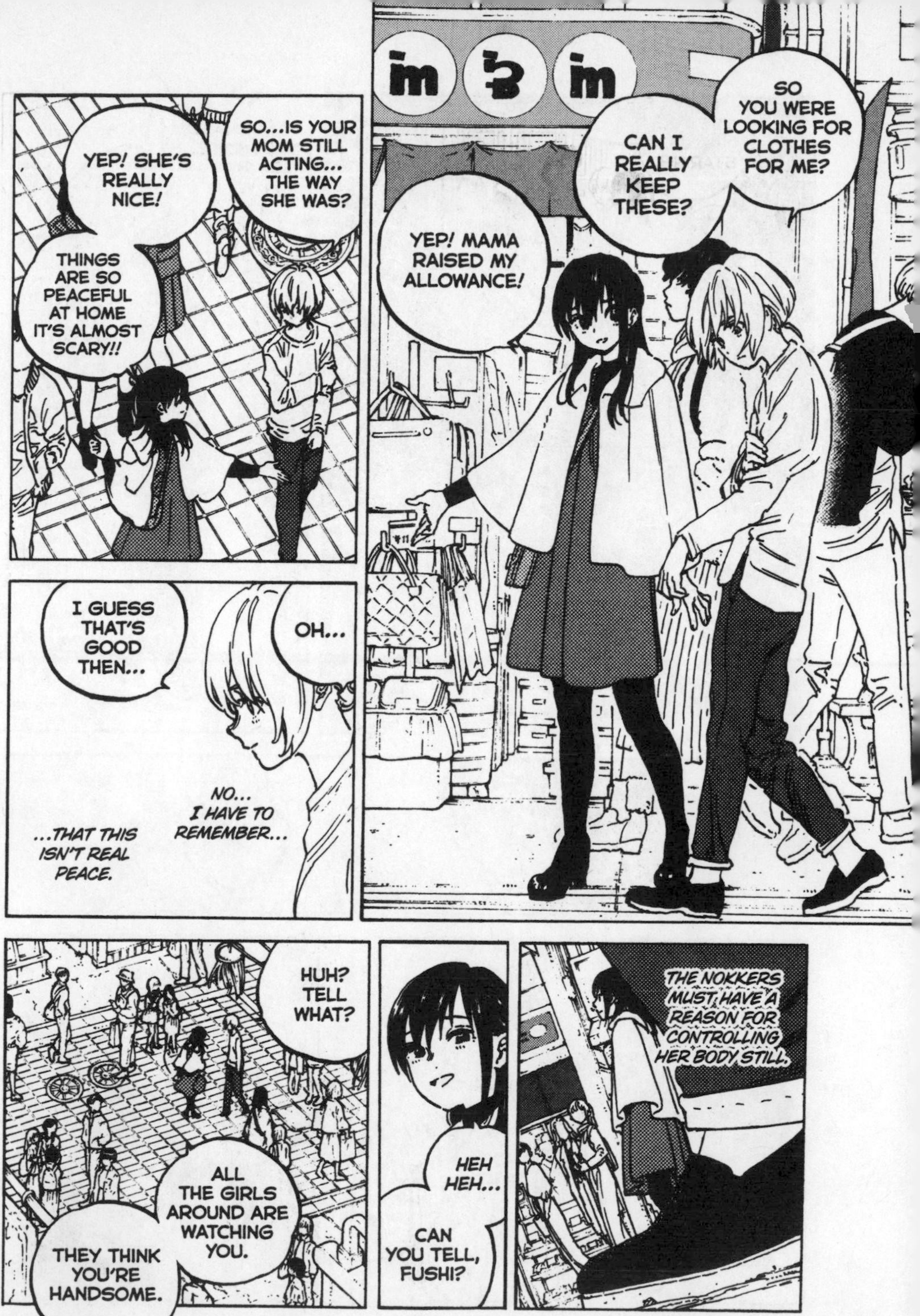
SO YOU WERE LOOKING FOR CLOTHES FOR ME?
CAN I REALLY KEEP THESE?
YEP! MAMA RAISED MY ALLOWANCE!
SO...IS YOUR MOM STILL ACTING... THE WAY SHE WAS?
YEP! SHE'S REALLY NICE!
THINGS ARE SO PEACEFUL AT HOME IT'S ALMOST SCARY!!
OH...
I GUESS THAT'S GOOD THEN...
NO... I HAVE TO REMEMBER...
...THAT THIS ISN'T REAL PEACE.
THE NOKKERS MUST HAVE A REASON FOR CONTROLLING HER BODY STILL.
HEH HEH...
CAN YOU TELL, FUSHI?
HUH? TELL WHAT?
ALL THE GIRLS AROUND ARE WATCHING YOU.
THEY THINK YOU'RE HANDSOME.

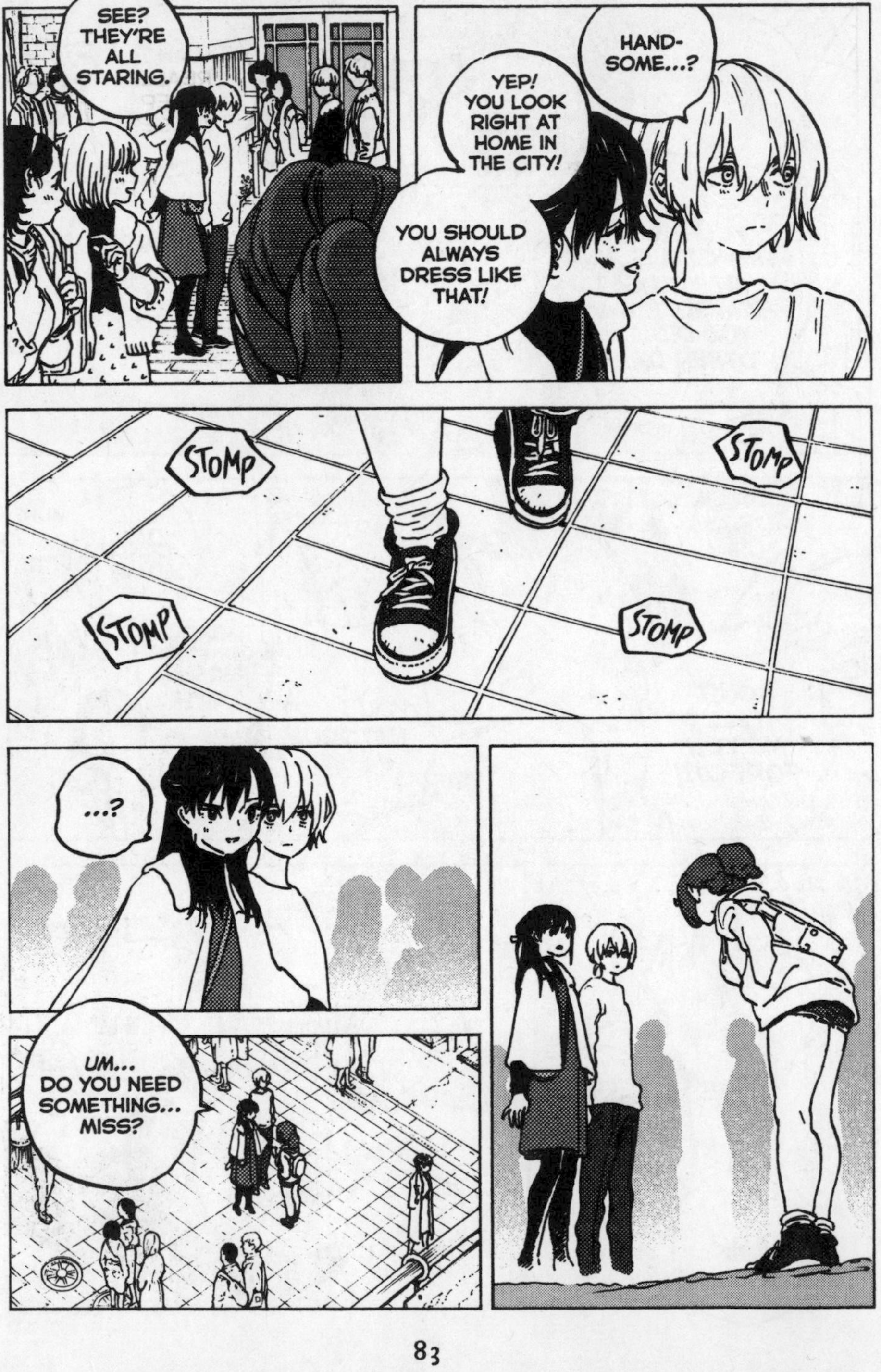
HAND-SOME...?
YEP! YOU LOOK RIGHT AT HOME IN THE CITY!
YOU SHOULD ALWAYS DRESS LIKE THAT!
SEE? THEY'RE ALL STARING.
STOMP
STOMP
STOMP
STOMP
...?
UM... DO YOU NEED SOMETHING... MISS?

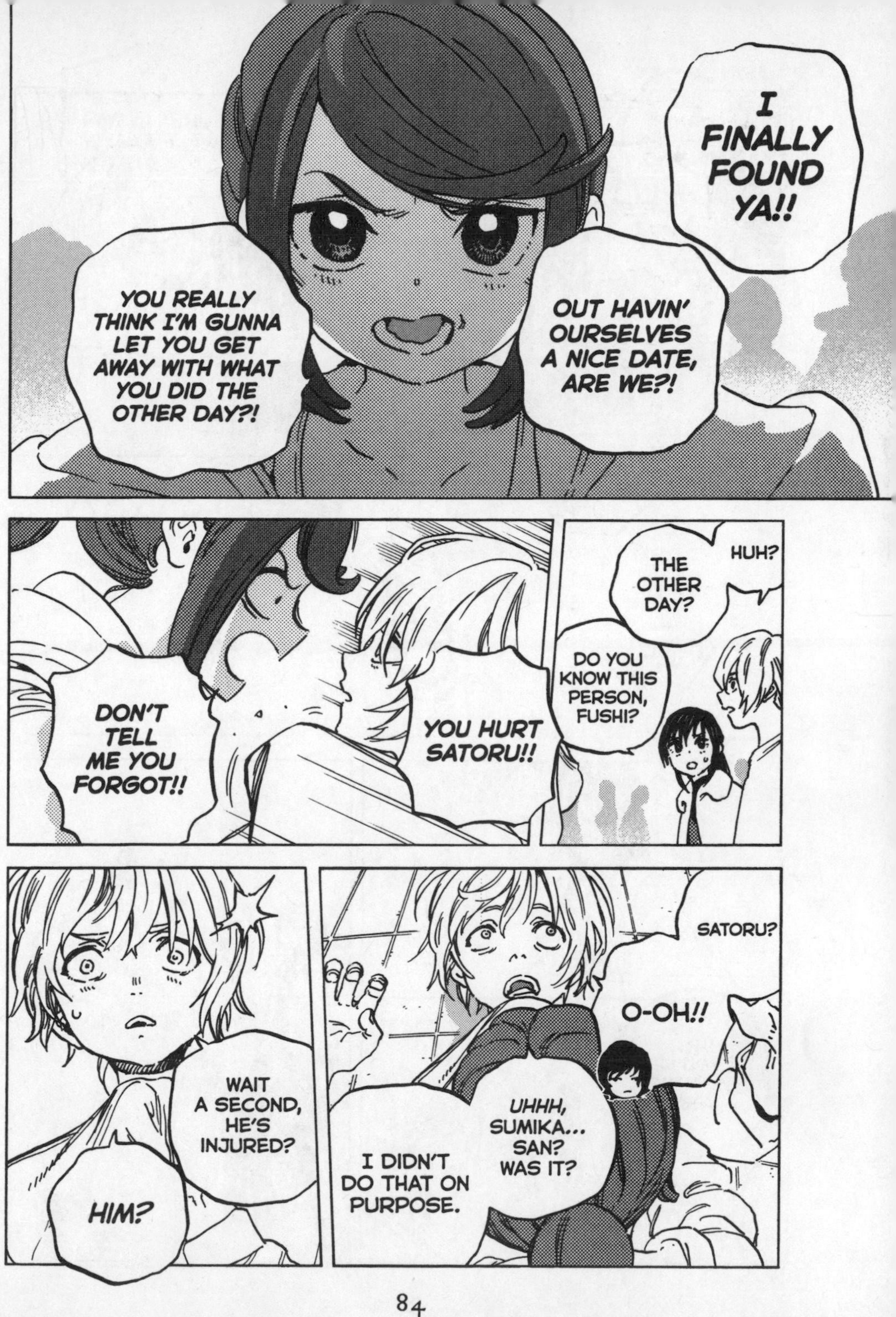
I FINALLY FOUND YA!!
OUT HAVIN' OURSELVES A NICE DATE, ARE WE?!
YOU REALLY THINK I'M GUNNA LET YOU GET AWAY WITH WHAT YOU DID THE OTHER DAY?!
HUH?
THE OTHER DAY?
DO YOU KNOW THIS PERSON, FUSHI?
YOU HURT SATORU!!
DON'T TELL ME YOU FORGOT!!
SATORU?
O-OH!!
UHHH, SUMIKA... SAN? WAS IT?
I DIDN'T DO THAT ON PURPOSE.
WAIT A SECOND, HE'S INJURED?
HIM?

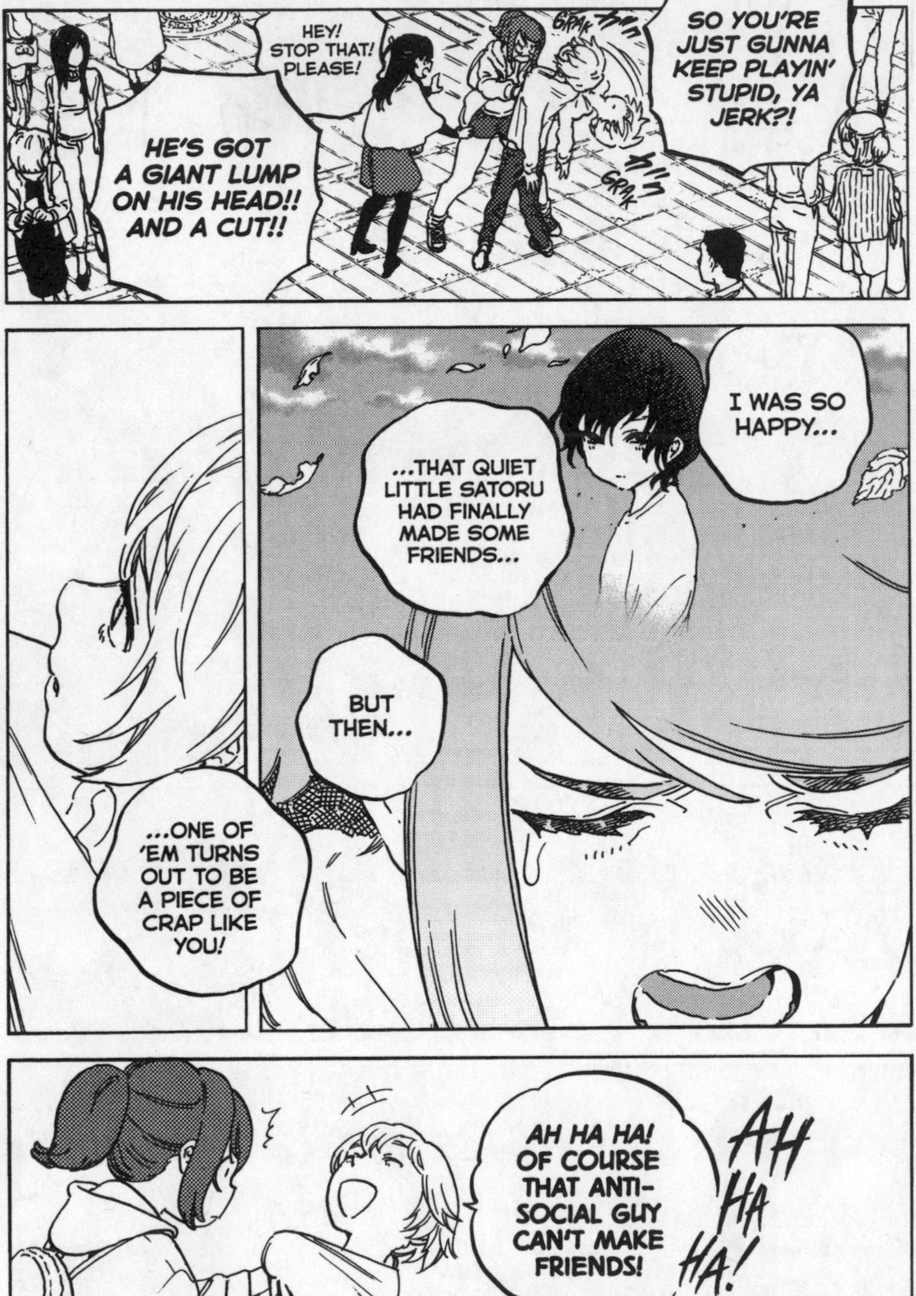
SO YOU'RE JUST GUNNA KEEP PLAYIN' STUPID, YA JERK?!
HEY! STOP THAT! PLEASE!
HE'S GOT A GIANT LUMP ON HIS HEAD!! AND A CUT!!
I WAS SO HAPPY...
...THAT QUIET LITTLE SATORU HAD FINALLY MADE SOME FRIENDS...
BUT THEN...
...ONE OF 'EM TURNS OUT TO BE A PIECE OF CRAP LIKE YOU!
AH HA HA! OF COURSE THAT ANTI-SOCIAL GUY CAN'T MAKE FRIENDS!
AH HA HA!

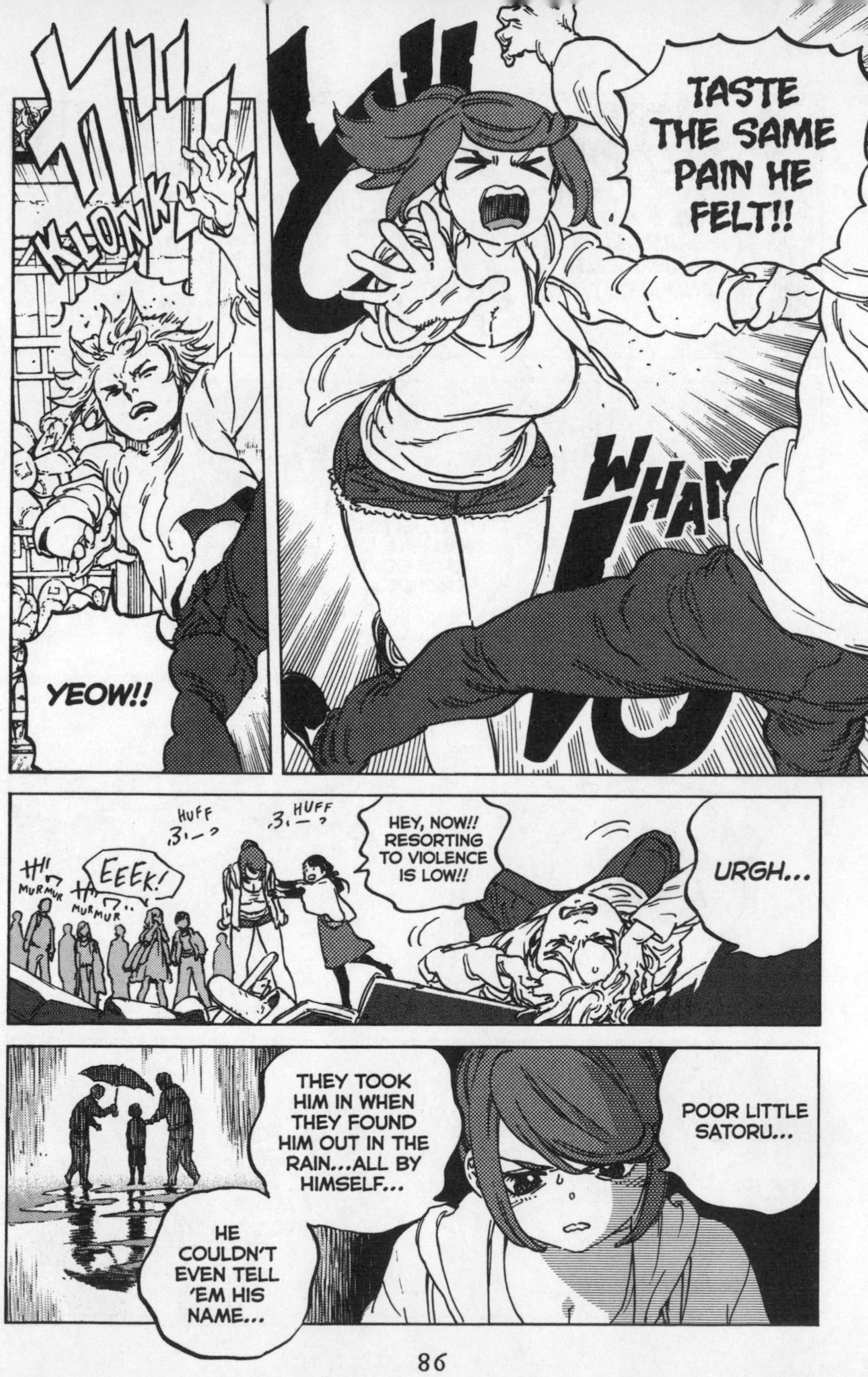
TASTE THE SAME PAIN HE FELT!!
WHAM
KLONK
YEOW!!
URGH...
HEY, NOW!! RESORTING TO VIOLENCE IS LOW!!
HUFF
HUFF
EEEK!
MURMUR
MURMUR
POOR LITTLE SATORU...
THEY TOOK HIM IN WHEN THEY FOUND HIM OUT IN THE RAIN...ALL BY HIMSELF...
HE COULDN'T EVEN TELL 'EM HIS NAME...

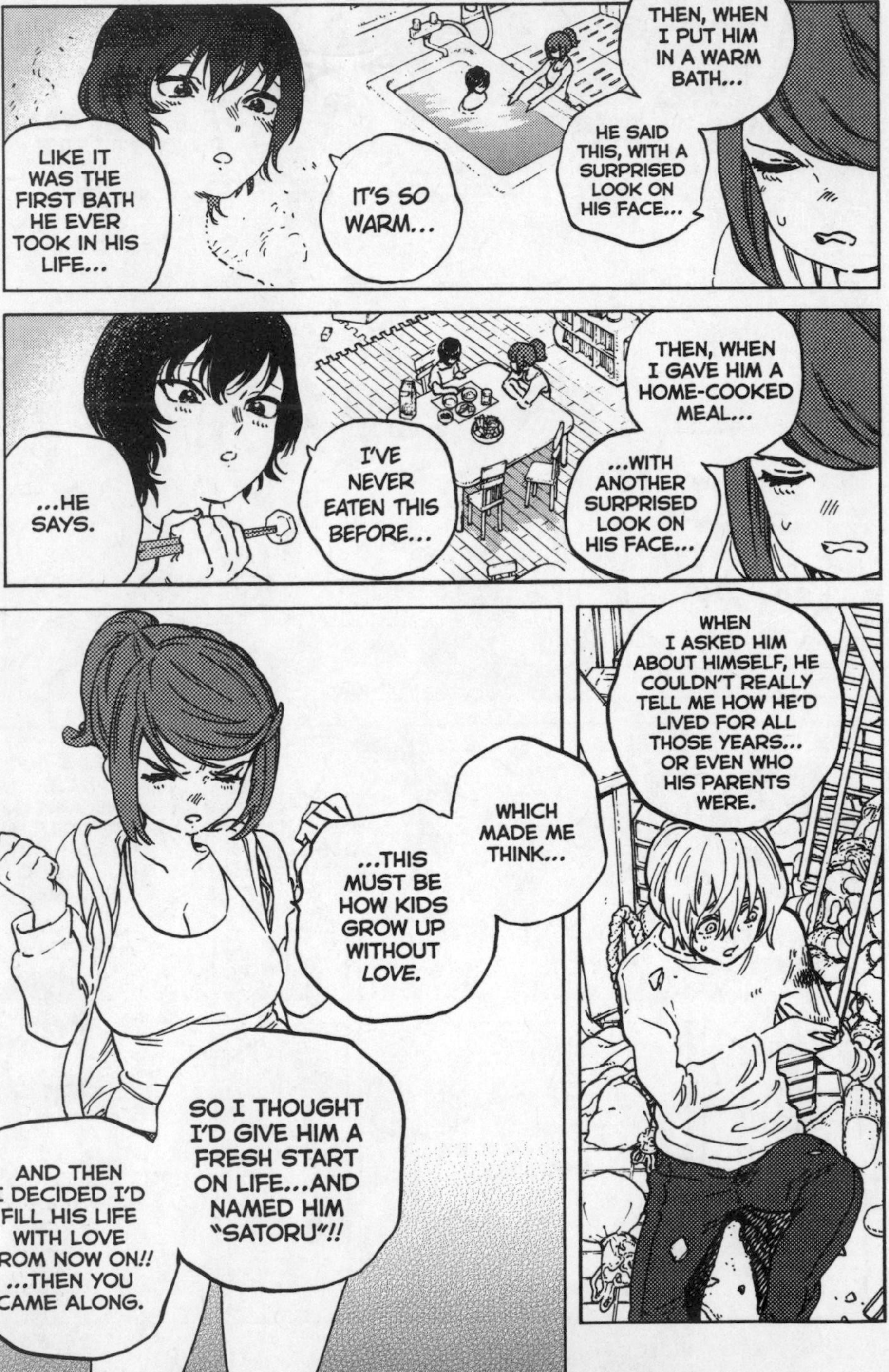

THEN, WHEN I PUT HIM IN A WARM BATH...
HE SAID THIS, WITH A SURPRISED LOOK ON HIS FACE...
IT'S SO WARM...
LIKE IT WAS THE FIRST BATH HE EVER TOOK IN HIS LIFE...
THEN, WHEN I GAVE HIM A HOME-COOKED MEAL...
...WITH ANOTHER SURPRISED LOOK ON HIS FACE...
I'VE NEVER EATEN THIS BEFORE...
...HE SAYS.
WHEN I ASKED HIM ABOUT HIMSELF, HE COULDN'T REALLY TELL ME HOW HE'D LIVED FOR ALL THOSE YEARS... OR EVEN WHO HIS PARENTS WERE.
WHICH MADE ME THINK...
...THIS MUST BE HOW KIDS GROW UP WITHOUT *LOVE*.
SO I THOUGHT I'D GIVE HIM A FRESH START ON LIFE...AND NAMED HIM "SATORU"!!
AND THEN I DECIDED I'D FILL HIS LIFE WITH LOVE FROM NOW ON!! ...THEN YOU CAME ALONG.

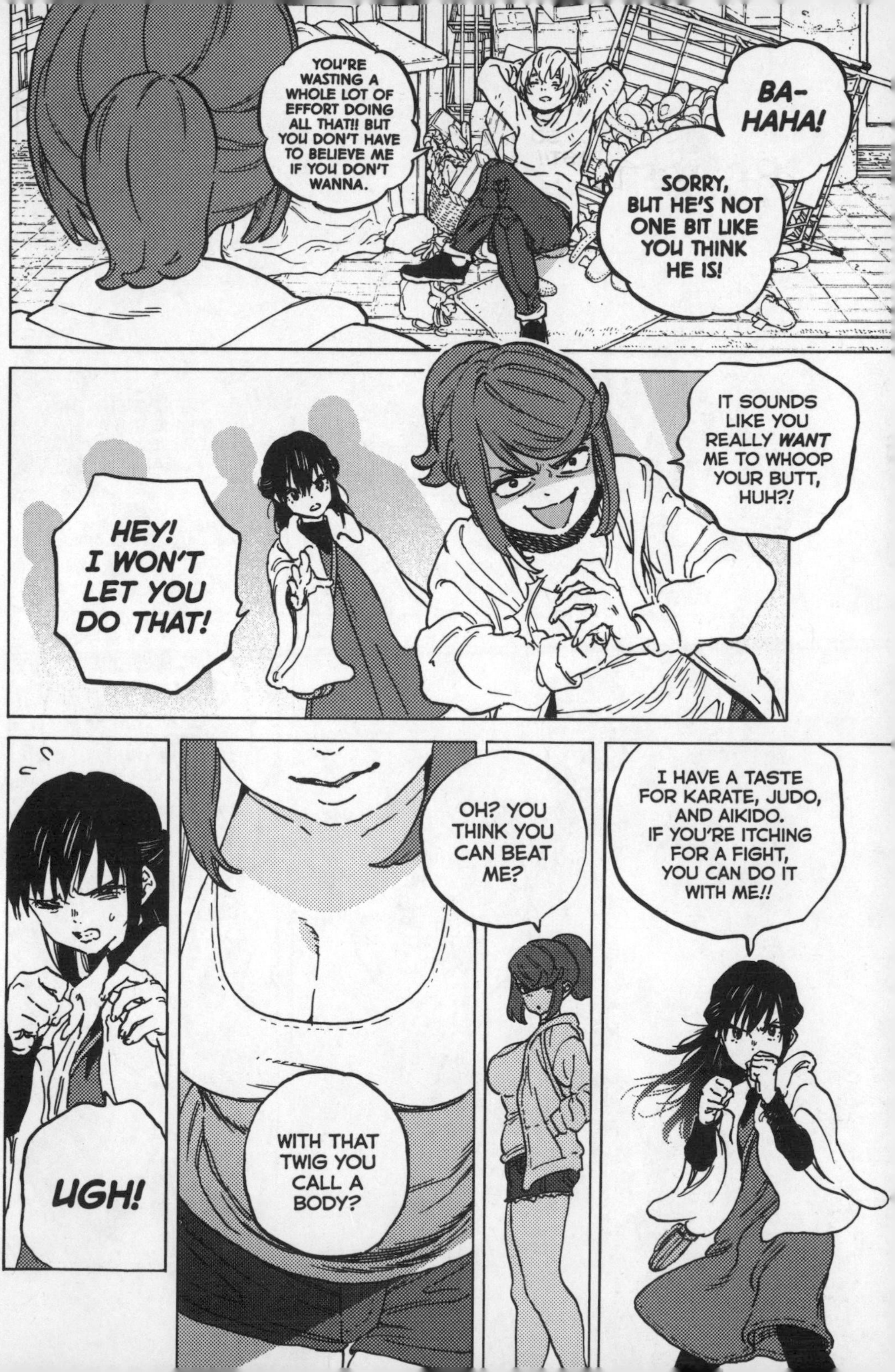
BA-HAHA!
SORRY, BUT HE'S NOT ONE BIT LIKE YOU THINK HE IS!
YOU'RE WASTING A WHOLE LOT OF EFFORT DOING ALL THAT!! BUT YOU DON'T HAVE TO BELIEVE ME IF YOU DON'T WANNA.
IT SOUNDS LIKE YOU REALLY *WANT* ME TO WHOOP YOUR BUTT, HUH?!
HEY! I WON'T LET YOU DO THAT!
I HAVE A TASTE FOR KARATE, JUDO, AND AIKIDO. IF YOU'RE ITCHING FOR A FIGHT, YOU CAN DO IT WITH ME!!
OH? YOU THINK YOU CAN BEAT ME?
WITH THAT TWIG YOU CALL A BODY?
UGH!

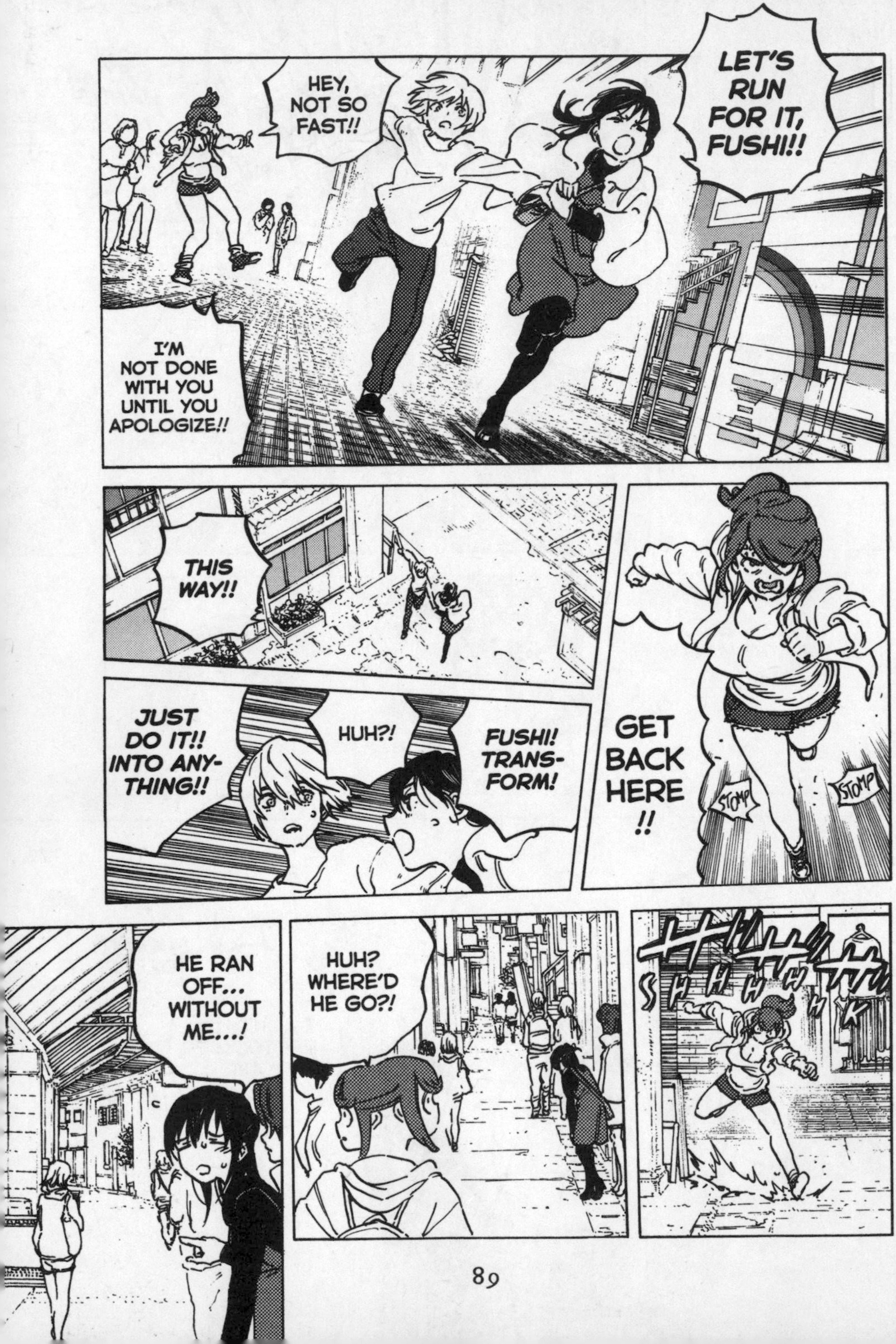
LET'S RUN FOR IT, FUSHI!!
HEY, NOT SO FAST!!
I'M NOT DONE WITH YOU UNTIL YOU APOLOGIZE!!
GET BACK HERE!!
STOMP
STOMP
THIS WAY!!
FUSHI! TRANS-FORM!
HUH?!
JUST DO IT!! INTO ANY-THING!!
SHHHHHK
HUH? WHERE'D HE GO?!
HE RAN OFF... WITHOUT ME...!

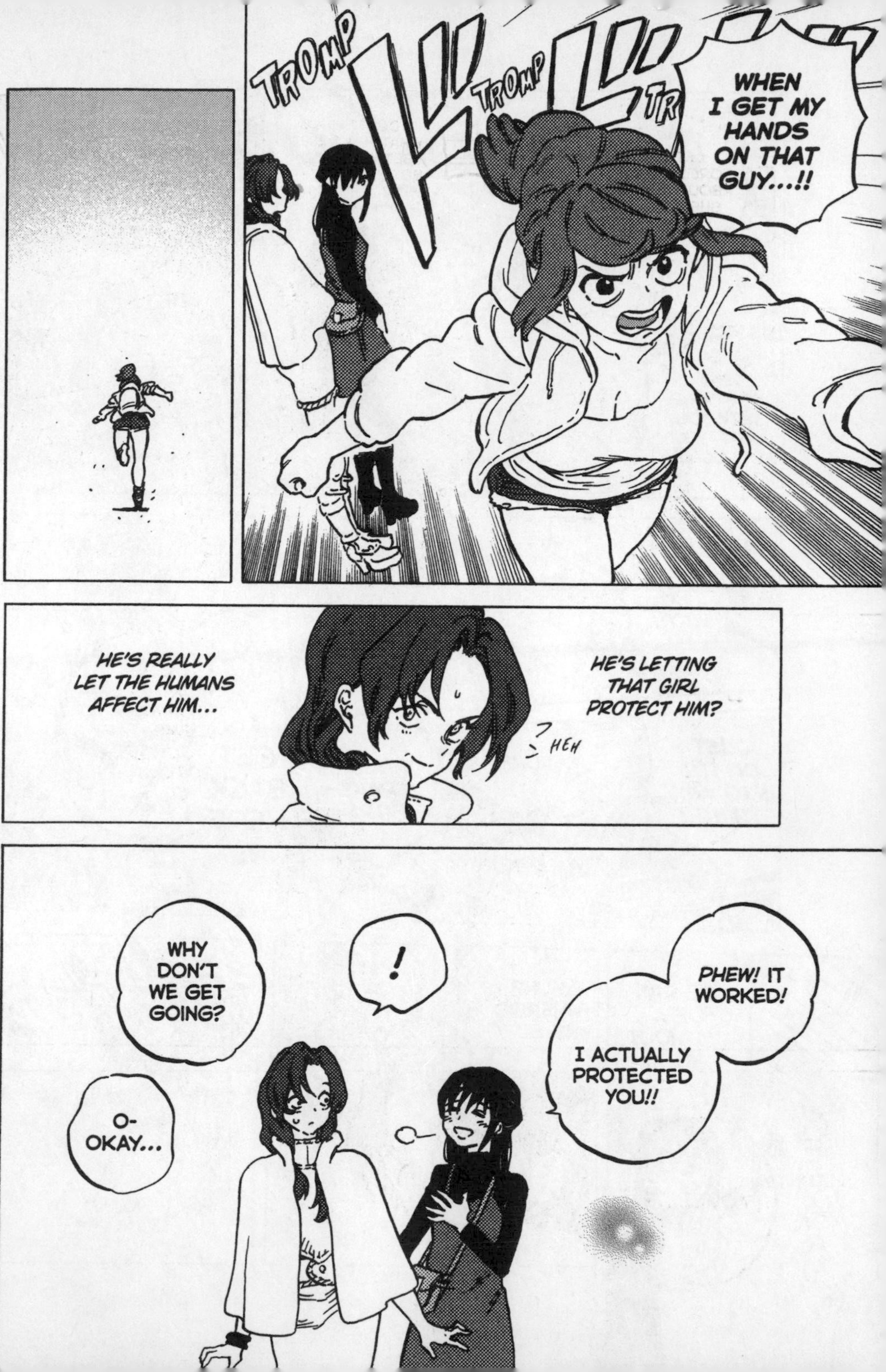
WHEN I GET MY HANDS ON THAT GUY...!!
TR
TROMP
TROMP
HE'S LETTING THAT GIRL PROTECT HIM?
HEH
HE'S REALLY LET THE HUMANS AFFECT HIM...
PHEW! IT WORKED!
I ACTUALLY PROTECTED YOU!!
!
WHY DON'T WE GET GOING?
O-OKAY...

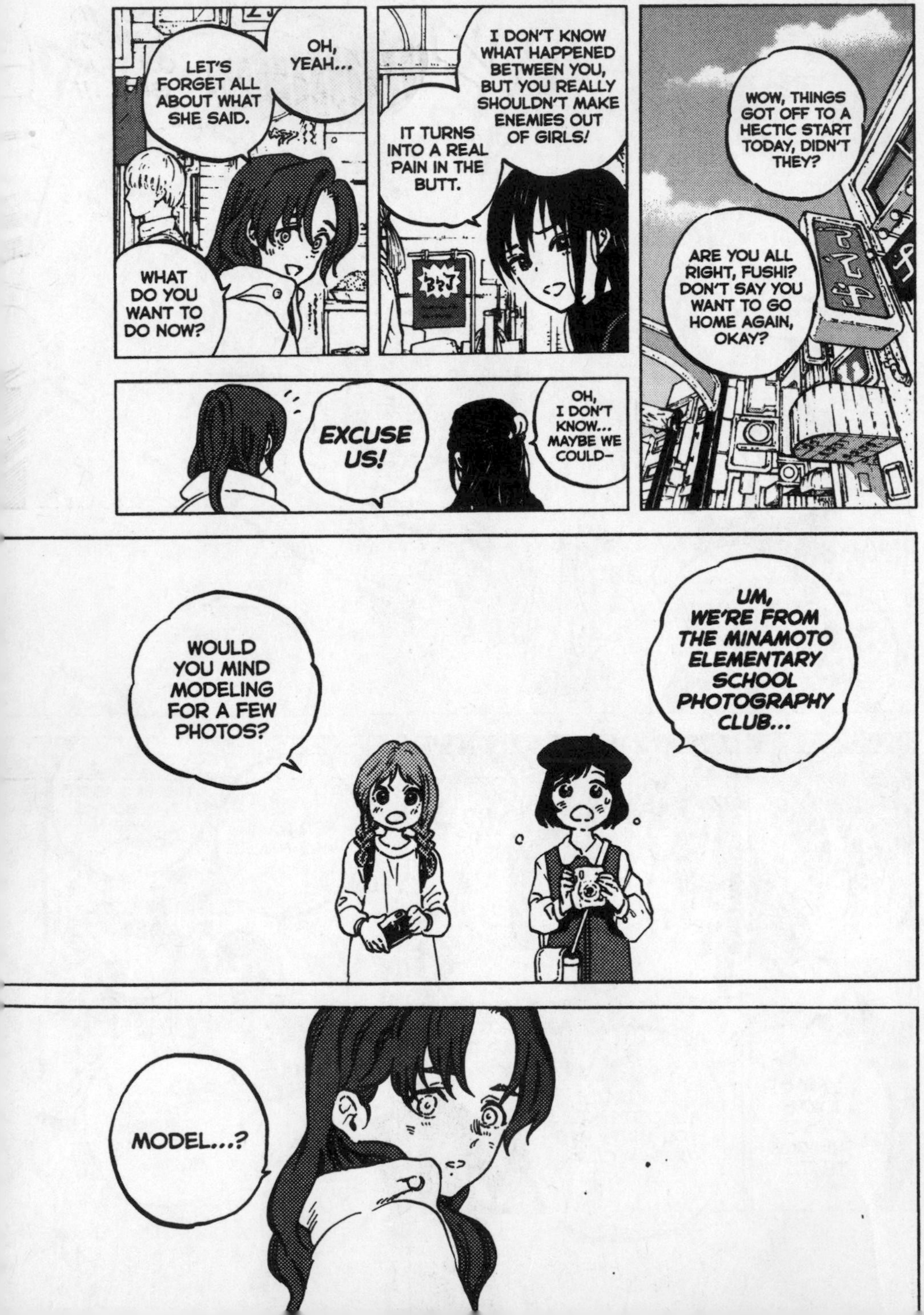
WOW, THINGS GOT OFF TO A HECTIC START TODAY, DIDN'T THEY?
ARE YOU ALL RIGHT, FUSHI? DON'T SAY YOU WANT TO GO HOME AGAIN, OKAY?
I DON'T KNOW WHAT HAPPENED BETWEEN YOU, BUT YOU REALLY SHOULDN'T MAKE ENEMIES OUT OF GIRLS!
IT TURNS INTO A REAL PAIN IN THE BUTT.
OH, YEAH...
LET'S FORGET ALL ABOUT WHAT SHE SAID.
WHAT DO YOU WANT TO DO NOW?
OH, I DON'T KNOW... MAYBE WE COULD–
EXCUSE US!
UM, WE'RE FROM THE MINAMOTO ELEMENTARY SCHOOL PHOTOGRAPHY CLUB...
WOULD YOU MIND MODELING FOR A FEW PHOTOS?
MODEL...?

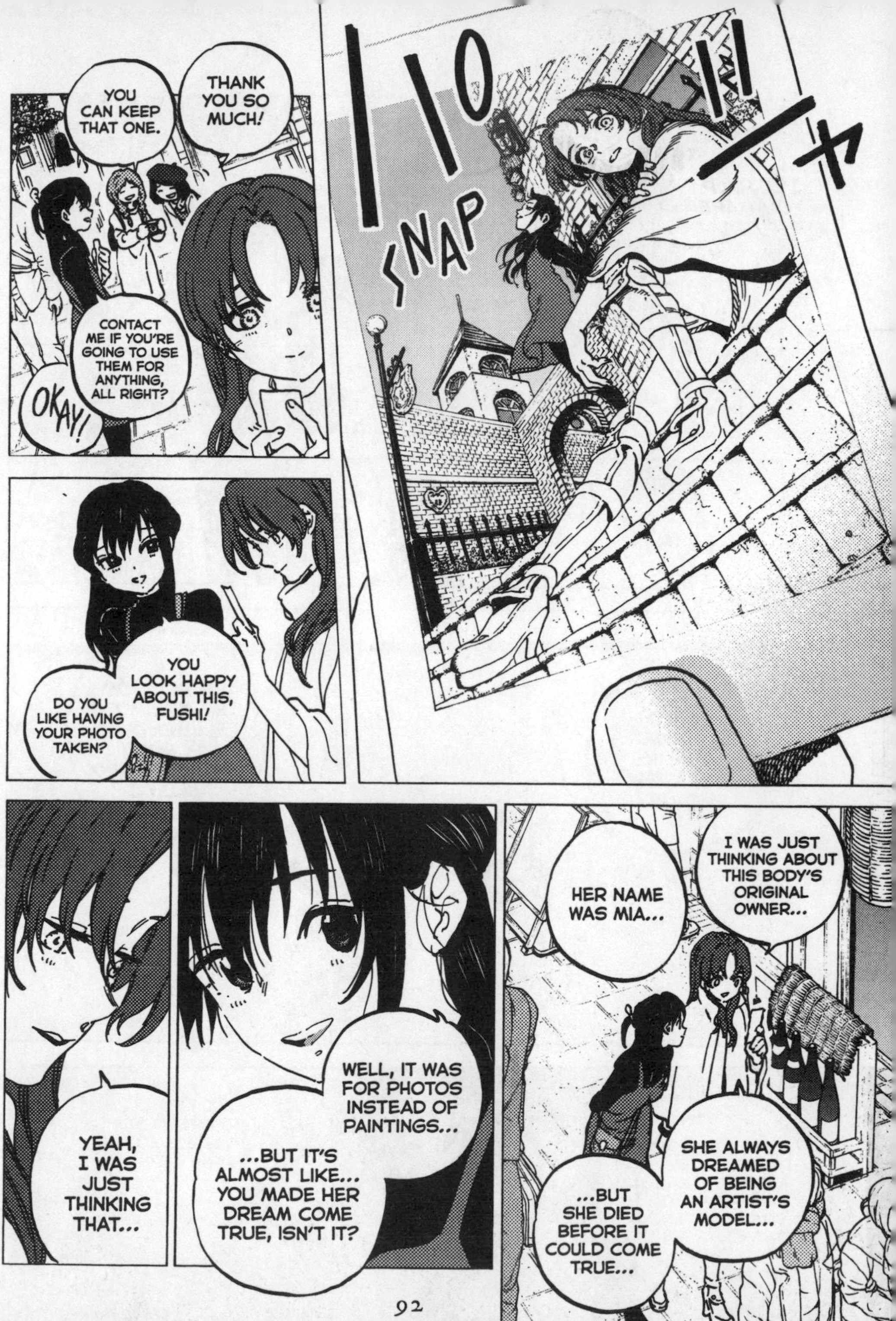
SNAP
THANK YOU SO MUCH!
YOU CAN KEEP THAT ONE.
CONTACT ME IF YOU'RE GOING TO USE THEM FOR ANYTHING, ALL RIGHT?
OKAY!
YOU LOOK HAPPY ABOUT THIS, FUSHI!
DO YOU LIKE HAVING YOUR PHOTO TAKEN?
I WAS JUST THINKING ABOUT THIS BODY'S ORIGINAL OWNER...
HER NAME WAS MIA...
SHE ALWAYS DREAMED OF BEING AN ARTIST'S MODEL...
...BUT SHE DIED BEFORE IT COULD COME TRUE...
WELL, IT WAS FOR PHOTOS INSTEAD OF PAINTINGS...
...BUT IT'S ALMOST LIKE... YOU MADE HER DREAM COME TRUE, ISN'T IT?
YEAH, I WAS JUST THINKING THAT...

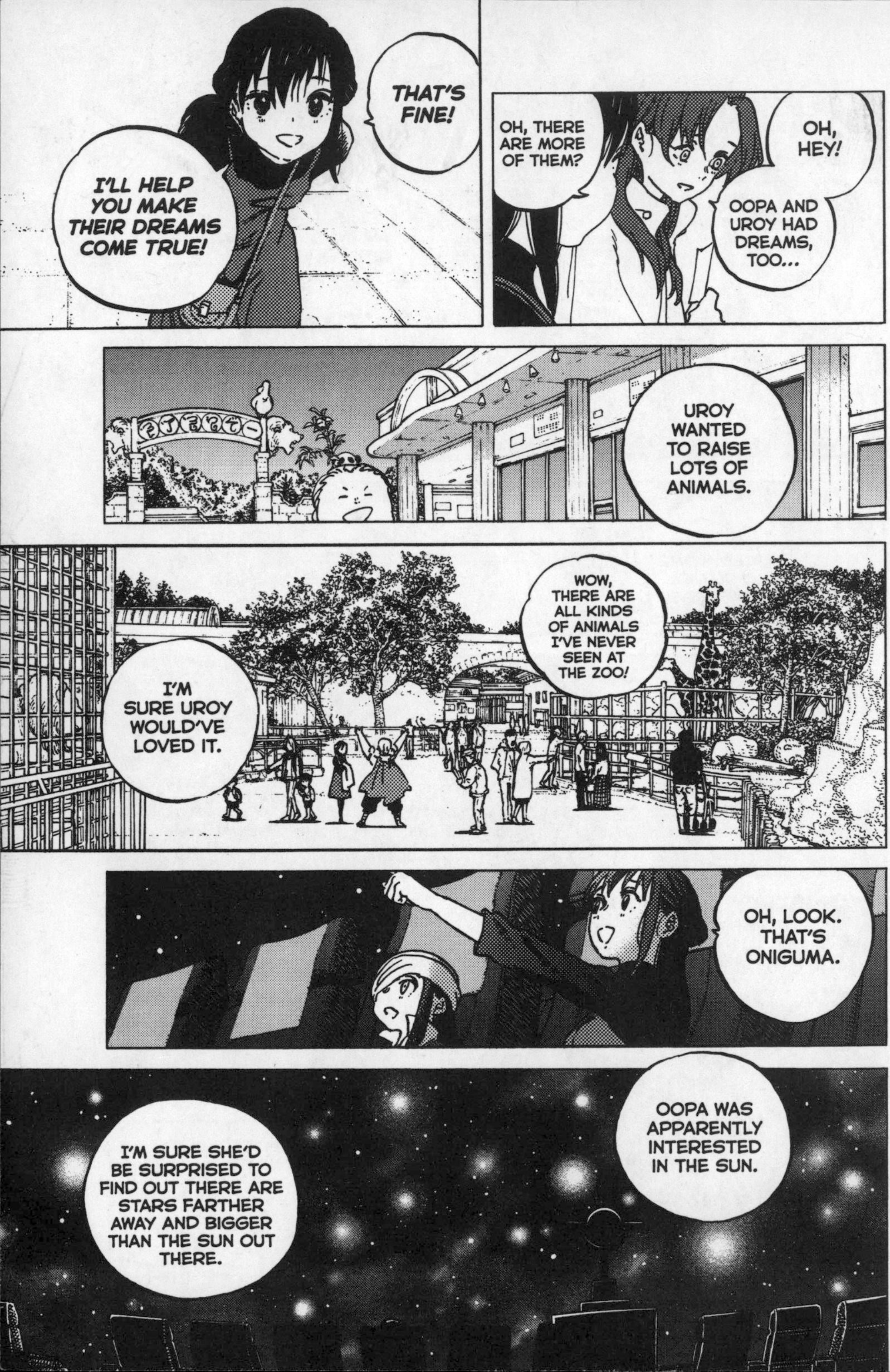
OH, HEY!
OOPA AND UROY HAD DREAMS, TOO...
OH, THERE ARE MORE OF THEM?
THAT'S FINE!
I'LL HELP YOU MAKE THEIR DREAMS COME TRUE!
UROY WANTED TO RAISE LOTS OF ANIMALS.
WOW, THERE ARE ALL KINDS OF ANIMALS I'VE NEVER SEEN AT THE ZOO!
I'M SURE UROY WOULD'VE LOVED IT.
OH, LOOK. THAT'S ONIGUMA.
OOPA WAS APPARENTLY INTERESTED IN THE SUN.
I'M SURE SHE'D BE SURPRISED TO FIND OUT THERE ARE STARS FARTHER AWAY AND BIGGER THAN THE SUN OUT THERE.

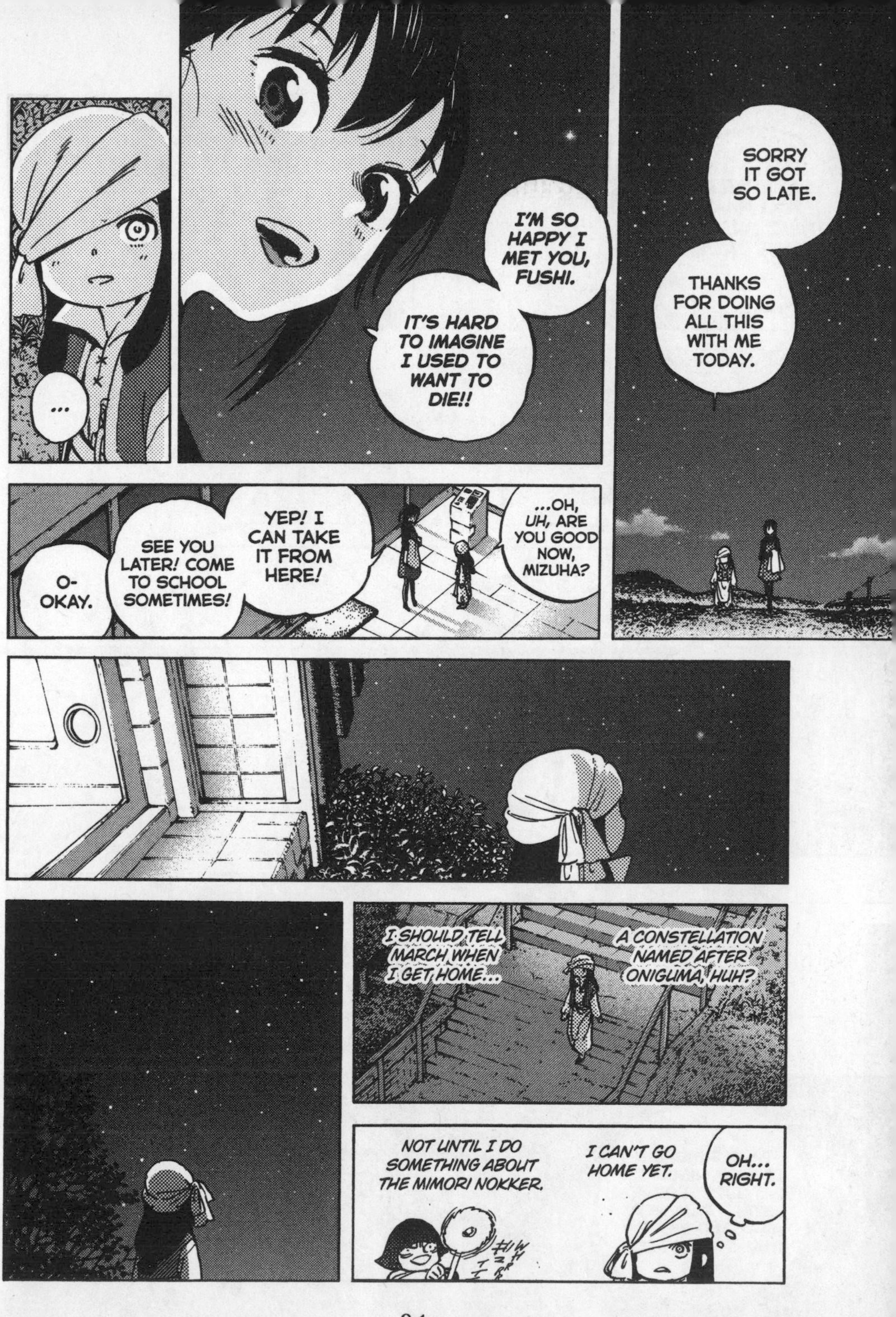
SORRY IT GOT SO LATE.
THANKS FOR DOING ALL THIS WITH ME TODAY.
I'M SO HAPPY I MET YOU, FUSHI.
IT'S HARD TO IMAGINE I USED TO WANT TO DIE!!
...
...OH, UH, ARE YOU GOOD NOW, MIZUHA?
YEP! I CAN TAKE IT FROM HERE!
SEE YOU LATER! COME TO SCHOOL SOMETIMES!
O-OKAY.
A CONSTELLATION NAMED AFTER ONIGUMA, HUH?
I SHOULD TELL MARCH WHEN I GET HOME...
OH... RIGHT.
I CAN'T GO HOME YET.
NOT UNTIL I DO SOMETHING ABOUT THE MIMORI NOKKER.

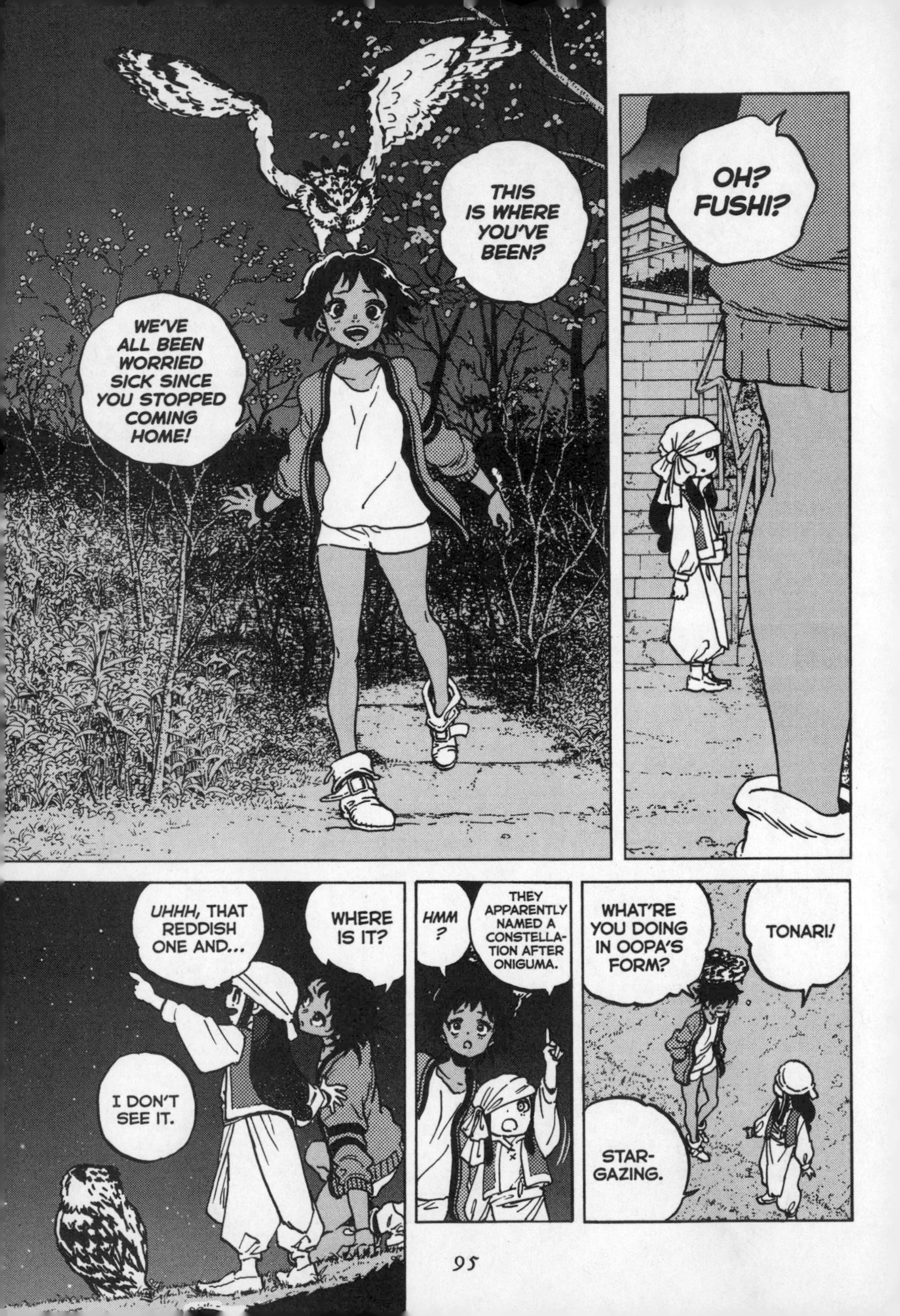
OH? FUSHI?
THIS IS WHERE YOU'VE BEEN?
WE'VE ALL BEEN WORRIED SICK SINCE YOU STOPPED COMING HOME!
TONARI!
WHAT'RE YOU DOING IN OOPA'S FORM?
STAR-GAZING.
THEY APPARENTLY NAMED A CONSTELLATION AFTER ONIGUMA.
HMM?
WHERE IS IT?
UHHH, THAT REDDISH ONE AND...
I DON'T SEE IT.

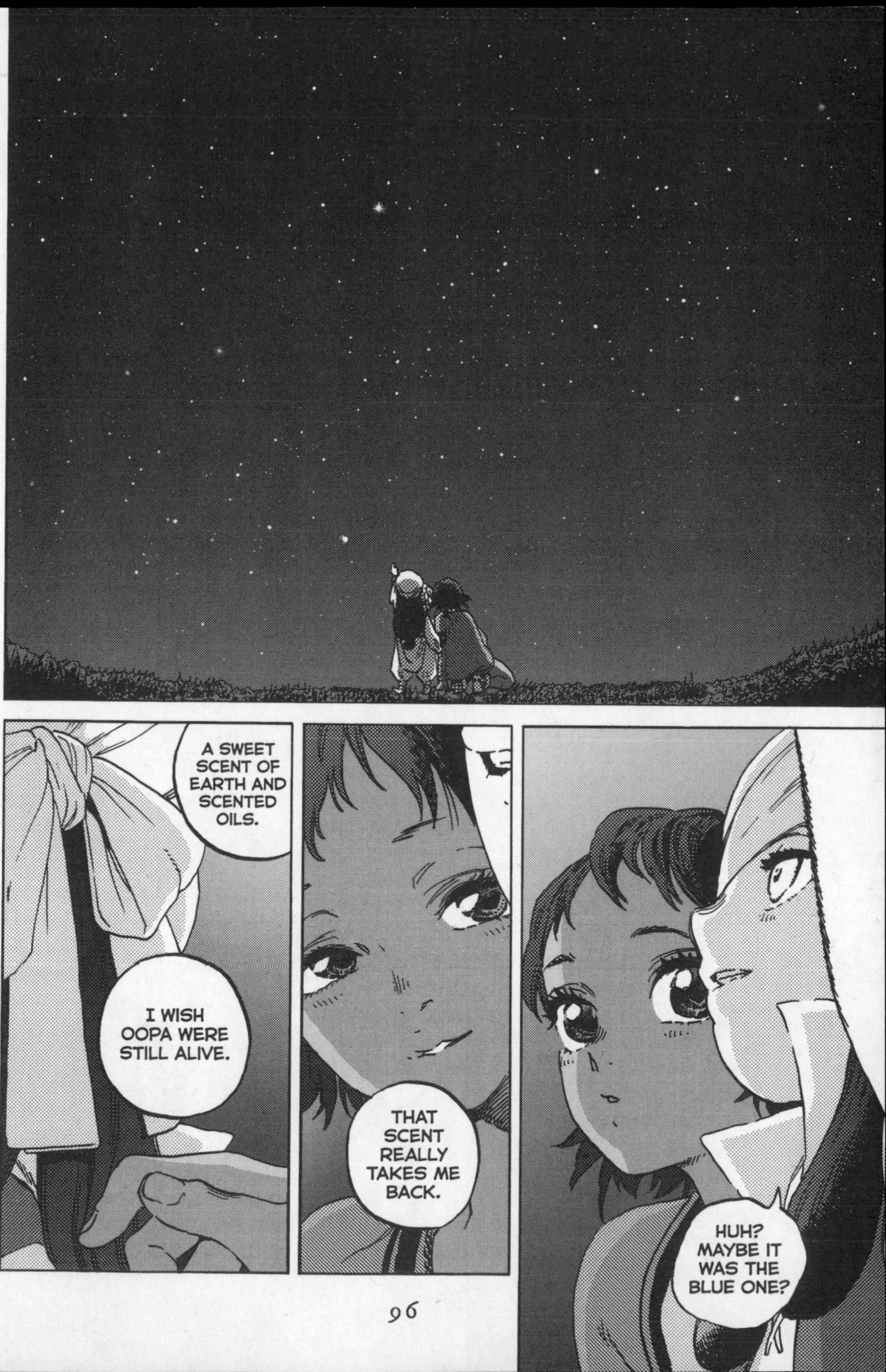
HUH? MAYBE IT WAS THE BLUE ONE?
THAT SCENT REALLY TAKES ME BACK.
A SWEET SCENT OF EARTH AND SCENTED OILS.
I WISH OOPA WERE STILL ALIVE.

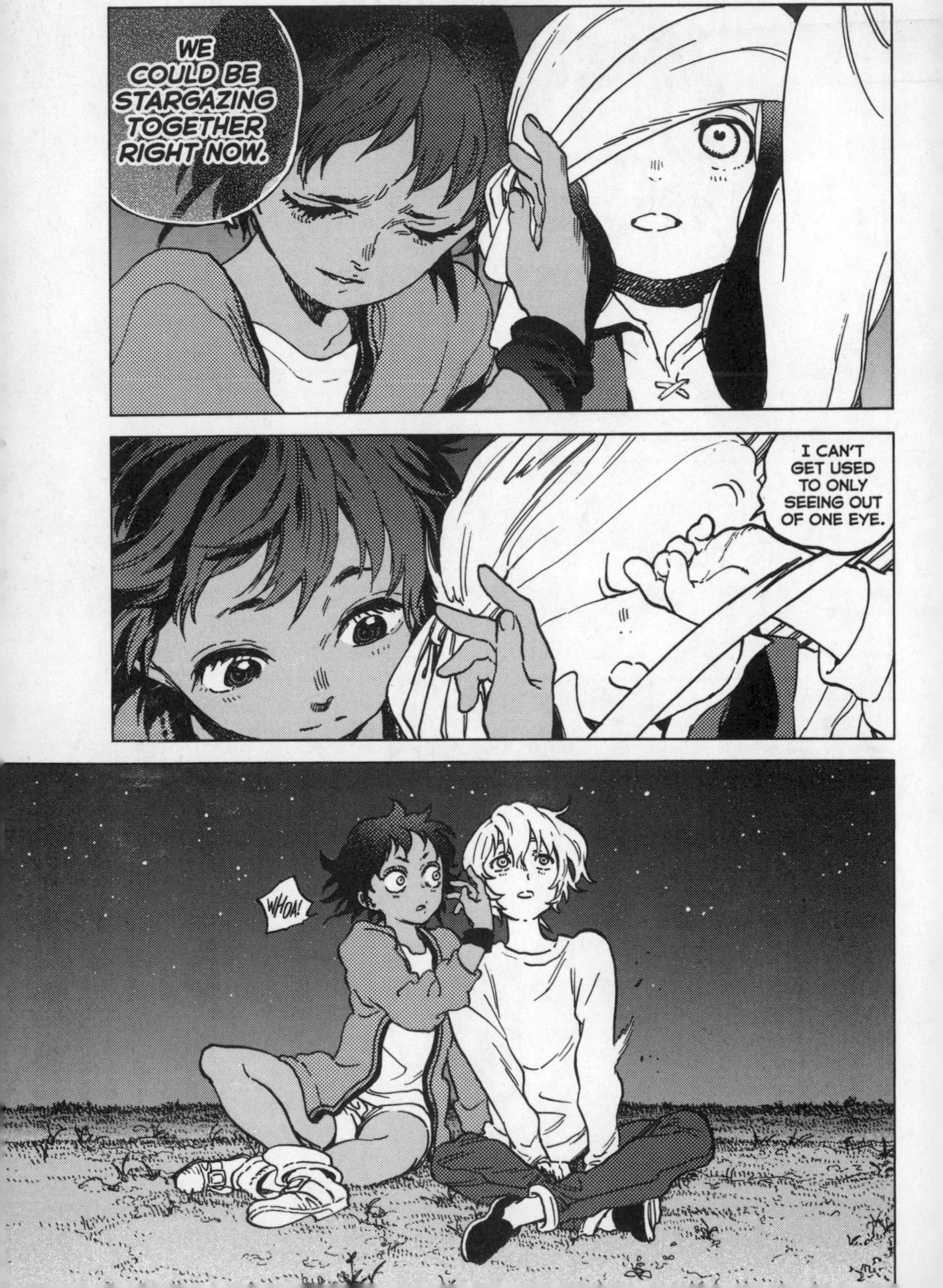
WE COULD BE STARGAZING TOGETHER RIGHT NOW.
I CAN'T GET USED TO ONLY SEEING OUT OF ONE EYE.
WHOA!

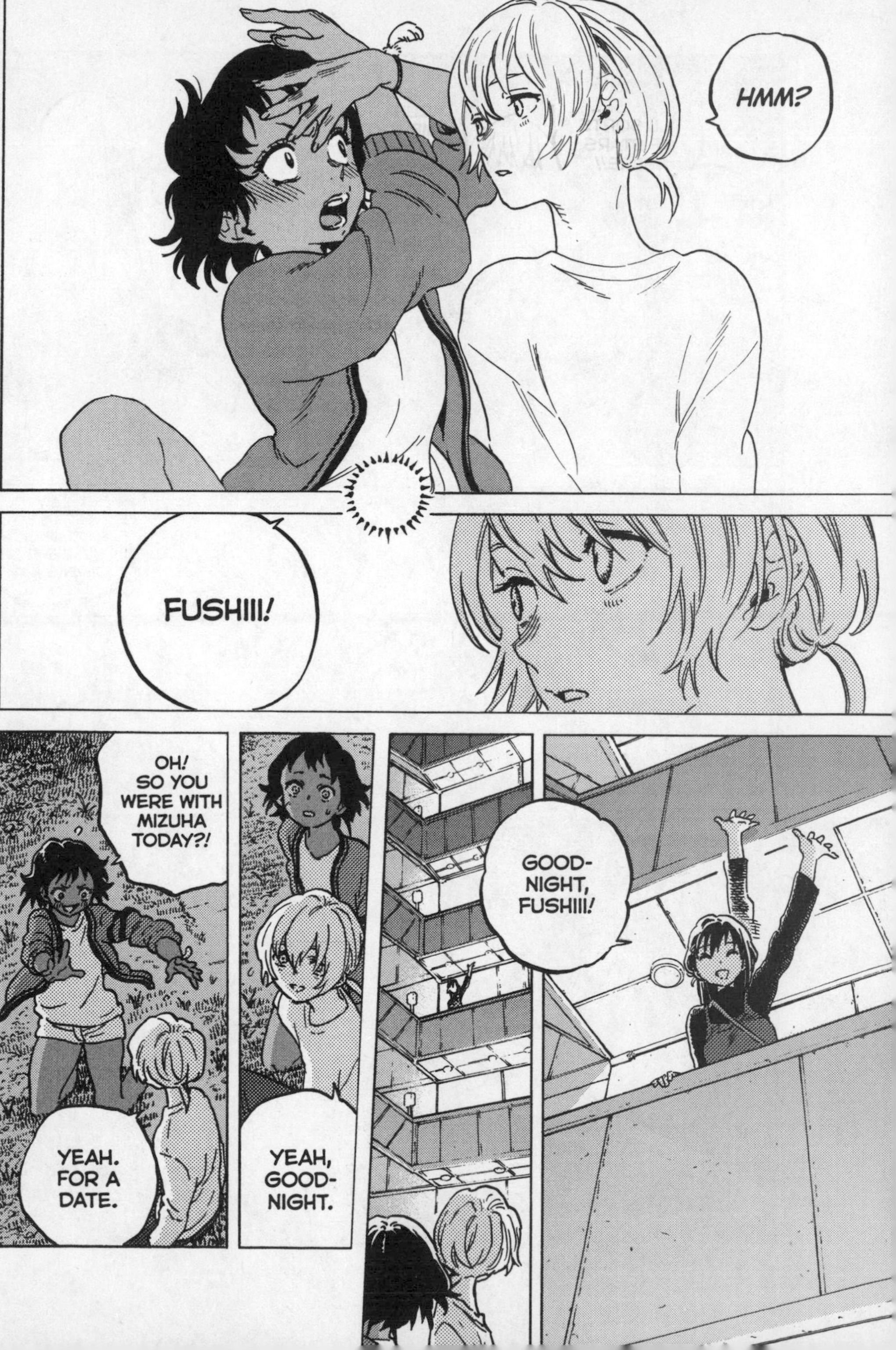
HMM?
FUSHIII!
GOOD-NIGHT, FUSHIII!
YEAH, GOOD-NIGHT.
OH! SO YOU WERE WITH MIZUHA TODAY?!
YEAH. FOR A DATE.

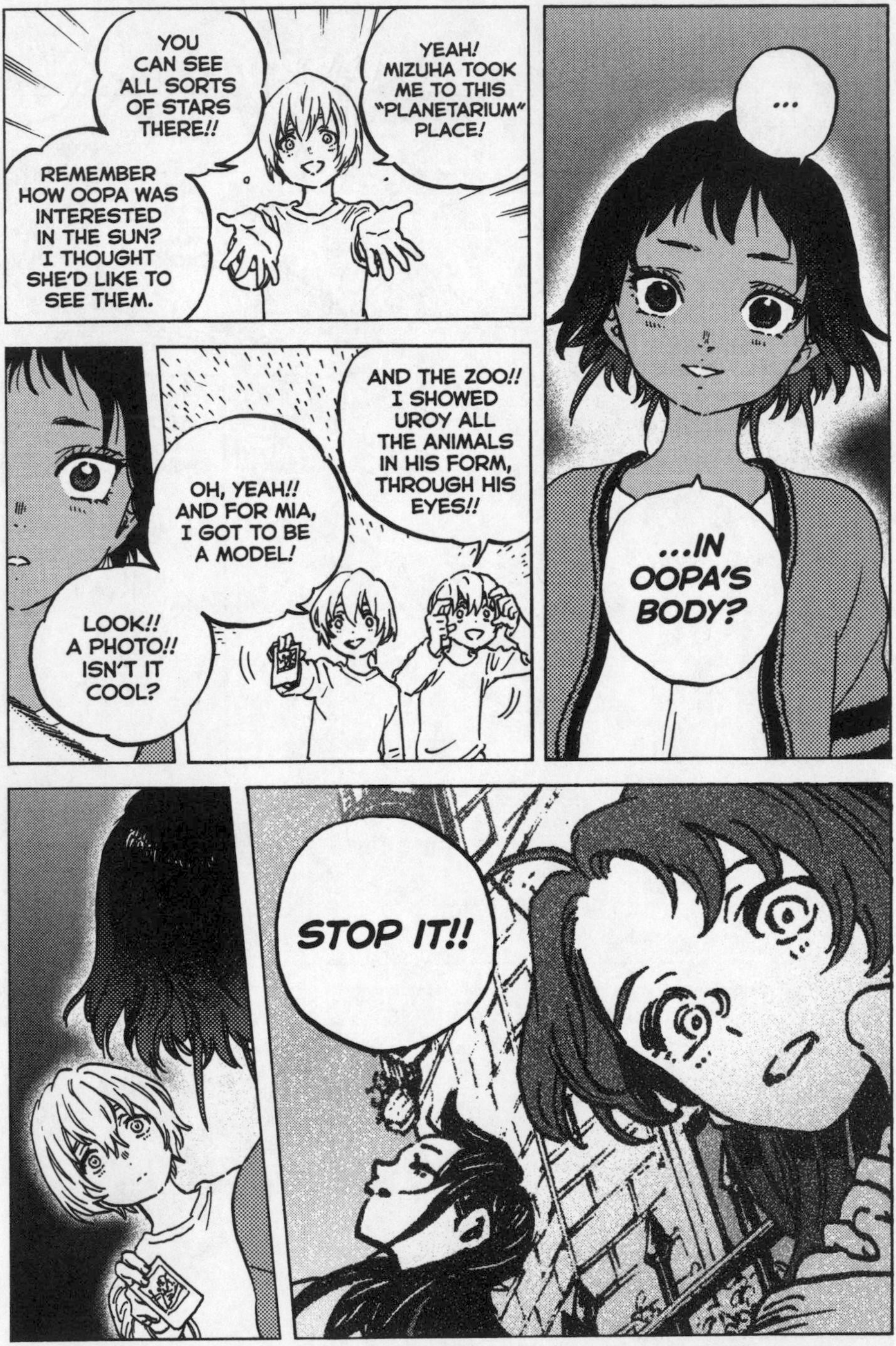
...
...IN OOPA'S BODY?
YEAH! MIZUHA TOOK ME TO THIS "PLANETARIUM" PLACE!
YOU CAN SEE ALL SORTS OF STARS THERE!!
REMEMBER HOW OOPA WAS INTERESTED IN THE SUN? I THOUGHT SHE'D LIKE TO SEE THEM.
AND THE ZOO!! I SHOWED UROY ALL THE ANIMALS IN HIS FORM, THROUGH HIS EYES!!
OH, YEAH!! AND FOR MIA, I GOT TO BE A MODEL!
LOOK!! A PHOTO!! ISN'T IT COOL?
STOP IT!!

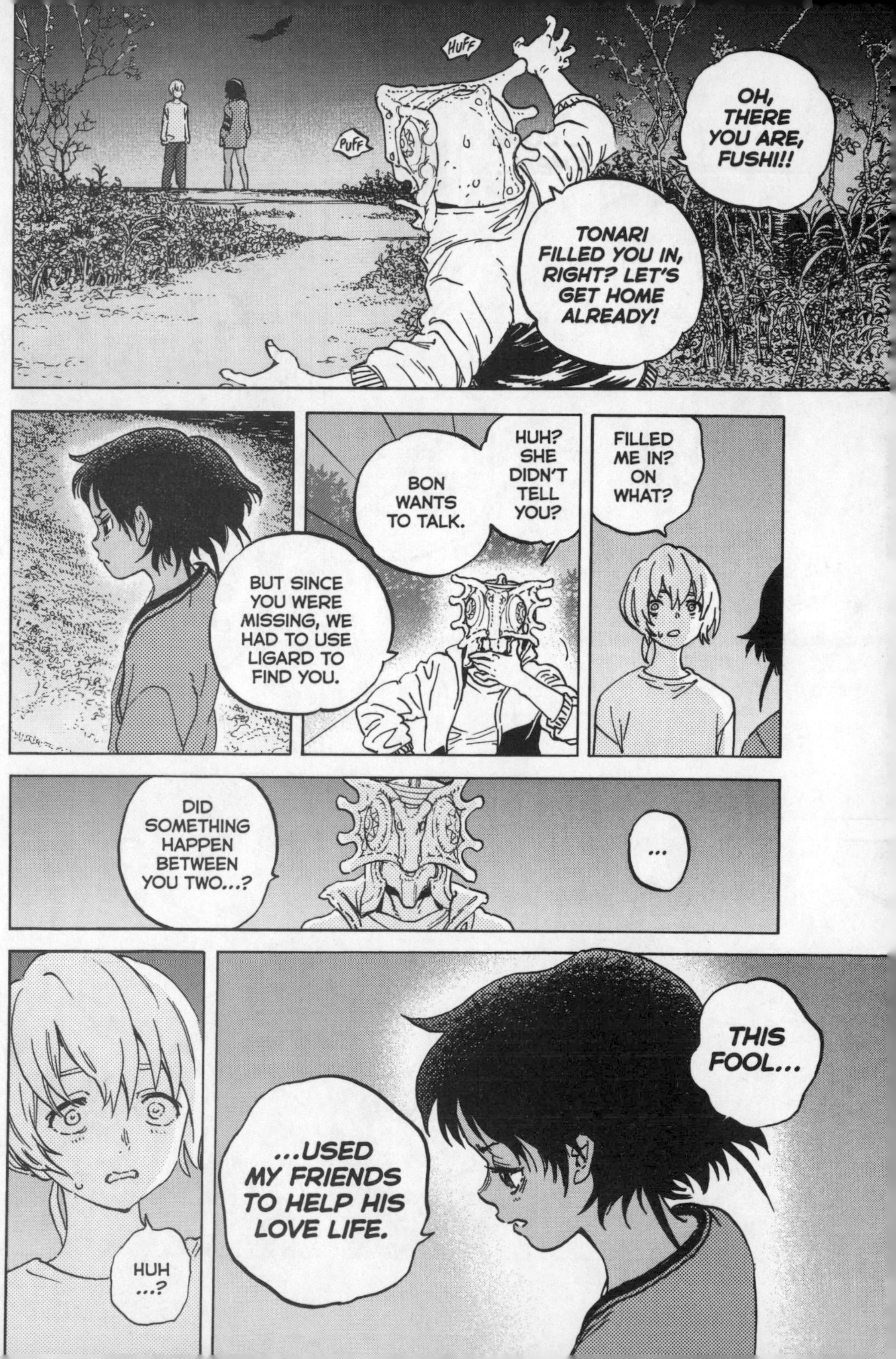
HUFF
PUFF
OH, THERE YOU ARE, FUSHI!!
TONARI FILLED YOU IN, RIGHT? LET'S GET HOME ALREADY!
FILLED ME IN? ON WHAT?
HUH? SHE DIDN'T TELL YOU?
BON WANTS TO TALK.
BUT SINCE YOU WERE MISSING, WE HAD TO USE LIGARD TO FIND YOU.
...
DID SOMETHING HAPPEN BETWEEN YOU TWO...?
THIS FOOL...
...USED MY FRIENDS TO HELP HIS LOVE LIFE.
HUH ...?

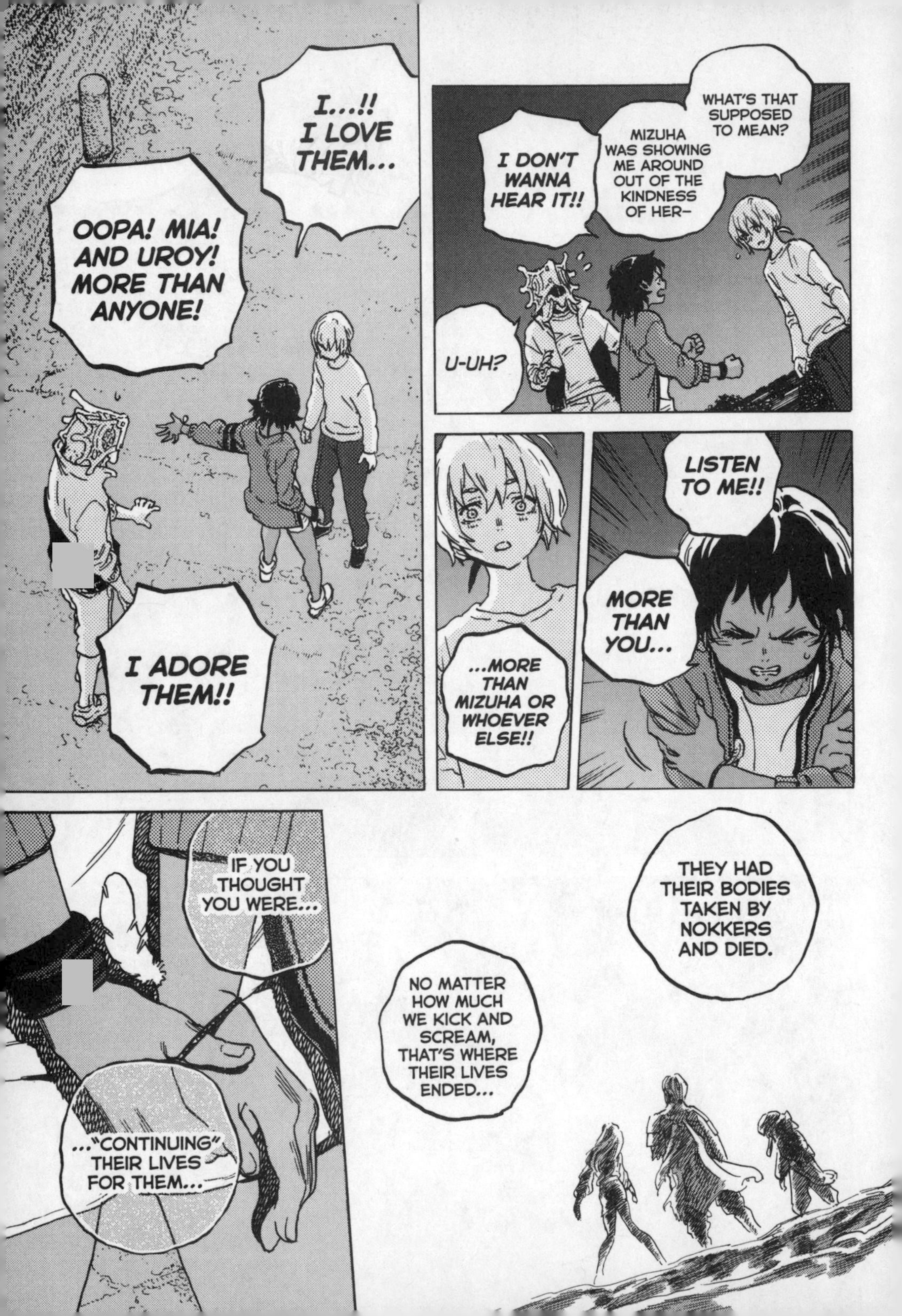

WHAT'S THAT SUPPOSED TO MEAN?
MIZUHA WAS SHOWING ME AROUND OUT OF THE KINDNESS OF HER–
I DON'T WANNA HEAR IT!!
U-UH?
LISTEN TO ME!!
MORE THAN YOU...
...MORE THAN MIZUHA OR WHOEVER ELSE!!
I...!! I LOVE THEM...
OOPA! MIA! AND UROY! MORE THAN ANYONE!
I ADORE THEM!!
THEY HAD THEIR BODIES TAKEN BY NOKKERS AND DIED.
NO MATTER HOW MUCH WE KICK AND SCREAM, THAT'S WHERE THEIR LIVES ENDED...
IF YOU THOUGHT YOU WERE...
..."CONTINUING" THEIR LIVES FOR THEM...

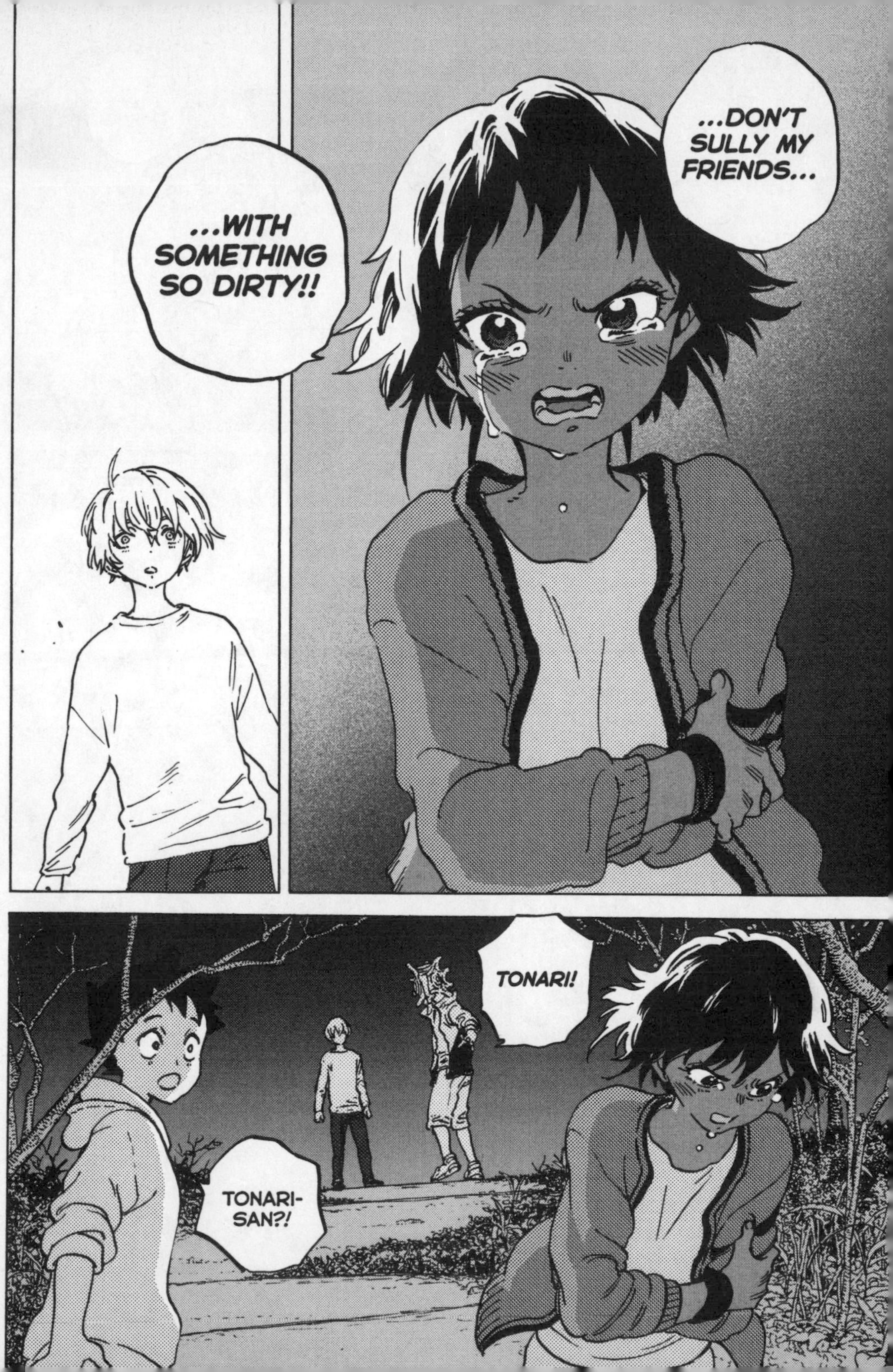
...DON'T SULLY MY FRIENDS...
...WITH SOMETHING SO DIRTY!!
TONARI!
TONARI-SAN?!

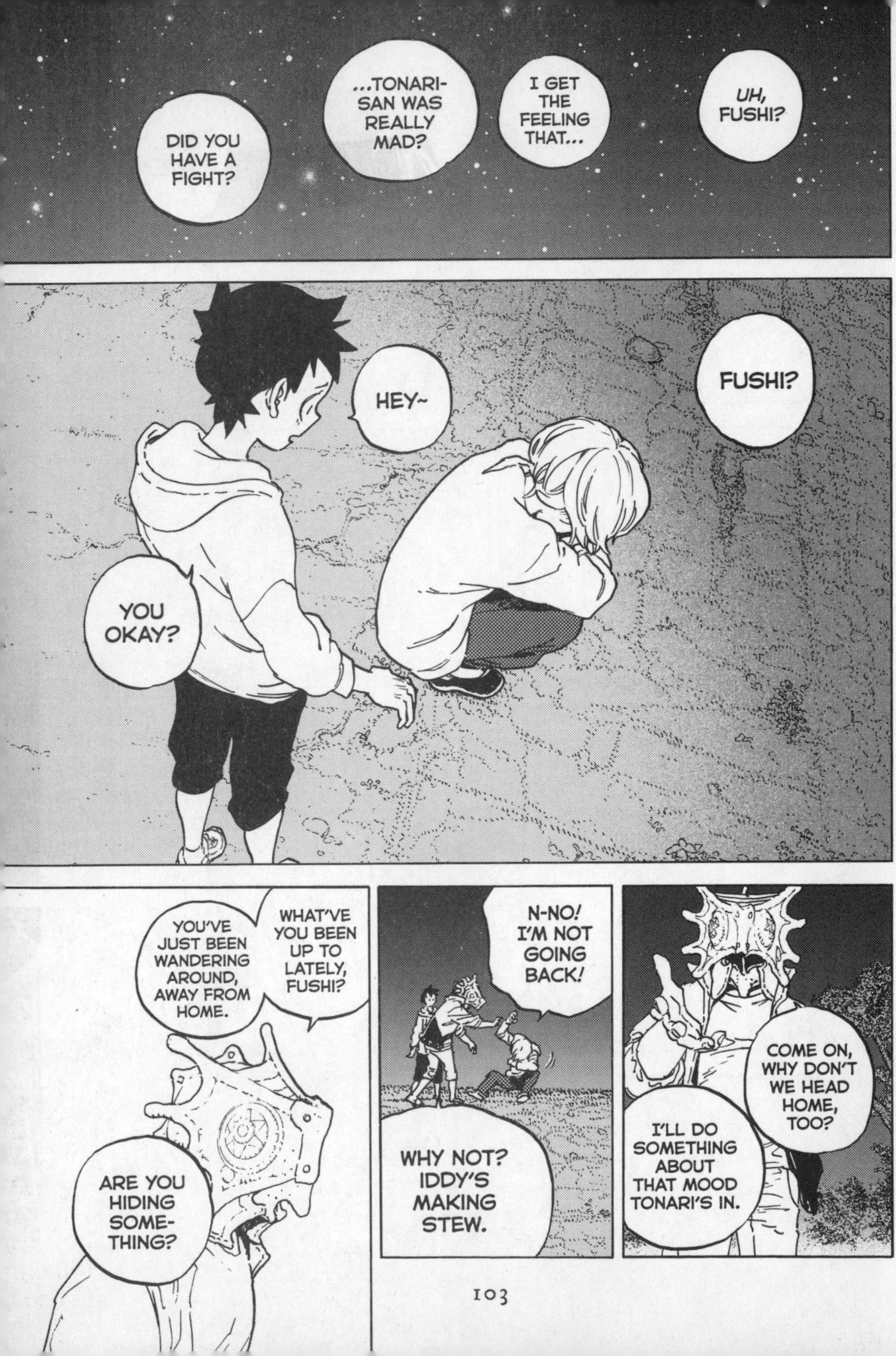
UH, FUSHI?
I GET THE FEELING THAT...
...TONARI-SAN WAS REALLY MAD?
DID YOU HAVE A FIGHT?
FUSHI?
HEY~
YOU OKAY?
COME ON, WHY DON'T WE HEAD HOME, TOO?
I'LL DO SOMETHING ABOUT THAT MOOD TONARI'S IN.
N-NO! I'M NOT GOING BACK!
WHY NOT? IDDY'S MAKING STEW.
WHAT'VE YOU BEEN UP TO LATELY, FUSHI?
YOU'VE JUST BEEN WANDERING AROUND, AWAY FROM HOME.
ARE YOU HIDING SOMETHING?

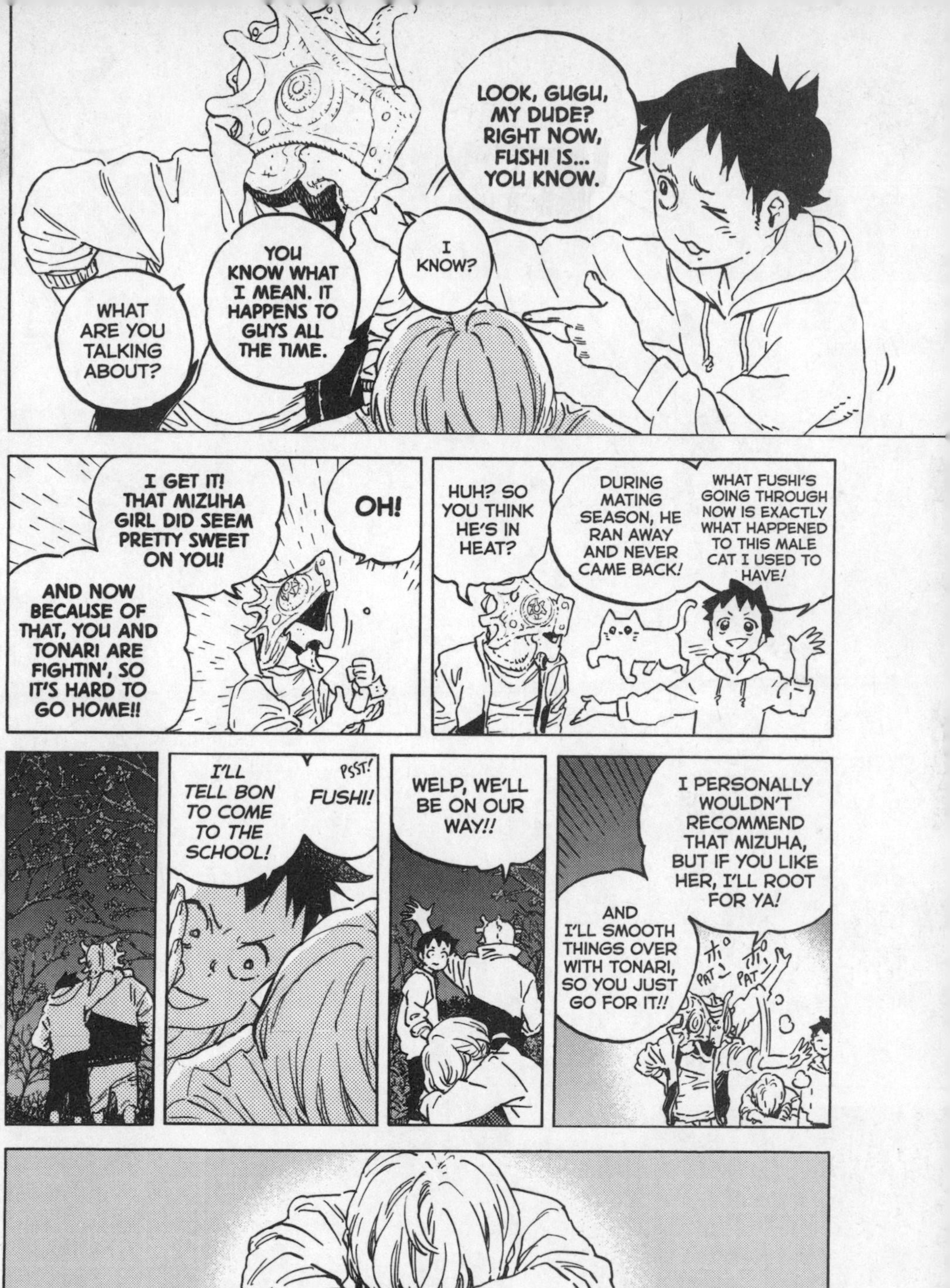
LOOK, GUGU, MY DUDE? RIGHT NOW, FUSHI IS... YOU KNOW.
I KNOW?
YOU KNOW WHAT I MEAN. IT HAPPENS TO GUYS ALL THE TIME.
WHAT ARE YOU TALKING ABOUT?
WHAT FUSHI'S GOING THROUGH NOW IS EXACTLY WHAT HAPPENED TO THIS MALE CAT I USED TO HAVE!
DURING MATING SEASON, HE RAN AWAY AND NEVER CAME BACK!
HUH? SO YOU THINK HE'S IN HEAT?
OH!
I GET IT! THAT MIZUHA GIRL DID SEEM PRETTY SWEET ON YOU!
AND NOW BECAUSE OF THAT, YOU AND TONARI ARE FIGHTIN', SO IT'S HARD TO GO HOME!!
I PERSONALLY WOULDN'T RECOMMEND THAT MIZUHA, BUT IF YOU LIKE HER, I'LL ROOT FOR YA!
AND I'LL SMOOTH THINGS OVER WITH TONARI, SO YOU JUST GO FOR IT!!
PAT PAT
WELP, WE'LL BE ON OUR WAY!!
PSST!
FUSHI!
I'LL TELL BON TO COME TO THE SCHOOL!

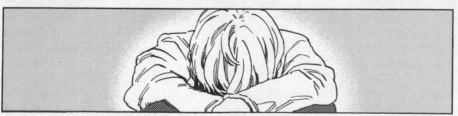

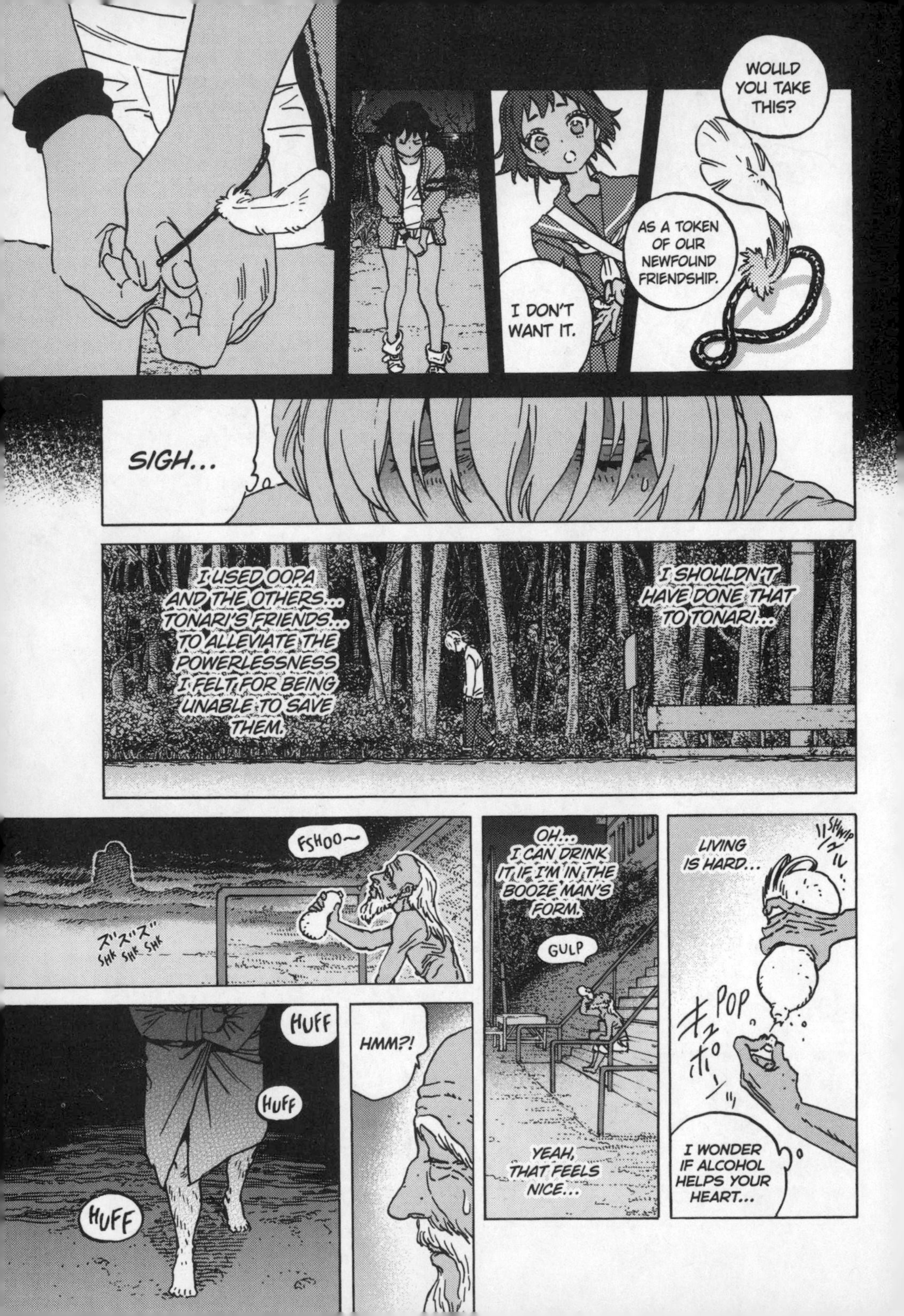
WOULD YOU TAKE THIS?
AS A TOKEN OF OUR NEWFOUND FRIENDSHIP.
I DON'T WANT IT.
SIGH...
I SHOULDN'T HAVE DONE THAT TO TONARI...
I USED OOPA AND THE OTHERS... TONARI'S FRIENDS... TO ALLEVIATE THE POWERLESSNESS I FELT FOR BEING UNABLE TO SAVE THEM.
SHWIP
LIVING IS HARD...
POP
I WONDER IF ALCOHOL HELPS YOUR HEART...
OH... I CAN DRINK IT IF I'M IN THE BOOZE MAN'S FORM.
GULP
YEAH, THAT FEELS NICE...
FSHOO~
SHK SHK SHK
HMM?!
HUFF
HUFF
HUFF

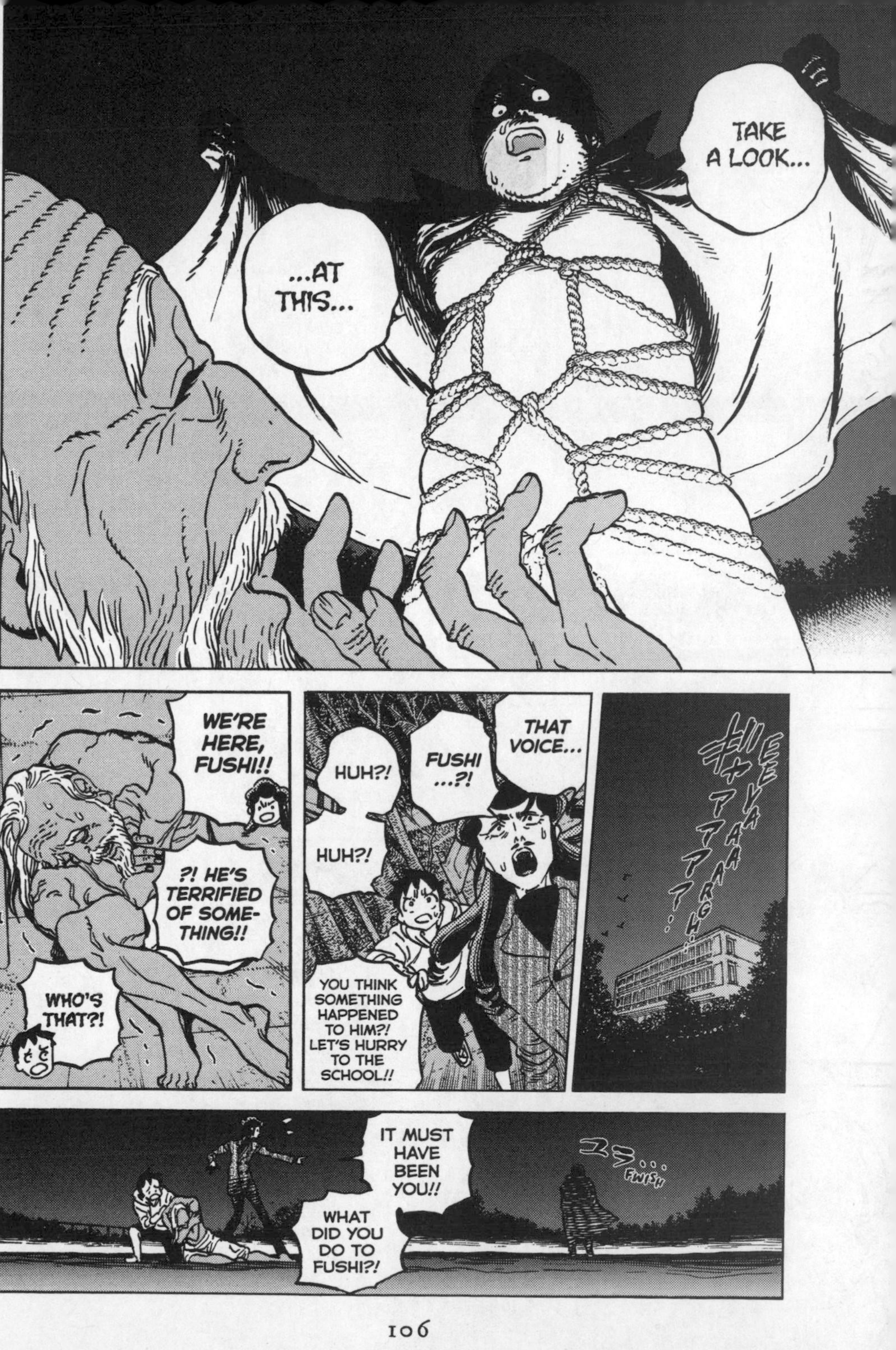
TAKE A LOOK...
...AT THIS...
ギャアアアア..
EEYAAAARGH!!
THAT VOICE...
FUSHI ...?!
HUH?!
HUH?!
YOU THINK SOMETHING HAPPENED TO HIM?! LET'S HURRY TO THE SCHOOL!!
WE'RE HERE, FUSHI!!
?! HE'S TERRIFIED OF SOME-THING!!
WHO'S THAT?!
ユラ...
FWISH
IT MUST HAVE BEEN YOU!!
WHAT DID YOU DO TO FUSHI?!

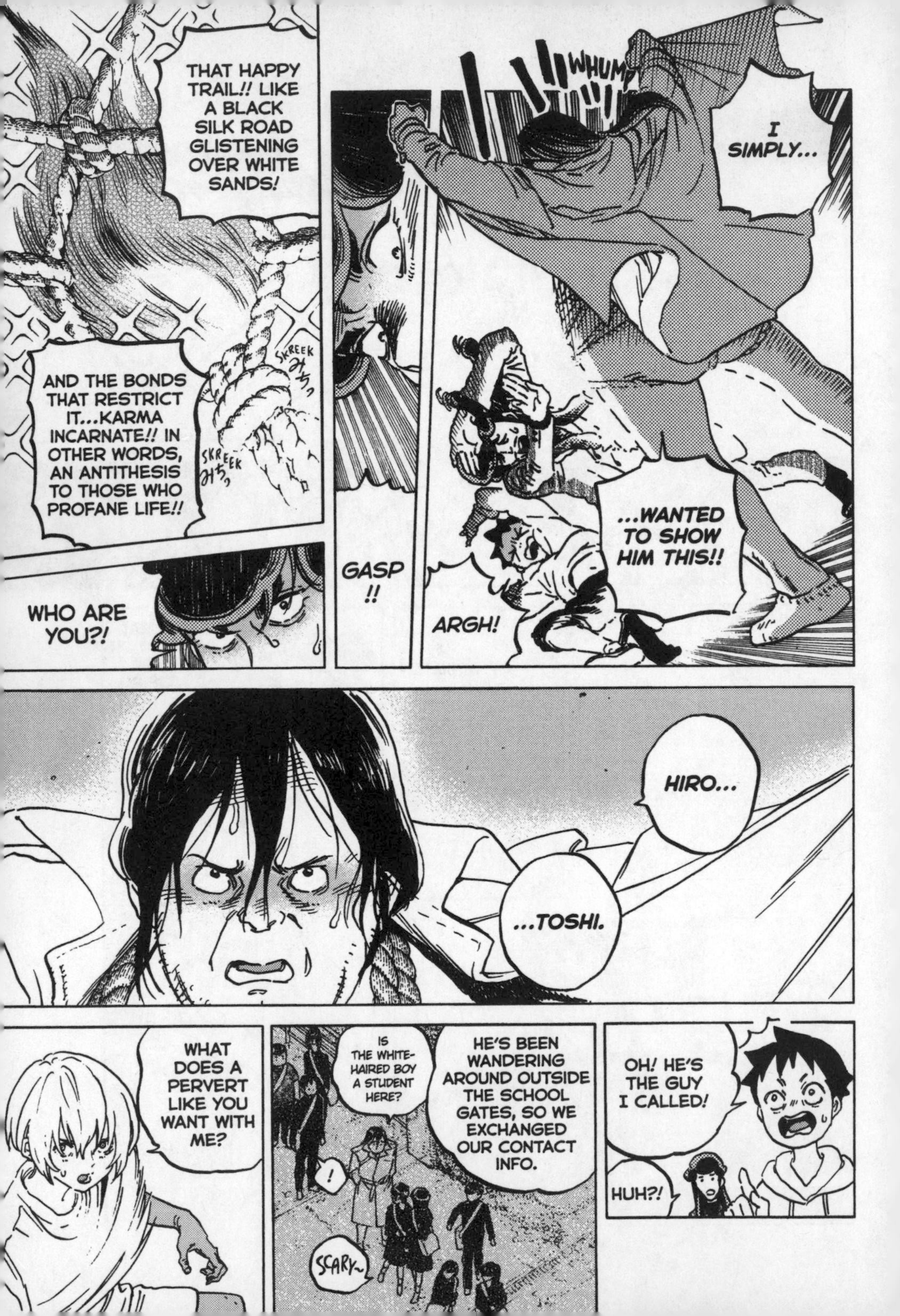
WHUMP
I SIMPLY...
...WANTED TO SHOW HIM THIS!!
ARGH!
GASP!!
THAT HAPPY TRAIL!! LIKE A BLACK SILK ROAD GLISTENING OVER WHITE SANDS!
SKREEK
AND THE BONDS THAT RESTRICT IT...KARMA INCARNATE!! IN OTHER WORDS, AN ANTITHESIS TO THOSE WHO PROFANE LIFE!!
SKREEK
WHO ARE YOU?!
HIRO...
...TOSHI.
OH! HE'S THE GUY I CALLED!
HUH?!
HE'S BEEN WANDERING AROUND OUTSIDE THE SCHOOL GATES, SO WE EXCHANGED OUR CONTACT INFO.
IS THE WHITE-HAIRED BOY A STUDENT HERE?
!
SCARY~
WHAT DOES A PERVERT LIKE YOU WANT WITH ME?

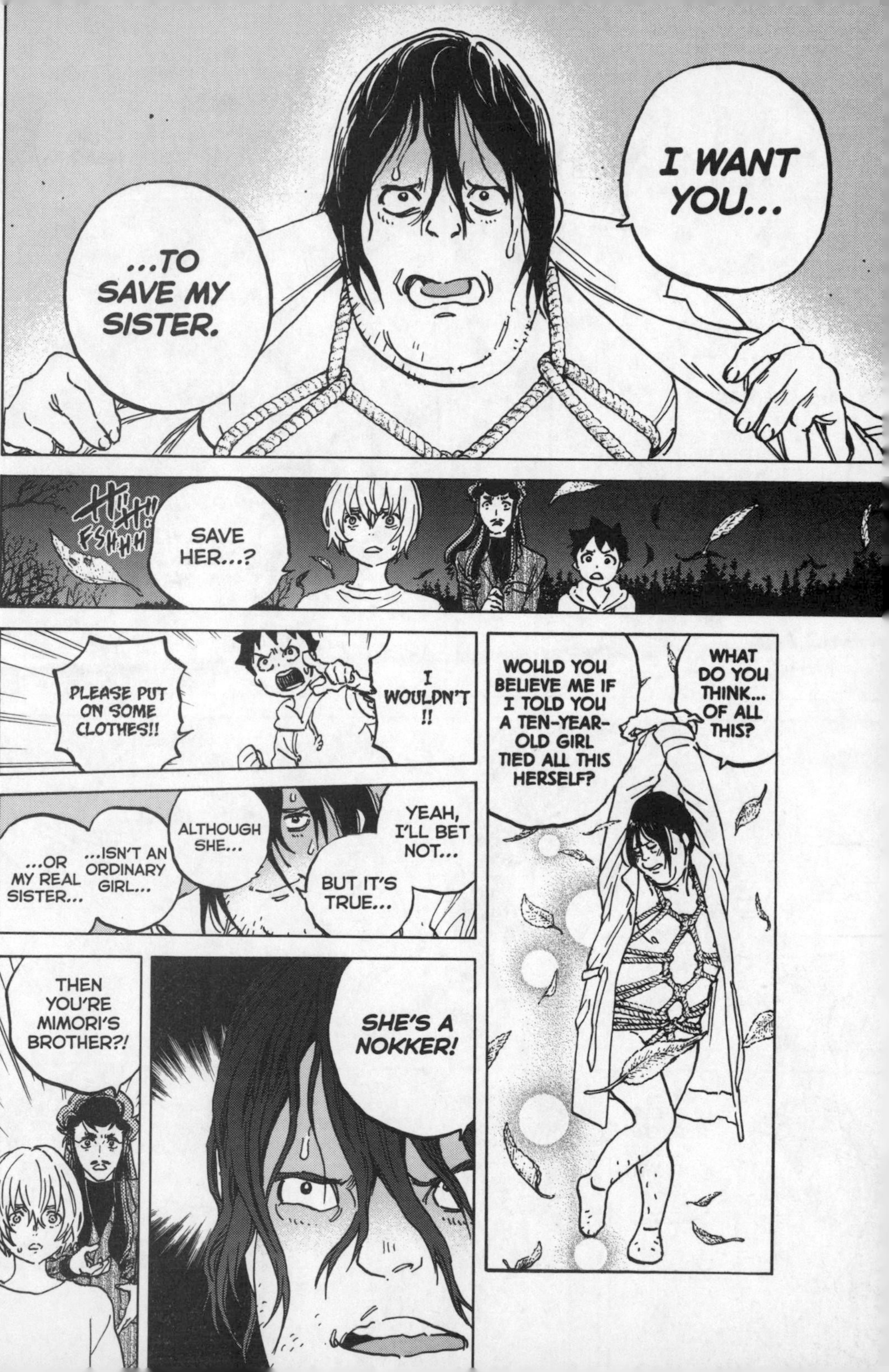
I WANT YOU...
...TO SAVE MY SISTER.
FSHHH
SAVE HER...?
WHAT DO YOU THINK... OF ALL THIS?
WOULD YOU BELIEVE ME IF I TOLD YOU A TEN-YEAR-OLD GIRL TIED ALL THIS HERSELF?
I WOULDN'T !!
PLEASE PUT ON SOME CLOTHES!!
YEAH, I'LL BET NOT...
BUT IT'S TRUE...
ALTHOUGH SHE...
...ISN'T AN ORDINARY GIRL...
...OR MY REAL SISTER...
SHE'S A NOKKER!
THEN YOU'RE MIMORI'S BROTHER?!

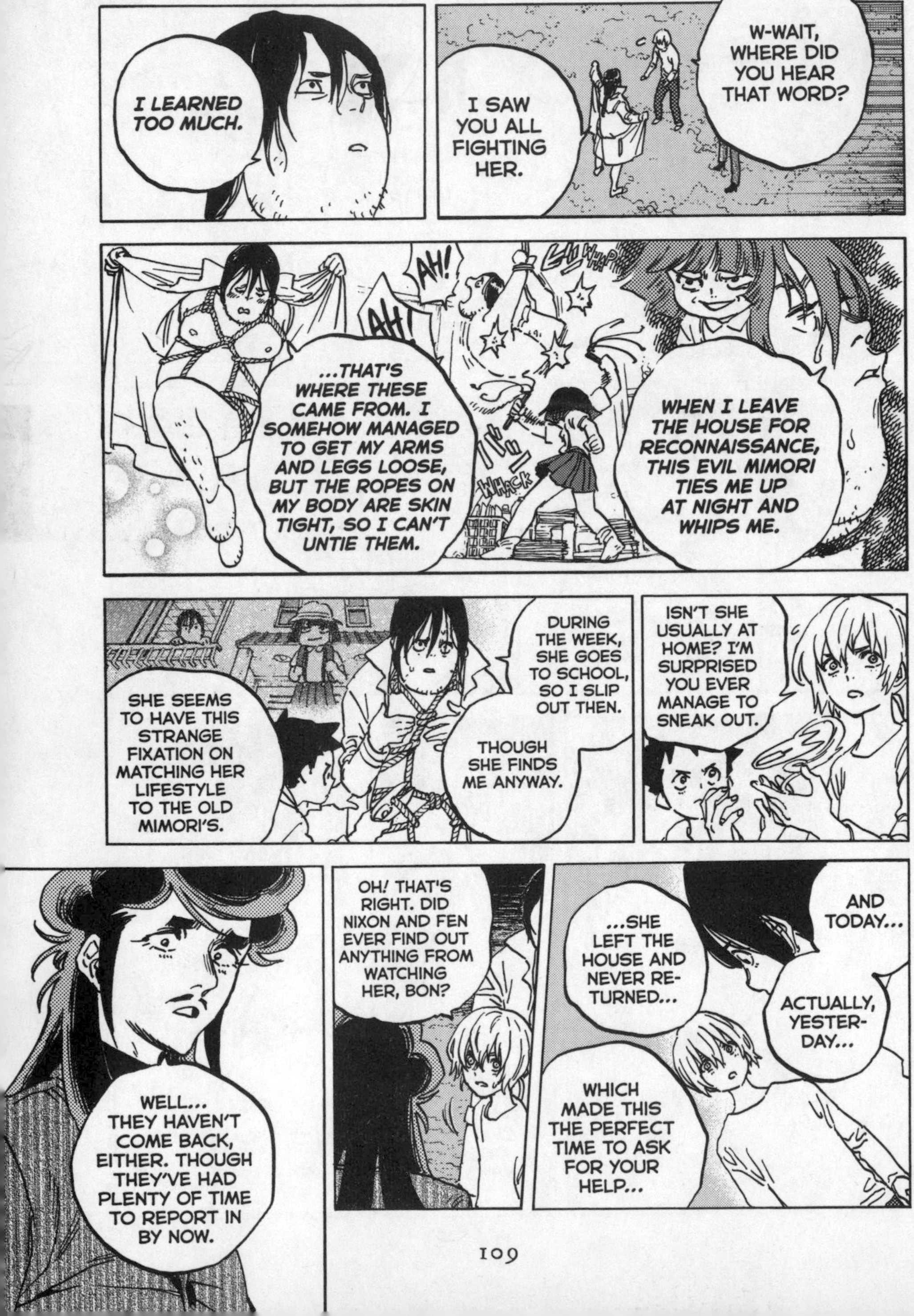
W-WAIT, WHERE DID YOU HEAR THAT WORD?
I SAW YOU ALL FIGHTING HER.
I LEARNED TOO MUCH.
WHIP
AH!
AH!
WHACK
WHEN I LEAVE THE HOUSE FOR RECONNAISSANCE, THIS EVIL MIMORI TIES ME UP AT NIGHT AND WHIPS ME.
...THAT'S WHERE THESE CAME FROM. I SOMEHOW MANAGED TO GET MY ARMS AND LEGS LOOSE, BUT THE ROPES ON MY BODY ARE SKIN TIGHT, SO I CAN'T UNTIE THEM.
ISN'T SHE USUALLY AT HOME? I'M SURPRISED YOU EVER MANAGE TO SNEAK OUT.
DURING THE WEEK, SHE GOES TO SCHOOL, SO I SLIP OUT THEN.
THOUGH SHE FINDS ME ANYWAY.
SHE SEEMS TO HAVE THIS STRANGE FIXATION ON MATCHING HER LIFESTYLE TO THE OLD MIMORI'S.
AND TODAY...
ACTUALLY, YESTERDAY...
...SHE LEFT THE HOUSE AND NEVER RETURNED...
WHICH MADE THIS THE PERFECT TIME TO ASK FOR YOUR HELP...
OH! THAT'S RIGHT. DID NIXON AND FEN EVER FIND OUT ANYTHING FROM WATCHING HER, BON?
WELL... THEY HAVEN'T COME BACK, EITHER. THOUGH THEY'VE HAD PLENTY OF TIME TO REPORT IN BY NOW.

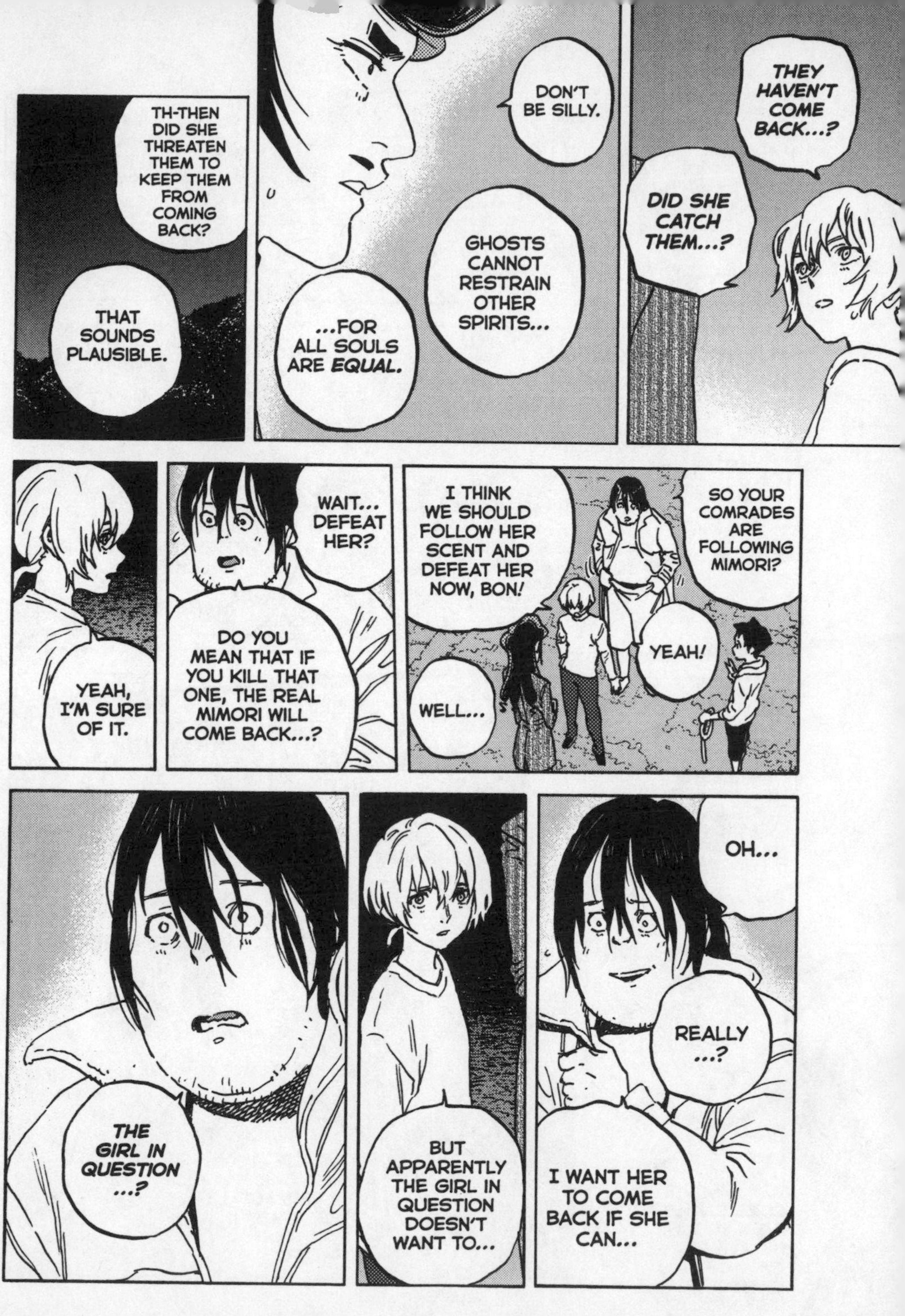
THEY HAVEN'T COME BACK...?
DID SHE CATCH THEM...?
DON'T BE SILLY.
GHOSTS CANNOT RESTRAIN OTHER SPIRITS...
...FOR ALL SOULS ARE EQUAL.
TH-THEN DID SHE THREATEN THEM TO KEEP THEM FROM COMING BACK?
THAT SOUNDS PLAUSIBLE.
SO YOUR COMRADES ARE FOLLOWING MIMORI?
I THINK WE SHOULD FOLLOW HER SCENT AND DEFEAT HER NOW, BON!
YEAH!
WELL...
WAIT... DEFEAT HER?
DO YOU MEAN THAT IF YOU KILL THAT ONE, THE REAL MIMORI WILL COME BACK...?
YEAH, I'M SURE OF IT.
OH...
REALLY ...?
I WANT HER TO COME BACK IF SHE CAN...
BUT APPARENTLY THE GIRL IN QUESTION DOESN'T WANT TO...
THE GIRL IN QUESTION ...?

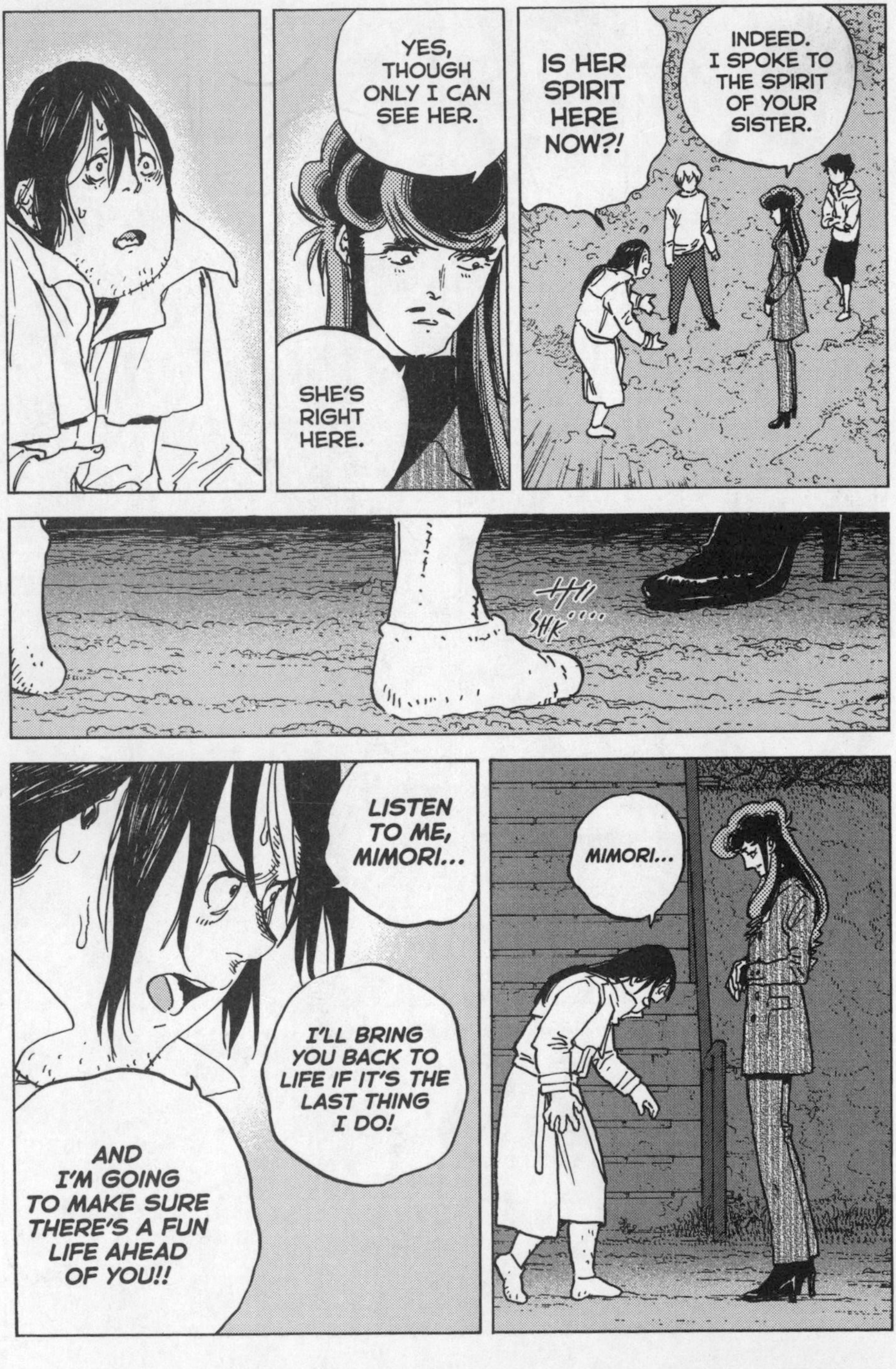
INDEED. I SPOKE TO THE SPIRIT OF YOUR SISTER.
IS HER SPIRIT HERE NOW?!
YES, THOUGH ONLY I CAN SEE HER.
SHE'S RIGHT HERE.
SHK....
MIMORI...
LISTEN TO ME, MIMORI...
I'LL BRING YOU BACK TO LIFE IF IT'S THE LAST THING I DO!
AND I'M GOING TO MAKE SURE THERE'S A FUN LIFE AHEAD OF YOU!!

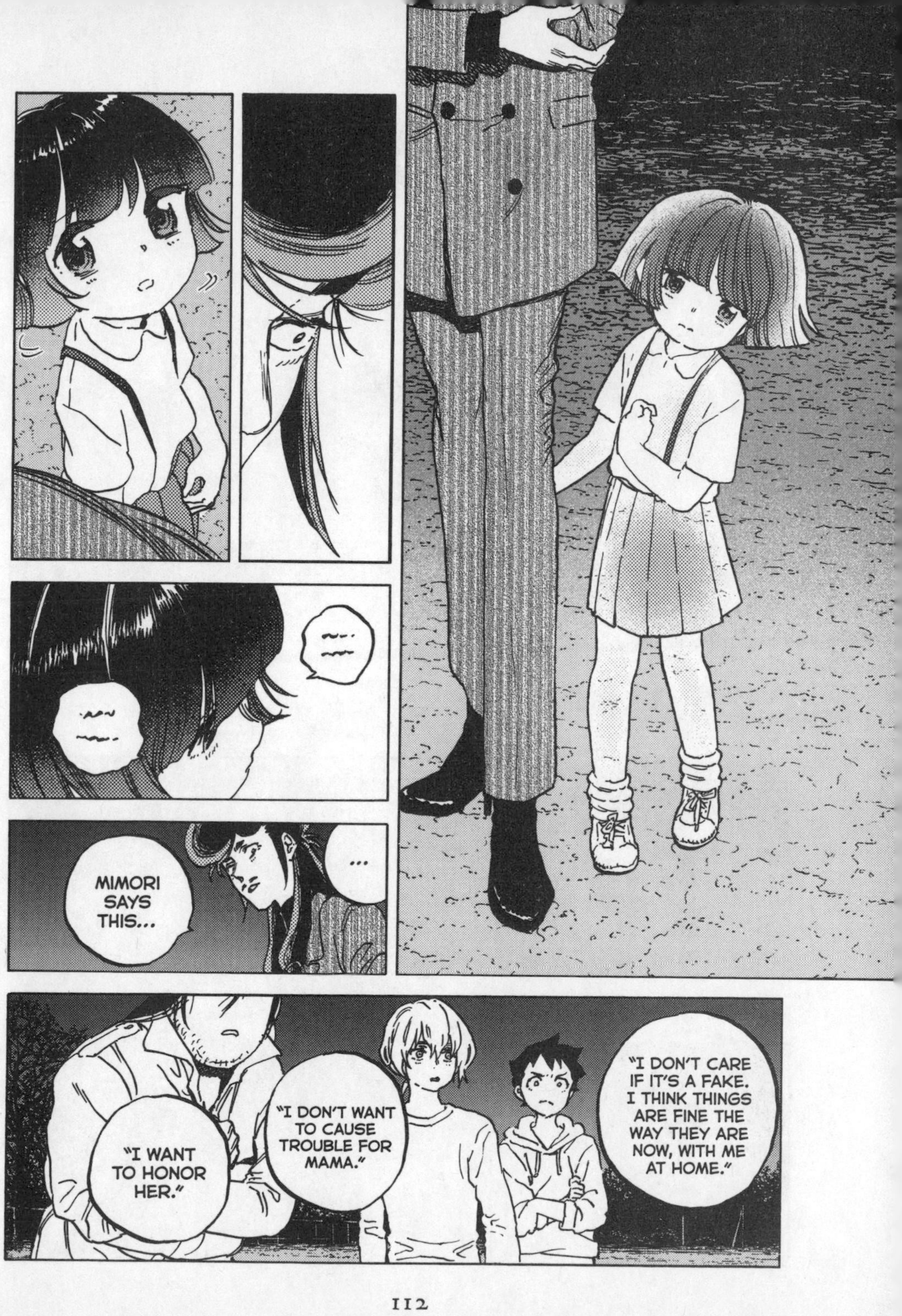
...
MIMORI SAYS THIS...
"I DON'T CARE IF IT'S A FAKE. I THINK THINGS ARE FINE THE WAY THEY ARE NOW, WITH ME AT HOME."
"I DON'T WANT TO CAUSE TROUBLE FOR MAMA."
"I WANT TO HONOR HER."

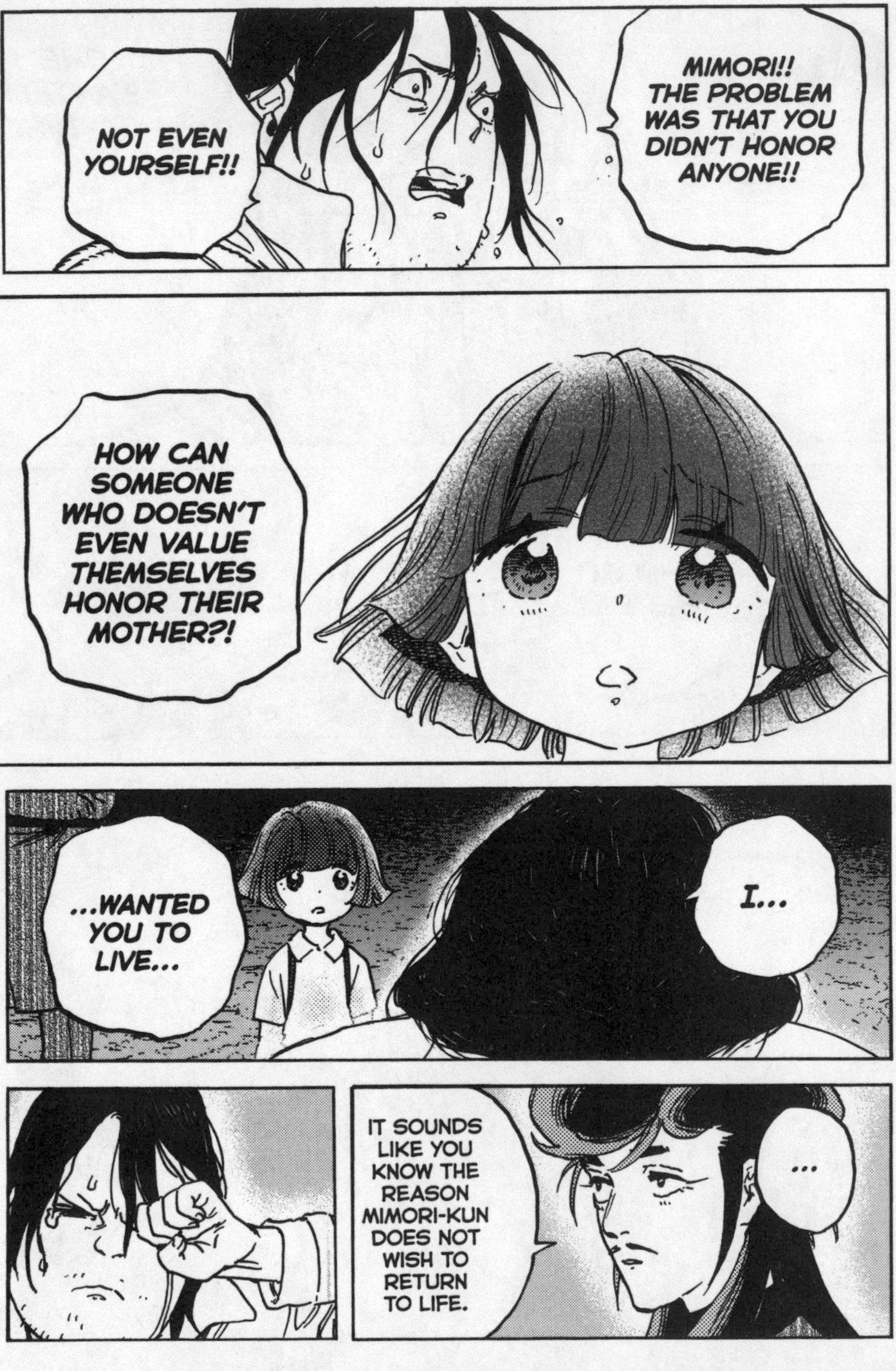
MIMORI!! THE PROBLEM WAS THAT YOU DIDN'T HONOR ANYONE!!
NOT EVEN YOURSELF!!
HOW CAN SOMEONE WHO DOESN'T EVEN VALUE THEMSELVES HONOR THEIR MOTHER?!
I...
...WANTED YOU TO LIVE...
...
IT SOUNDS LIKE YOU KNOW THE REASON MIMORI-KUN DOES NOT WISH TO RETURN TO LIFE.

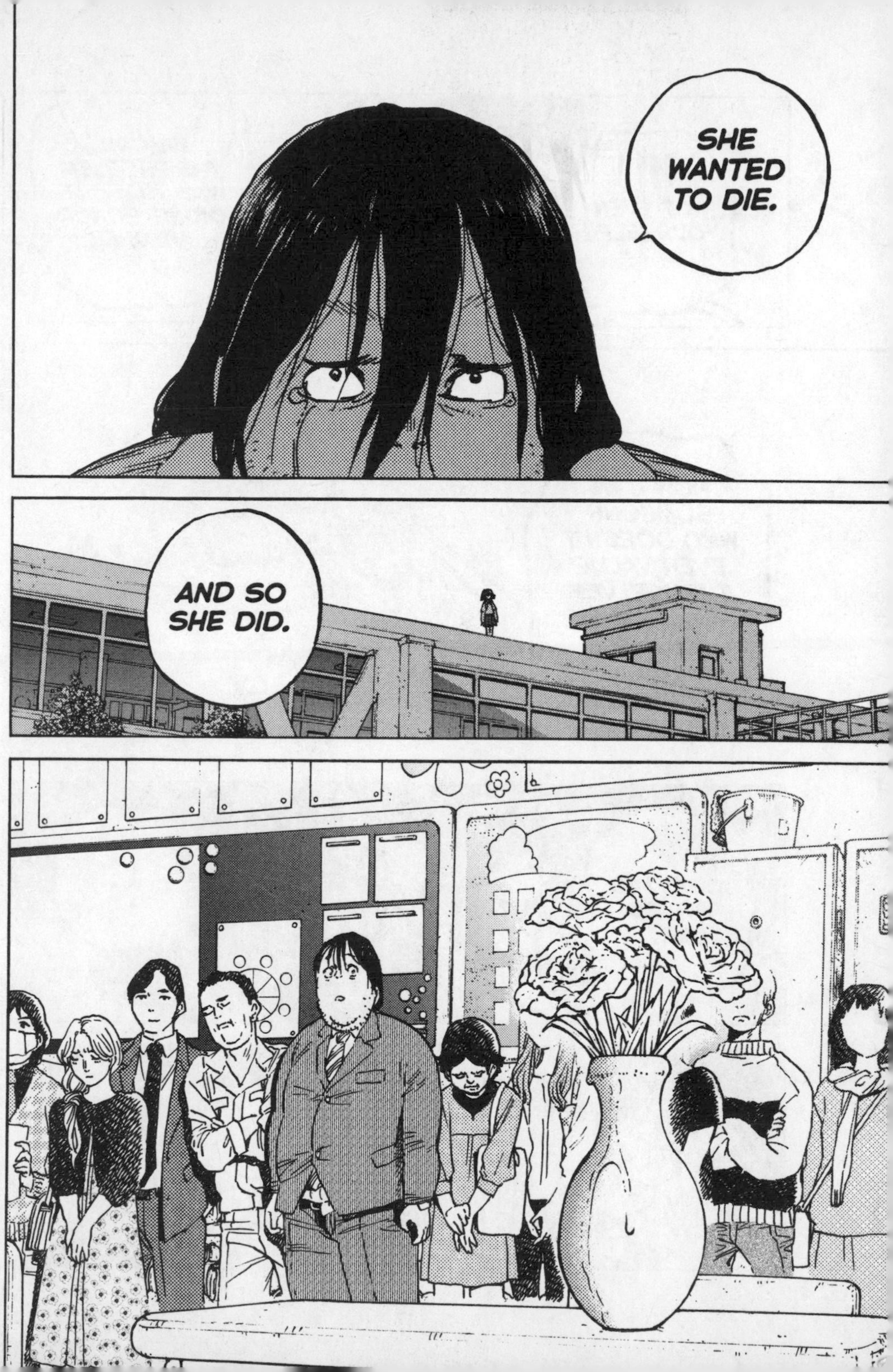
SHE WANTED TO DIE.
AND SO SHE DID.

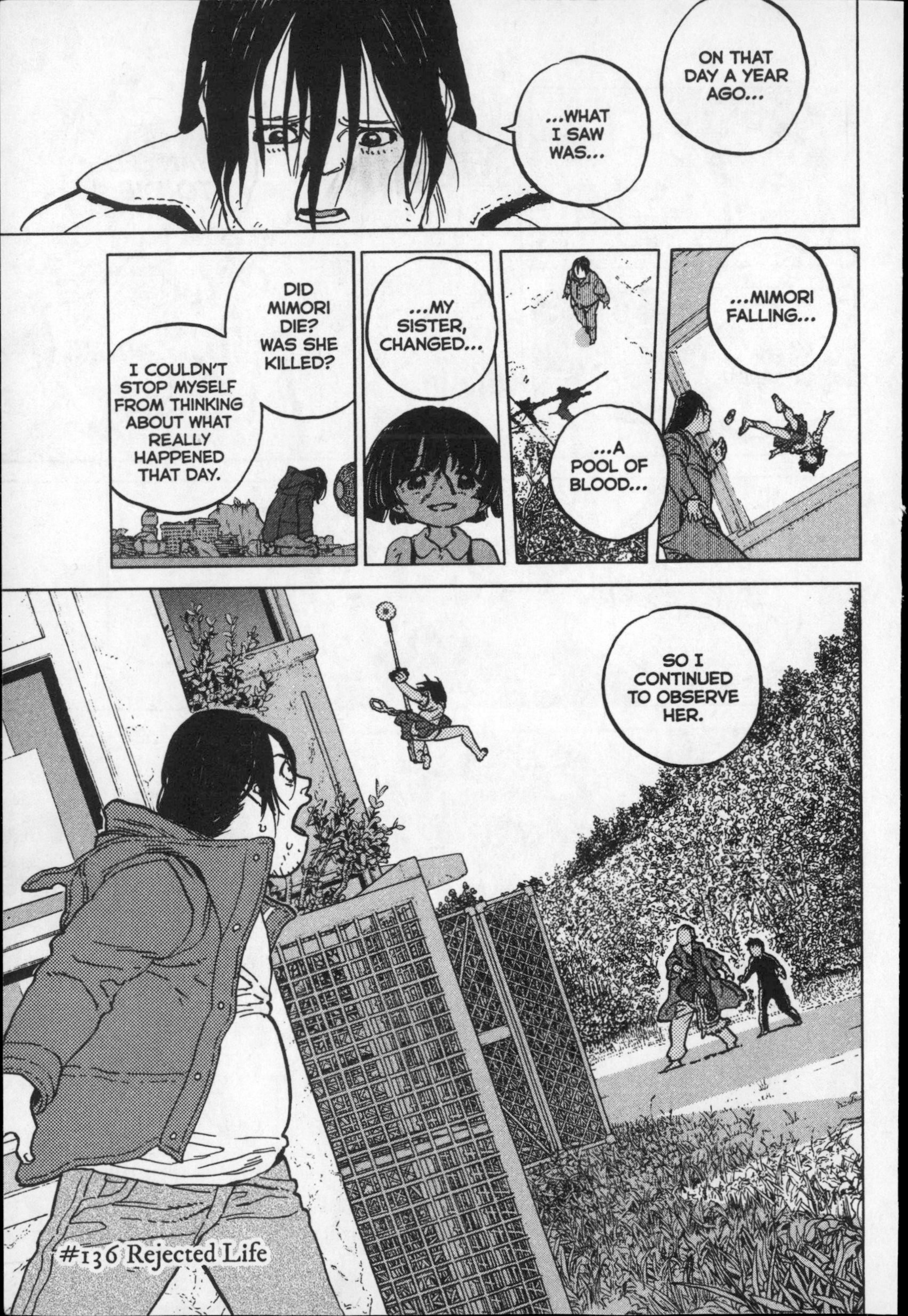
ON THAT DAY A YEAR AGO...
...WHAT I SAW WAS...
...MIMORI FALLING...
...A POOL OF BLOOD...
...MY SISTER, CHANGED...
DID MIMORI DIE? WAS SHE KILLED?
I COULDN'T STOP MYSELF FROM THINKING ABOUT WHAT REALLY HAPPENED THAT DAY.
SO I CONTINUED TO OBSERVE HER.

#136 Rejected Life

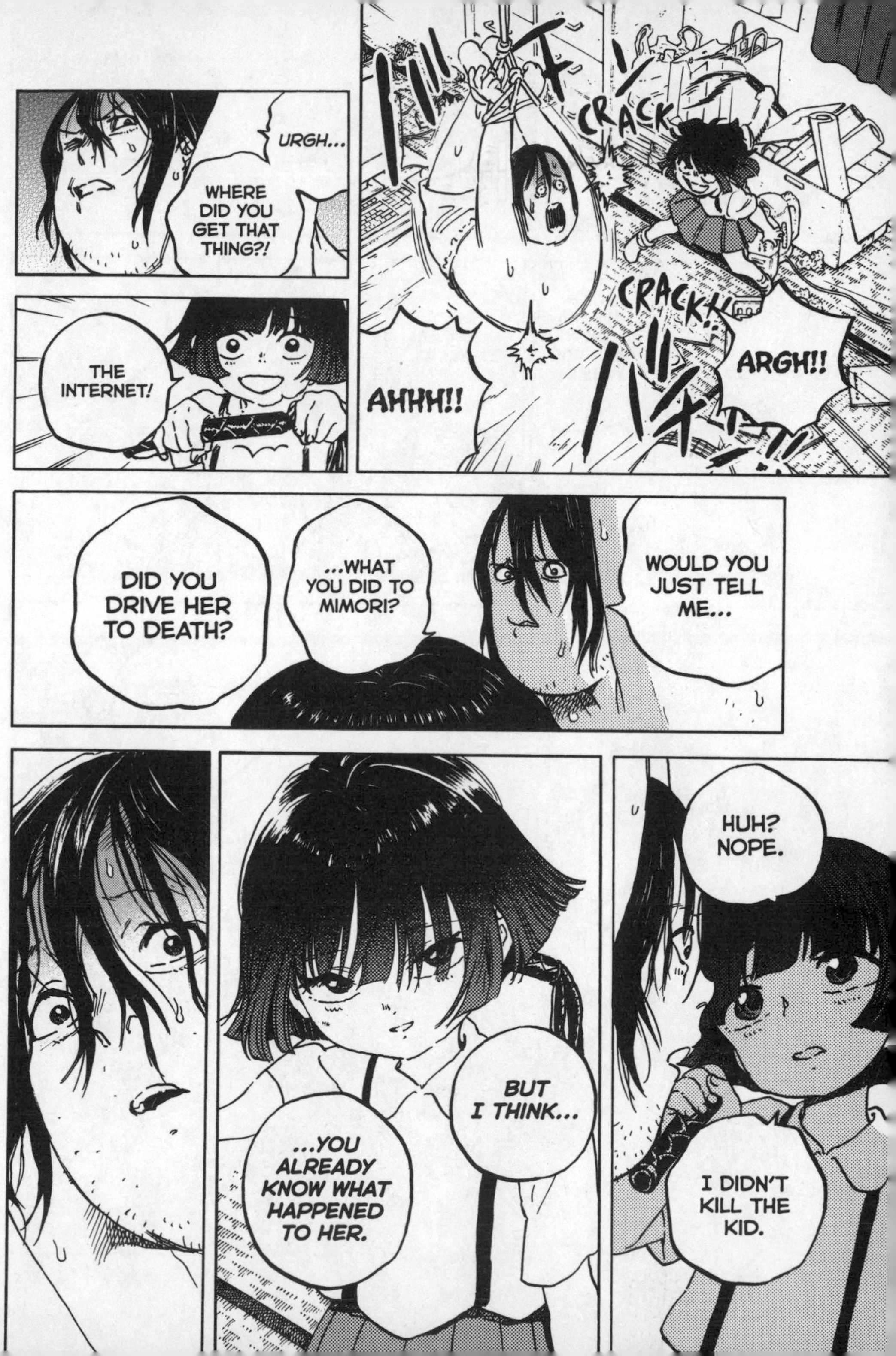
CRACK
CRACK!!
ARGH!!
AHHH!!
URGH...
WHERE DID YOU GET THAT THING?!
THE INTERNET!
WOULD YOU JUST TELL ME...
...WHAT YOU DID TO MIMORI?
DID YOU DRIVE HER TO DEATH?
HUH? NOPE.
I DIDN'T KILL THE KID.
BUT I THINK...
...YOU ALREADY KNOW WHAT HAPPENED TO HER.

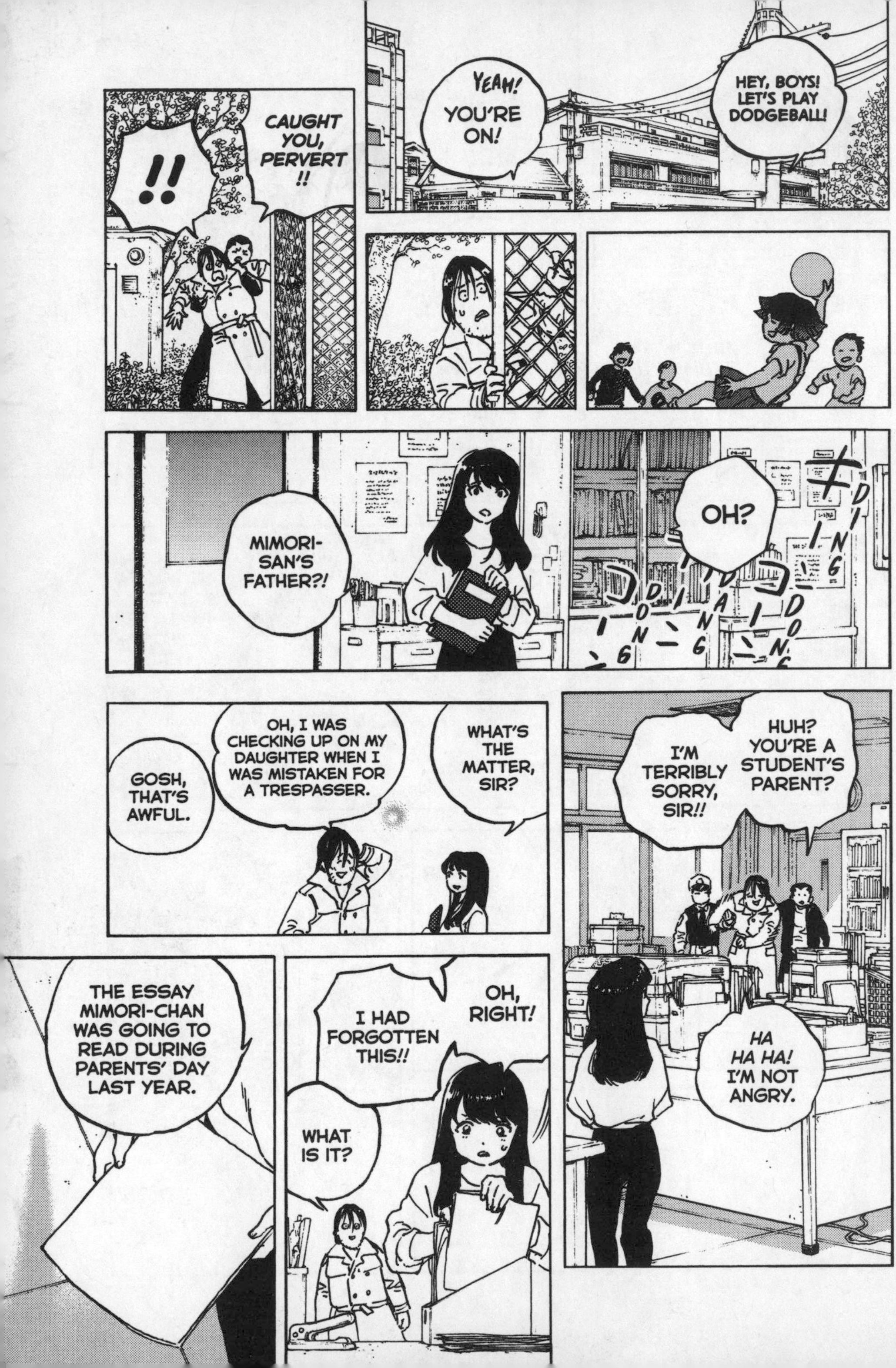
HEY, BOYS! LET'S PLAY DODGEBALL!
YEAH! YOU'RE ON!
CAUGHT YOU, PERVERT !!
!!
OH?
DING DONG DING DONG
MIMORI-SAN'S FATHER?!
HUH? YOU'RE A STUDENT'S PARENT?
I'M TERRIBLY SORRY, SIR!!
HA HA HA! I'M NOT ANGRY.
WHAT'S THE MATTER, SIR?
OH, I WAS CHECKING UP ON MY DAUGHTER WHEN I WAS MISTAKEN FOR A TRESPASSER.
GOSH, THAT'S AWFUL.
OH, RIGHT!
I HAD FORGOTTEN THIS!!
WHAT IS IT?
THE ESSAY MIMORI-CHAN WAS GOING TO READ DURING PARENTS' DAY LAST YEAR.

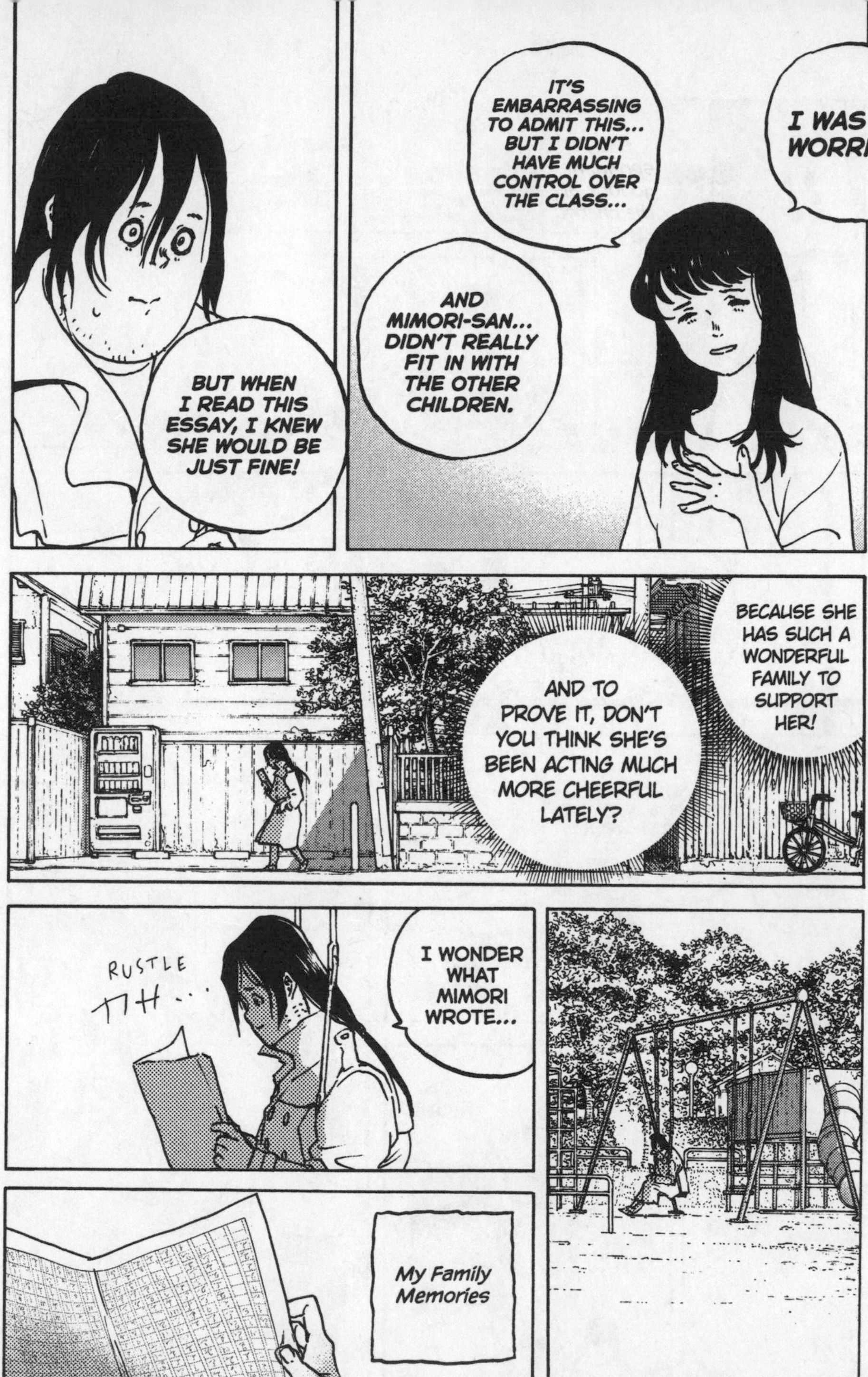
I WAS SO WORRIED.
IT'S EMBARRASSING TO ADMIT THIS... BUT I DIDN'T HAVE MUCH CONTROL OVER THE CLASS...
AND MIMORI-SAN... DIDN'T REALLY FIT IN WITH THE OTHER CHILDREN.
BUT WHEN I READ THIS ESSAY, I KNEW SHE WOULD BE JUST FINE!
BECAUSE SHE HAS SUCH A WONDERFUL FAMILY TO SUPPORT HER!
AND TO PROVE IT, DON'T YOU THINK SHE'S BEEN ACTING MUCH MORE CHEERFUL LATELY?
I WONDER WHAT MIMORI WROTE...
RUSTLE
My Family Memories

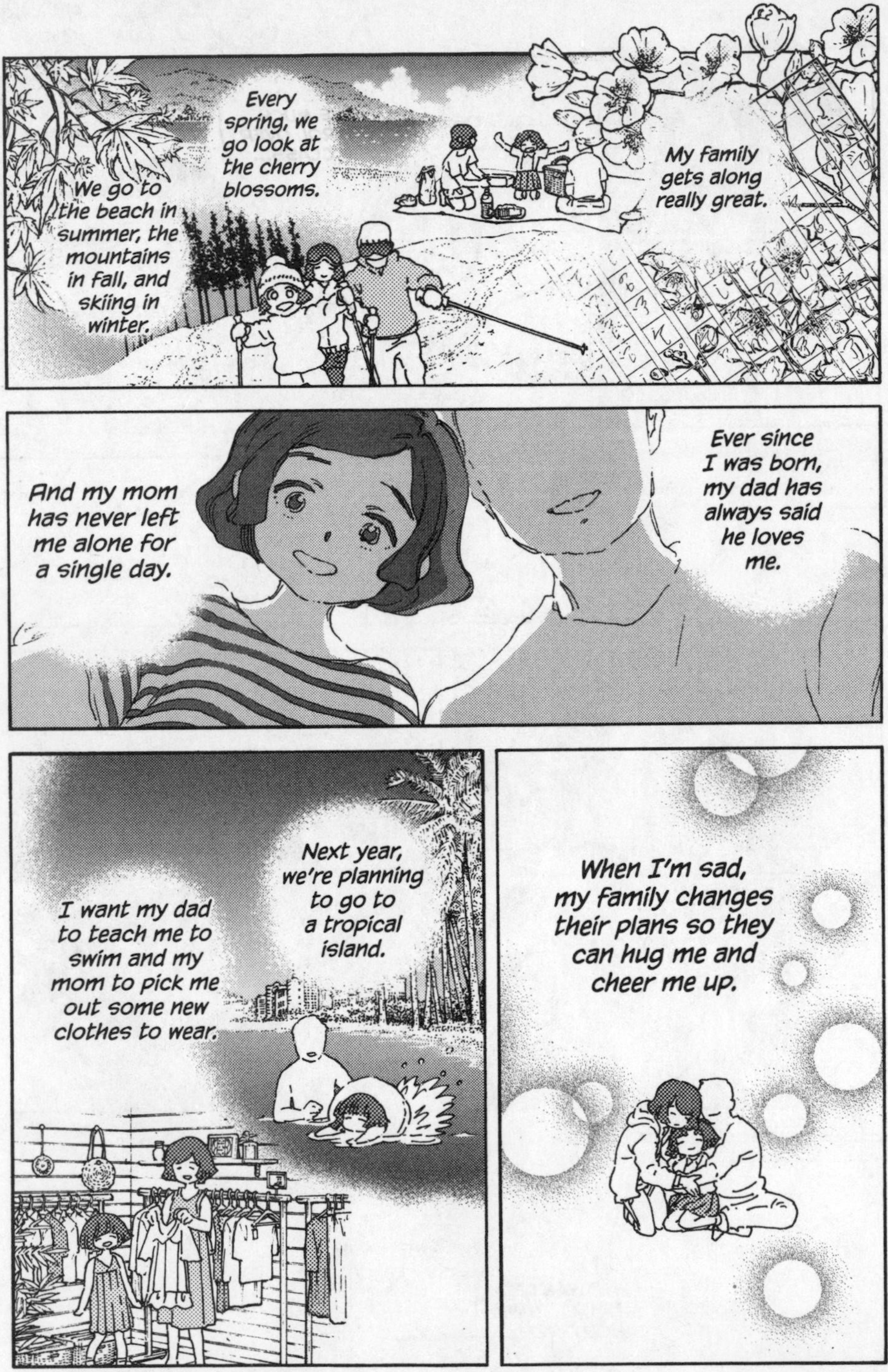
My family gets along really great.
Every spring, we go look at the cherry blossoms.
We go to the beach in summer, the mountains in fall, and skiing in winter.
Ever since I was born, my dad has always said he loves me.
And my mom has never left me alone for a single day.
When I'm sad, my family changes their plans so they can hug me and cheer me up.
Next year, we're planning to go to a tropical island.
I want my dad to teach me to swim and my mom to pick me out some new clothes to wear.

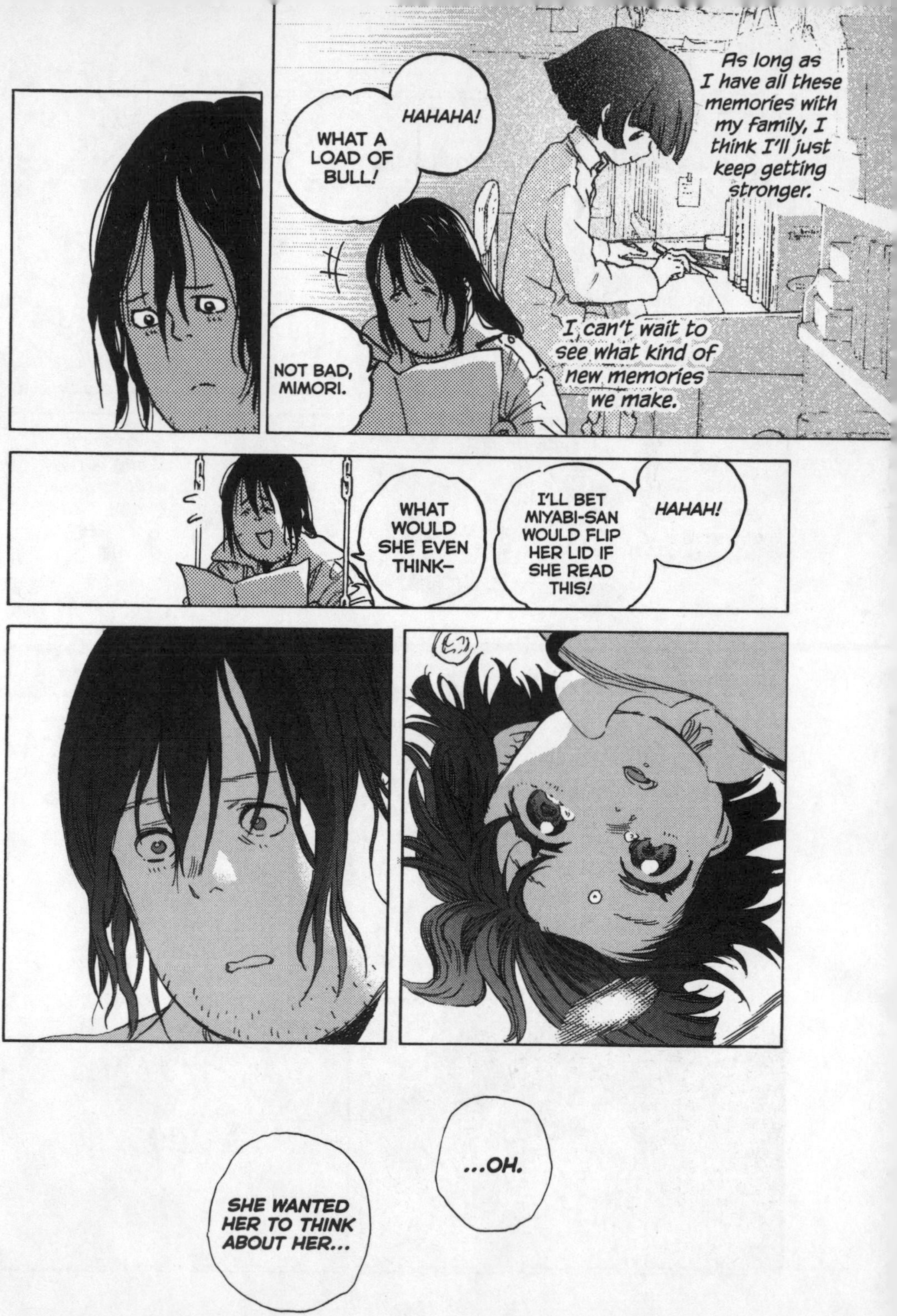
As long as I have all these memories with my family, I think I'll just keep getting stronger.
HAHAHA!
WHAT A LOAD OF BULL!
I can't wait to see what kind of new memories we make.
NOT BAD, MIMORI.
HAHAH!
I'LL BET MIYABI-SAN WOULD FLIP HER LID IF SHE READ THIS!
WHAT WOULD SHE EVEN THINK–
...OH.
SHE WANTED HER TO THINK ABOUT HER...

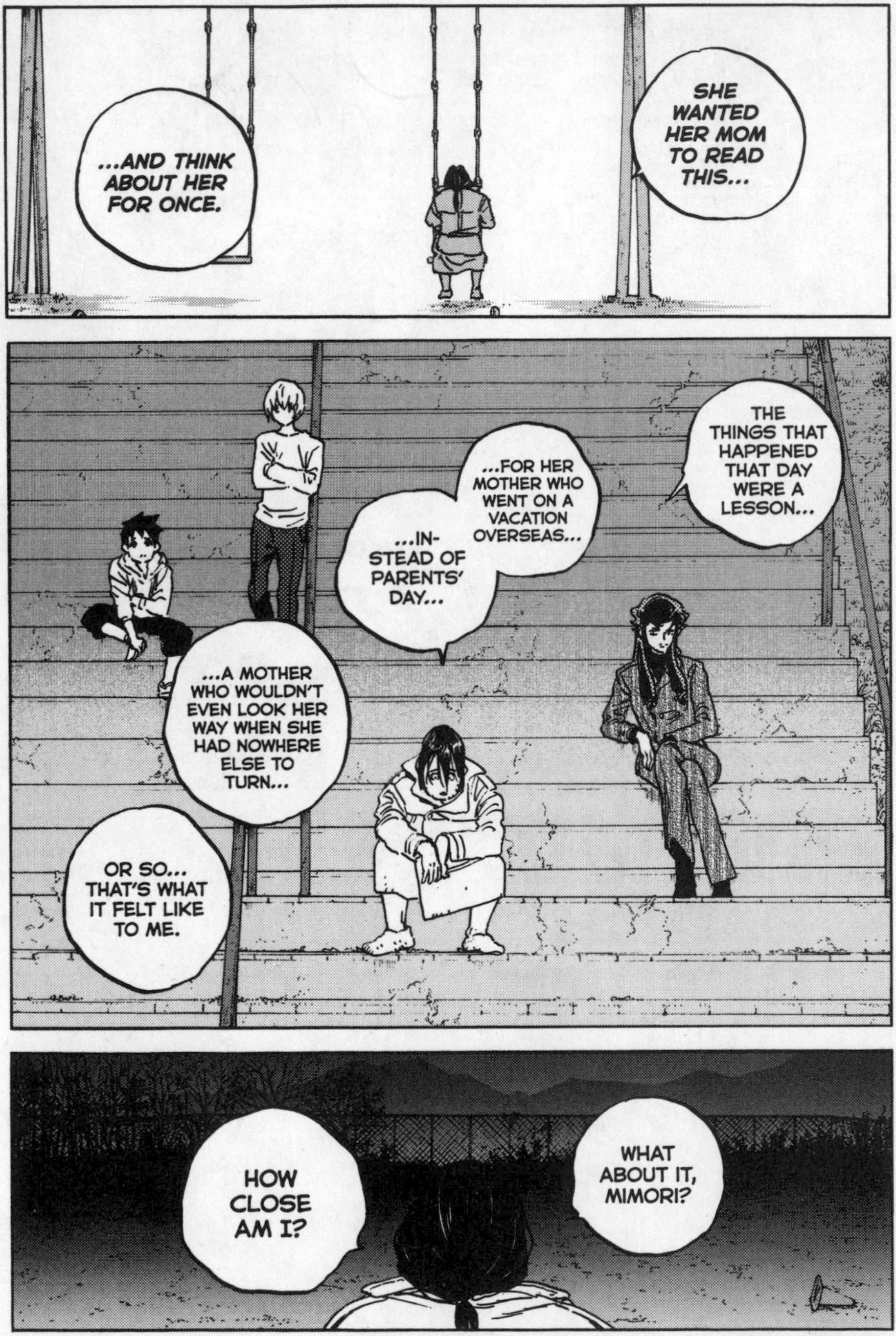
SHE WANTED HER MOM TO READ THIS...
...AND THINK ABOUT HER FOR ONCE.
THE THINGS THAT HAPPENED THAT DAY WERE A LESSON...
...FOR HER MOTHER WHO WENT ON A VACATION OVERSEAS...
...IN-STEAD OF PARENTS' DAY...
...A MOTHER WHO WOULDN'T EVEN LOOK HER WAY WHEN SHE HAD NOWHERE ELSE TO TURN...
OR SO... THAT'S WHAT IT FELT LIKE TO ME.
WHAT ABOUT IT, MIMORI?
HOW CLOSE AM I?

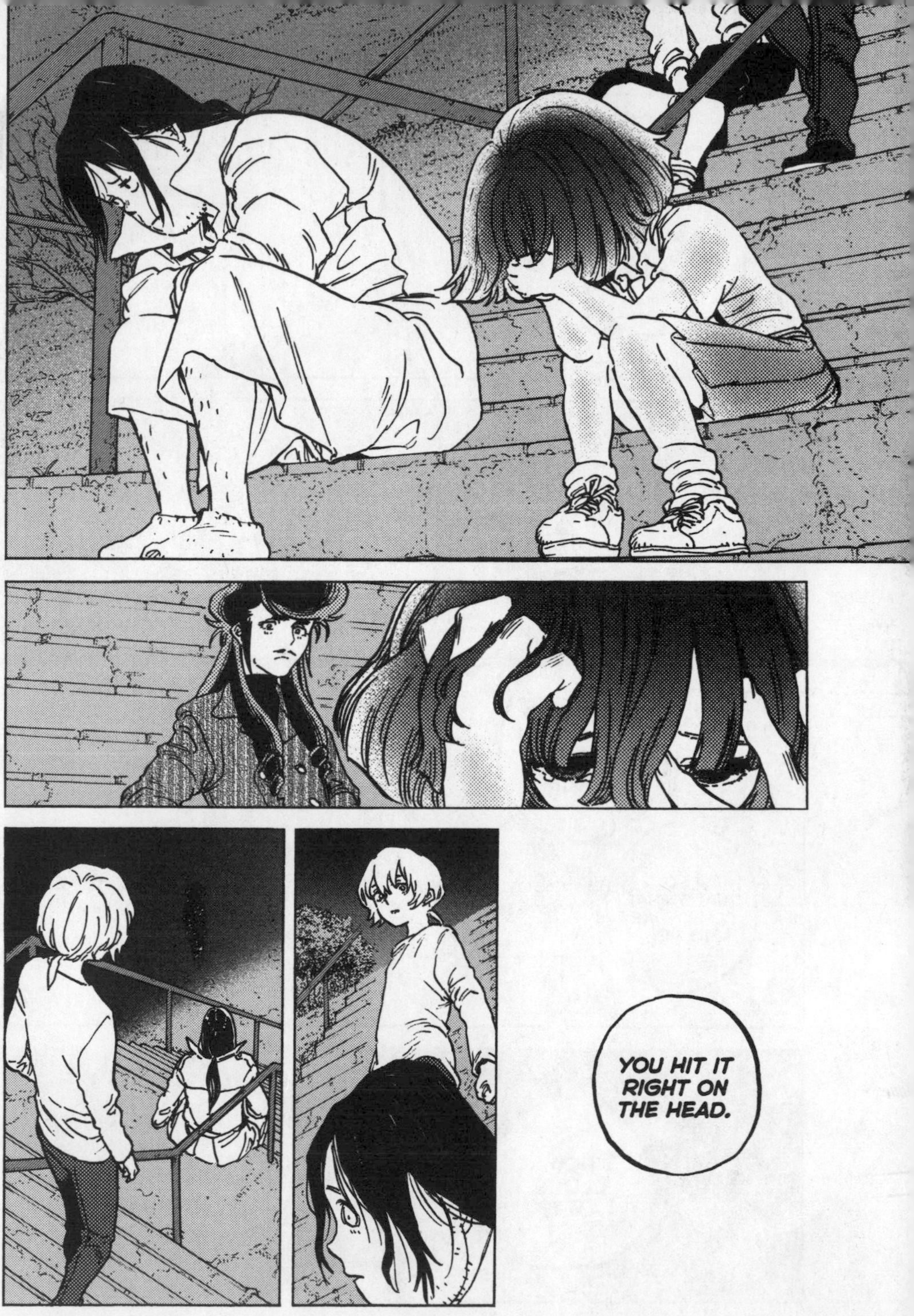
YOU HIT IT RIGHT ON THE HEAD.

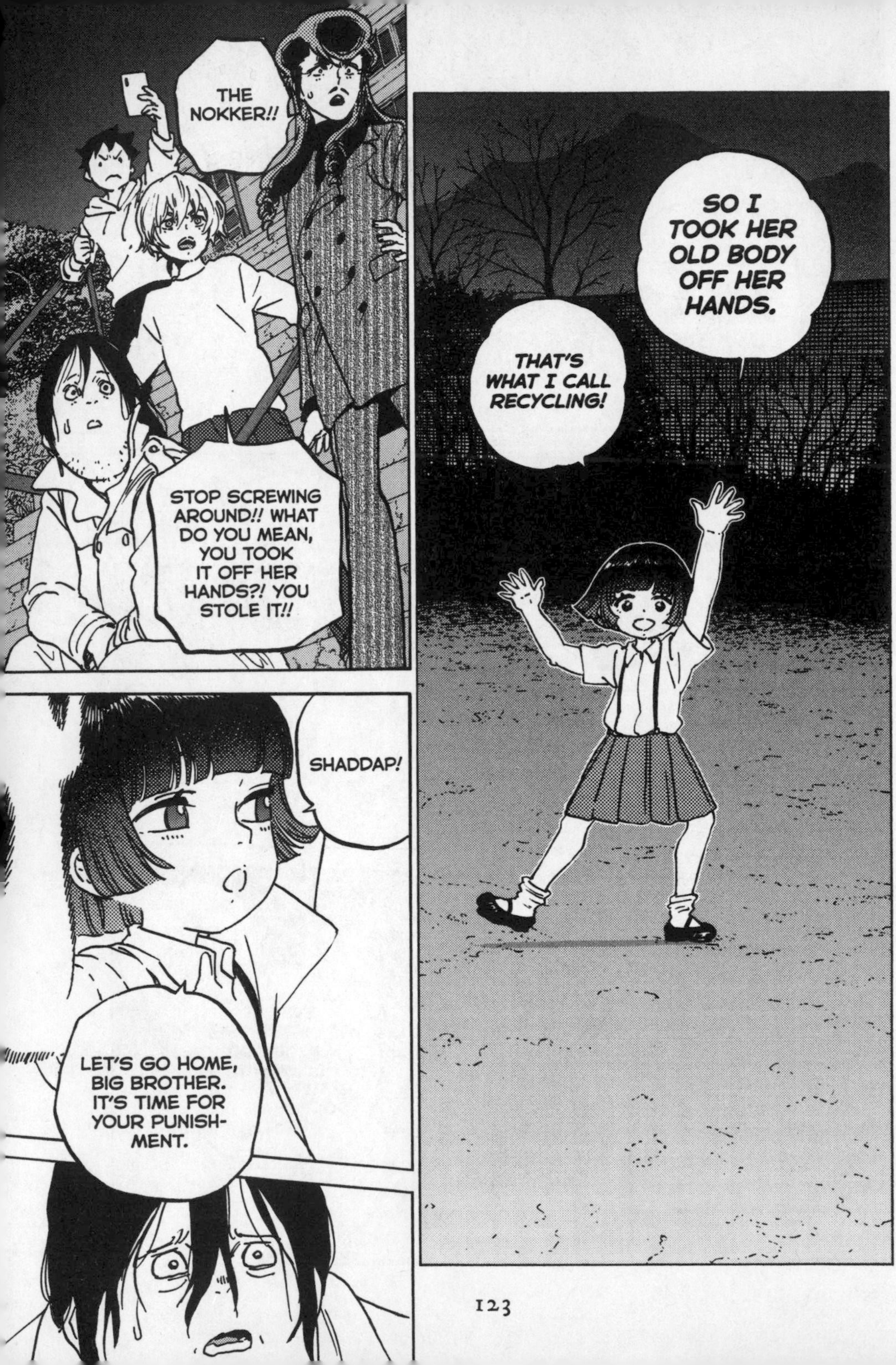

SO I TOOK HER OLD BODY OFF HER HANDS.
THAT'S WHAT I CALL RECYCLING!
THE NOKKER!!
STOP SCREWING AROUND!! WHAT DO YOU MEAN, YOU TOOK IT OFF HER HANDS?! YOU STOLE IT!!
SHADDAP!
LET'S GO HOME, BIG BROTHER. IT'S TIME FOR YOUR PUNISH-MENT.

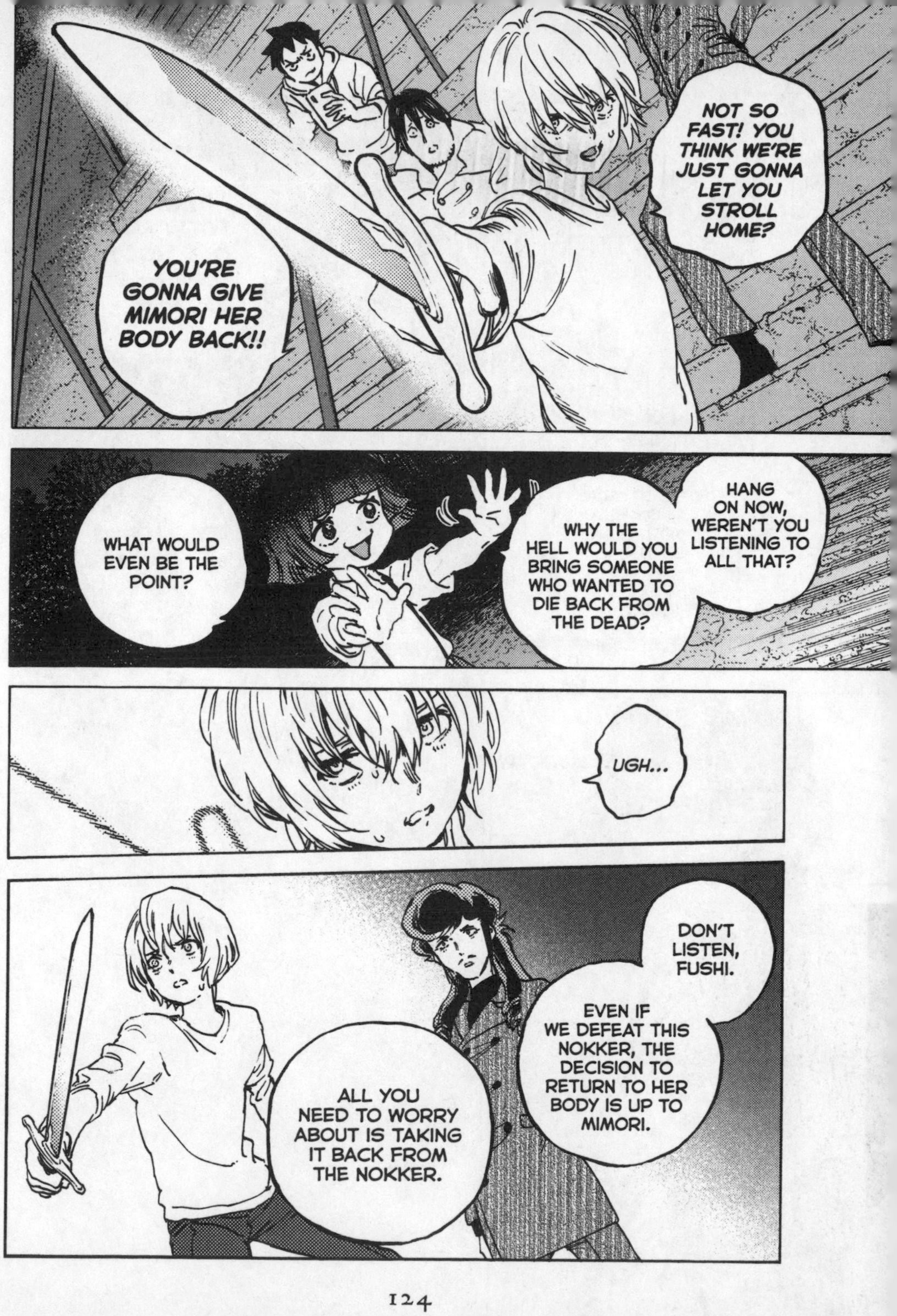
NOT SO FAST! YOU THINK WE'RE JUST GONNA LET YOU STROLL HOME?
YOU'RE GONNA GIVE MIMORI HER BODY BACK!!
HANG ON NOW, WEREN'T YOU LISTENING TO ALL THAT?
WHY THE HELL WOULD YOU BRING SOMEONE WHO WANTED TO DIE BACK FROM THE DEAD?
WHAT WOULD EVEN BE THE POINT?
UGH...
DON'T LISTEN, FUSHI.
EVEN IF WE DEFEAT THIS NOKKER, THE DECISION TO RETURN TO HER BODY IS UP TO MIMORI.
ALL YOU NEED TO WORRY ABOUT IS TAKING IT BACK FROM THE NOKKER.

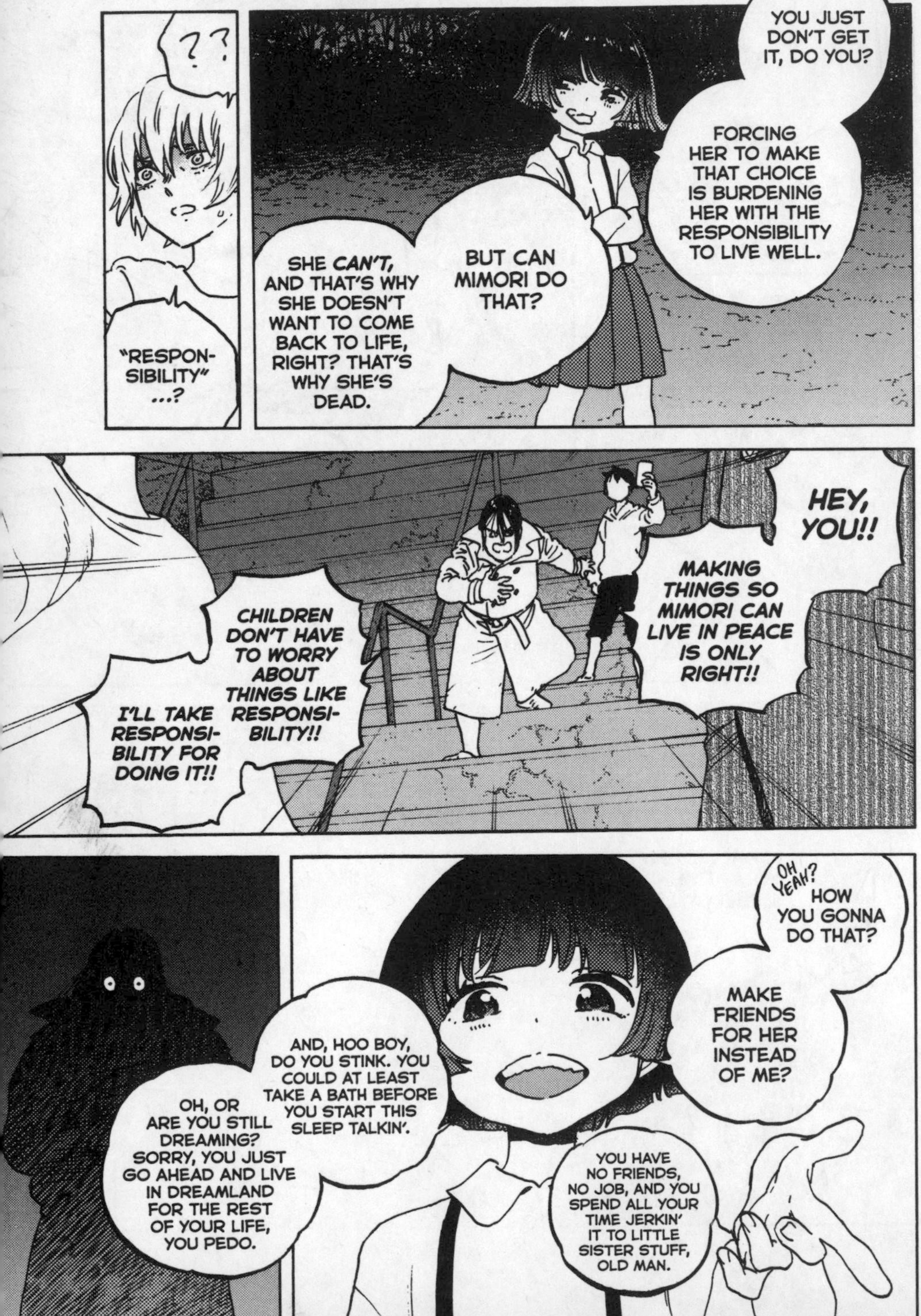
YOU JUST DON'T GET IT, DO YOU?
FORCING HER TO MAKE THAT CHOICE IS BURDENING HER WITH THE RESPONSIBILITY TO LIVE WELL.
BUT CAN MIMORI DO THAT?
SHE *CAN'T,* AND THAT'S WHY SHE DOESN'T WANT TO COME BACK TO LIFE, RIGHT? THAT'S WHY SHE'S DEAD.
??
"RESPON-SIBILITY" ...?
HEY, YOU!!
MAKING THINGS SO MIMORI CAN LIVE IN PEACE IS ONLY RIGHT!!
CHILDREN DON'T HAVE TO WORRY ABOUT THINGS LIKE RESPONSI-BILITY!!
I'LL TAKE RESPONSI-BILITY FOR DOING IT!!
OH YEAH? HOW YOU GONNA DO THAT?
MAKE FRIENDS FOR HER INSTEAD OF ME?
YOU HAVE NO FRIENDS, NO JOB, AND YOU SPEND ALL YOUR TIME JERKIN' IT TO LITTLE SISTER STUFF, OLD MAN.
AND, HOO BOY, DO YOU STINK. YOU COULD AT LEAST TAKE A BATH BEFORE YOU START THIS SLEEP TALKIN'.
OH, OR ARE YOU STILL DREAMING? SORRY, YOU JUST GO AHEAD AND LIVE IN DREAMLAND FOR THE REST OF YOUR LIFE, YOU PEDO.

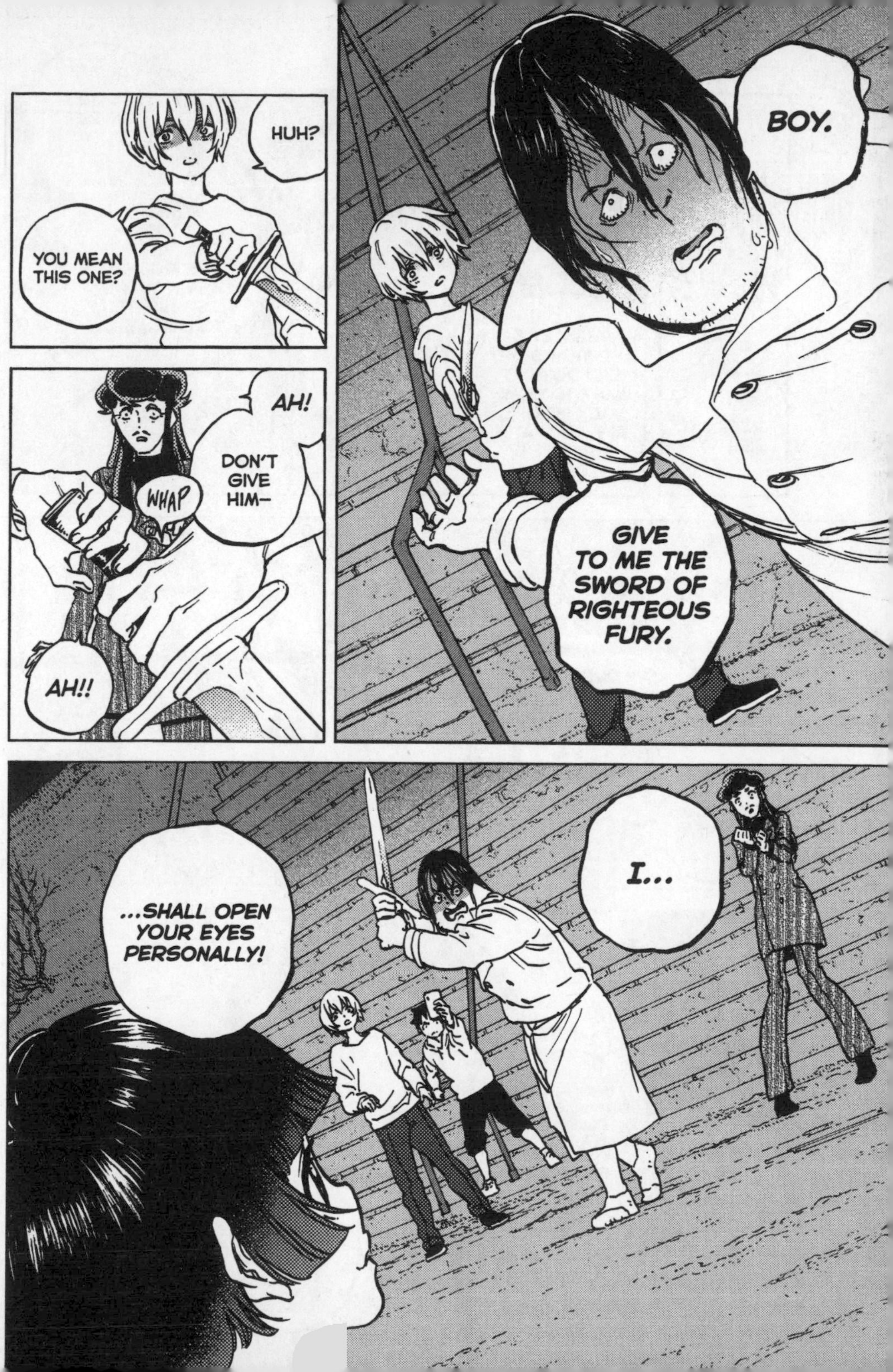
BOY.
GIVE TO ME THE SWORD OF RIGHTEOUS FURY.
HUH?
YOU MEAN THIS ONE?
AH!
DON'T GIVE HIM–
WHAP
AH!!
I...
...SHALL OPEN YOUR EYES PERSONALLY!

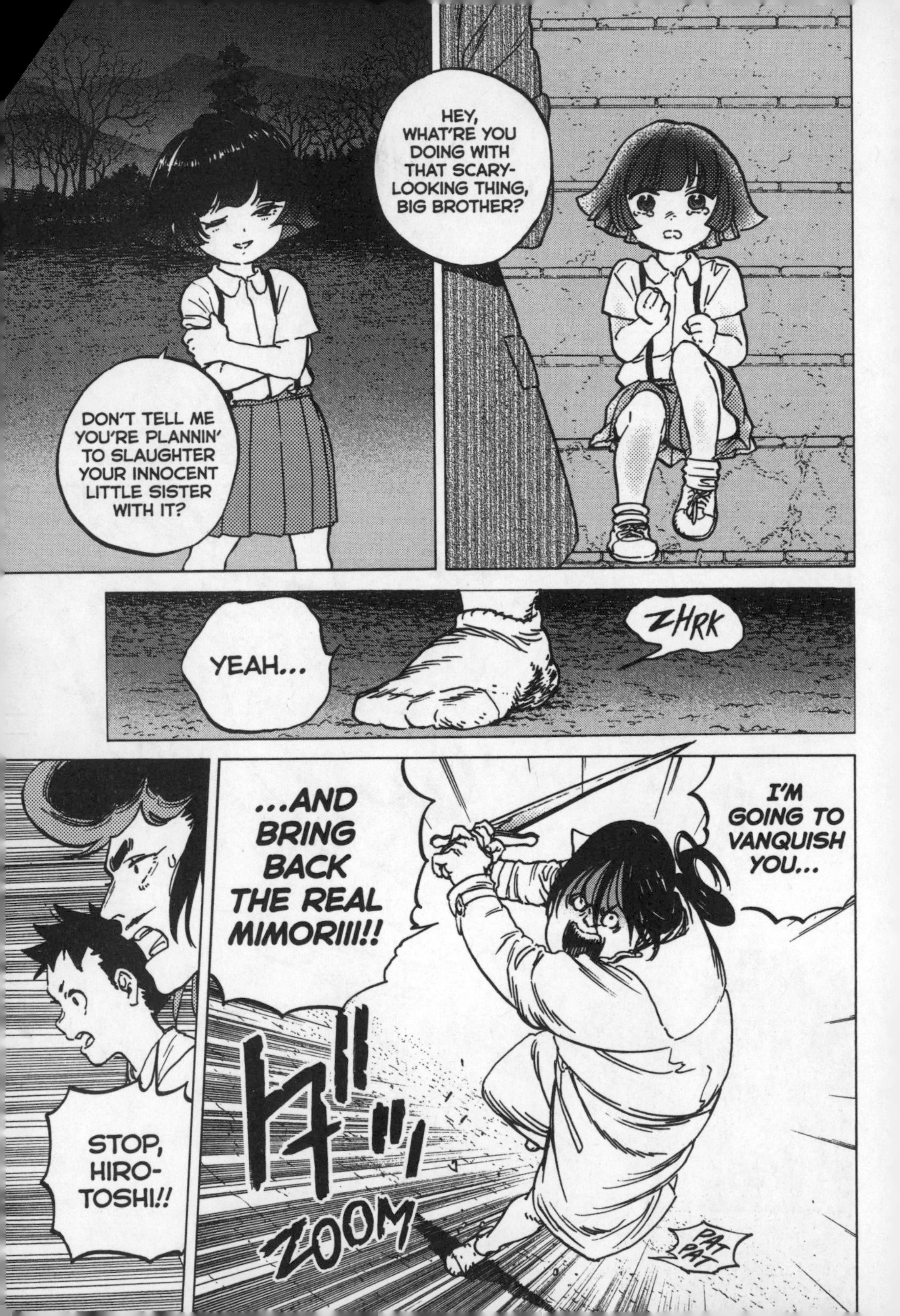
HEY, WHAT'RE YOU DOING WITH THAT SCARY-LOOKING THING, BIG BROTHER?
DON'T TELL ME YOU'RE PLANNIN' TO SLAUGHTER YOUR INNOCENT LITTLE SISTER WITH IT?
ZHRK
YEAH...
I'M GOING TO VANQUISH YOU...
...AND BRING BACK THE REAL MIMORIII!!
ZOOM
PAT PAT
STOP, HIRO-TOSHI!!

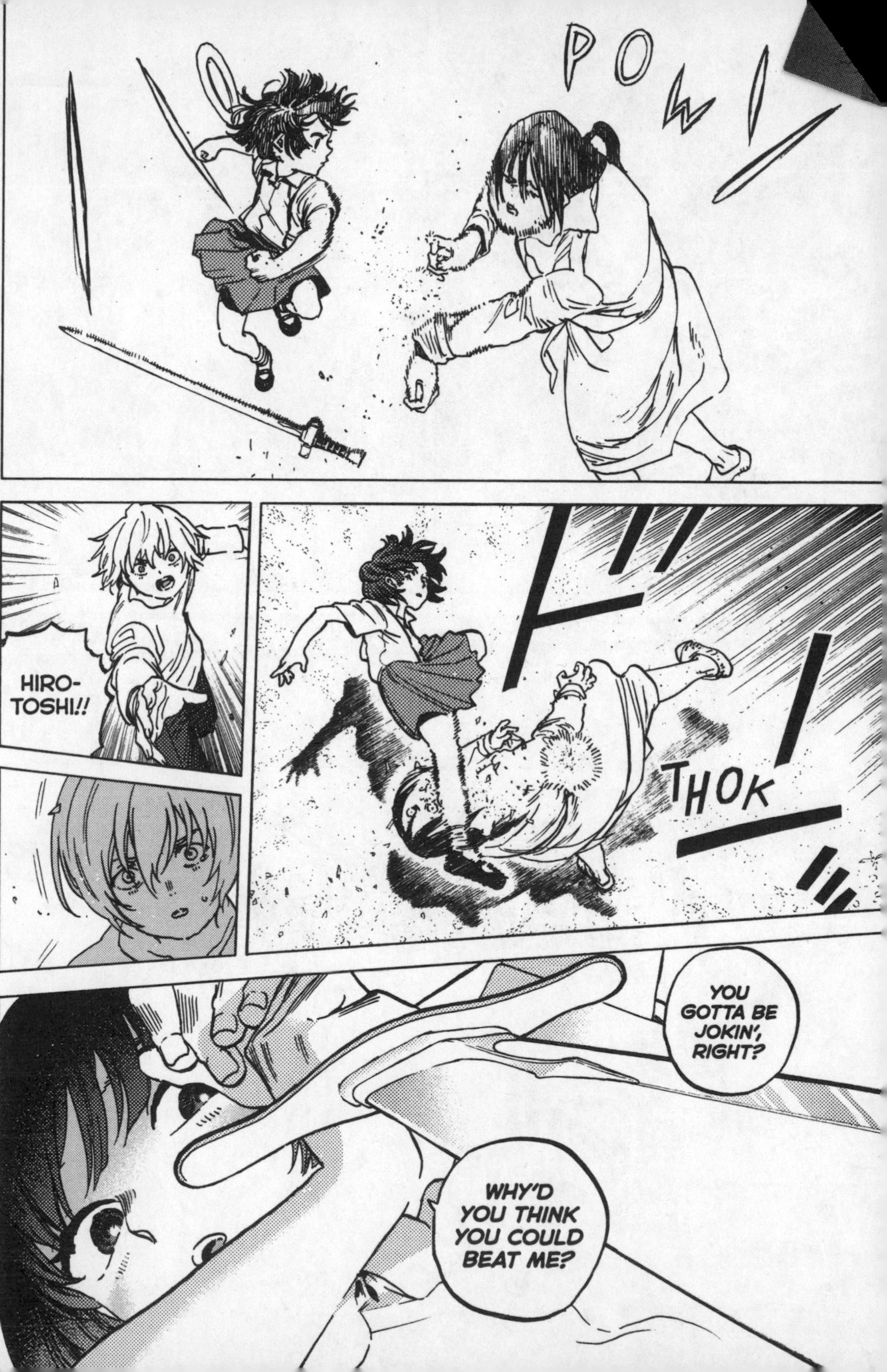
POW
THOK
HIRO-TOSHI!!
YOU GOTTA BE JOKIN', RIGHT?
WHY'D YOU THINK YOU COULD BEAT ME?

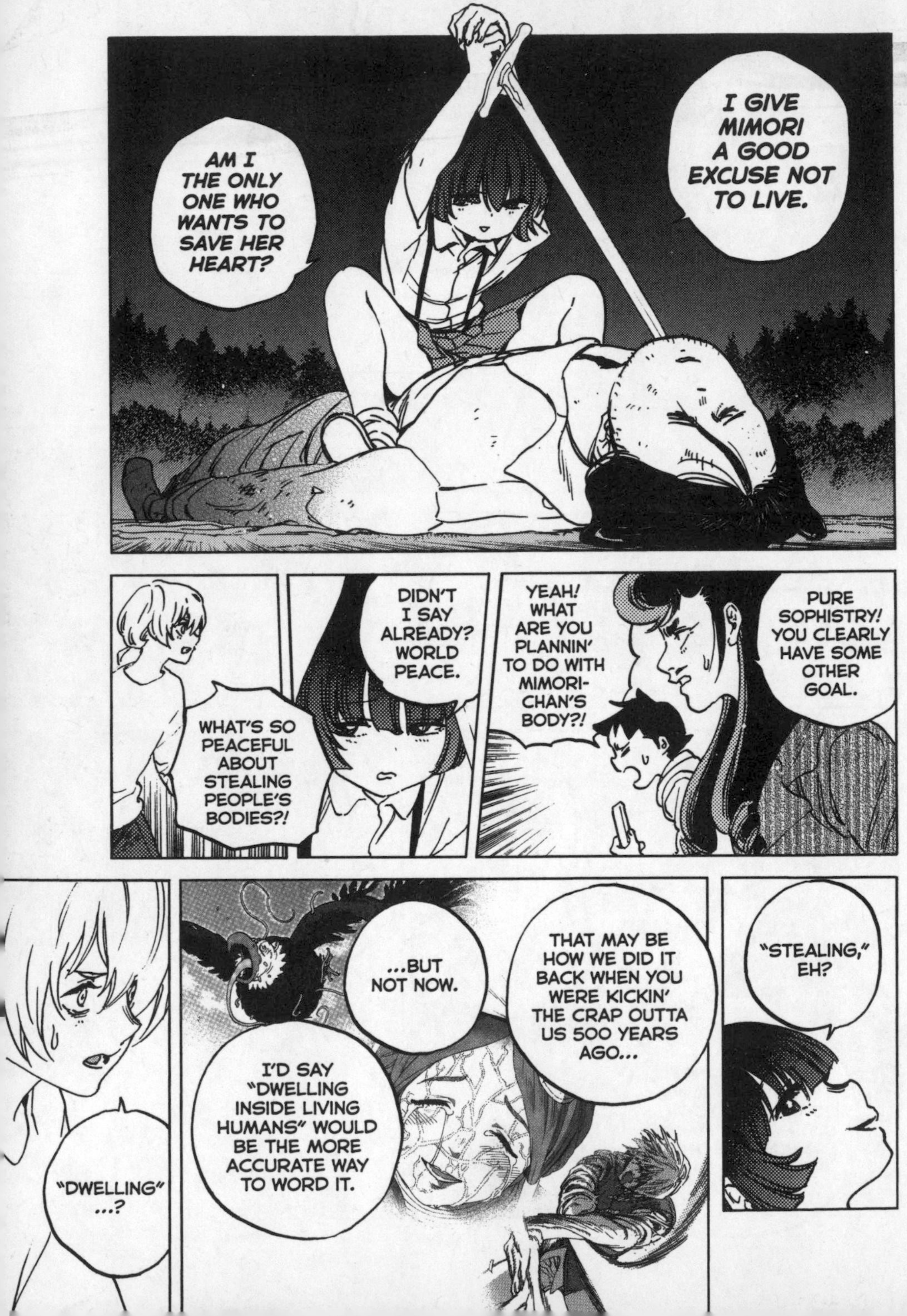
I GIVE MIMORI A GOOD EXCUSE NOT TO LIVE.
AM I THE ONLY ONE WHO WANTS TO SAVE HER HEART?
PURE SOPHISTRY! YOU CLEARLY HAVE SOME OTHER GOAL.
YEAH! WHAT ARE YOU PLANNIN' TO DO WITH MIMORI-CHAN'S BODY?!
DIDN'T I SAY ALREADY? WORLD PEACE.
WHAT'S SO PEACEFUL ABOUT STEALING PEOPLE'S BODIES?!
"STEALING," EH?
THAT MAY BE HOW WE DID IT BACK WHEN YOU WERE KICKIN' THE CRAP OUTTA US 500 YEARS AGO...
...BUT NOT NOW.
I'D SAY "DWELLING INSIDE LIVING HUMANS" WOULD BE THE MORE ACCURATE WAY TO WORD IT.
"DWELLING" ...?

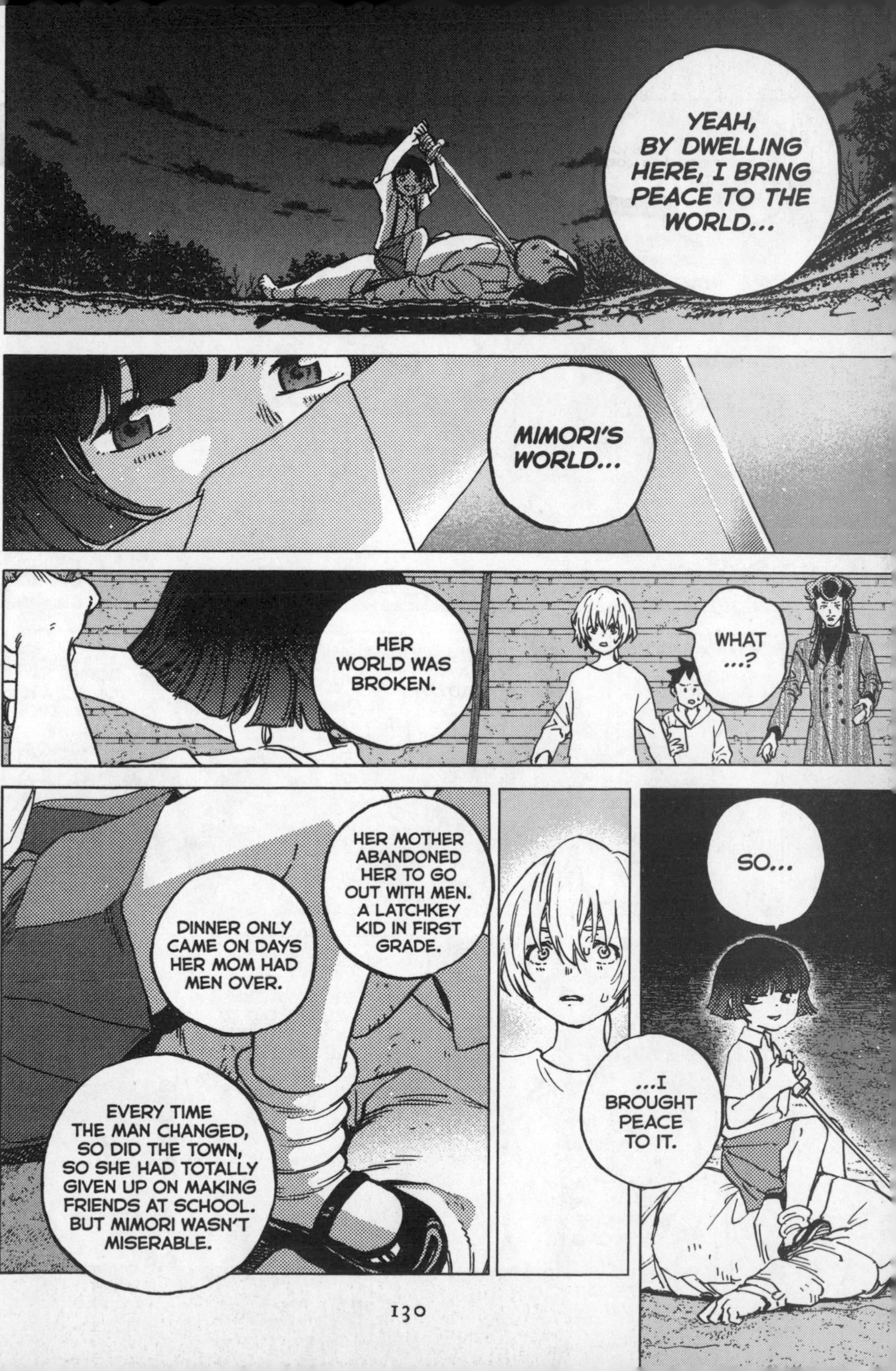
YEAH, BY DWELLING HERE, I BRING PEACE TO THE WORLD...
MIMORI'S WORLD...
WHAT ...?
HER WORLD WAS BROKEN.
SO...
...I BROUGHT PEACE TO IT.
HER MOTHER ABANDONED HER TO GO OUT WITH MEN. A LATCHKEY KID IN FIRST GRADE.
DINNER ONLY CAME ON DAYS HER MOM HAD MEN OVER.
EVERY TIME THE MAN CHANGED, SO DID THE TOWN, SO SHE HAD TOTALLY GIVEN UP ON MAKING FRIENDS AT SCHOOL. BUT MIMORI WASN'T MISERABLE.

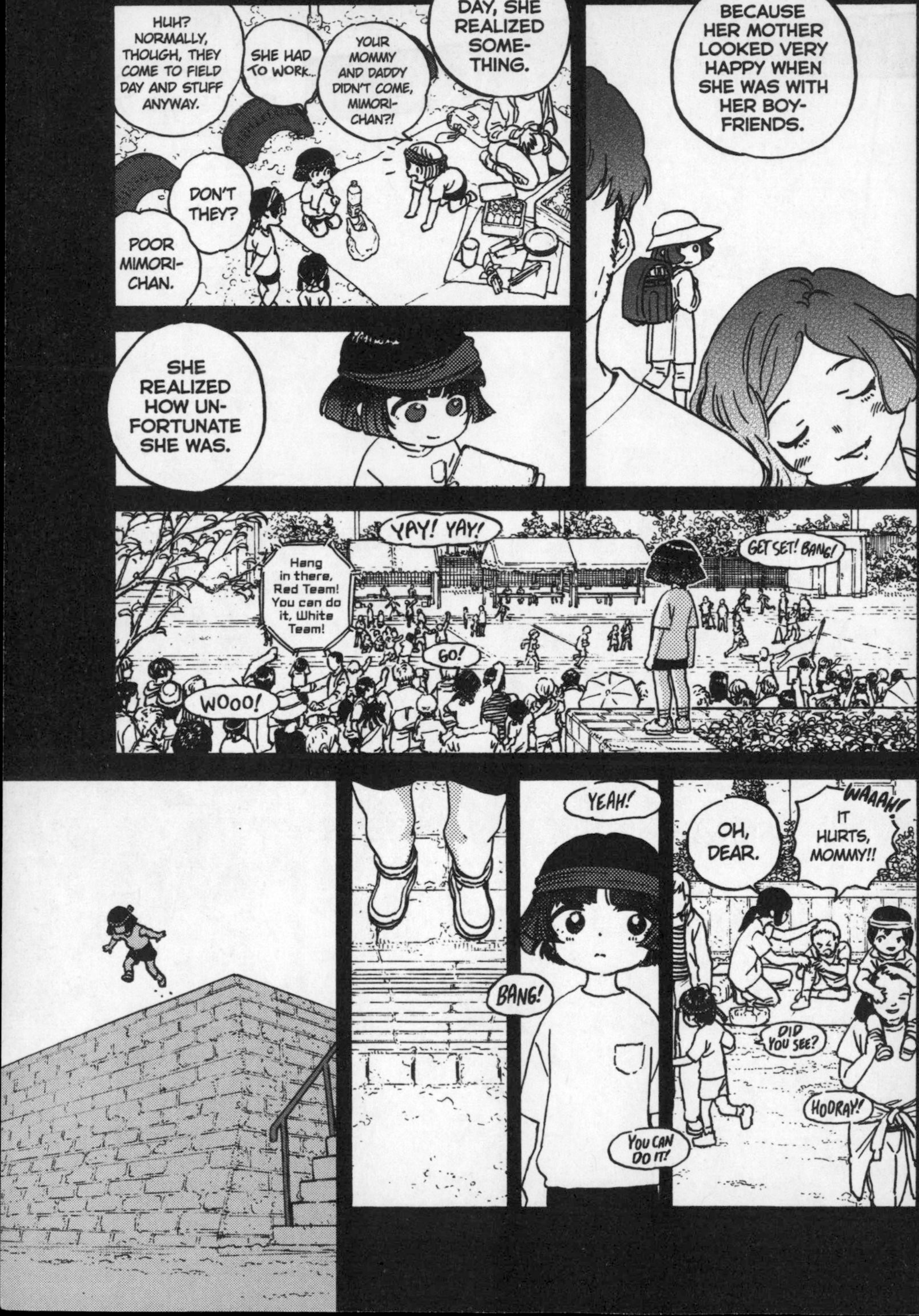
BECAUSE HER MOTHER LOOKED VERY HAPPY WHEN SHE WAS WITH HER BOY-FRIENDS.
BUT ONE DAY, SHE REALIZED SOME-THING.
YOUR MOMMY AND DADDY DIDN'T COME, MIMORI-CHAN?!
SHE HAD TO WORK...
HUH? NORMALLY, THOUGH, THEY COME TO FIELD DAY AND STUFF ANYWAY.
DON'T THEY?
POOR MIMORI-CHAN.
SHE REALIZED HOW UN-FORTUNATE SHE WAS.
GET SET! BANG!
YAY! YAY!
Hang in there, Red Team! You can do it, White Team!
GO!
WOOO!
WAAAH!
IT HURTS, MOMMY!!
OH, DEAR.
DID YOU SEE?
HOORAY!
YEAH!
BANG!
YOU CAN DO IT!

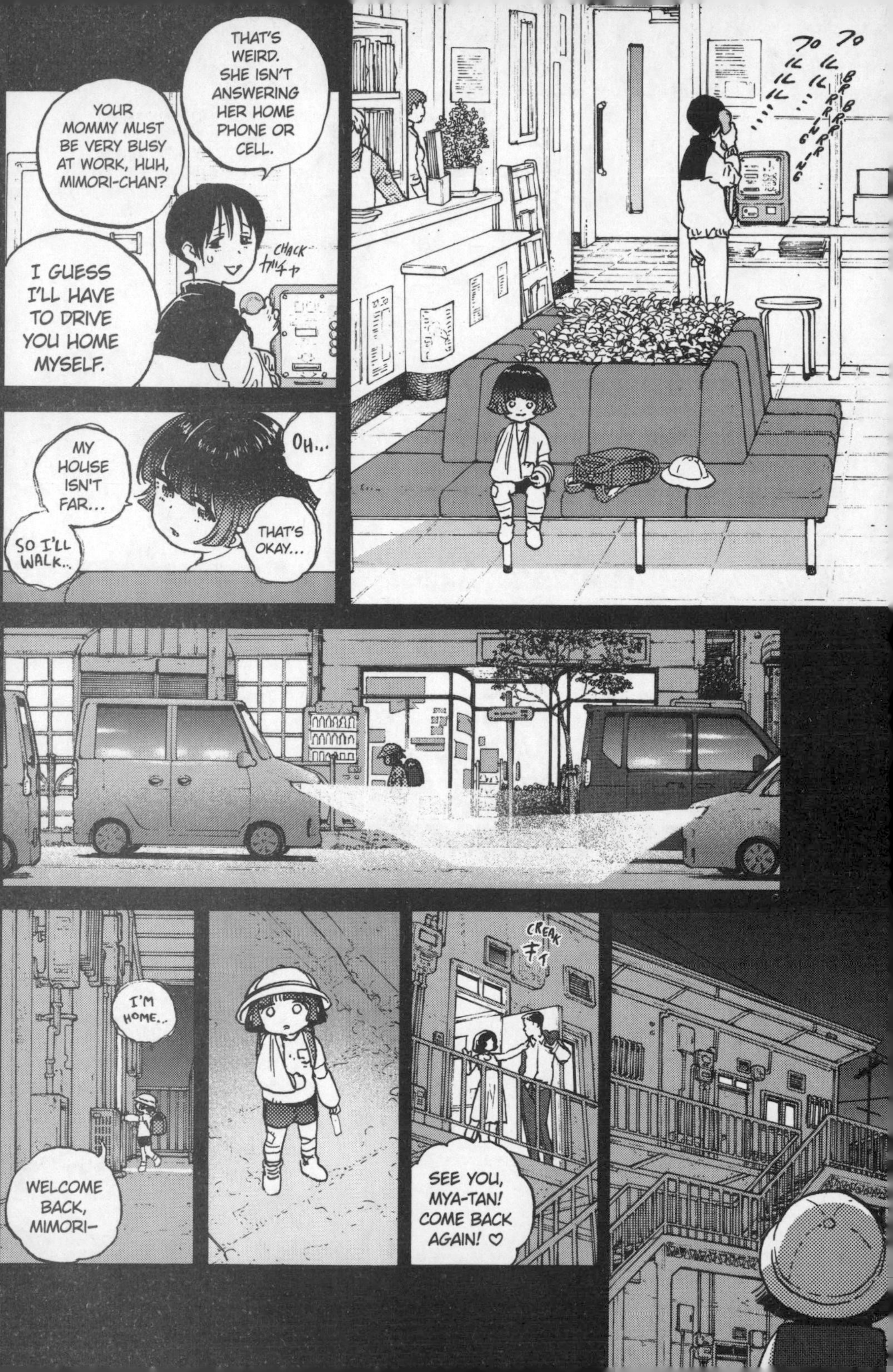
BRRRING
BRRRRRING
THAT'S WEIRD. SHE ISN'T ANSWERING HER HOME PHONE OR CELL.
YOUR MOMMY MUST BE VERY BUSY AT WORK, HUH, MIMORI-CHAN?
CHACK
I GUESS I'LL HAVE TO DRIVE YOU HOME MYSELF.
OH...
THAT'S OKAY...
MY HOUSE ISN'T FAR...
SO I'LL WALK..
CREAK
SEE YOU, MYA-TAN! COME BACK AGAIN! ♡
I'M HOME..
WELCOME BACK, MIMORI-

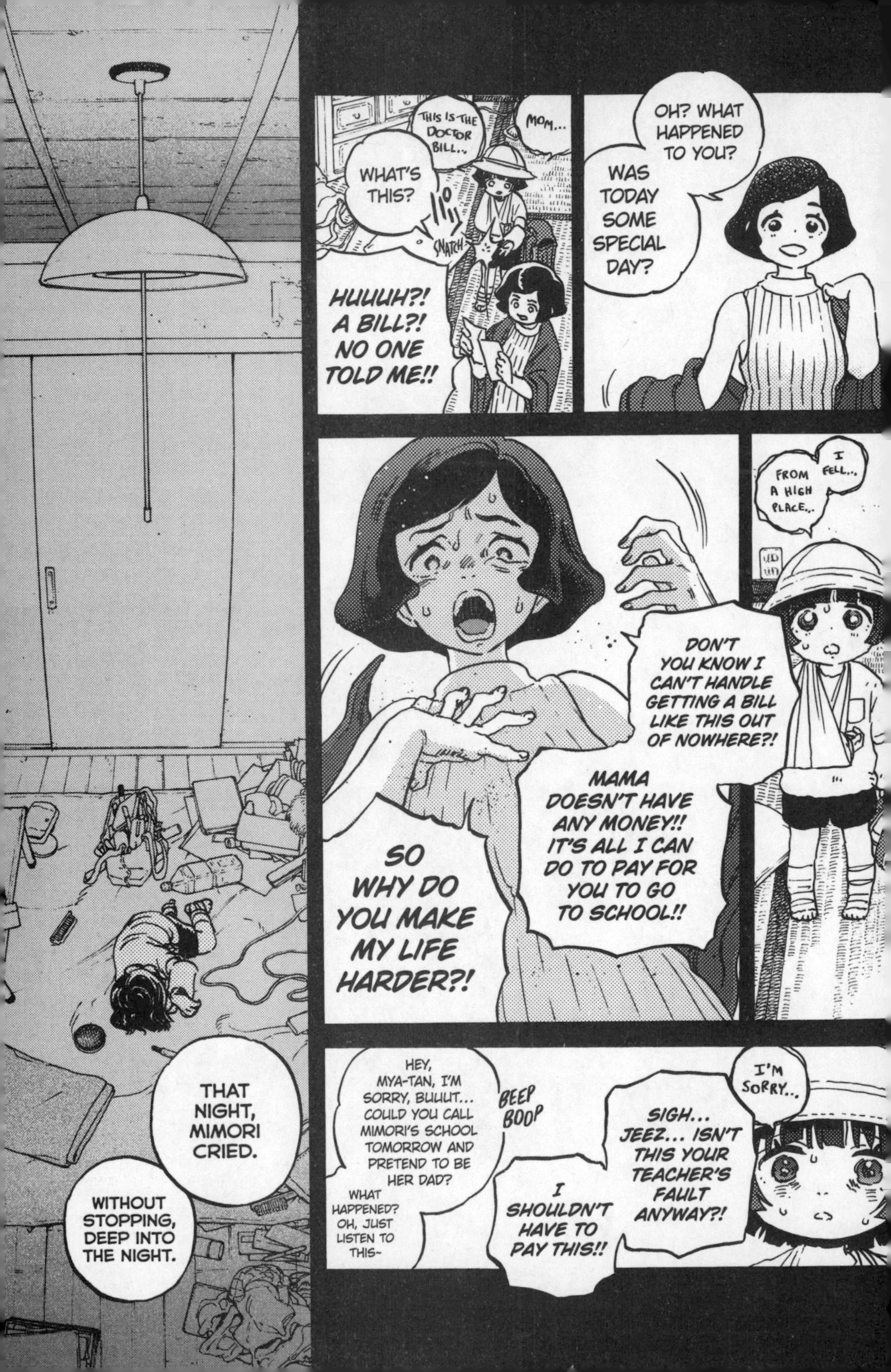
OH? WHAT HAPPENED TO YOU?
WAS TODAY SOME SPECIAL DAY?
MOM...
THIS IS THE DOCTOR BILL...
WHAT'S THIS?
SNATCH
HUUUH?! A BILL?! NO ONE TOLD ME!!
I FELL...
FROM A HIGH PLACE...
DON'T YOU KNOW I CAN'T HANDLE GETTING A BILL LIKE THIS OUT OF NOWHERE?!
MAMA DOESN'T HAVE ANY MONEY!! IT'S ALL I CAN DO TO PAY FOR YOU TO GO TO SCHOOL!!
SO WHY DO YOU MAKE MY LIFE HARDER?!
I'M SORRY...
SIGH... JEEZ... ISN'T THIS YOUR TEACHER'S FAULT ANYWAY?!
I SHOULDN'T HAVE TO PAY THIS!!
BEEP BOOP
HEY, MYA-TAN, I'M SORRY, BUUUT... COULD YOU CALL MIMORI'S SCHOOL TOMORROW AND PRETEND TO BE HER DAD?
WHAT HAPPENED? OH, JUST LISTEN TO THIS~
THAT NIGHT, MIMORI CRIED.
WITHOUT STOPPING, DEEP INTO THE NIGHT.

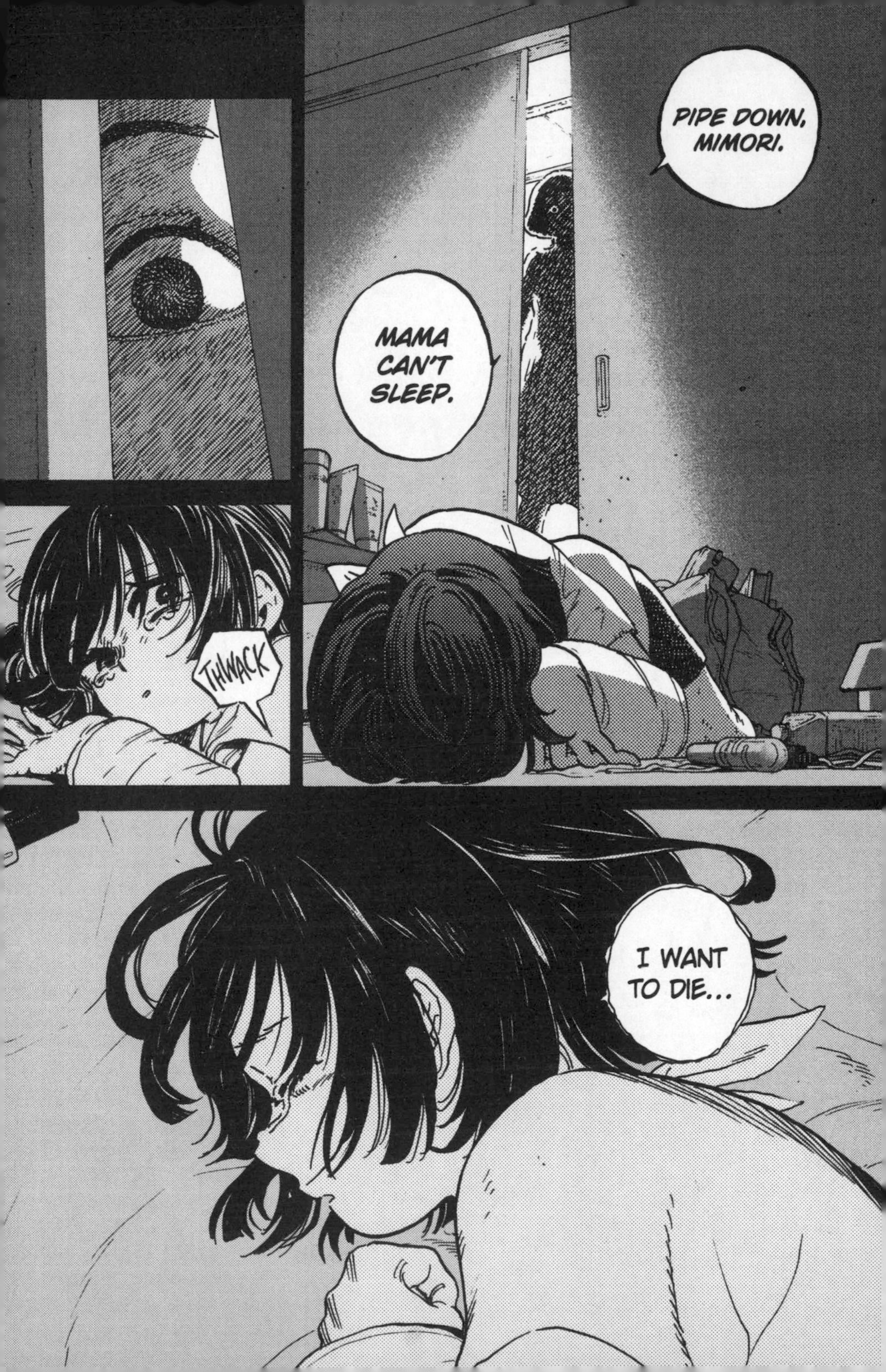
PIPE DOWN, MIMORI.
MAMA CAN'T SLEEP.
THWACK
I WANT TO DIE...

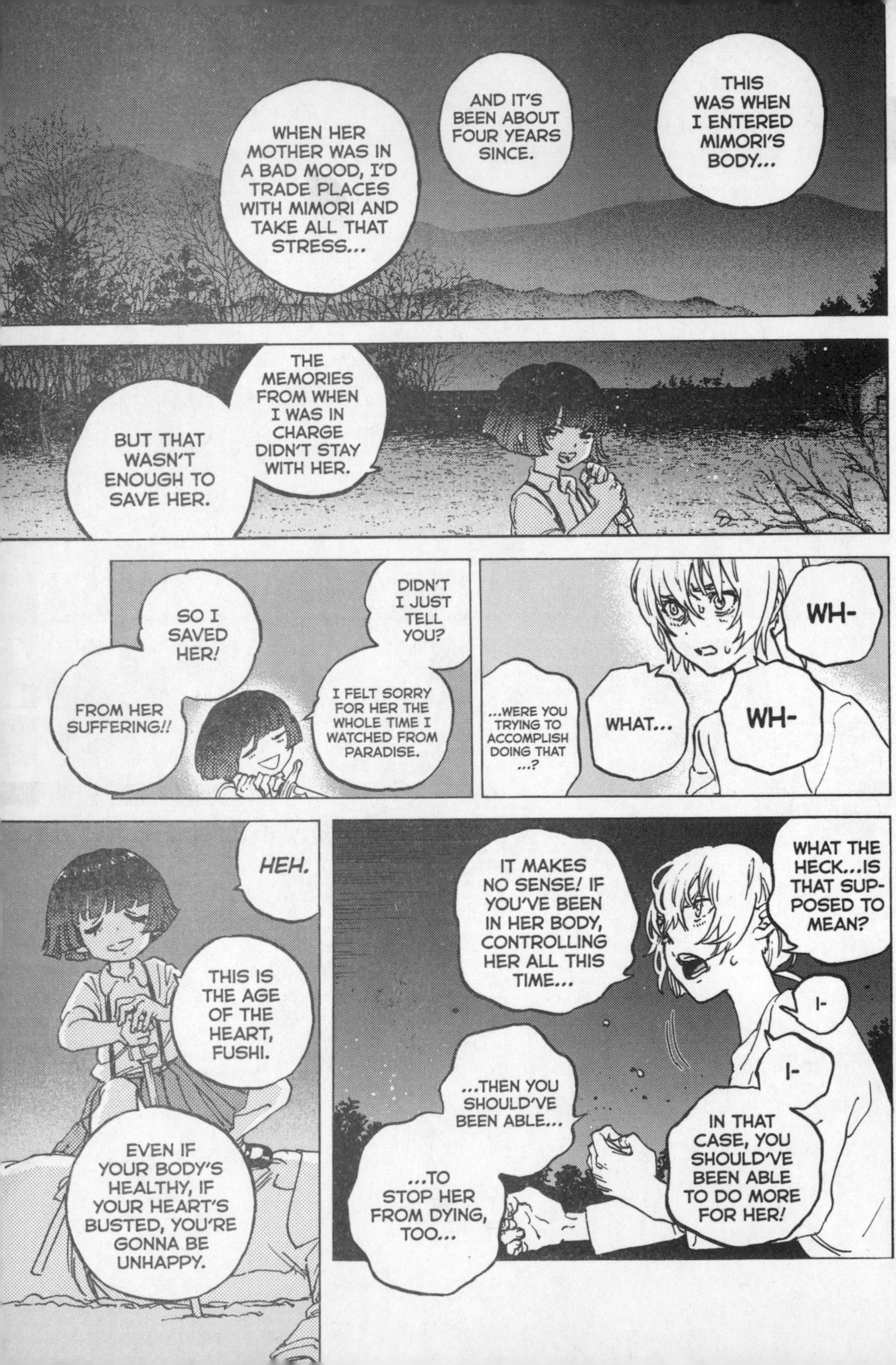
THIS WAS WHEN I ENTERED MIMORI'S BODY...
AND IT'S BEEN ABOUT FOUR YEARS SINCE.
WHEN HER MOTHER WAS IN A BAD MOOD, I'D TRADE PLACES WITH MIMORI AND TAKE ALL THAT STRESS...
THE MEMORIES FROM WHEN I WAS IN CHARGE DIDN'T STAY WITH HER.
BUT THAT WASN'T ENOUGH TO SAVE HER.
WH-
WH-
WHAT...
...WERE YOU TRYING TO ACCOMPLISH DOING THAT ...?
DIDN'T I JUST TELL YOU?
SO I SAVED HER!
FROM HER SUFFERING!!
I FELT SORRY FOR HER THE WHOLE TIME I WATCHED FROM PARADISE.
WHAT THE HECK...IS THAT SUP-POSED TO MEAN?
I-
I-
IN THAT CASE, YOU SHOULD'VE BEEN ABLE TO DO MORE FOR HER!
IT MAKES NO SENSE! IF YOU'VE BEEN IN HER BODY, CONTROLLING HER ALL THIS TIME...
...THEN YOU SHOULD'VE BEEN ABLE...
...TO STOP HER FROM DYING, TOO...
HEH.
THIS IS THE AGE OF THE HEART, FUSHI.
EVEN IF YOUR BODY'S HEALTHY, IF YOUR HEART'S BUSTED, YOU'RE GONNA BE UNHAPPY.

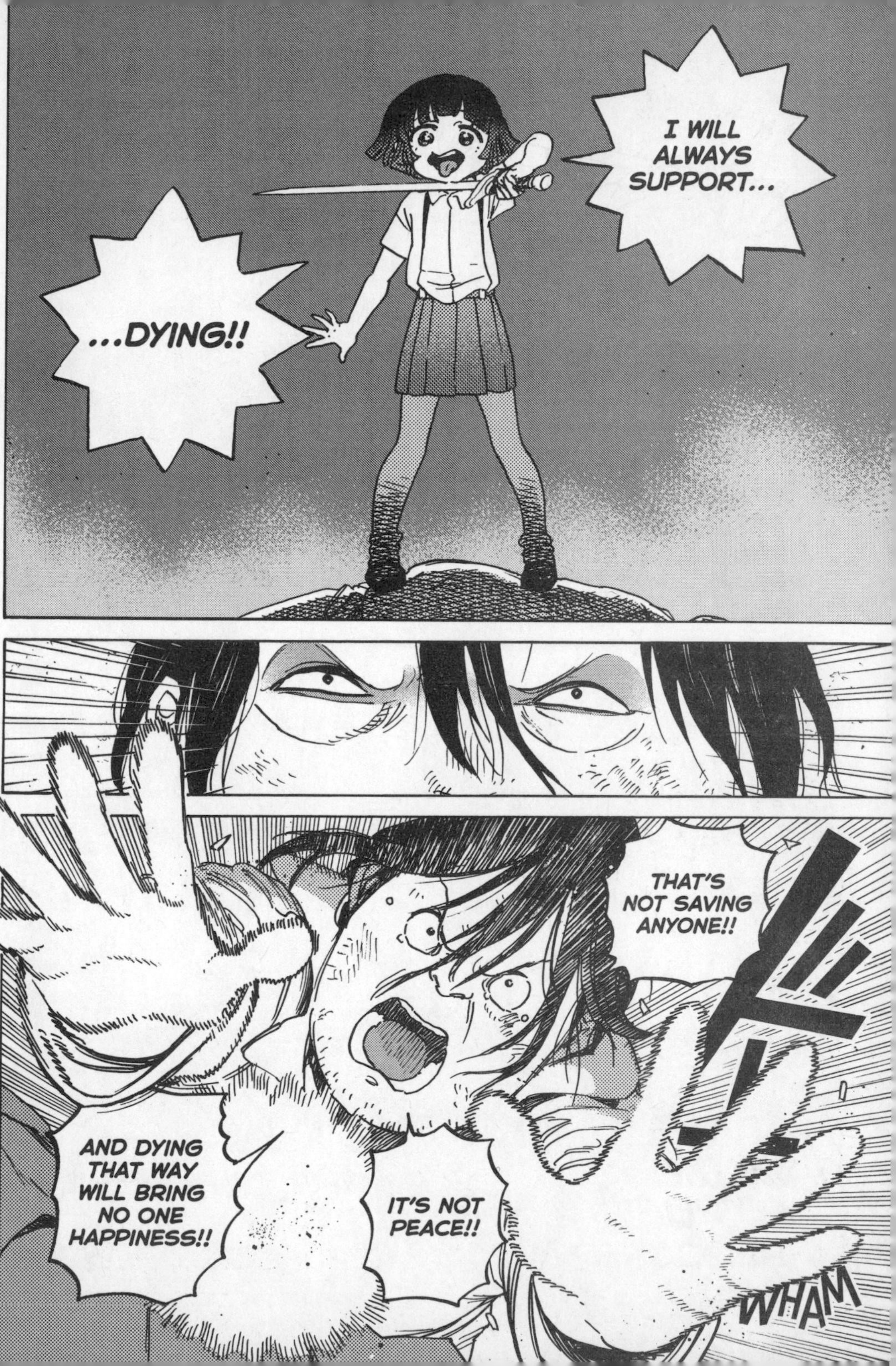
I WILL ALWAYS SUPPORT...
...DYING!!
THAT'S NOT SAVING ANYONE!!
IT'S NOT PEACE!!
AND DYING THAT WAY WILL BRING NO ONE HAPPINESS!!
WHAM

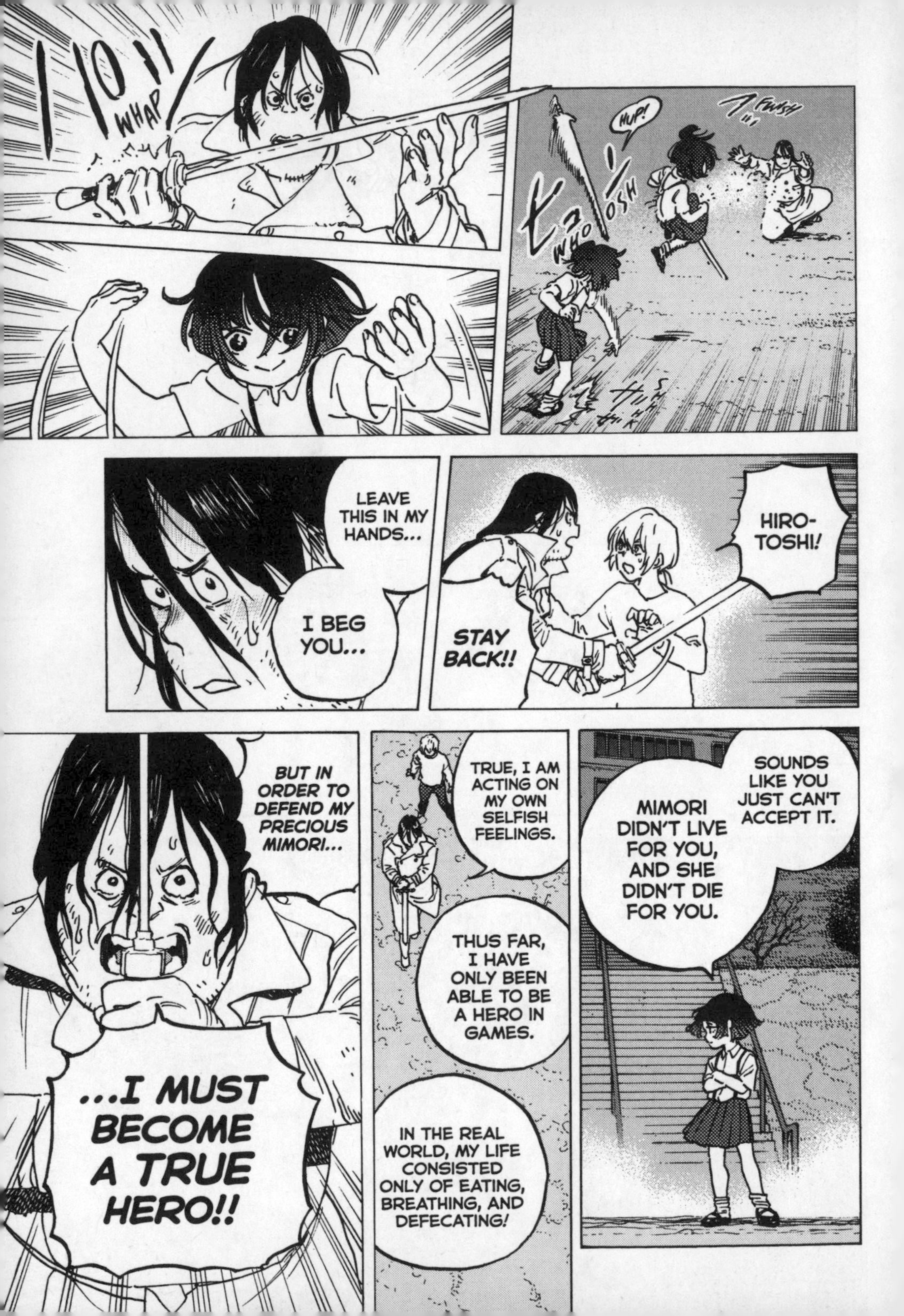
HUP!
FWISH
WHOOSH
SHHK
WHAP
HIRO-TOSHI!
STAY BACK!!
LEAVE THIS IN MY HANDS...
I BEG YOU...
SOUNDS LIKE YOU JUST CAN'T ACCEPT IT.
MIMORI DIDN'T LIVE FOR YOU, AND SHE DIDN'T DIE FOR YOU.
TRUE, I AM ACTING ON MY OWN SELFISH FEELINGS.
THUS FAR, I HAVE ONLY BEEN ABLE TO BE A HERO IN GAMES.
IN THE REAL WORLD, MY LIFE CONSISTED ONLY OF EATING, BREATHING, AND DEFECATING!
BUT IN ORDER TO DEFEND MY PRECIOUS MIMORI...
...I MUST BECOME A TRUE HERO!!

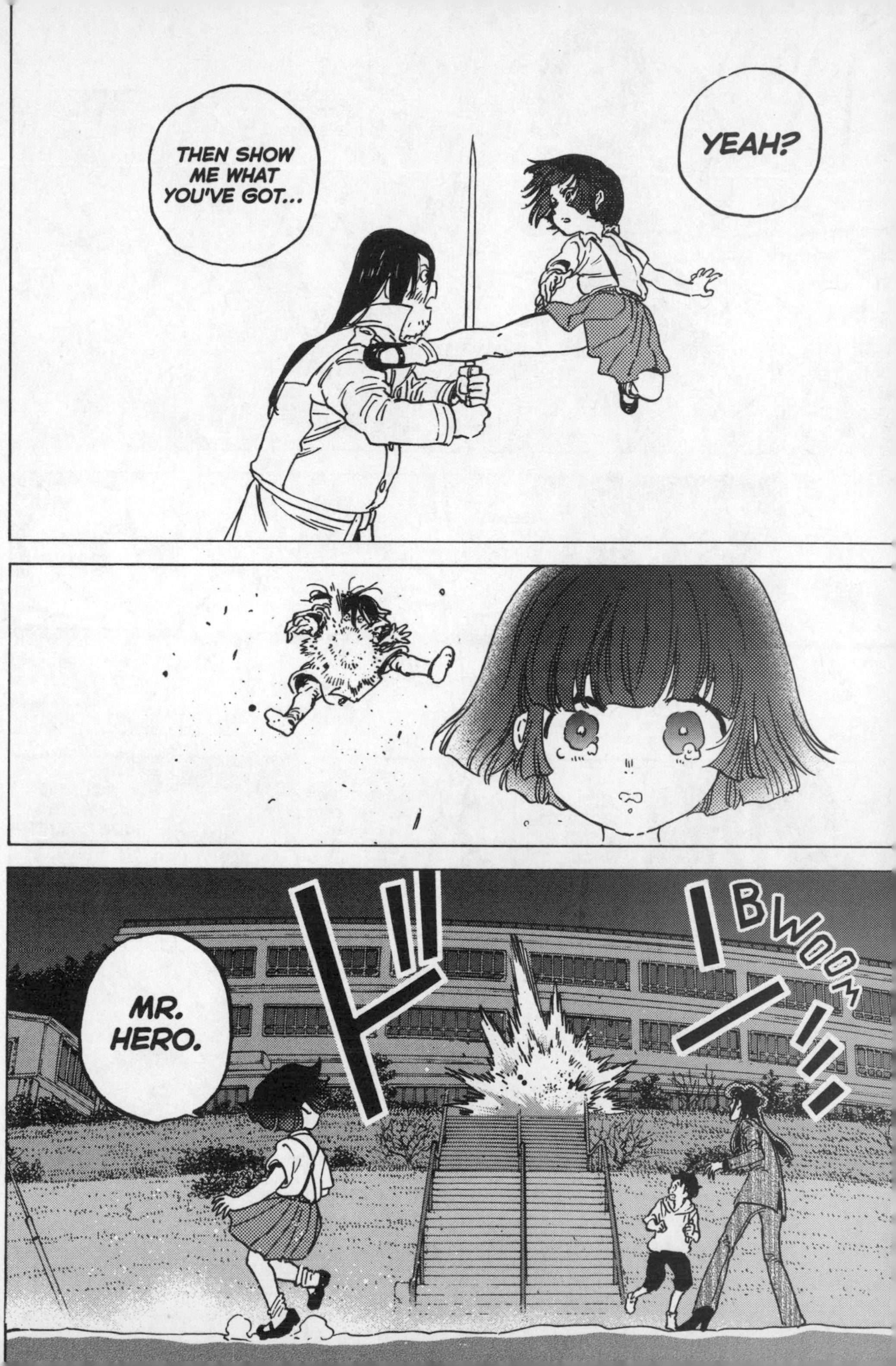
YEAH?
THEN SHOW ME WHAT YOU'VE GOT...
BWOOM
ド
MR. HERO.

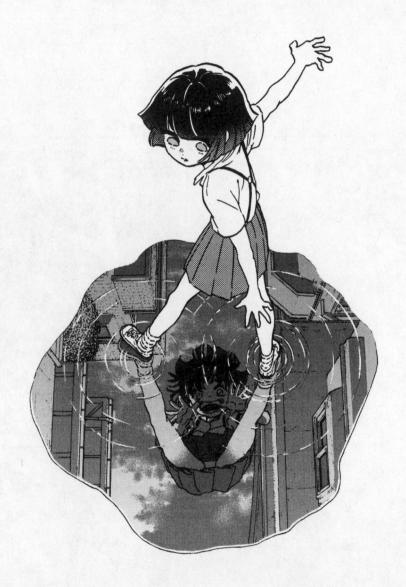

#137 A Say

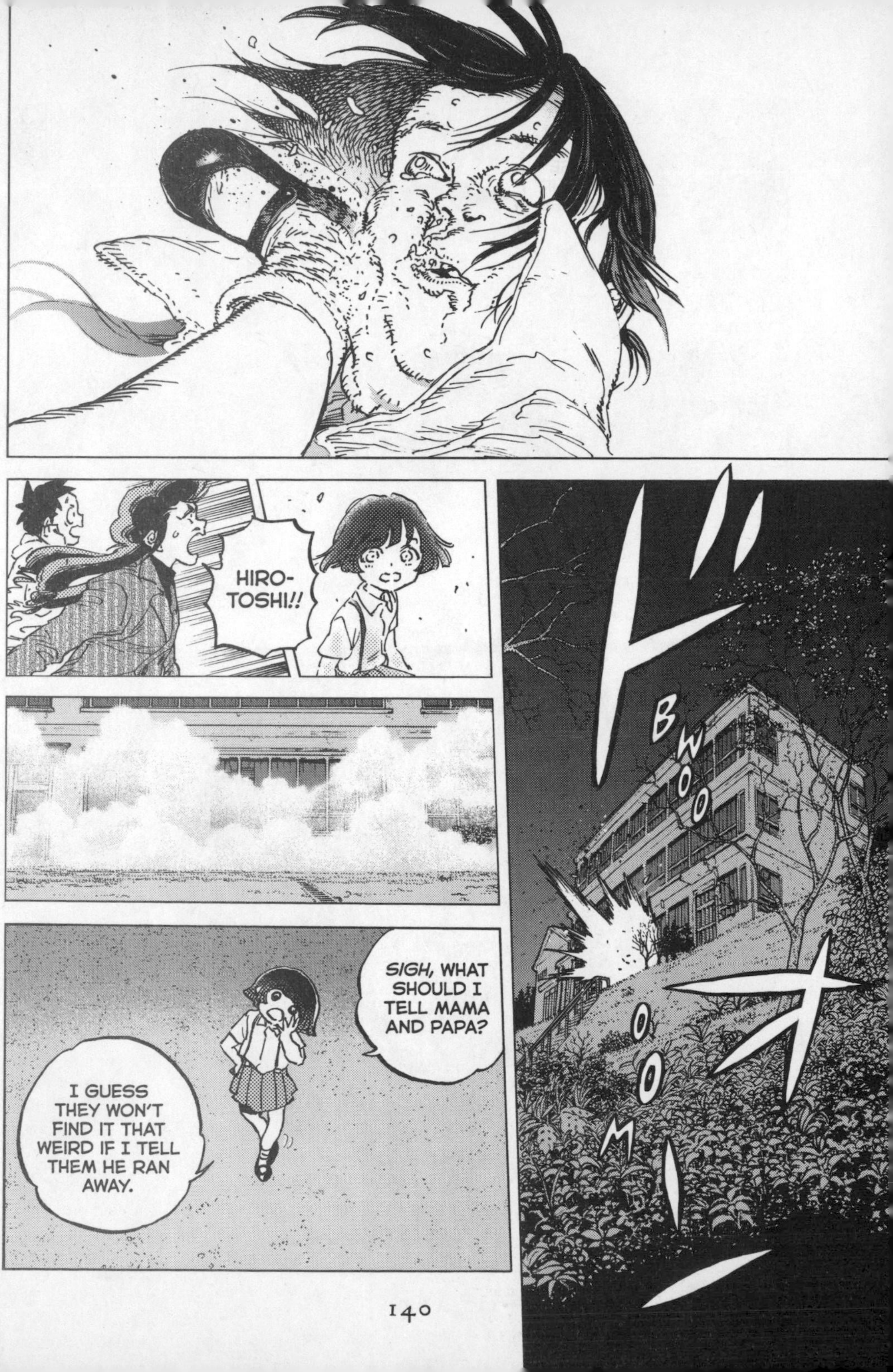
BWOOOOM
HIRO-TOSHI!!
SIGH, WHAT SHOULD I TELL MAMA AND PAPA?
I GUESS THEY WON'T FIND IT THAT WEIRD IF I TELL THEM HE RAN AWAY.

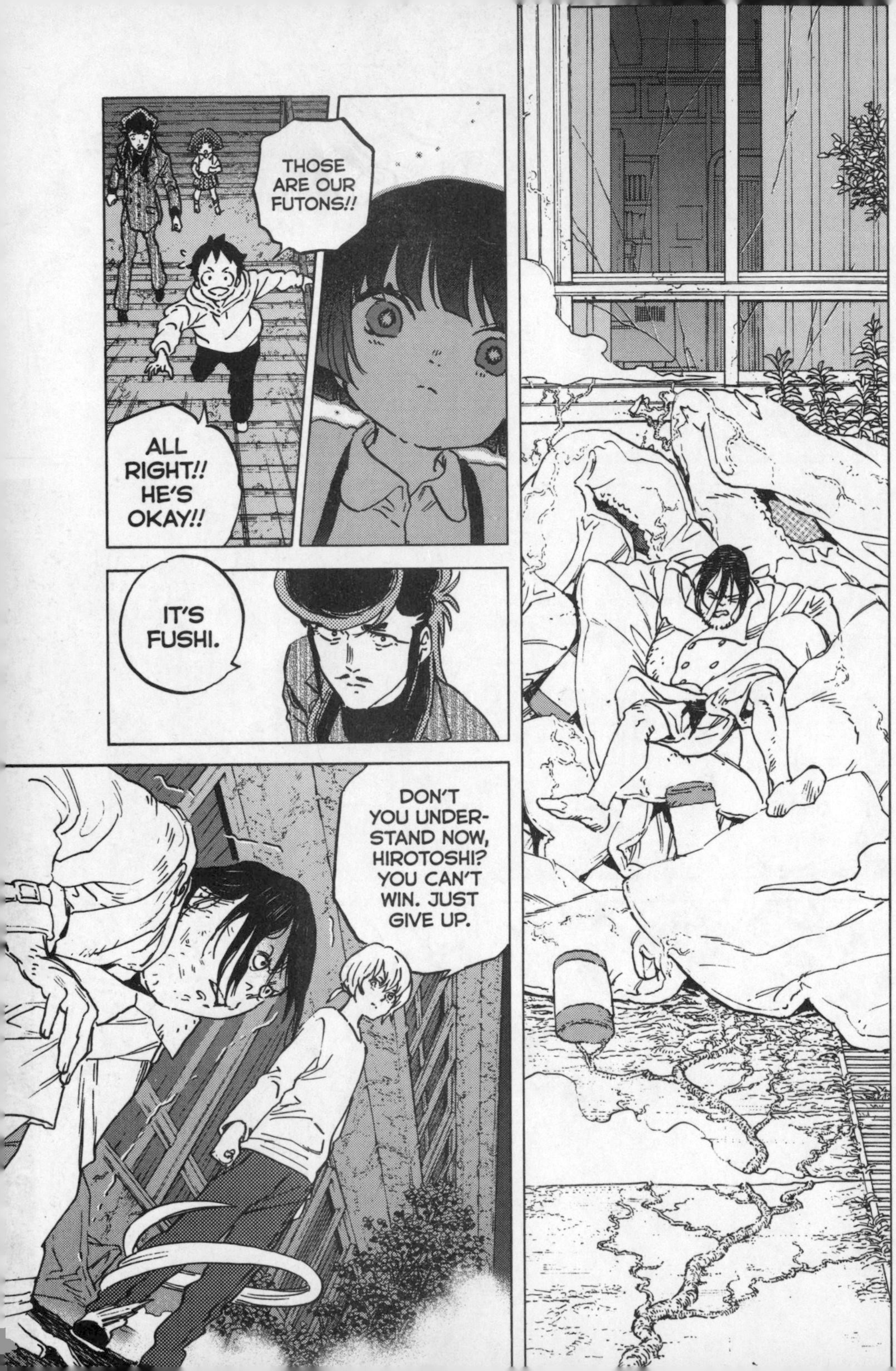
THOSE ARE OUR FUTONS!!
ALL RIGHT!! HE'S OKAY!!
IT'S FUSHI.
DON'T YOU UNDERSTAND NOW, HIROTOSHI? YOU CAN'T WIN. JUST GIVE UP.

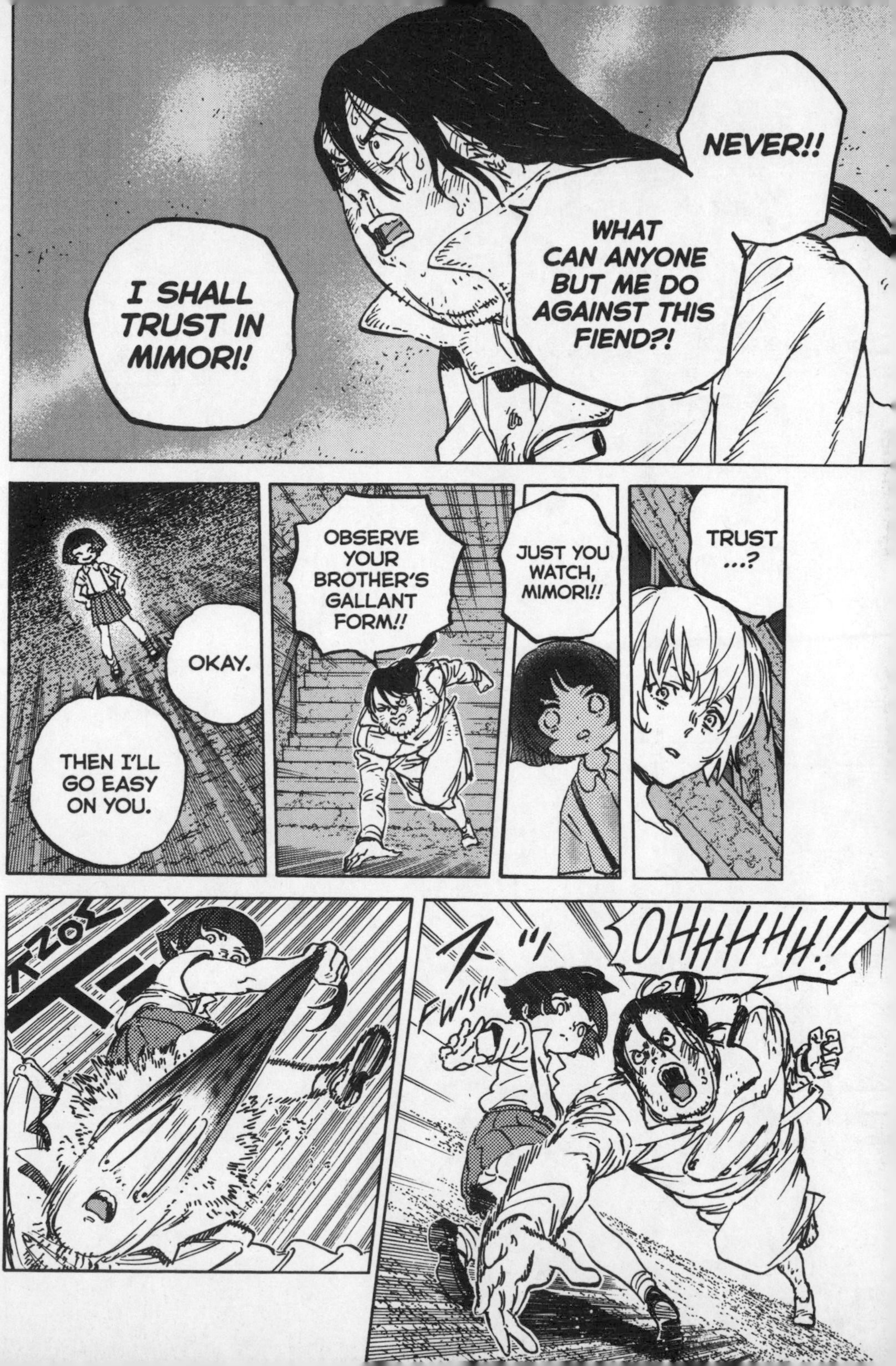
NEVER!!
WHAT CAN ANYONE BUT ME DO AGAINST THIS FIEND?!
I SHALL TRUST IN MIMORI!
TRUST ...?
JUST YOU WATCH, MIMORI!!
OBSERVE YOUR BROTHER'S GALLANT FORM!!
OKAY.
THEN I'LL GO EASY ON YOU.
OHHHHHH!!
FWISH

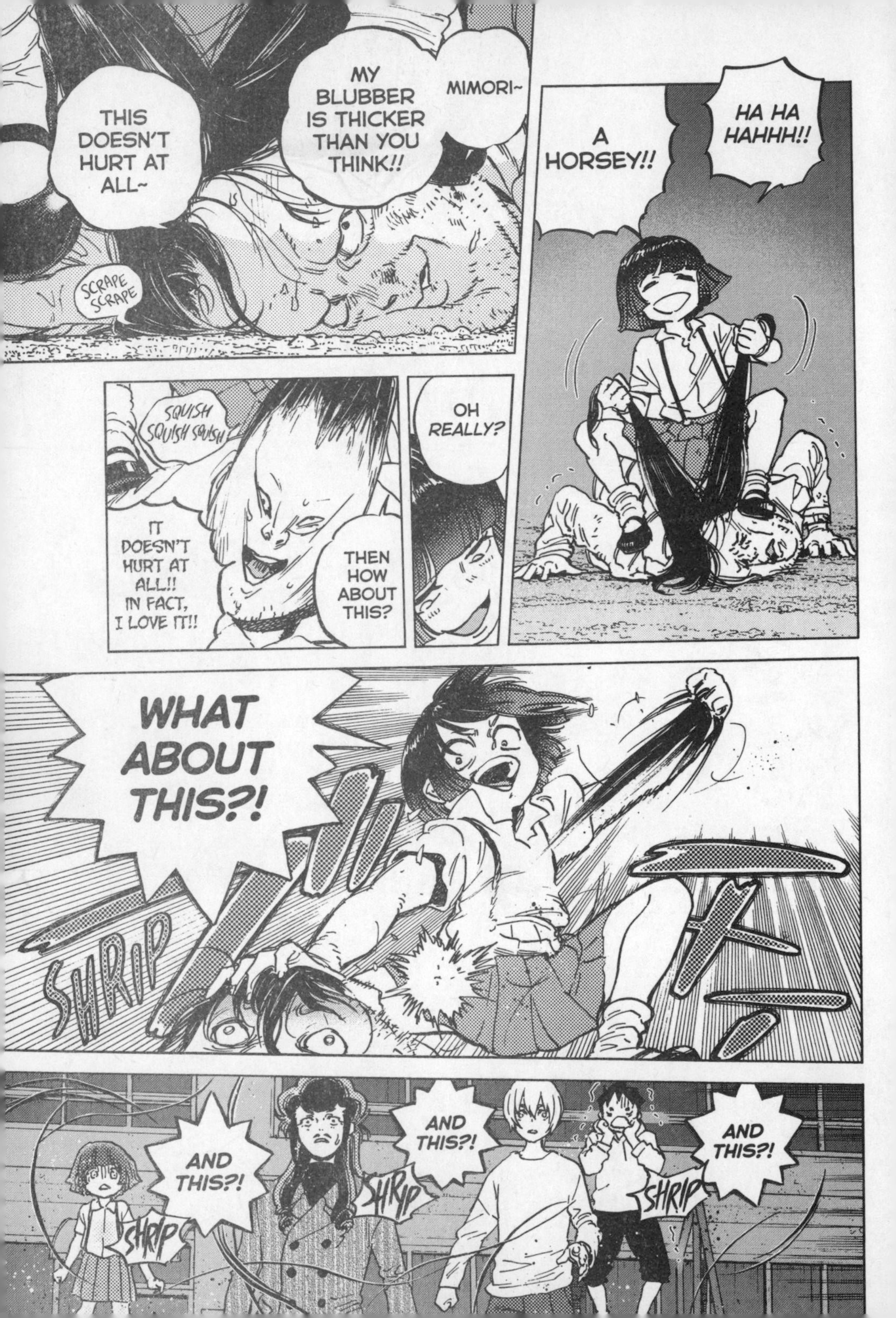
HA HA HAHHH!!
A HORSEY!!
MIMORI~
MY BLUBBER IS THICKER THAN YOU THINK!!
THIS DOESN'T HURT AT ALL~
SCRAPE SCRAPE
OH REALLY?
THEN HOW ABOUT THIS?
SQUISH SQUISH SQUISH
IT DOESN'T HURT AT ALL!! IN FACT, I LOVE IT!!
WHAT ABOUT THIS?!
SHRIP
AND THIS?!
SHRIP
AND THIS?!
SHRIP
AND THIS?!
SHRIP

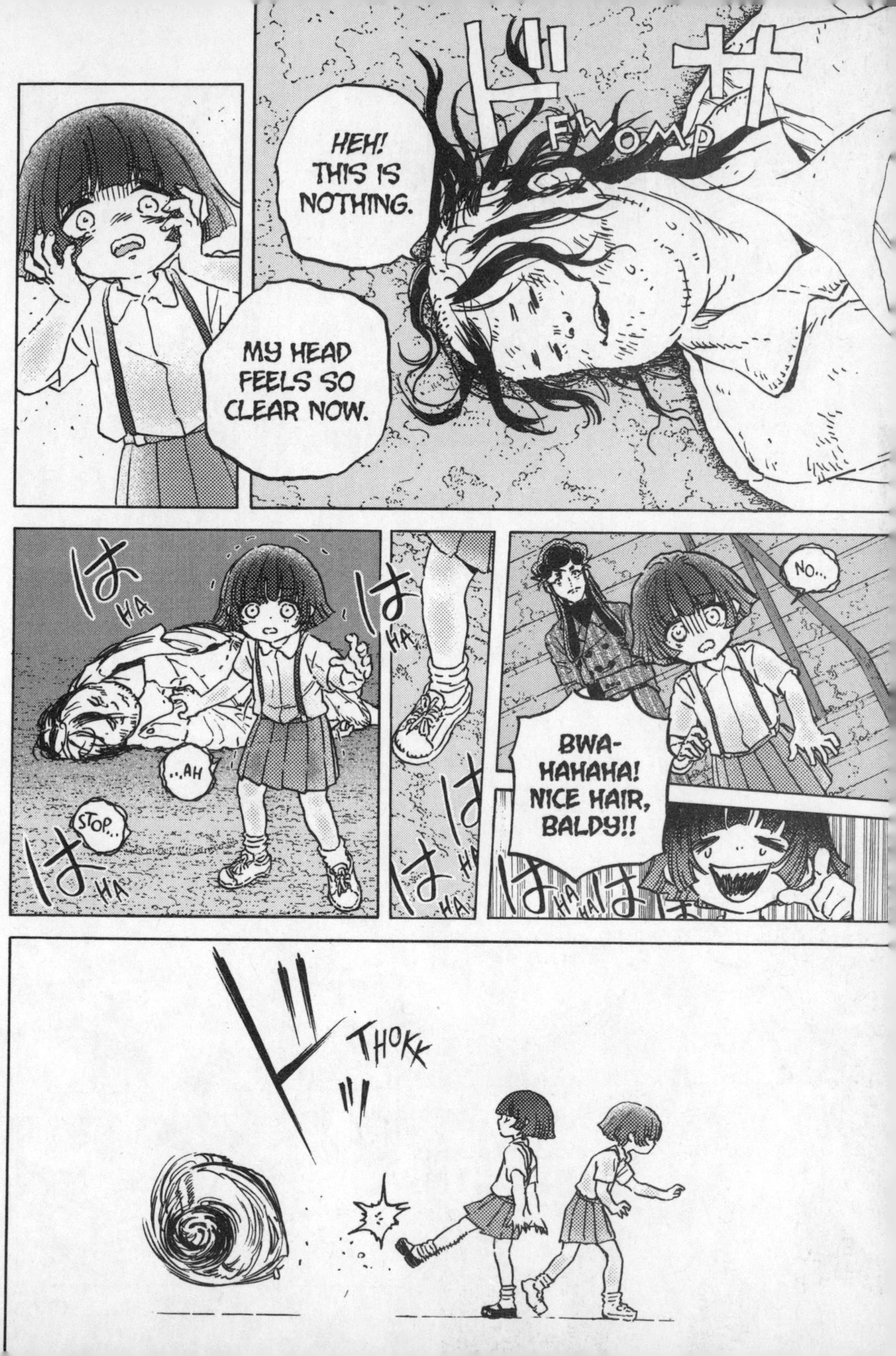

ドサ
FWOMP
HEH! THIS IS NOTHING.
MY HEAD FEELS SO CLEAR NOW.
NO...
BWA-HAHAHA! NICE HAIR, BALDY!!
はははは
HA HA HA
はは
HA HA
はは
HA HA
...AH
STOP...
ド
THOKK

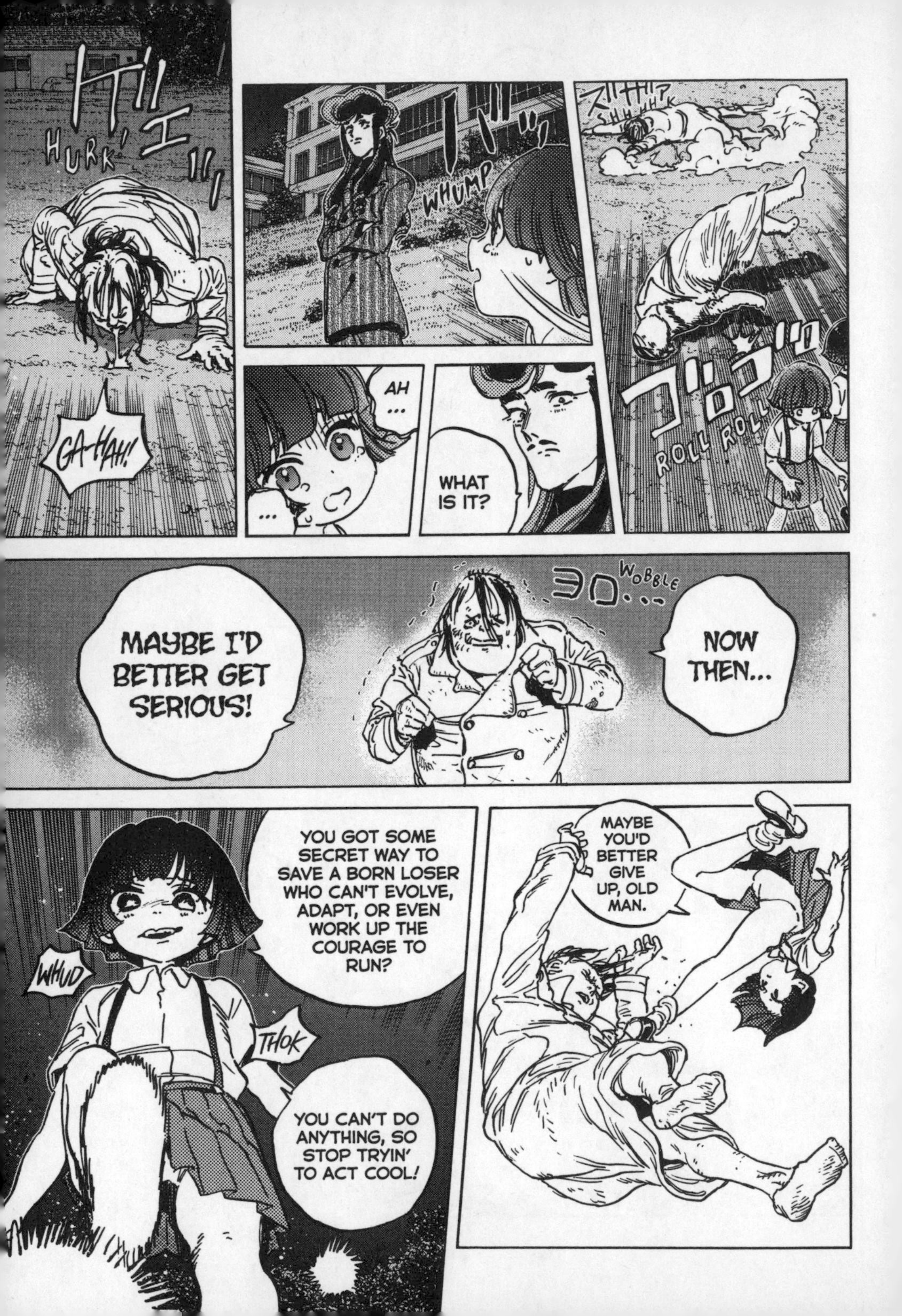
SHHHHK
ゴロゴロ
ROLL ROLL
WHUMP
WHAT IS IT?
AH ...
...
HURK!
GA-HAH!
ヨロ...
WOBBLE
NOW THEN...
MAYBE I'D BETTER GET SERIOUS!
MAYBE YOU'D BETTER GIVE UP, OLD MAN.
YOU GOT SOME SECRET WAY TO SAVE A BORN LOSER WHO CAN'T EVOLVE, ADAPT, OR EVEN WORK UP THE COURAGE TO RUN?
WHUD
THOK
YOU CAN'T DO ANYTHING, SO STOP TRYIN' TO ACT COOL!

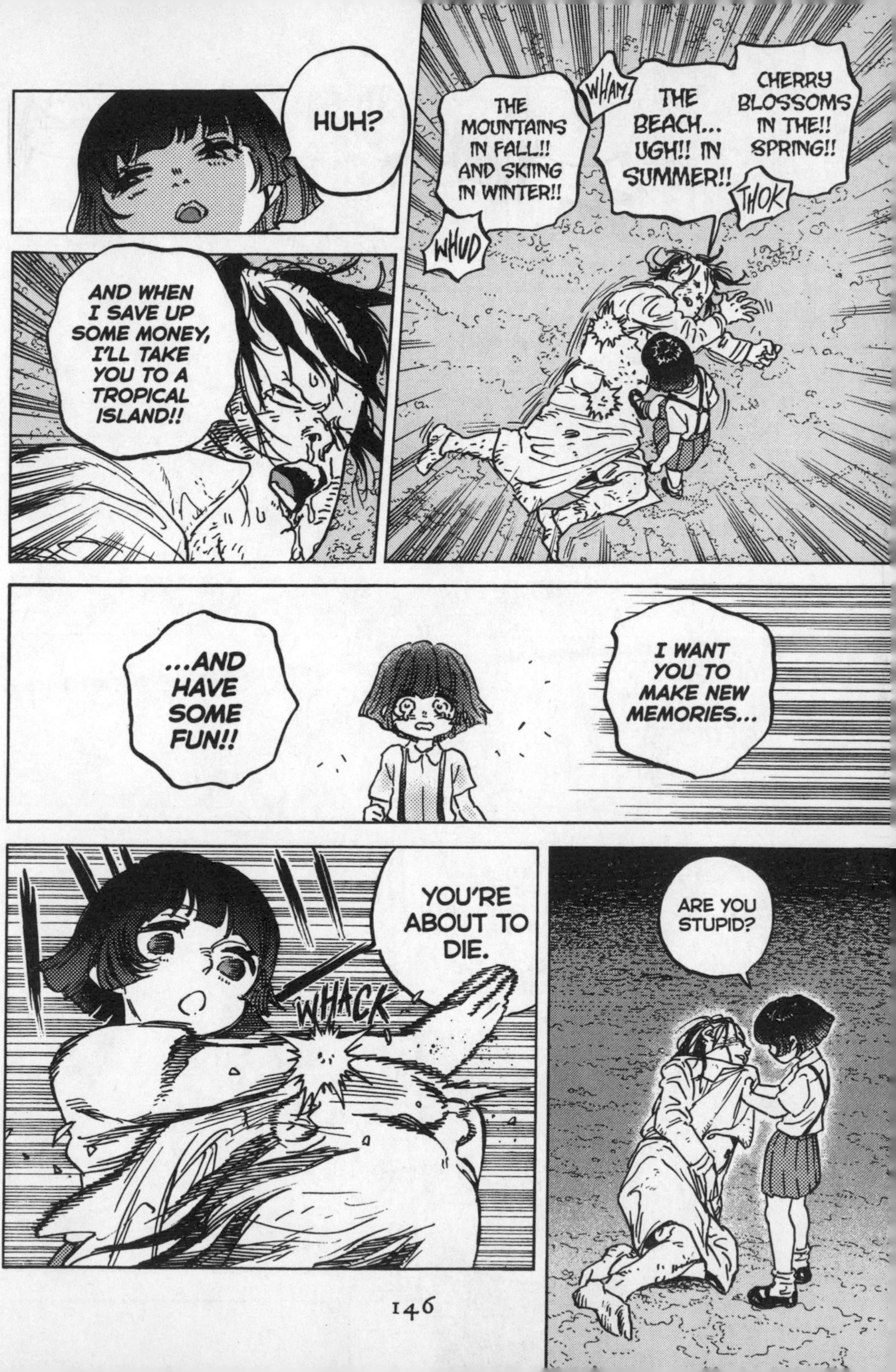

CHERRY BLOSSOMS IN THE!! SPRING!!
WHAM
THE BEACH... UGH!! IN SUMMER!!
THOK
THE MOUNTAINS IN FALL!! AND SKIING IN WINTER!!
WHUD
HUH?
AND WHEN I SAVE UP SOME MONEY, I'LL TAKE YOU TO A TROPICAL ISLAND!!
I WANT YOU TO MAKE NEW MEMORIES...
...AND HAVE SOME FUN!!
ARE YOU STUPID?
YOU'RE ABOUT TO DIE.
WHACK

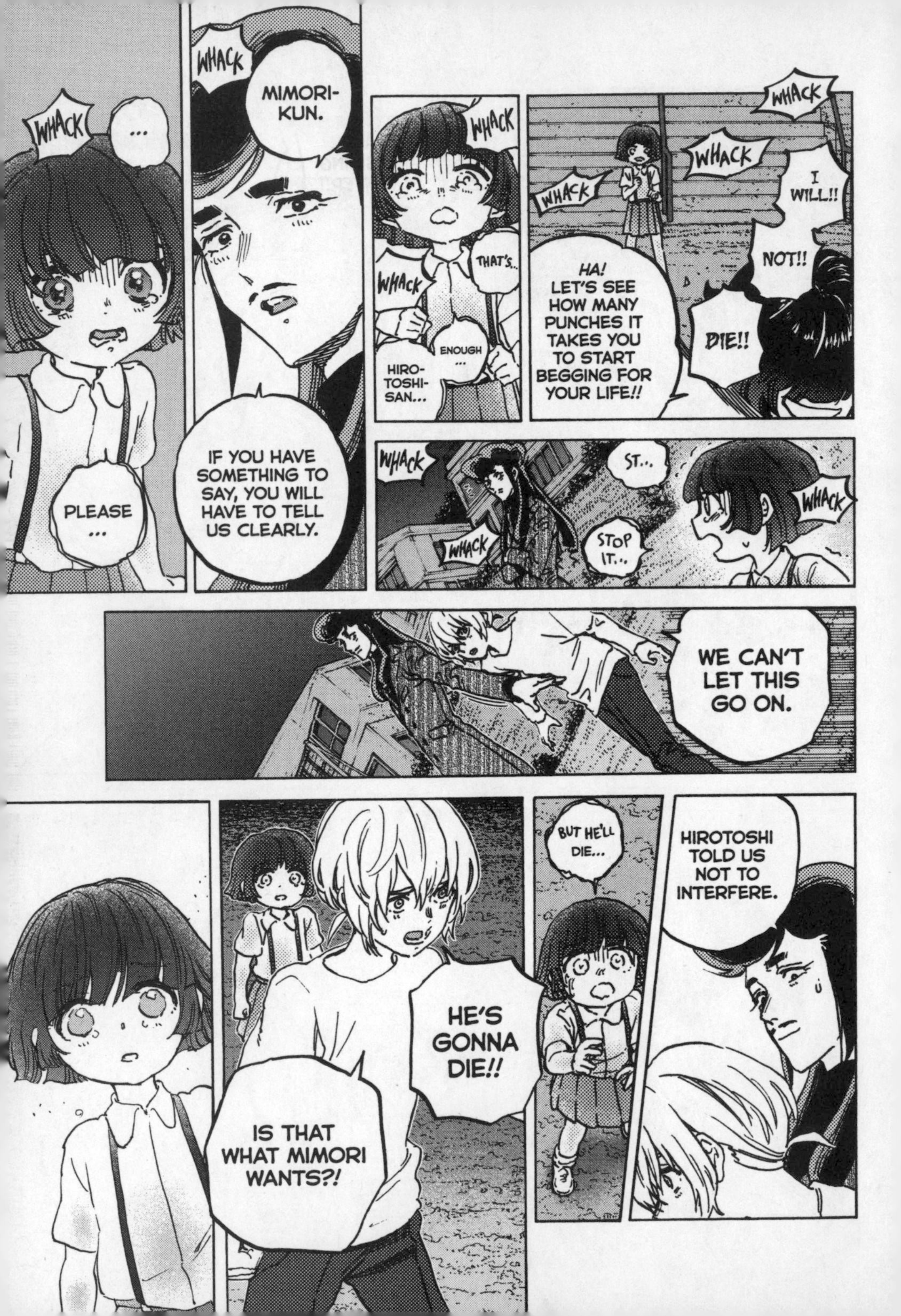
WHACK
WHACK
WHACK
I WILL!!
NOT!!
DIE!!
HA! LET'S SEE HOW MANY PUNCHES IT TAKES YOU TO START BEGGING FOR YOUR LIFE!!
WHACK
WHACK
THAT'S...
ENOUGH...
HIROTOSHI-SAN...
WHACK
ST...
WHACK
STOP IT...
WHACK
WHACK
MIMORI-KUN.
IF YOU HAVE SOMETHING TO SAY, YOU WILL HAVE TO TELL US CLEARLY.
WHACK
...
PLEASE...
WE CAN'T LET THIS GO ON.
HIROTOSHI TOLD US NOT TO INTERFERE.
BUT HE'LL DIE...
HE'S GONNA DIE!!
IS THAT WHAT MIMORI WANTS?!

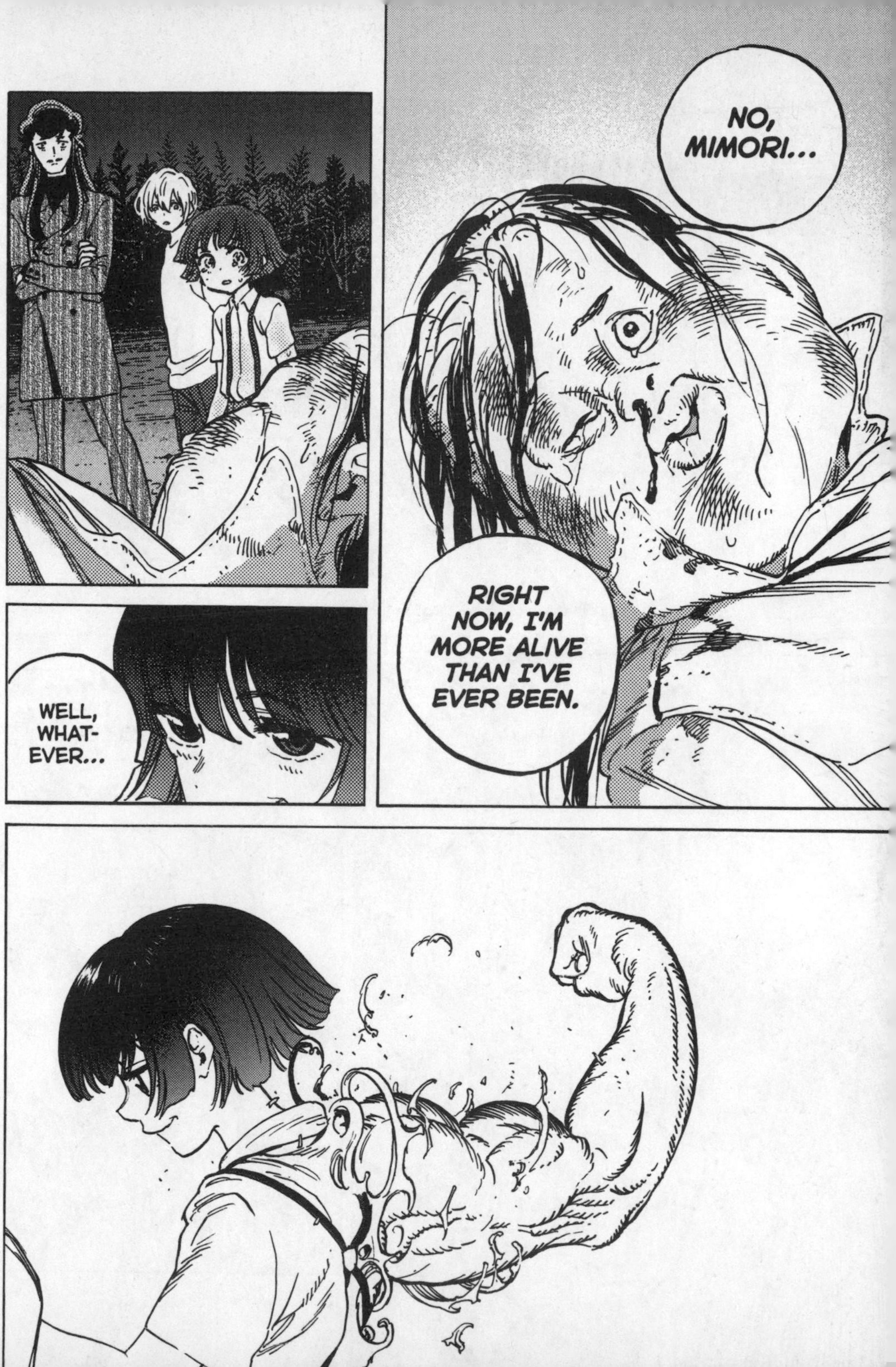
NO, MIMORI...
RIGHT NOW, I'M MORE ALIVE THAN I'VE EVER BEEN.
WELL, WHATEVER...

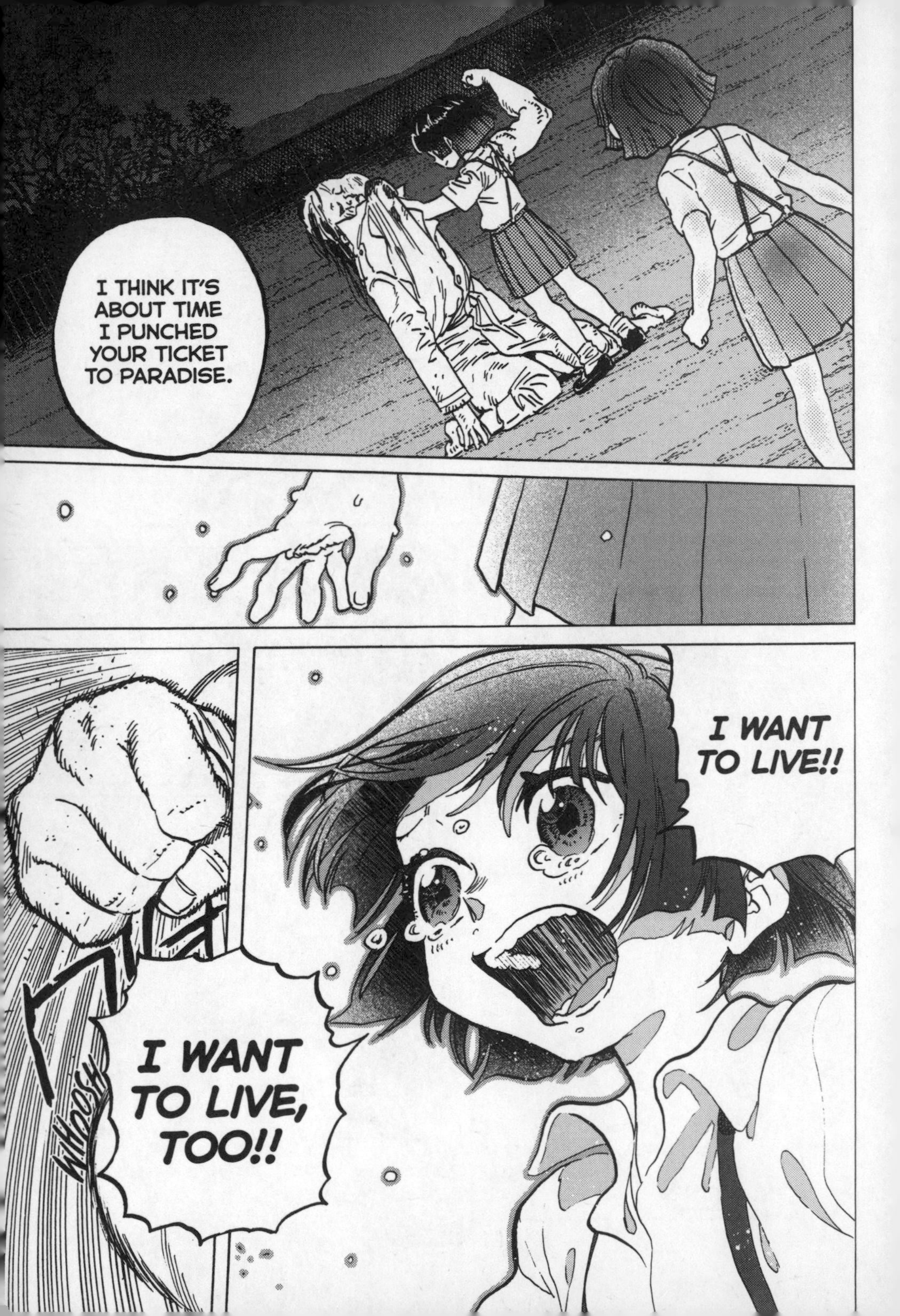
I THINK IT'S ABOUT TIME I PUNCHED YOUR TICKET TO PARADISE.
I WANT TO LIVE!!
I WANT TO LIVE, TOO!!
WHOOSH

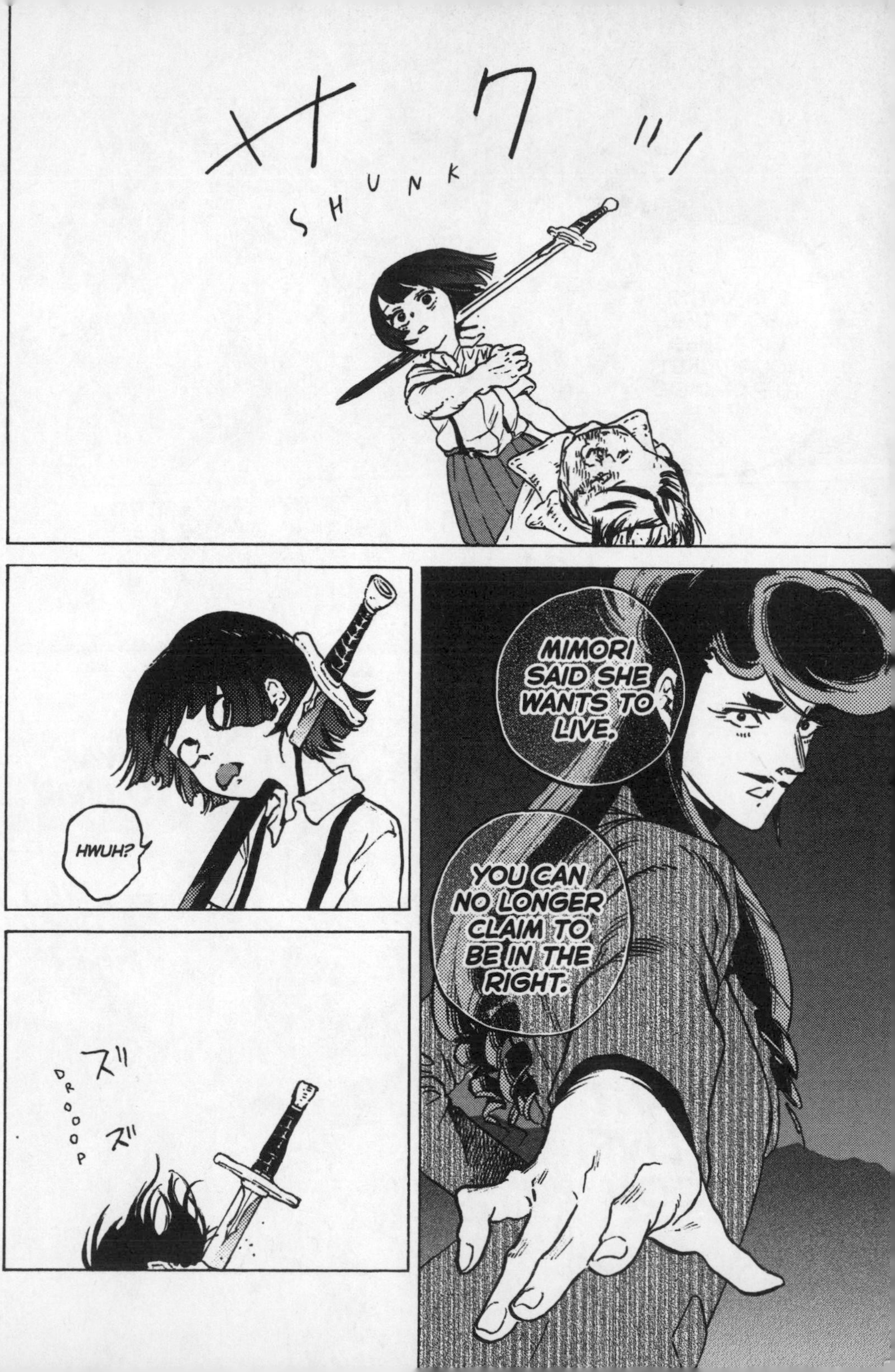
SHUNK
MIMORI SAID SHE WANTS TO LIVE.
YOU CAN NO LONGER CLAIM TO BE IN THE RIGHT.
HWUH?
DROOOP

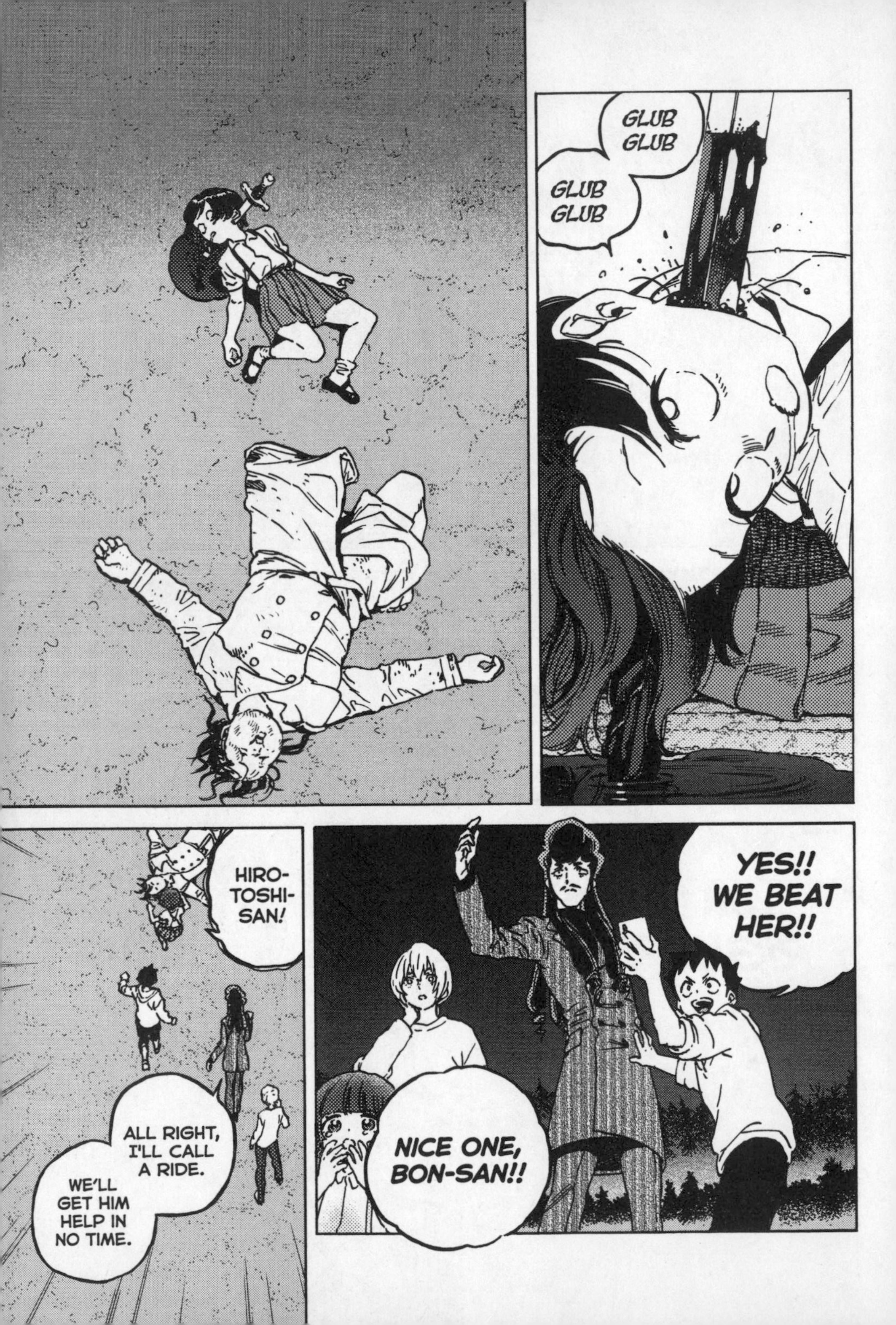
GLUB GLUB
GLUB GLUB
YES!! WE BEAT HER!!
NICE ONE, BON-SAN!!
HIRO-TOSHI-SAN!
ALL RIGHT, I'LL CALL A RIDE.
WE'LL GET HIM HELP IN NO TIME.

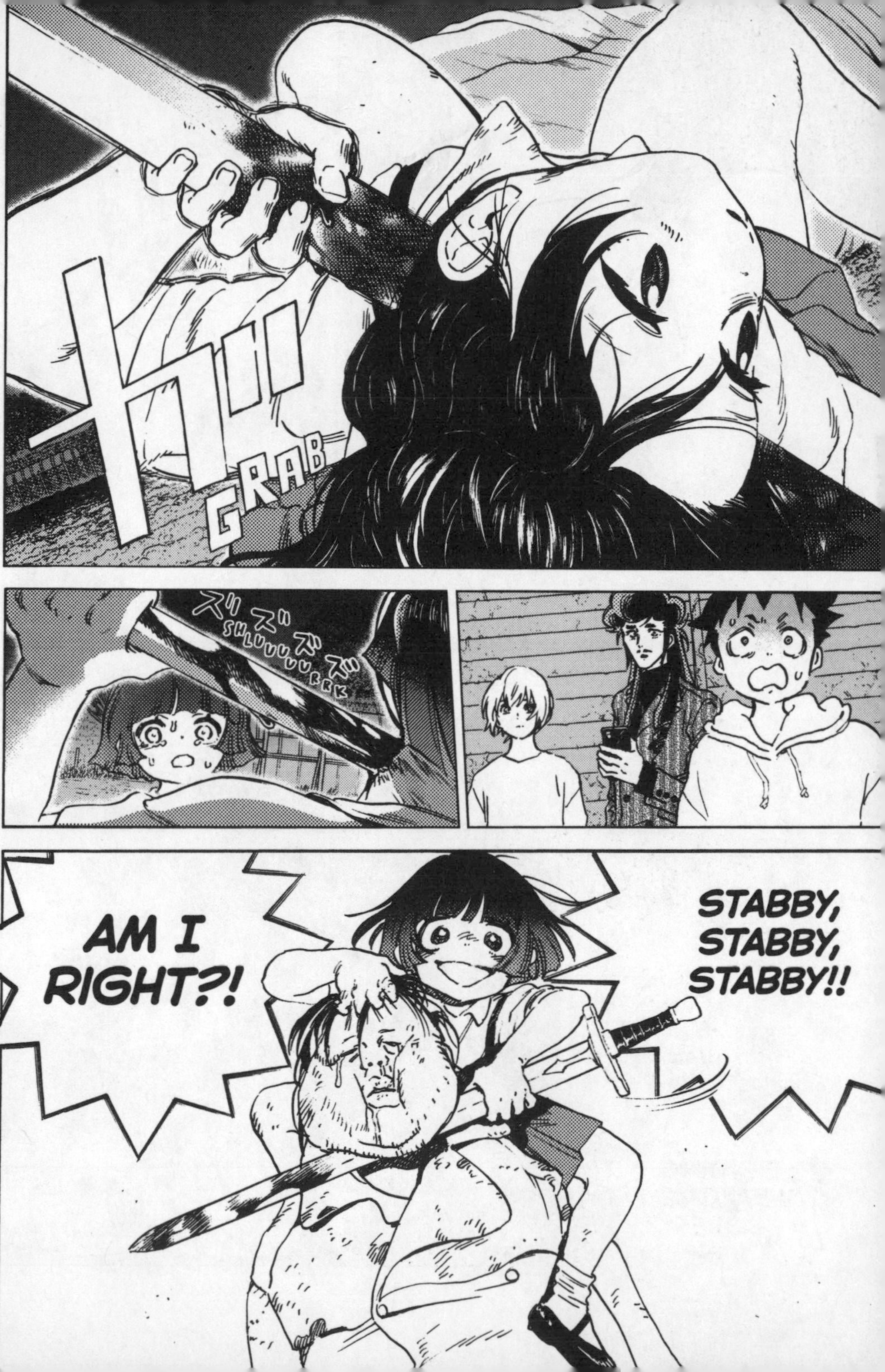
GRAB
SHLUUUUURRK
STABBY, STABBY, STABBY!!
AM I RIGHT?!

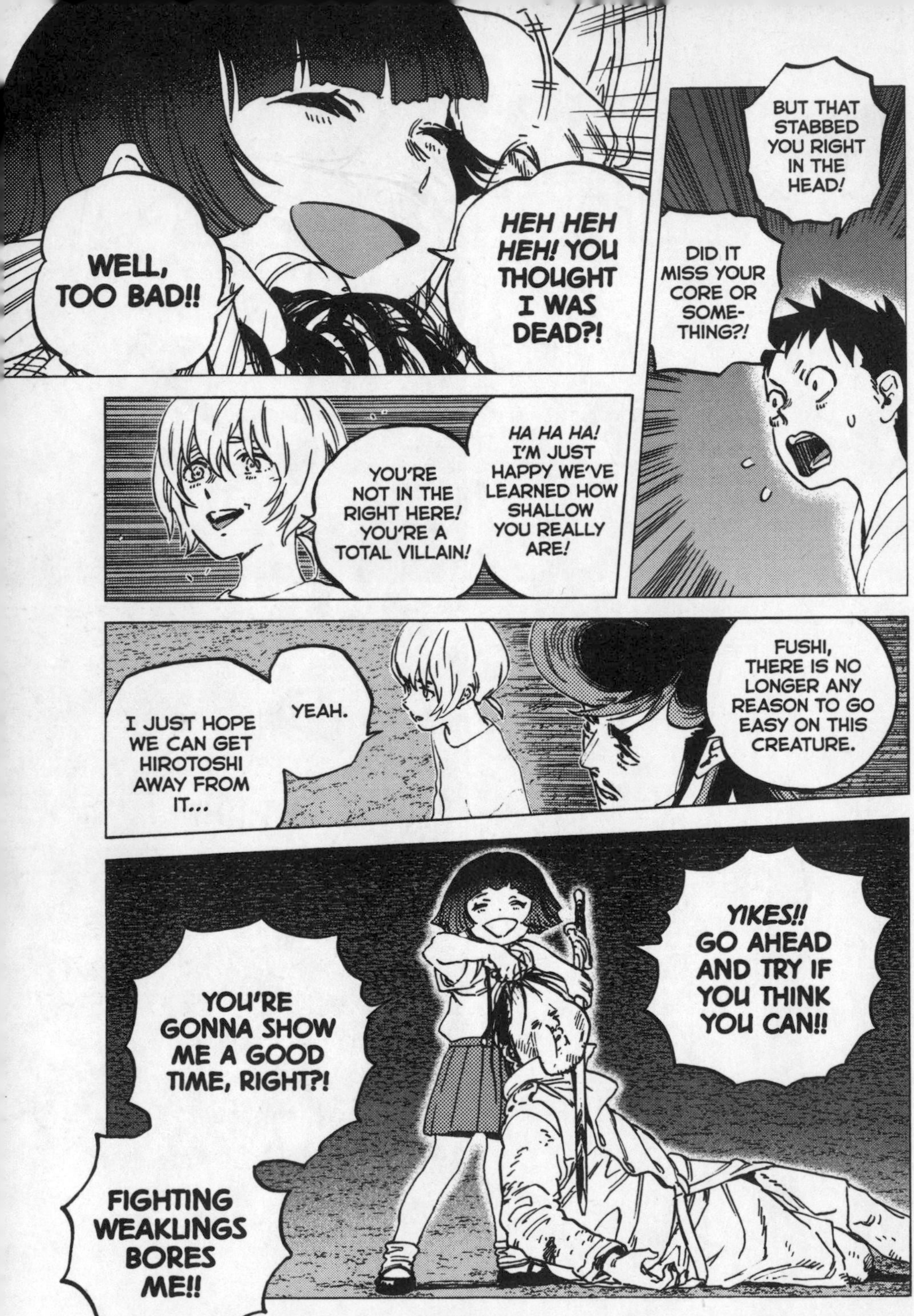
BUT THAT STABBED YOU RIGHT IN THE HEAD!
DID IT MISS YOUR CORE OR SOME-THING?!
HEH HEH HEH! YOU THOUGHT I WAS DEAD?!
WELL, TOO BAD!!
HA HA HA! I'M JUST HAPPY WE'VE LEARNED HOW SHALLOW YOU REALLY ARE!
YOU'RE NOT IN THE RIGHT HERE! YOU'RE A TOTAL VILLAIN!
FUSHI, THERE IS NO LONGER ANY REASON TO GO EASY ON THIS CREATURE.
YEAH.
I JUST HOPE WE CAN GET HIROTOSHI AWAY FROM IT...
YIKES!! GO AHEAD AND TRY IF YOU THINK YOU CAN!!
YOU'RE GONNA SHOW ME A GOOD TIME, RIGHT?!
FIGHTING WEAKLINGS BORES ME!!

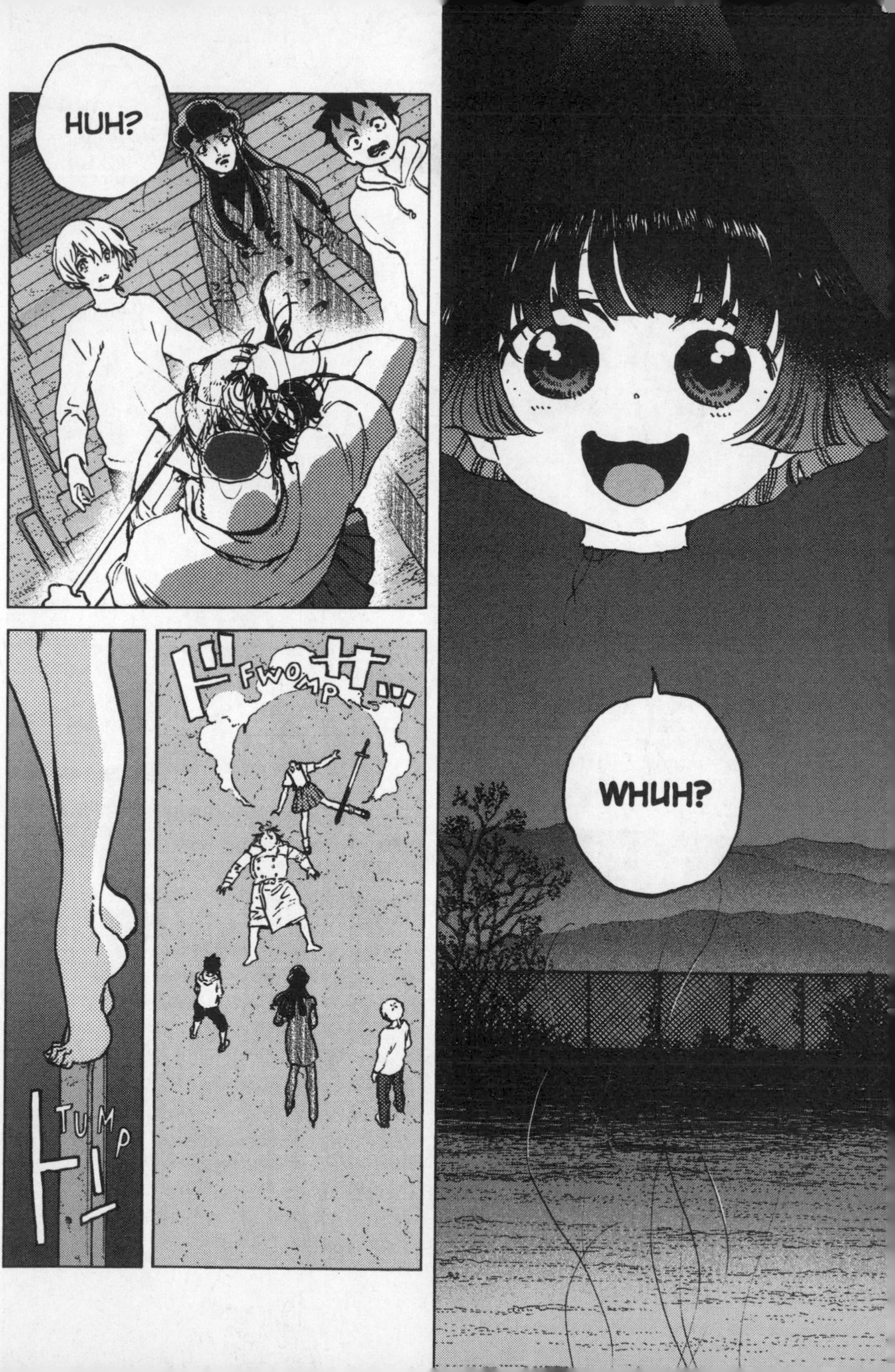
WHUH?
HUH?
FWOMP
TUMP

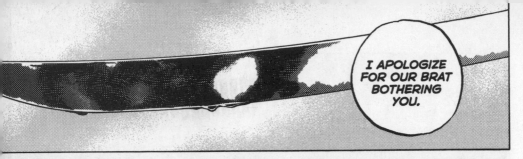

I APOLOGIZE FOR OUR BRAT BOTHERING YOU.

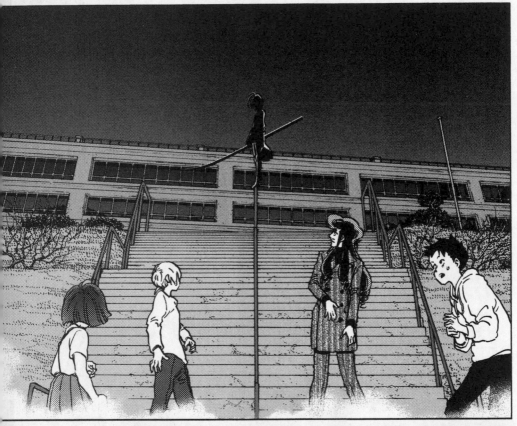

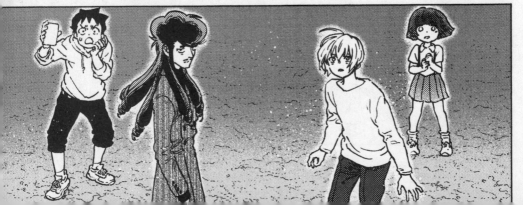

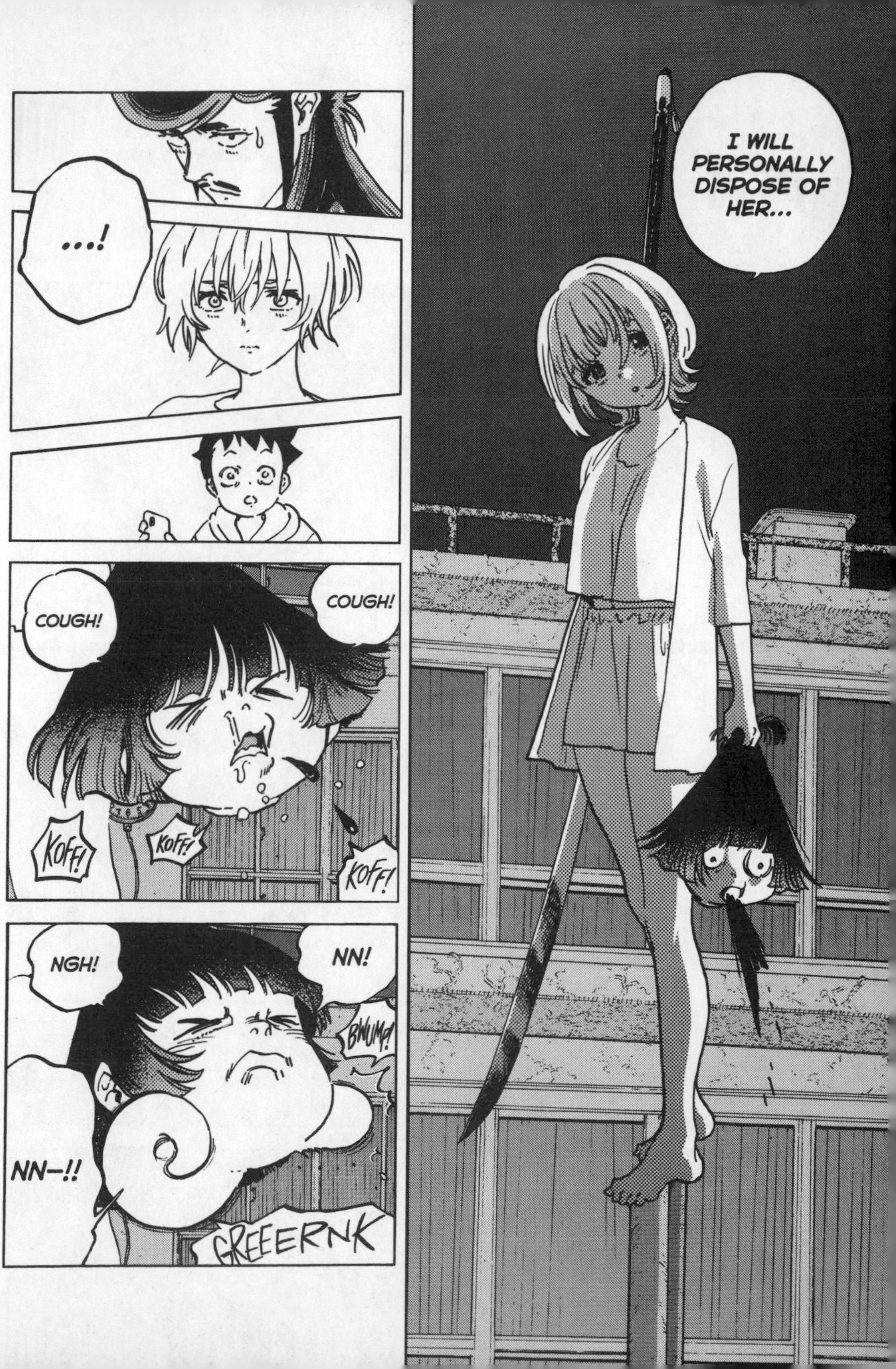
I WILL PERSONALLY DISPOSE OF HER...
...!
COUGH!
COUGH!
KOFF!
KOFF!
KOFF!
NN!
NGH!
BWUMP!
NN-!!
GREEERNK

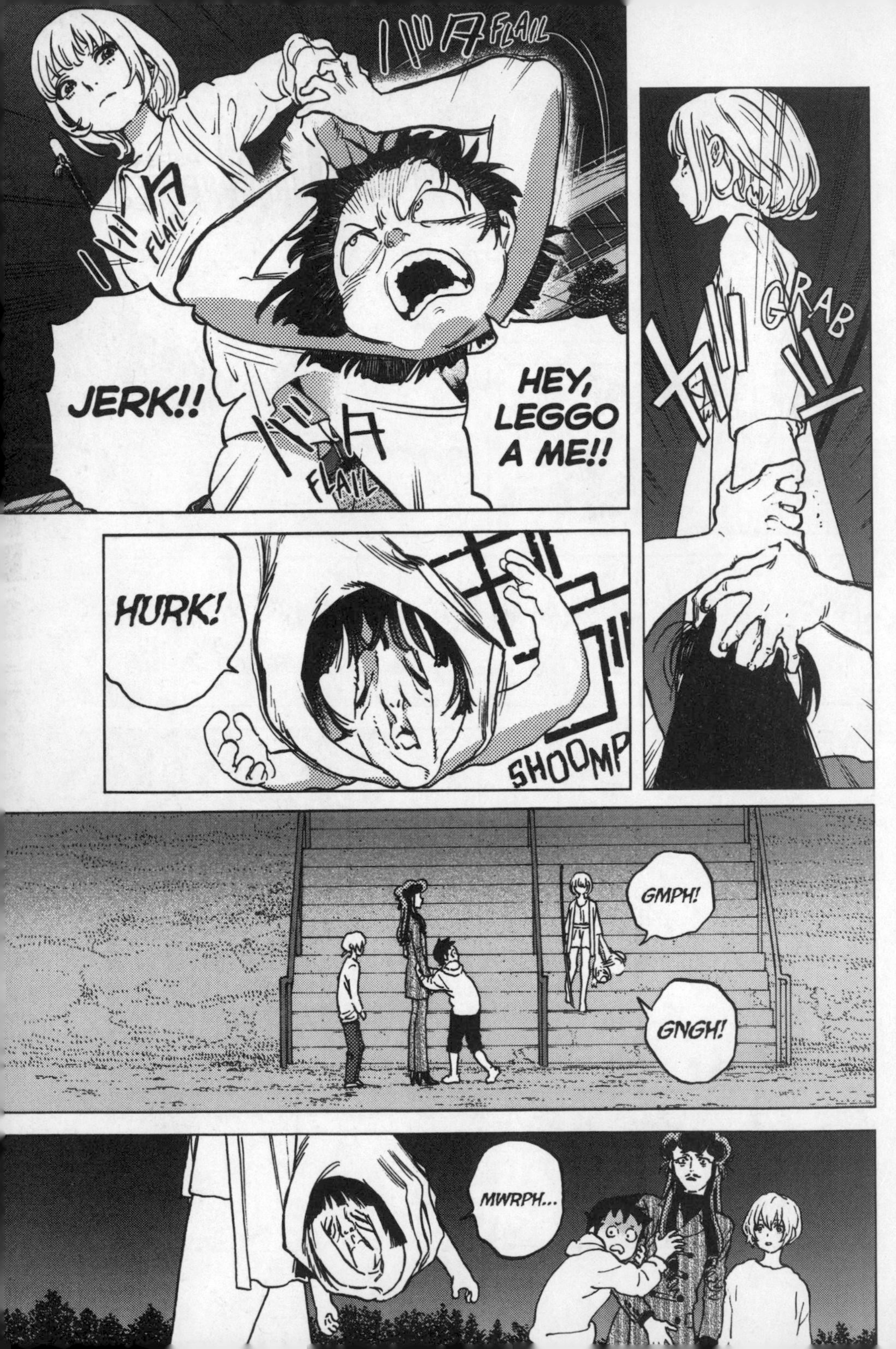
GRAB
FLAIL
HEY, LEGGO A ME!!
FLAIL
JERK!!
FLAIL
HURK!
SHOOMP
GMPH!
GNGH!
MWRPH...

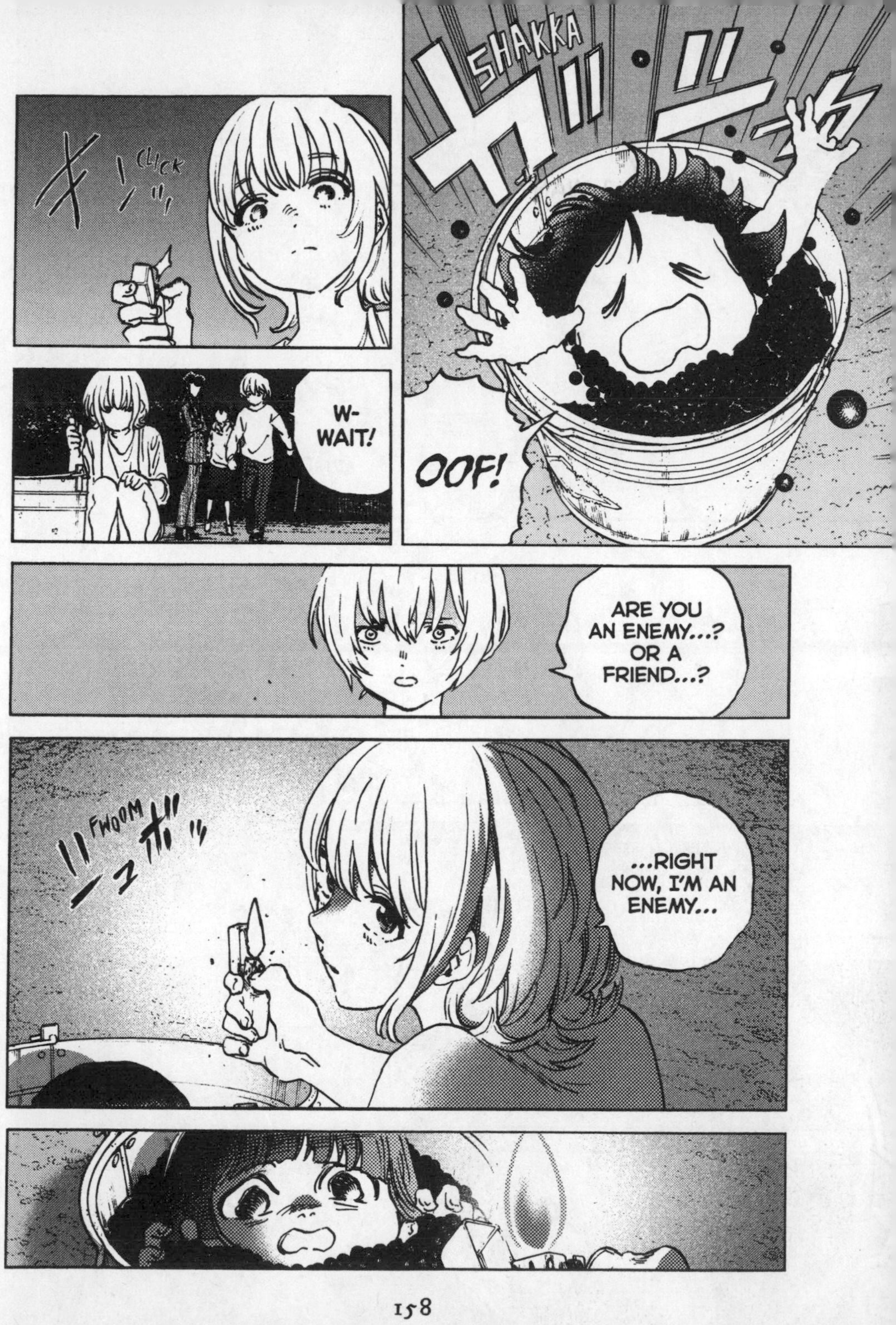
SHAKKA
OOF!
CLICK
W-WAIT!
ARE YOU AN ENEMY...? OR A FRIEND...?
FWOOM
...RIGHT NOW, I'M AN ENEMY...

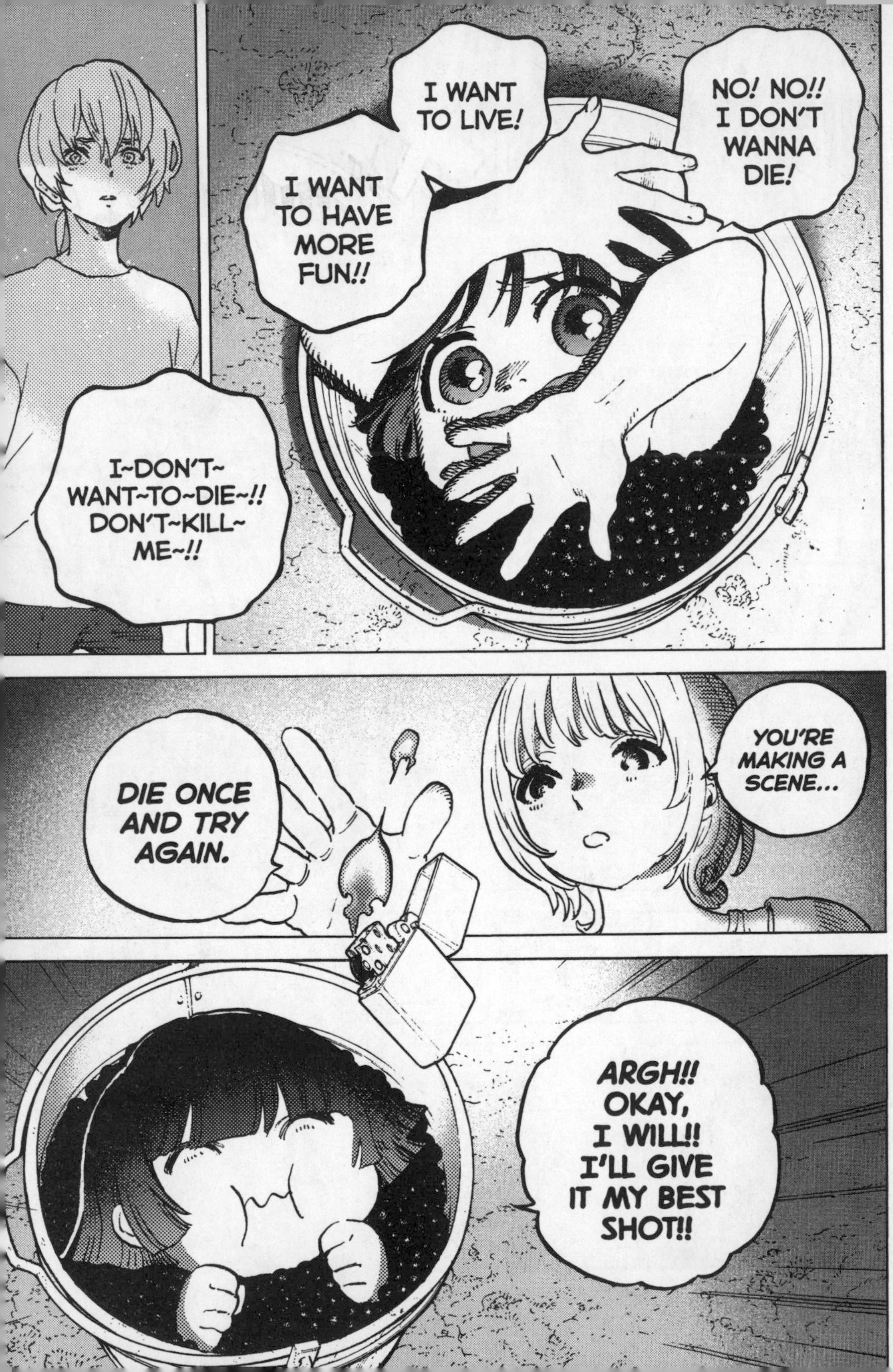
NO! NO!! I DON'T WANNA DIE!
I WANT TO LIVE!
I WANT TO HAVE MORE FUN!!
I~DON'T~WANT~TO~DIE~!! DON'T~KILL~ME~!!
YOU'RE MAKING A SCENE...
DIE ONCE AND TRY AGAIN.
ARGH!! OKAY, I WILL!! I'LL GIVE IT MY BEST SHOT!!

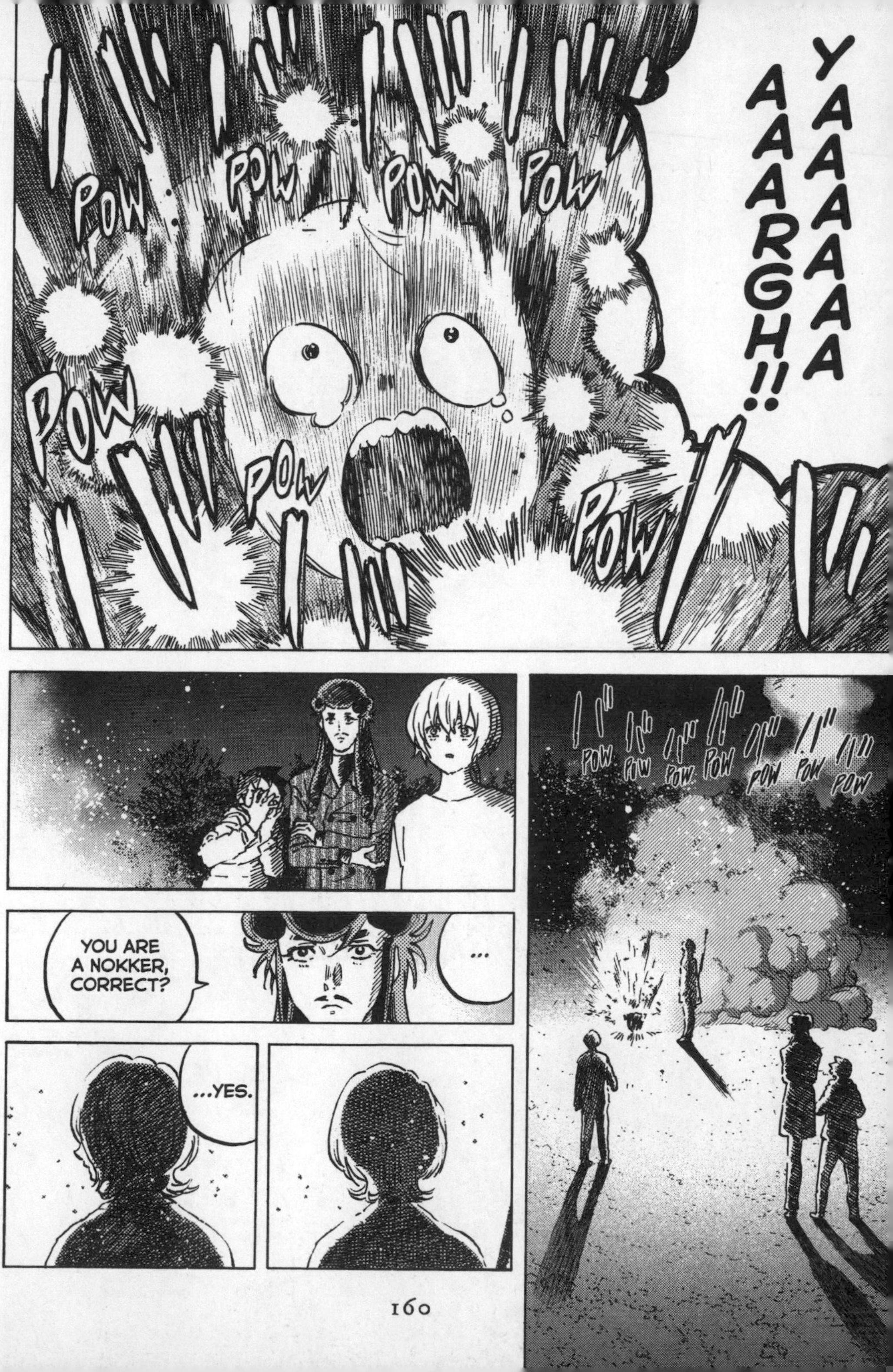
YAAAAAAAAARGH!!
POW
POW
POW
POW
POW
POW
POW
POW
POW
POW
POW
POW
POW
POW
POW
YOU ARE A NOKKER, CORRECT?
...
...YES.

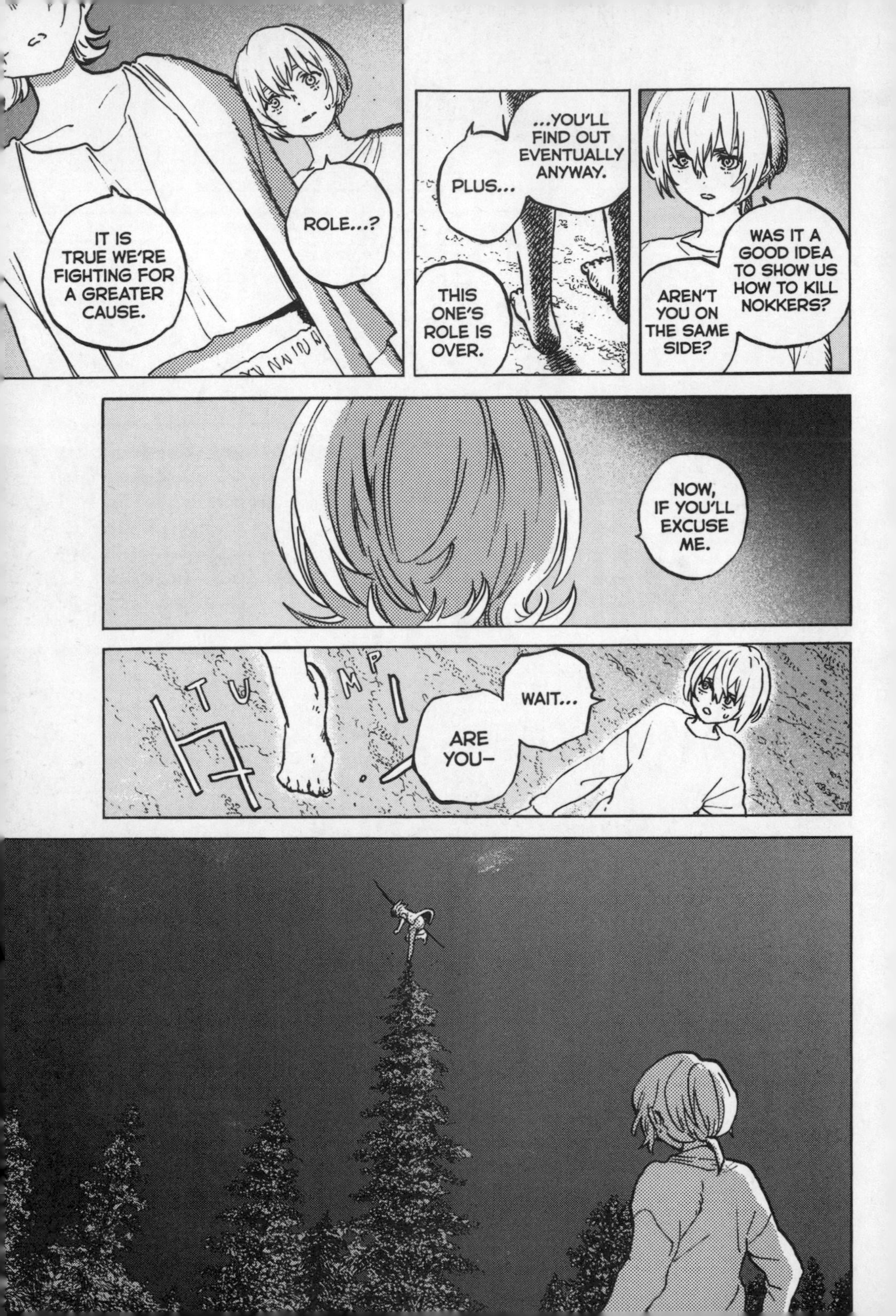
WAS IT A GOOD IDEA TO SHOW US HOW TO KILL NOKKERS?
AREN'T YOU ON THE SAME SIDE?
...YOU'LL FIND OUT EVENTUALLY ANYWAY.
PLUS...
THIS ONE'S ROLE IS OVER.
ROLE...?
IT IS TRUE WE'RE FIGHTING FOR A GREATER CAUSE.
NOW, IF YOU'LL EXCUSE ME.
WAIT...
ARE YOU–
TUMP!

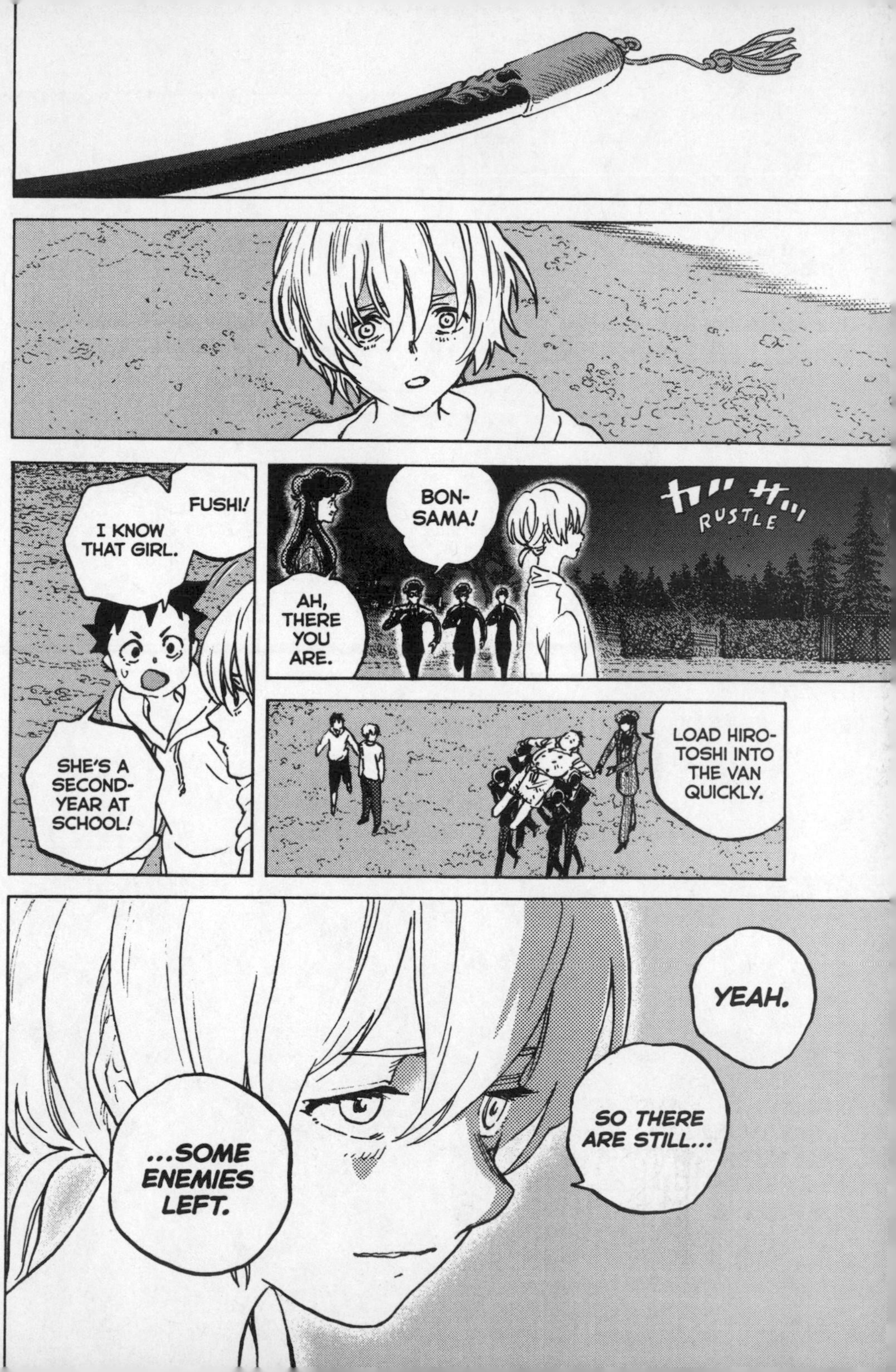
RUSTLE
BON-SAMA!
AH, THERE YOU ARE.
LOAD HIROTOSHI INTO THE VAN QUICKLY.
FUSHI! I KNOW THAT GIRL.
SHE'S A SECOND-YEAR AT SCHOOL!
YEAH.
SO THERE ARE STILL...
...SOME ENEMIES LEFT.

TO YOUR ETERNITY

TO YOUR ETERNITY

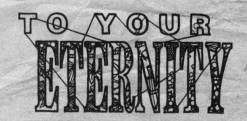

#138 Enemy's Den

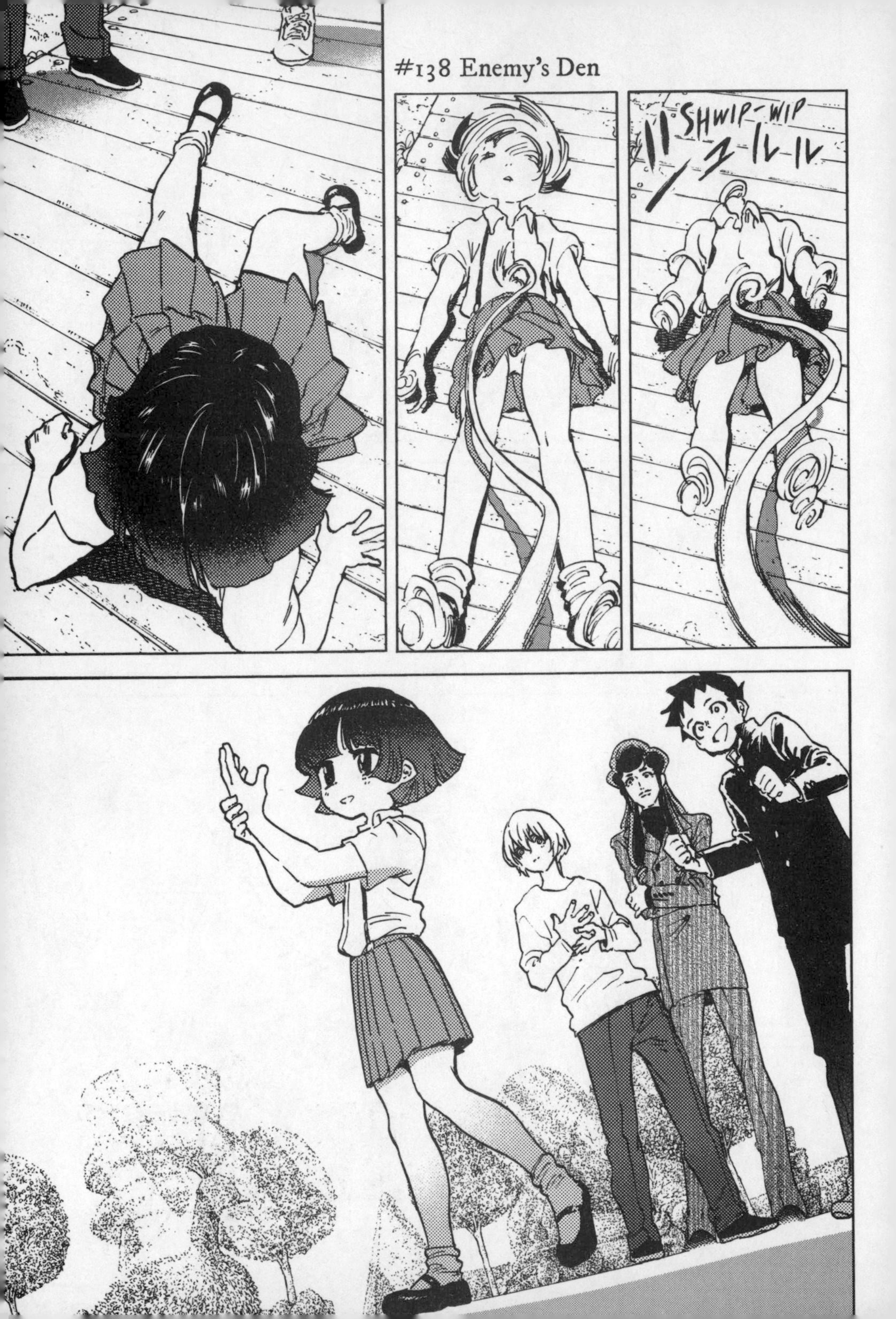
SHWIP-WIP

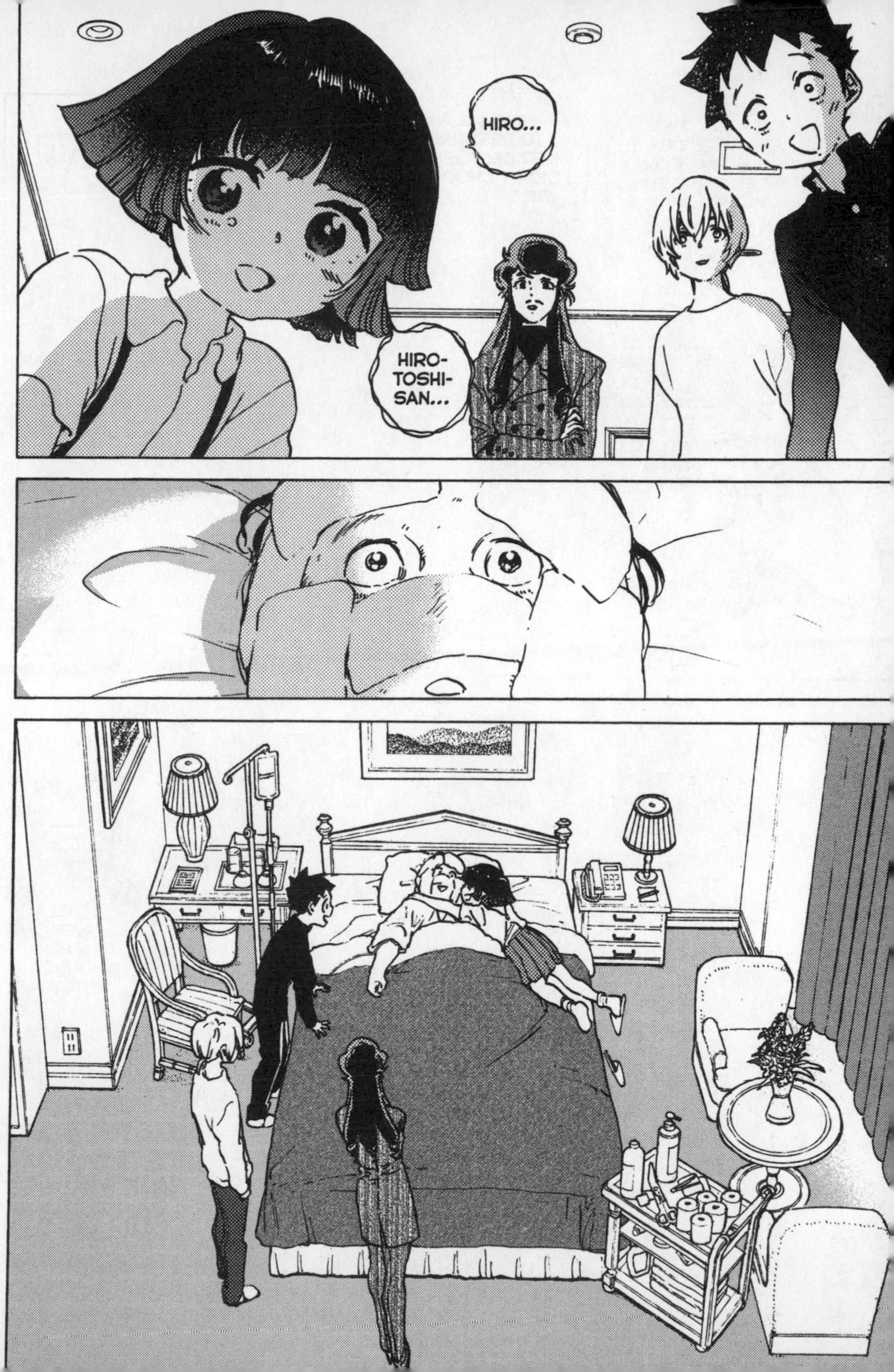
HIRO...
HIRO-TOSHI-SAN...

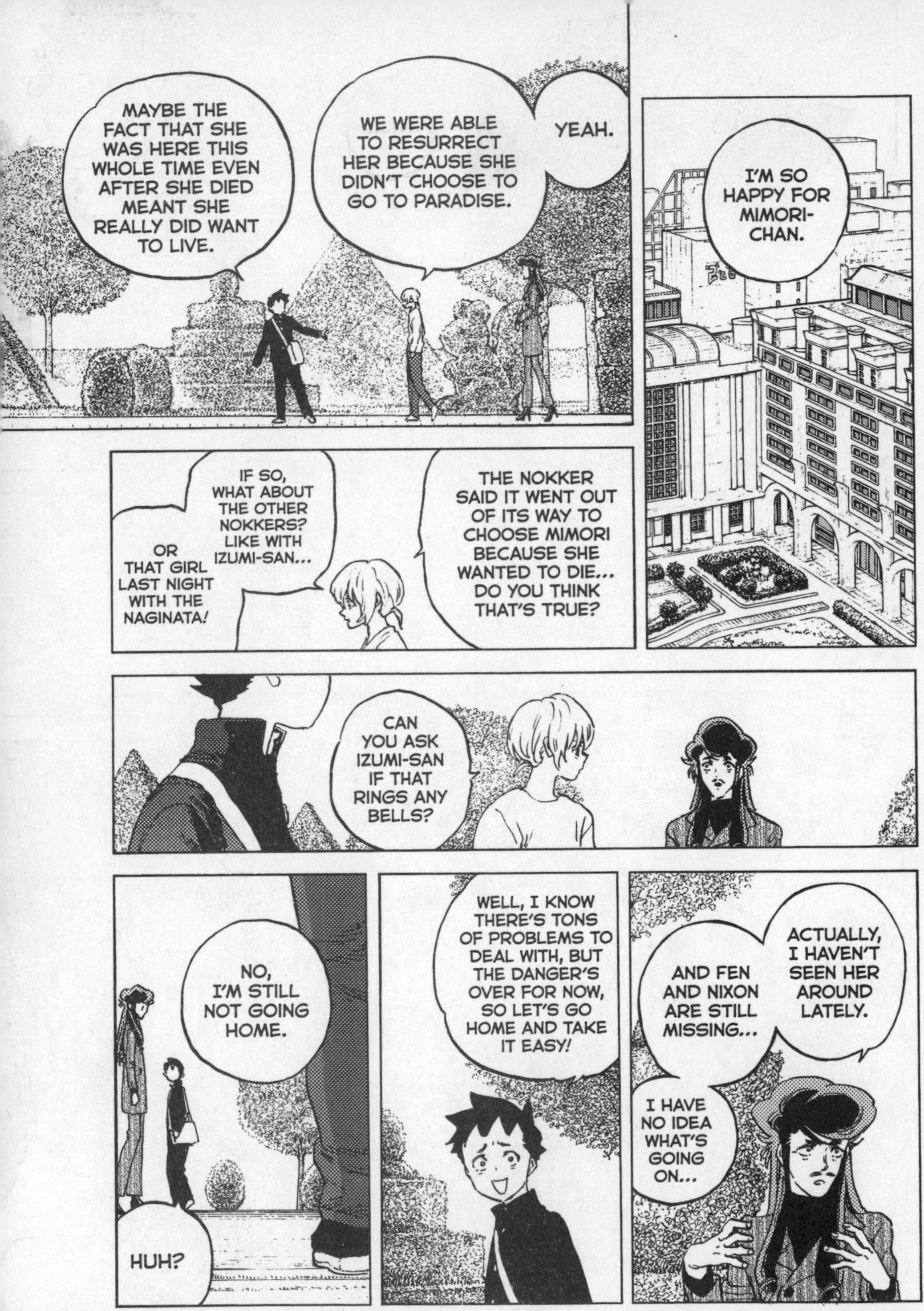
I'M SO HAPPY FOR MIMORI-CHAN.
YEAH.
WE WERE ABLE TO RESURRECT HER BECAUSE SHE DIDN'T CHOOSE TO GO TO PARADISE.
MAYBE THE FACT THAT SHE WAS HERE THIS WHOLE TIME EVEN AFTER SHE DIED MEANT SHE REALLY DID WANT TO LIVE.
THE NOKKER SAID IT WENT OUT OF ITS WAY TO CHOOSE MIMORI BECAUSE SHE WANTED TO DIE... DO YOU THINK THAT'S TRUE?
IF SO, WHAT ABOUT THE OTHER NOKKERS? LIKE WITH IZUMI-SAN...
OR THAT GIRL LAST NIGHT WITH THE NAGINATA!
CAN YOU ASK IZUMI-SAN IF THAT RINGS ANY BELLS?
ACTUALLY, I HAVEN'T SEEN HER AROUND LATELY.
AND FEN AND NIXON ARE STILL MISSING...
I HAVE NO IDEA WHAT'S GOING ON...
WELL, I KNOW THERE'S TONS OF PROBLEMS TO DEAL WITH, BUT THE DANGER'S OVER FOR NOW, SO LET'S GO HOME AND TAKE IT EASY!
NO, I'M STILL NOT GOING HOME.
HUH?

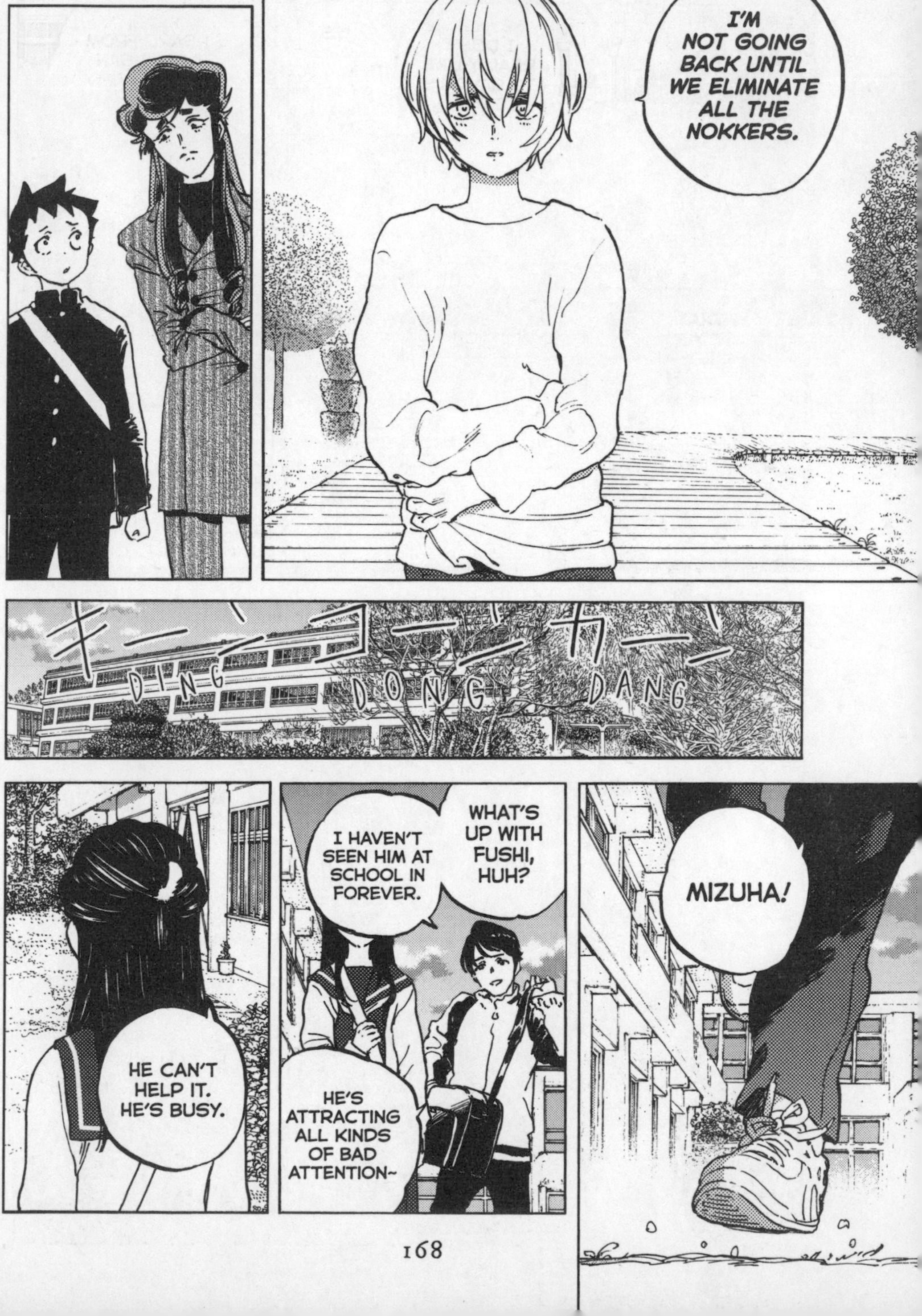
I'M NOT GOING BACK UNTIL WE ELIMINATE ALL THE NOKKERS.
キーンコーンカーン
DING DONG DANG
MIZUHA!
WHAT'S UP WITH FUSHI, HUH?
I HAVEN'T SEEN HIM AT SCHOOL IN FOREVER.
HE'S ATTRACTING ALL KINDS OF BAD ATTENTION~
HE CAN'T HELP IT. HE'S BUSY.

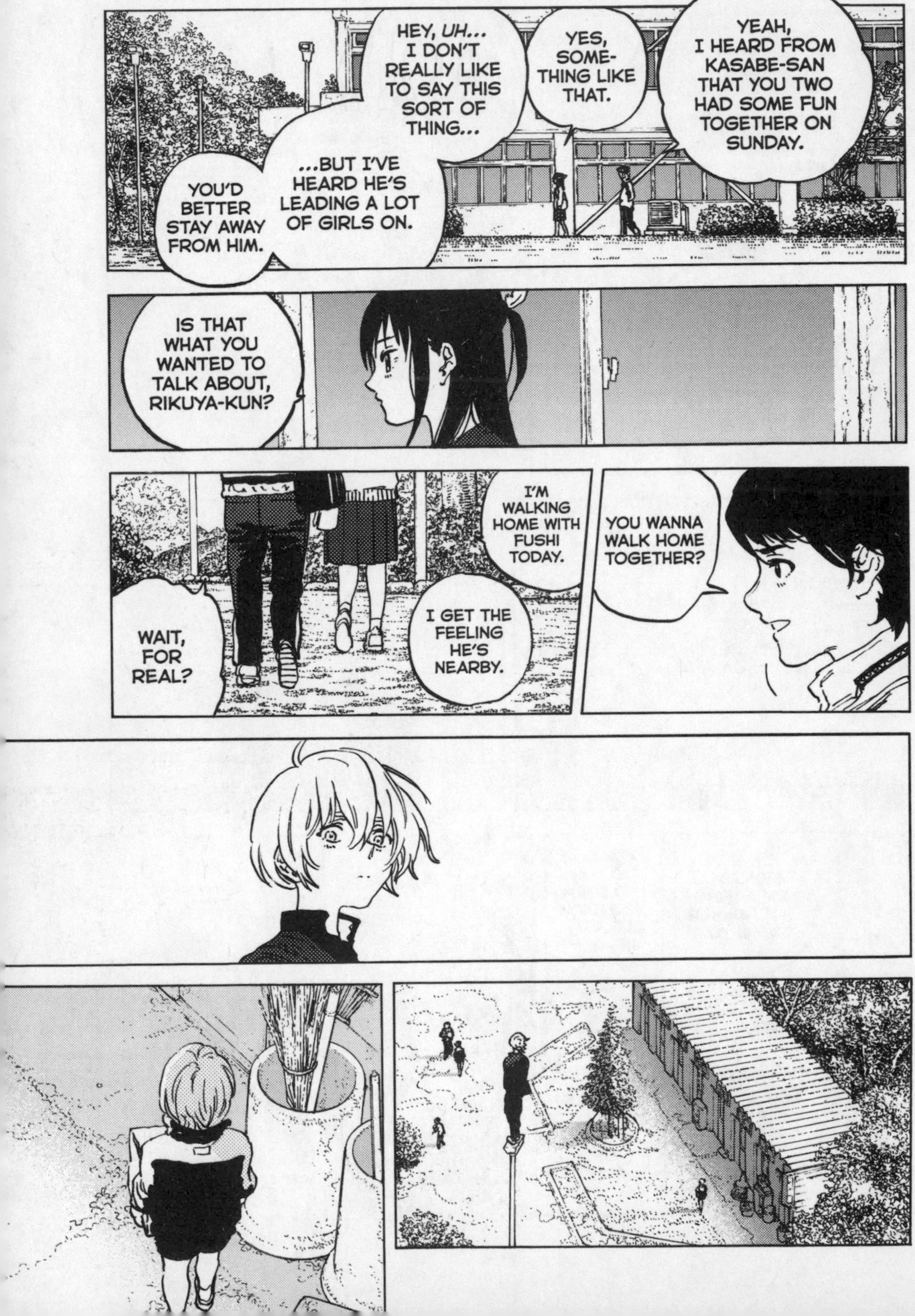
YEAH, I HEARD FROM KASABE-SAN THAT YOU TWO HAD SOME FUN TOGETHER ON SUNDAY.
YES, SOME-THING LIKE THAT.
HEY, *UH*... I DON'T REALLY LIKE TO SAY THIS SORT OF THING...
...BUT I'VE HEARD HE'S LEADING A LOT OF GIRLS ON.
YOU'D BETTER STAY AWAY FROM HIM.
IS THAT WHAT YOU WANTED TO TALK ABOUT, RIKUYA-KUN?
YOU WANNA WALK HOME TOGETHER?
I'M WALKING HOME WITH FUSHI TODAY.
I GET THE FEELING HE'S NEARBY.
WAIT, FOR REAL?

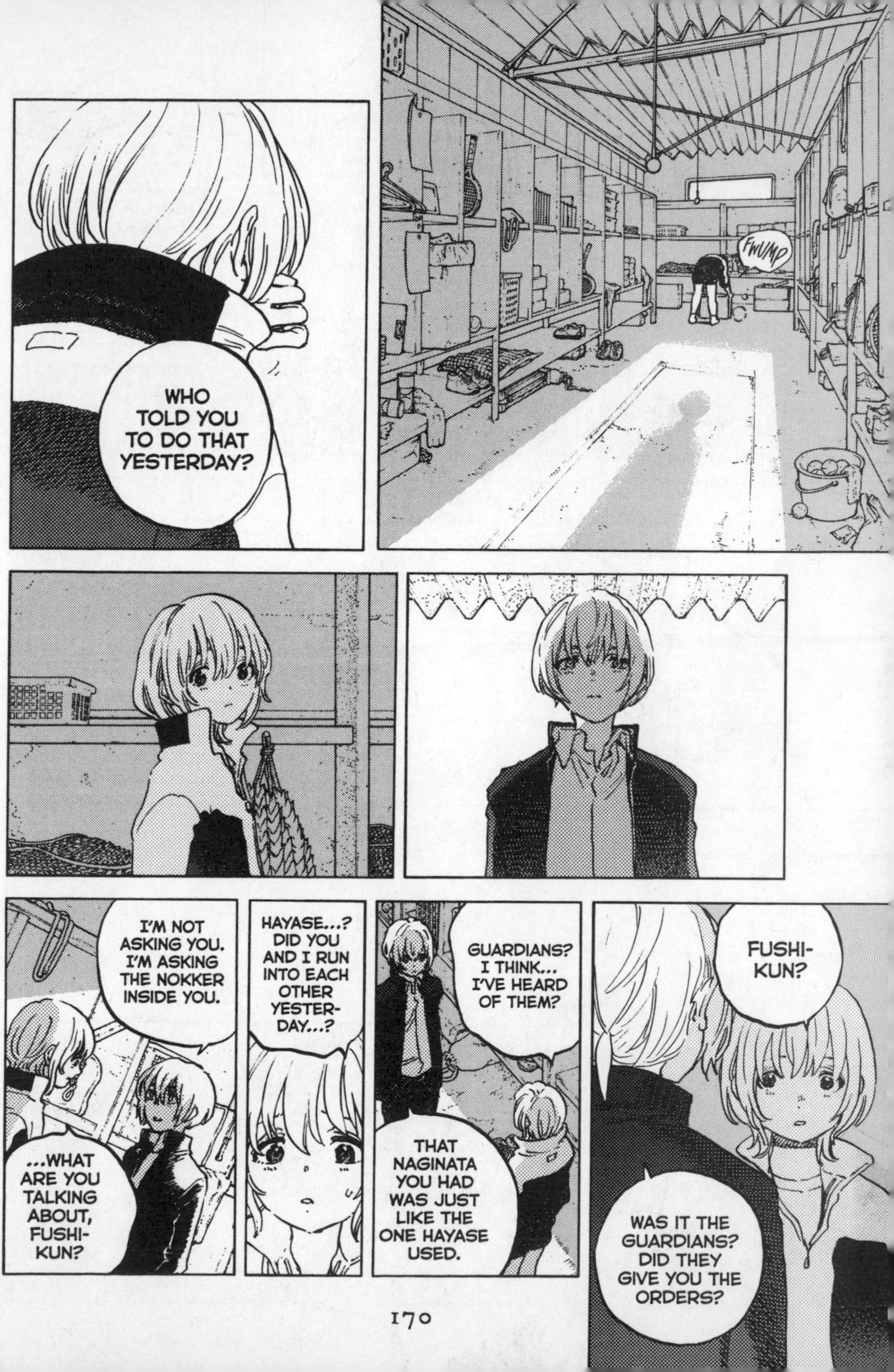
FWUMP
WHO TOLD YOU TO DO THAT YESTERDAY?
FUSHI-KUN?
WAS IT THE GUARDIANS? DID THEY GIVE YOU THE ORDERS?
GUARDIANS? I THINK... I'VE HEARD OF THEM?
THAT NAGINATA YOU HAD WAS JUST LIKE THE ONE HAYASE USED.
HAYASE...? DID YOU AND I RUN INTO EACH OTHER YESTER-DAY...?
I'M NOT ASKING YOU. I'M ASKING THE NOKKER INSIDE YOU.
...WHAT ARE YOU TALKING ABOUT, FUSHI-KUN?

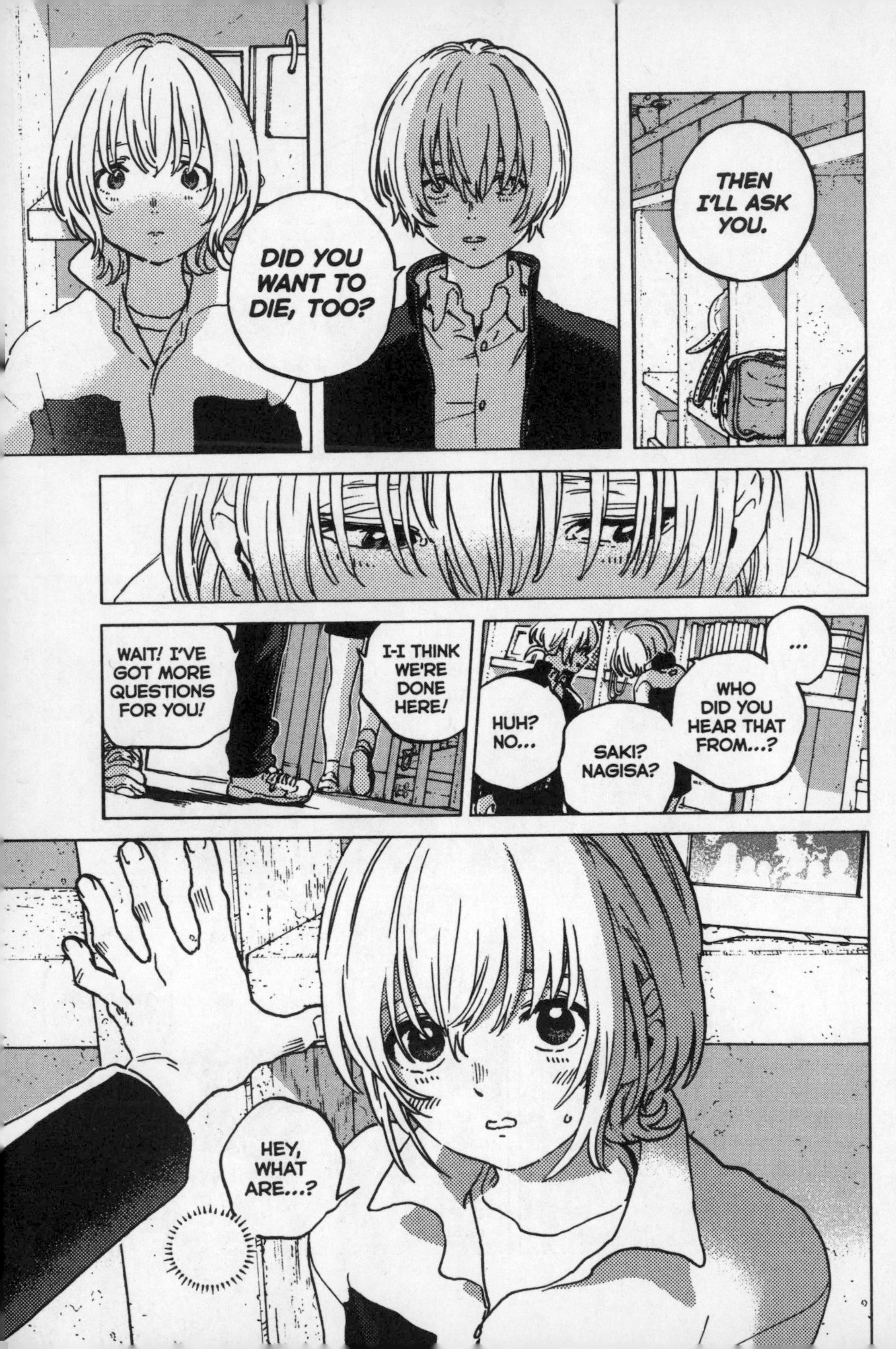
THEN I'LL ASK YOU.
DID YOU WANT TO DIE, TOO?
...
WHO DID YOU HEAR THAT FROM...?
SAKI? NAGISA?
HUH? NO...
I-I THINK WE'RE DONE HERE!
WAIT! I'VE GOT MORE QUESTIONS FOR YOU!
HEY, WHAT ARE...?

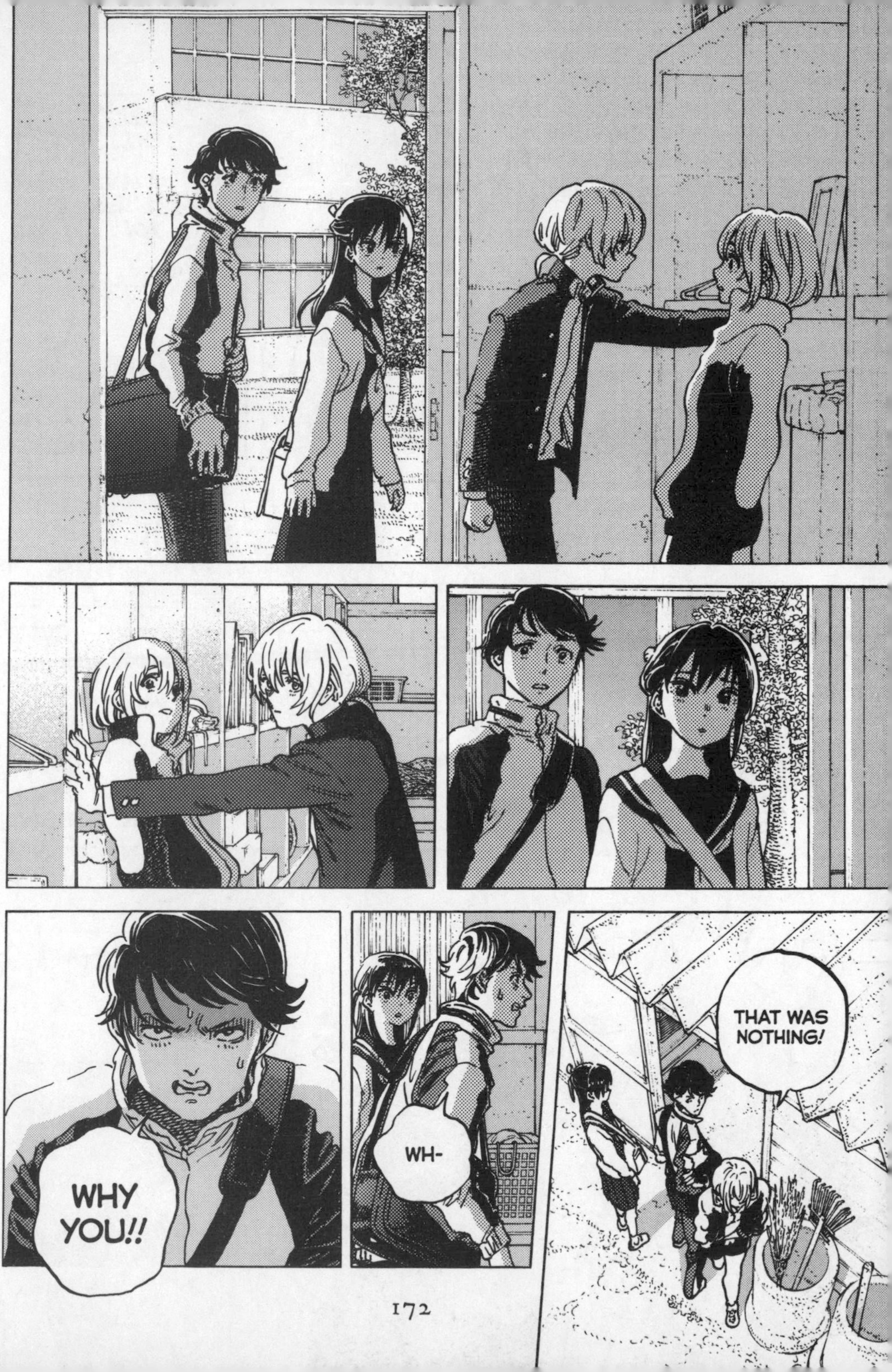
THAT WAS NOTHING!
WH-
WHY YOU!!

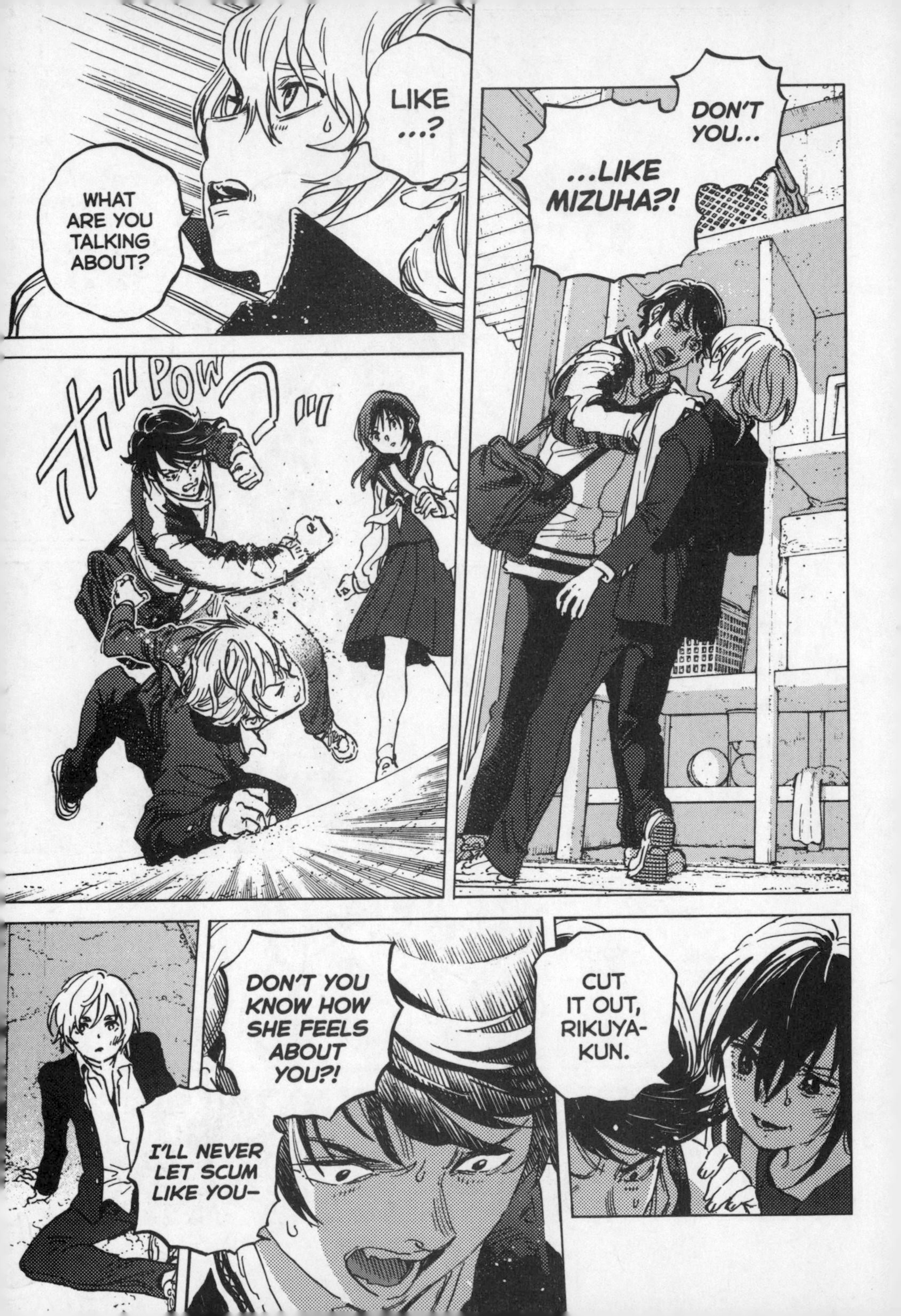
DON'T YOU...
...LIKE MIZUHA?!
LIKE ...?
WHAT ARE YOU TALKING ABOUT?
POW
CUT IT OUT, RIKUYA-KUN.
DON'T YOU KNOW HOW SHE FEELS ABOUT YOU?!
I'LL NEVER LET SCUM LIKE YOU–

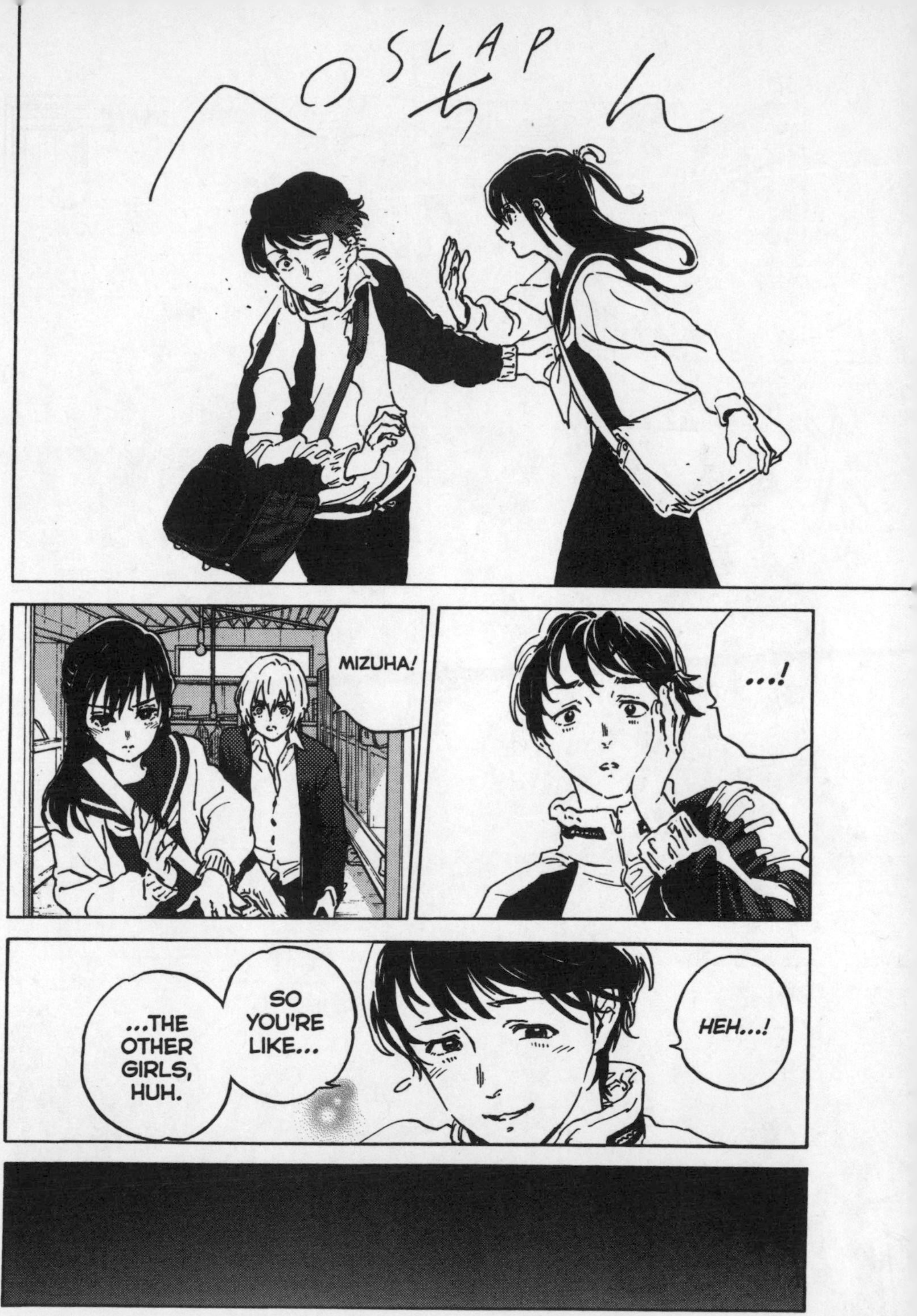
SLAP
ちん
...!
MIZUHA!
HEH...!
SO YOU'RE LIKE...
...THE OTHER GIRLS, HUH.

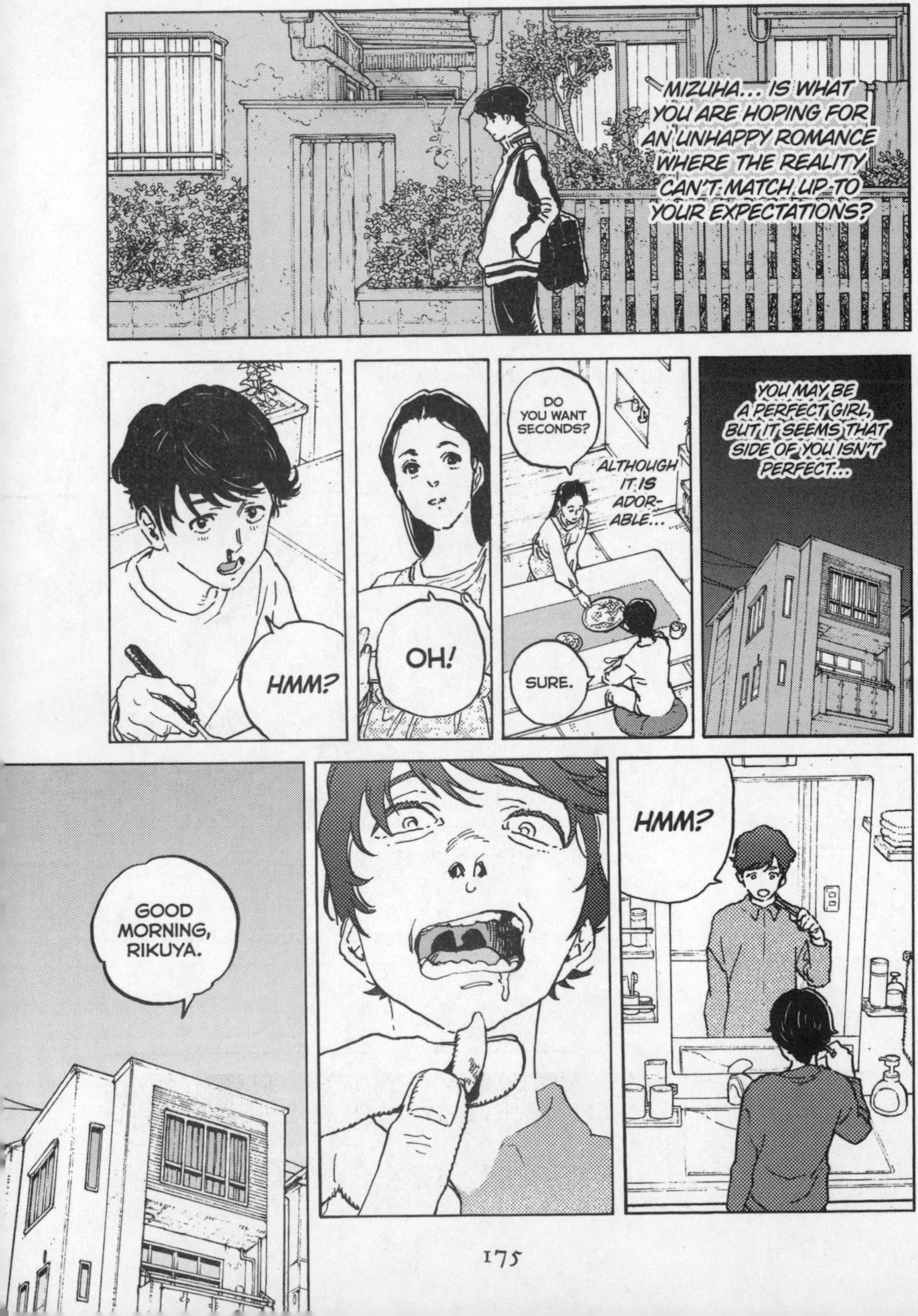
MIZUHA... IS WHAT YOU ARE HOPING FOR AN UNHAPPY ROMANCE WHERE THE REALITY CAN'T MATCH UP TO YOUR EXPECTATIONS?
YOU MAY BE A PERFECT GIRL, BUT IT SEEMS THAT SIDE OF YOU ISN'T PERFECT...
DO YOU WANT SECONDS?
ALTHOUGH IT IS ADOR-ABLE...
SURE.
OH!
HMM?
HMM?
GOOD MORNING, RIKUYA.

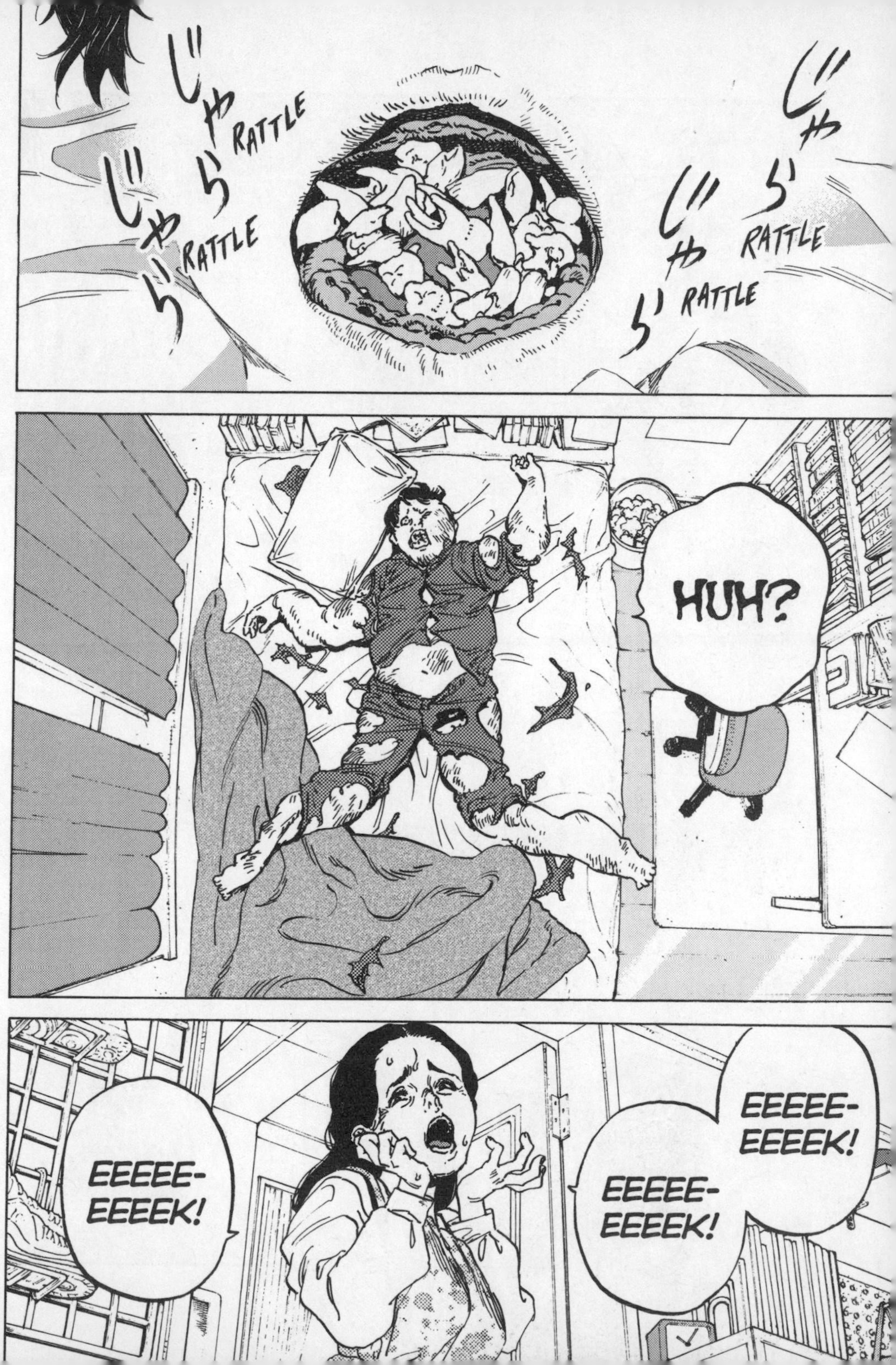

じゃら RATTLE
じゃら RATTLE
じゃら RATTLE
じゃら RATTLE
HUH?
EEEEE-EEEEK!
EEEEE-EEEEK!
EEEEE-EEEEK!

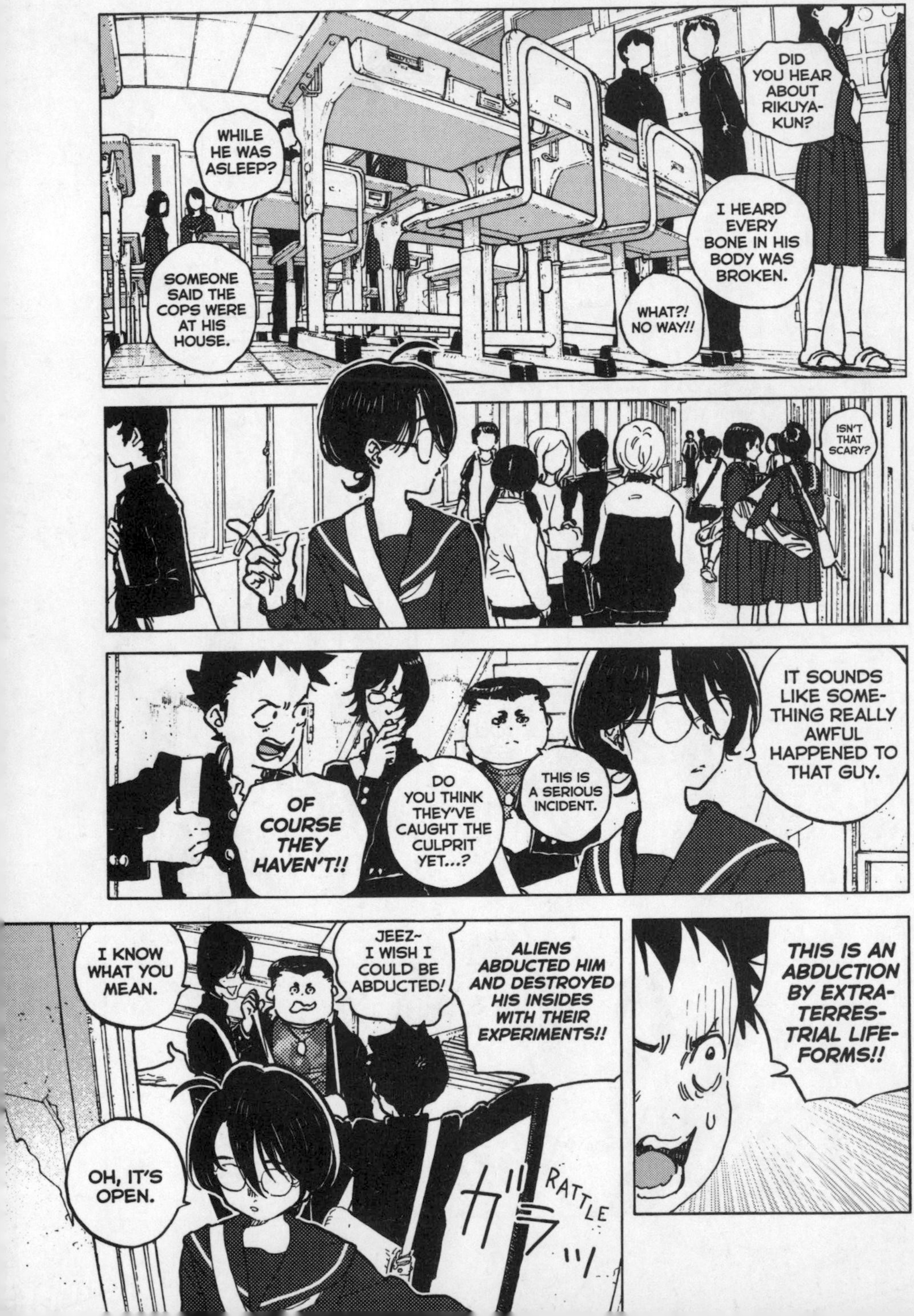
DID YOU HEAR ABOUT RIKUYA-KUN?
I HEARD EVERY BONE IN HIS BODY WAS BROKEN.
WHAT?! NO WAY!!
WHILE HE WAS ASLEEP?
SOMEONE SAID THE COPS WERE AT HIS HOUSE.
ISN'T THAT SCARY?
IT SOUNDS LIKE SOMETHING REALLY AWFUL HAPPENED TO THAT GUY.
THIS IS A SERIOUS INCIDENT.
DO YOU THINK THEY'VE CAUGHT THE CULPRIT YET...?
OF COURSE THEY HAVEN'T!!
THIS IS AN ABDUCTION BY EXTRATERRESTRIAL LIFEFORMS!!
ALIENS ABDUCTED HIM AND DESTROYED HIS INSIDES WITH THEIR EXPERIMENTS!!
JEEZ~ I WISH I COULD BE ABDUCTED!
I KNOW WHAT YOU MEAN.
OH, IT'S OPEN.
RATTLE

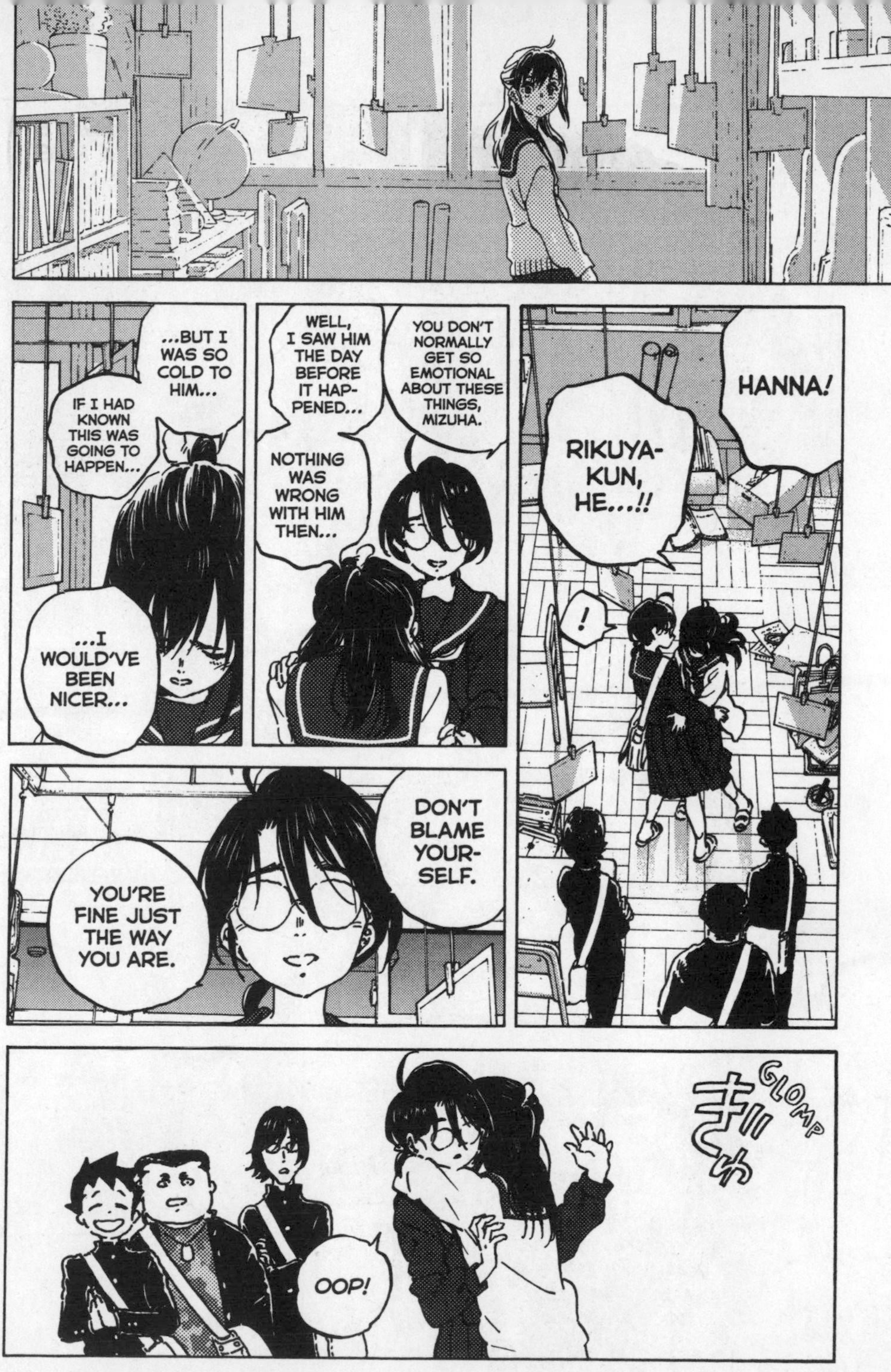
HANNA!
RIKUYA-KUN, HE...!!
!
YOU DON'T NORMALLY GET SO EMOTIONAL ABOUT THESE THINGS, MIZUHA.
WELL, I SAW HIM THE DAY BEFORE IT HAPPENED...
NOTHING WAS WRONG WITH HIM THEN...
...BUT I WAS SO COLD TO HIM...
IF I HAD KNOWN THIS WAS GOING TO HAPPEN...
...I WOULD'VE BEEN NICER...
DON'T BLAME YOURSELF.
YOU'RE FINE JUST THE WAY YOU ARE.
GLOMP
OOP!

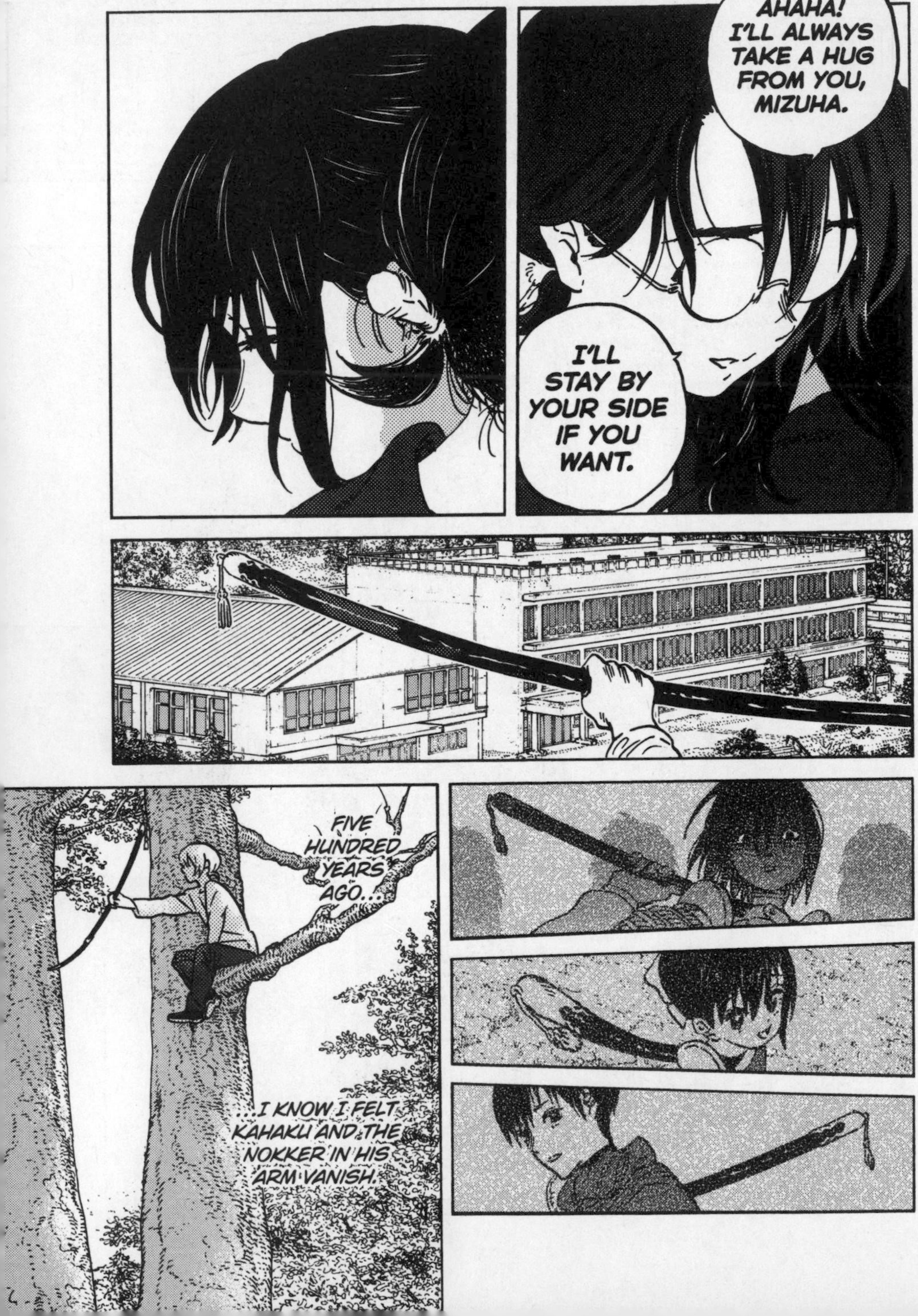
AHAHA! I'LL ALWAYS TAKE A HUG FROM YOU, MIZUHA.
I'LL STAY BY YOUR SIDE IF YOU WANT.
FIVE HUNDRED YEARS AGO...
...I KNOW I FELT KAHAKU AND THE NOKKER IN HIS ARM VANISH.

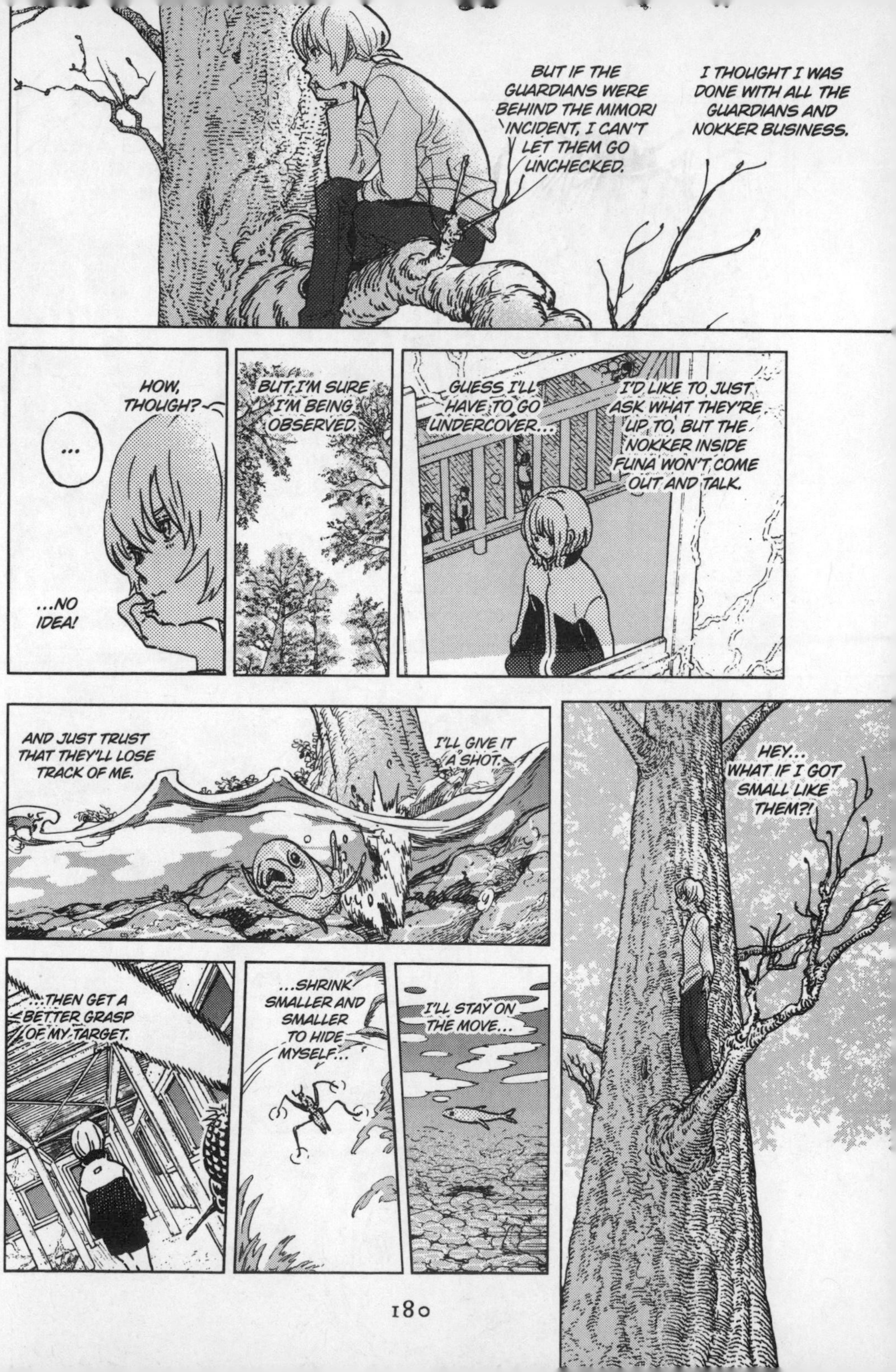
I THOUGHT I WAS DONE WITH ALL THE GUARDIANS AND NOKKER BUSINESS.
BUT IF THE GUARDIANS WERE BEHIND THE MIMORI INCIDENT, I CAN'T LET THEM GO UNCHECKED.
I'D LIKE TO JUST ASK WHAT THEY'RE UP TO, BUT THE NOKKER INSIDE FUNA WON'T COME OUT AND TALK.
GUESS I'LL HAVE TO GO UNDERCOVER...
BUT I'M SURE I'M BEING OBSERVED.
HOW, THOUGH?
...
...NO IDEA!
HEY... WHAT IF I GOT SMALL LIKE THEM?!
I'LL GIVE IT A SHOT.
AND JUST TRUST THAT THEY'LL LOSE TRACK OF ME.
I'LL STAY ON THE MOVE...
...SHRINK SMALLER AND SMALLER TO HIDE MYSELF...
...THEN GET A BETTER GRASP OF MY TARGET.

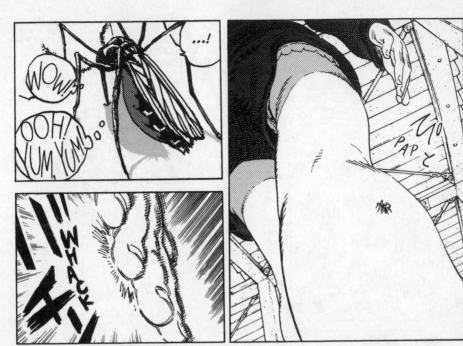

WOW!!

OOH!
YUM, YUM.

....!

WHACK!!

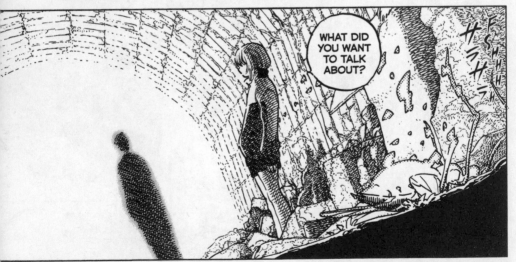

WHAT DID
YOU WANT
TO TALK
ABOUT?

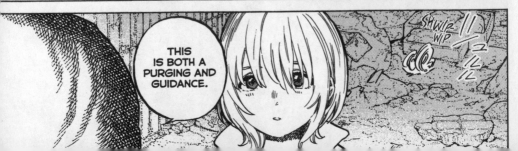

THIS
IS BOTH A
PURGING AND
GUIDANCE.

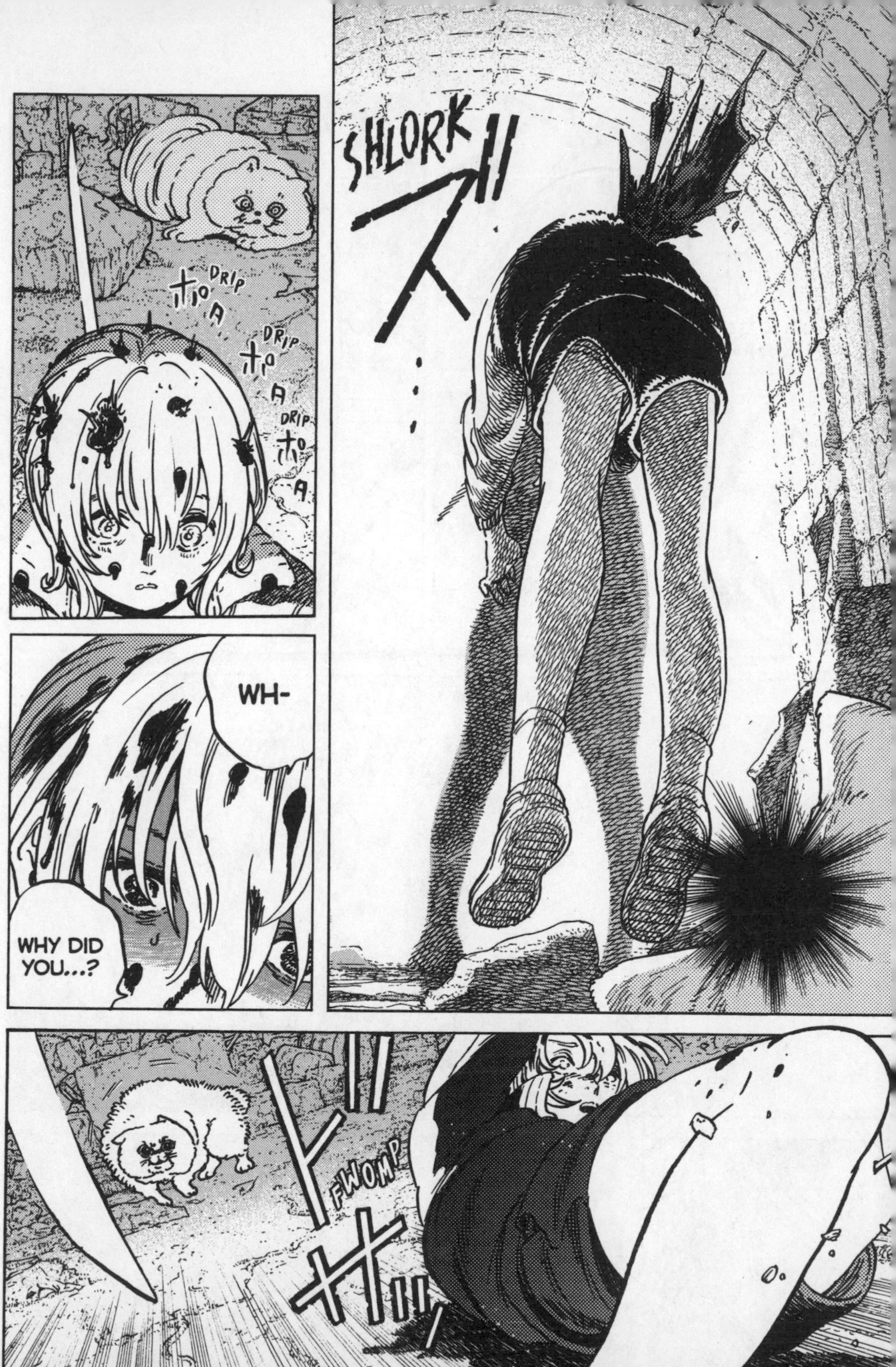
SHLORK
DRIP
DRIP
DRIP
WH-
WHY DID YOU...?
FWOMP

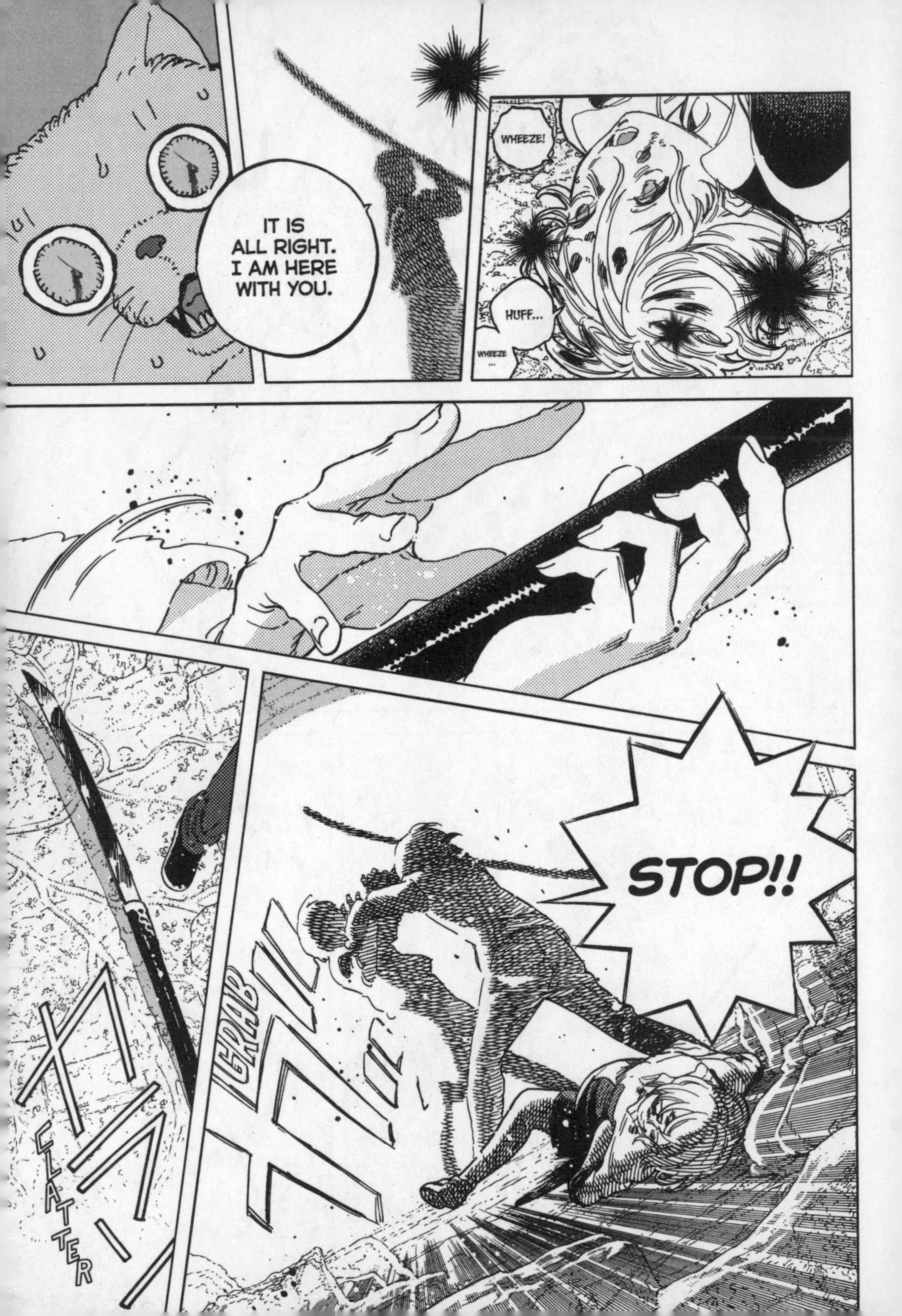

WHEEZE!
HUFF...
WHEEZE ...
IT IS ALL RIGHT. I AM HERE WITH YOU.
STOP!!
GRAB
CLATTER

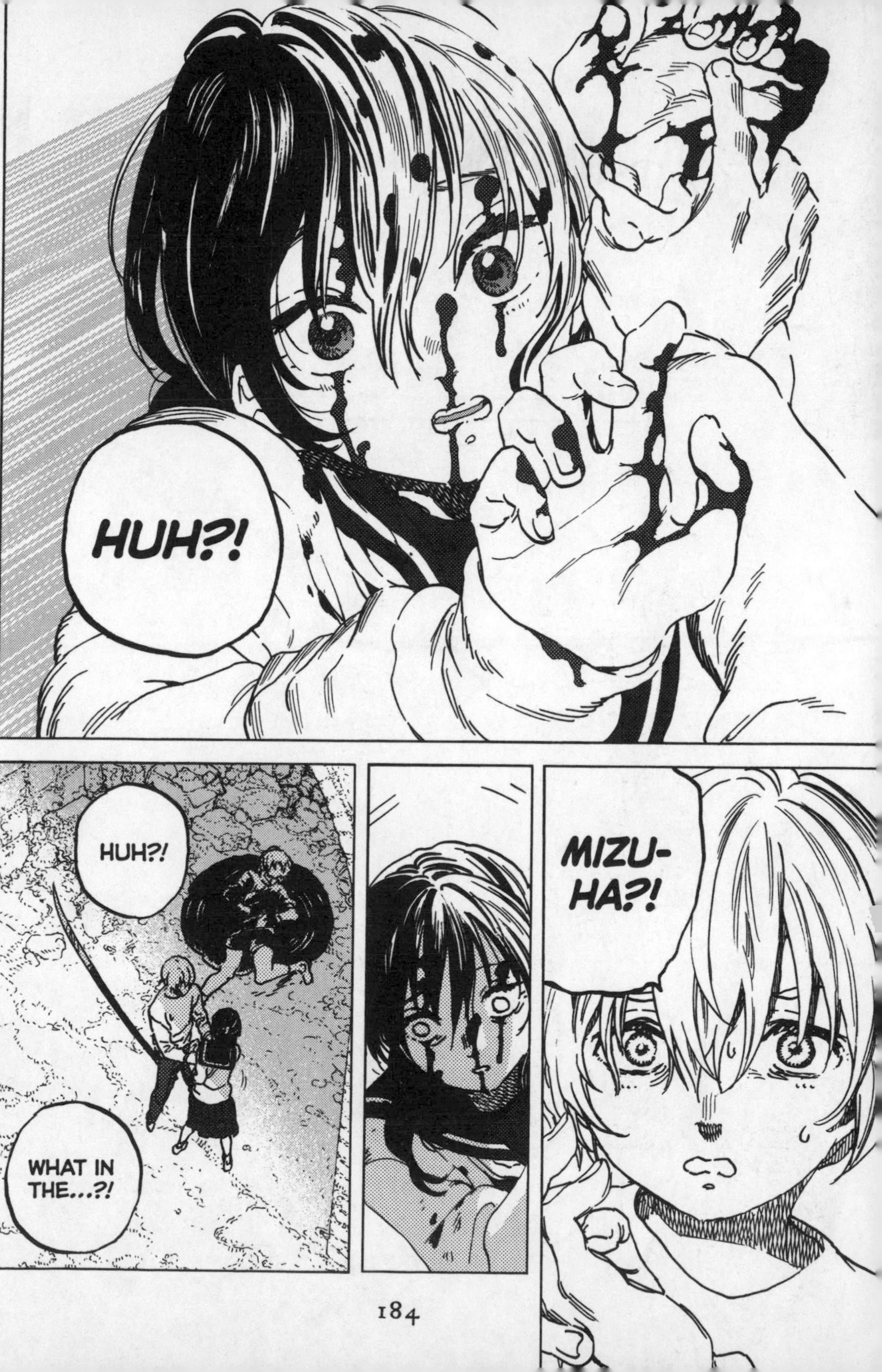
HUH?!
MIZU-HA?!
HUH?!
WHAT IN THE...?!

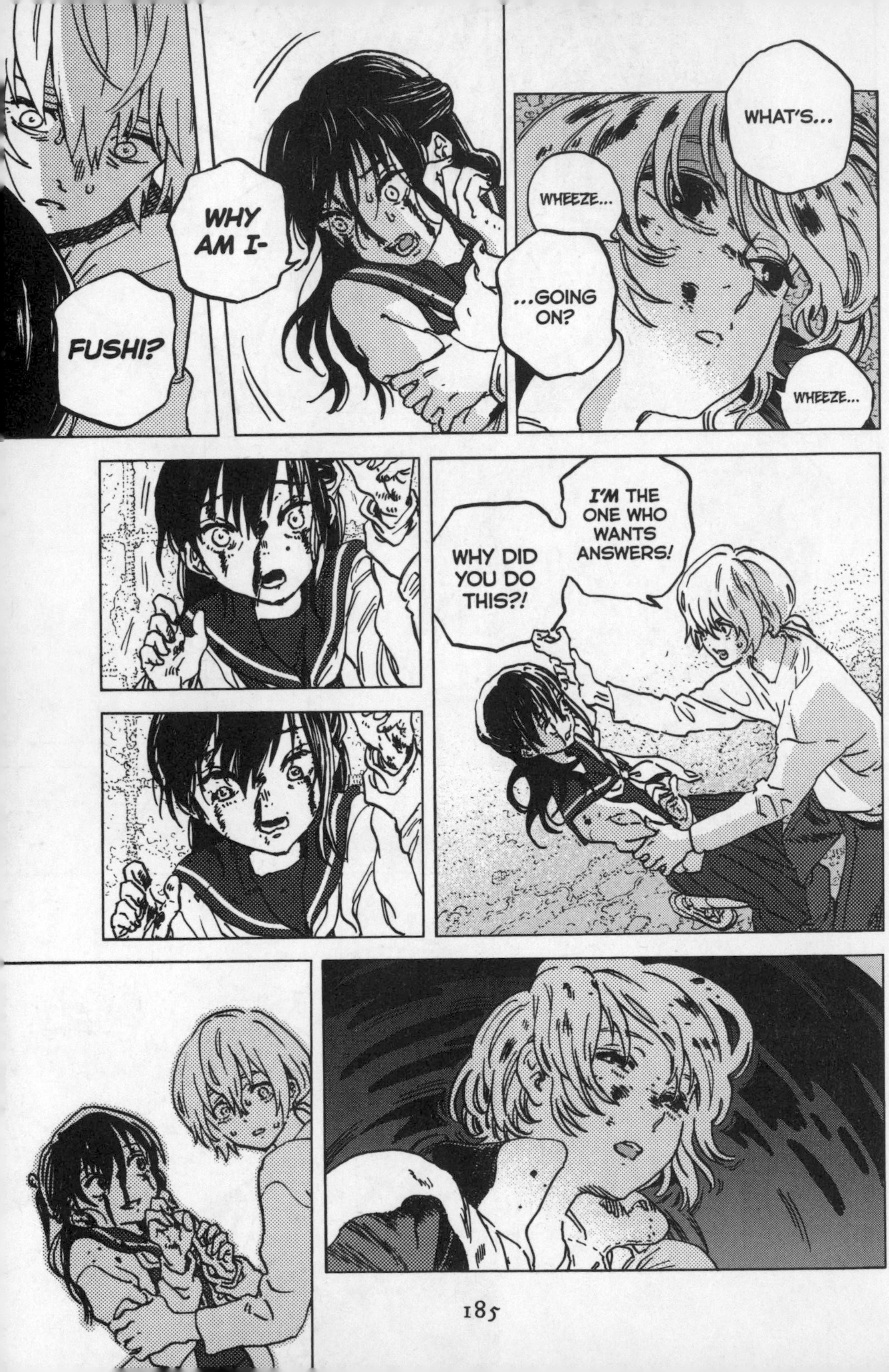
WHAT'S...
WHEEZE...
...GOING ON?
WHEEZE...
WHY AM I-
FUSHI?
I'M THE ONE WHO WANTS ANSWERS!
WHY DID YOU DO THIS?!

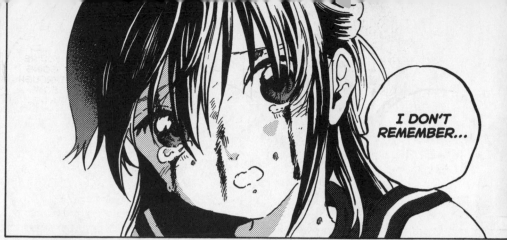

I DON'T REMEMBER...

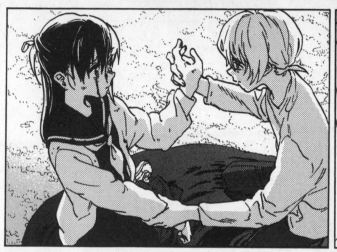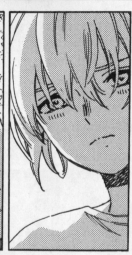

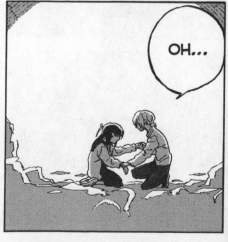

OH...

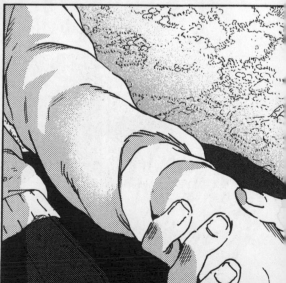

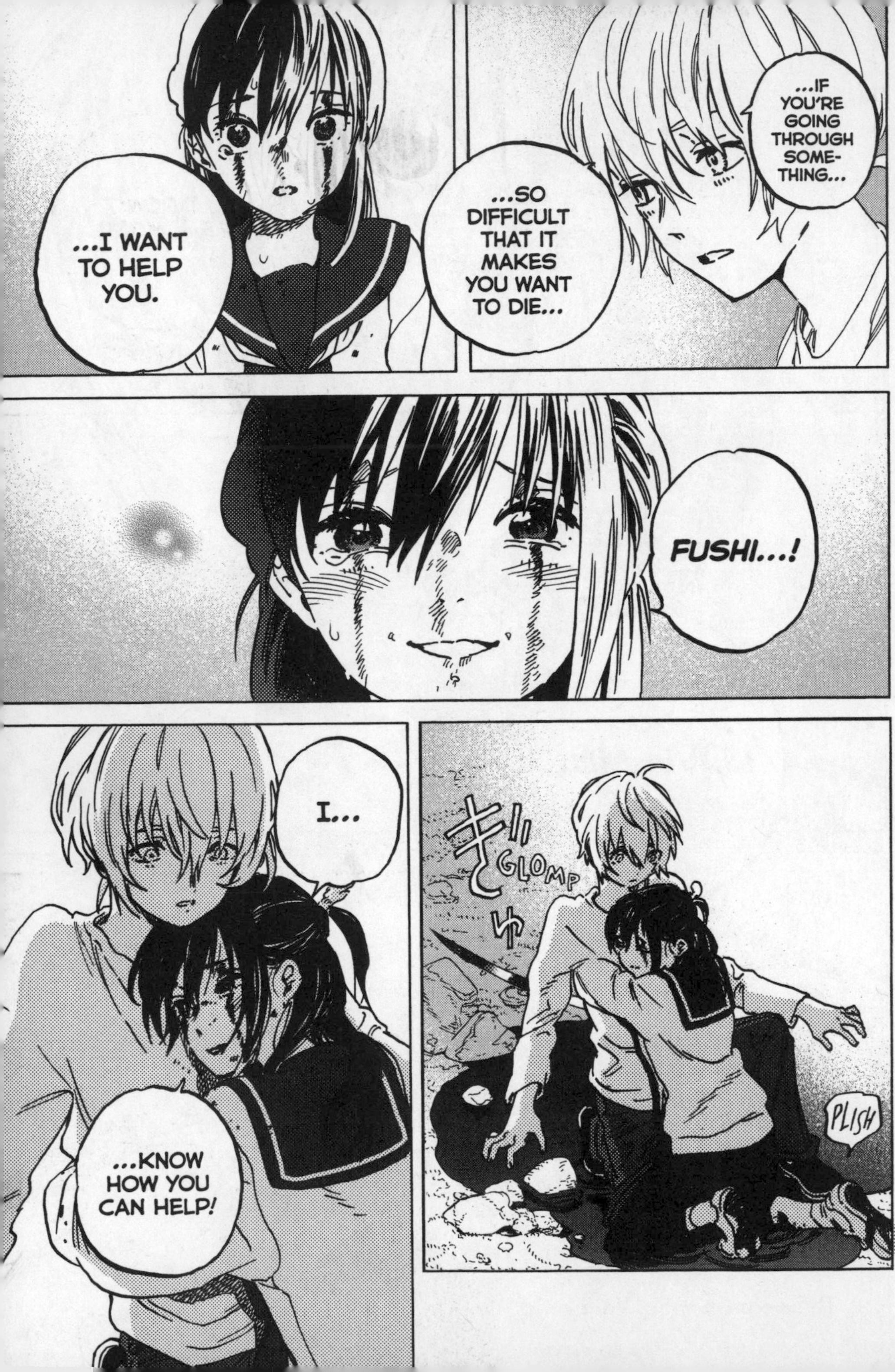
...IF YOU'RE GOING THROUGH SOME-THING...
...SO DIFFICULT THAT IT MAKES YOU WANT TO DIE...
...I WANT TO HELP YOU.
FUSHI...!
GLOMP
PLISH
I...
...KNOW HOW YOU CAN HELP!

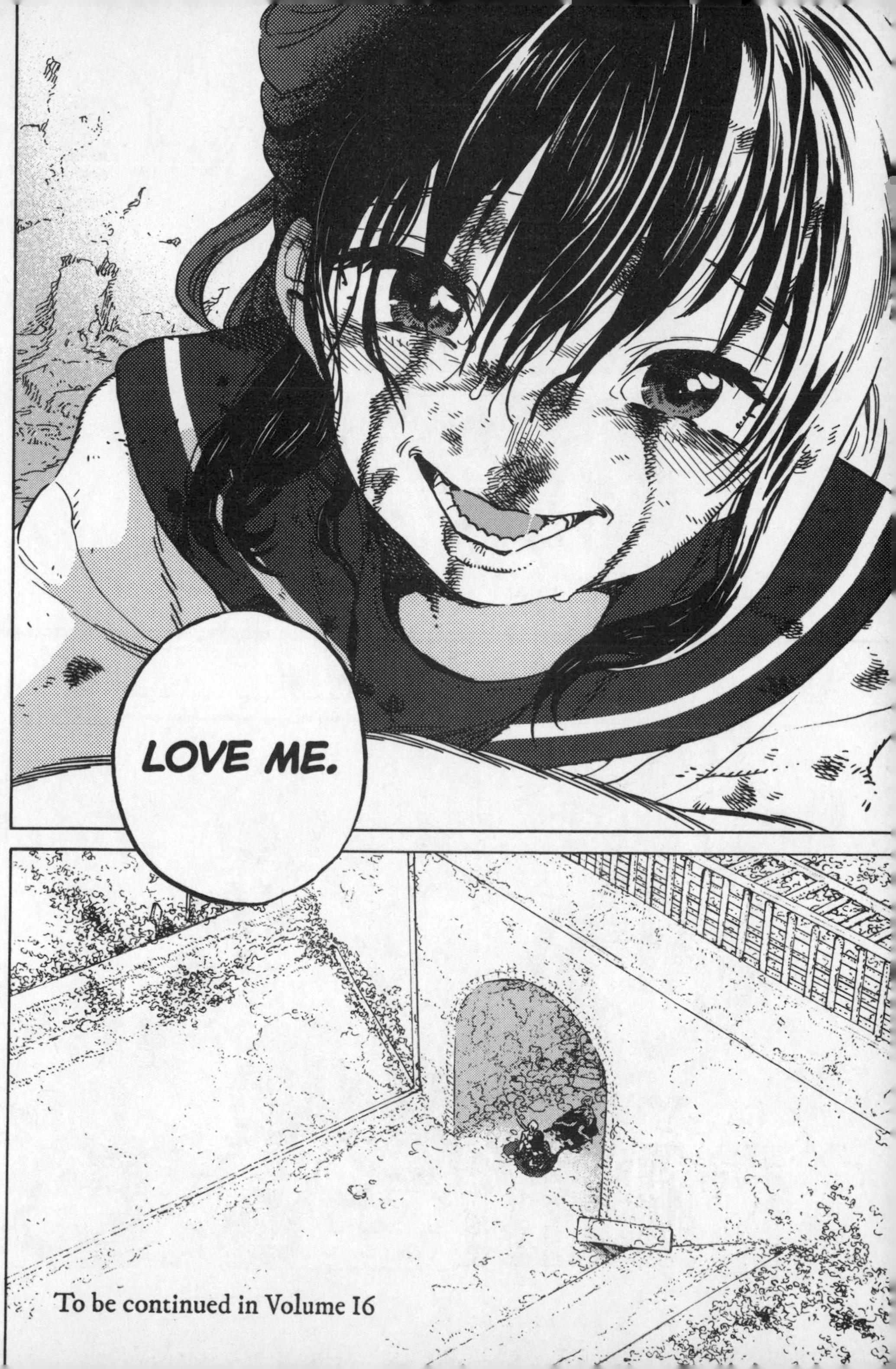
LOVE ME.
To be continued in Volume 16

TO YOUR ETERNITY

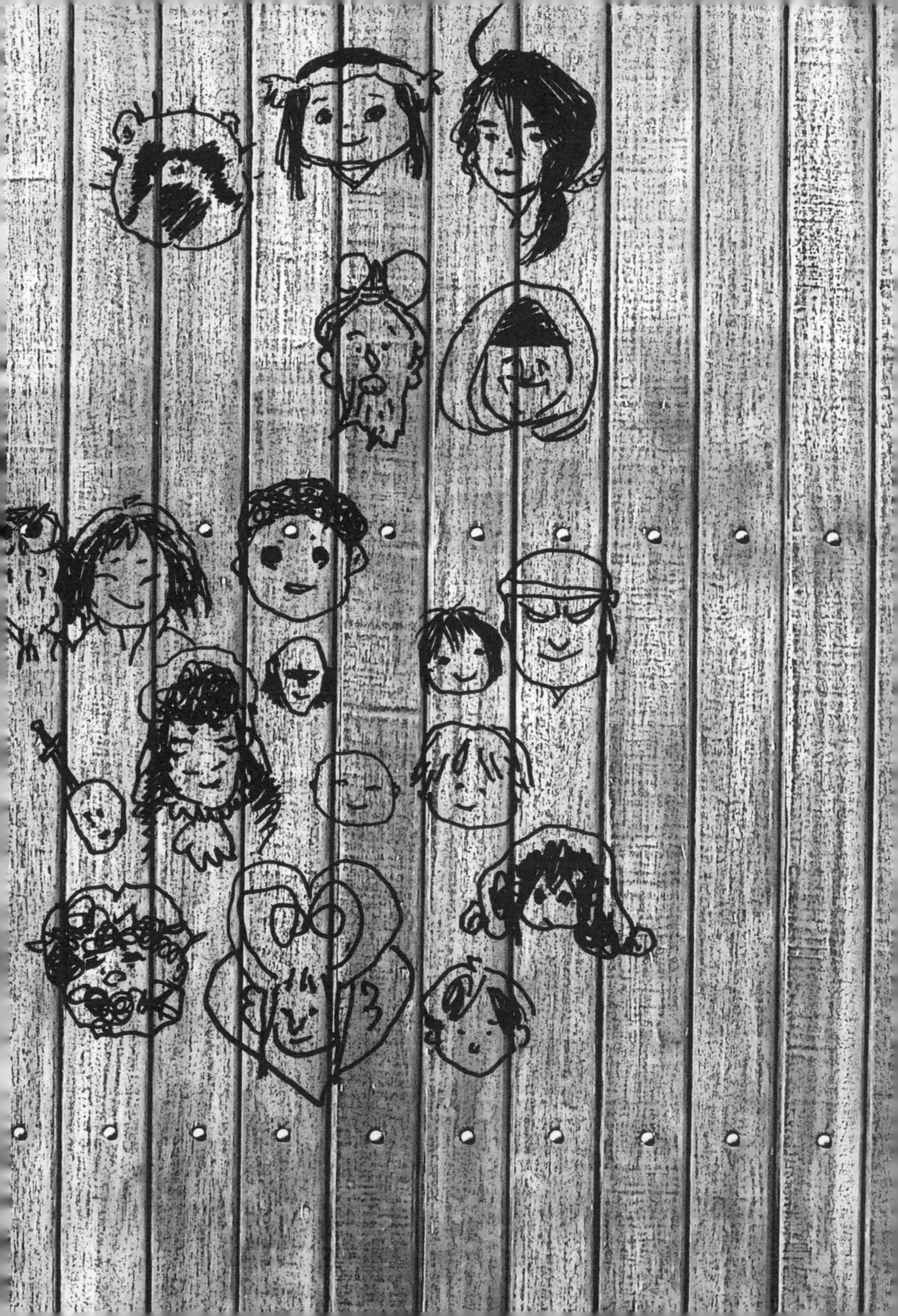

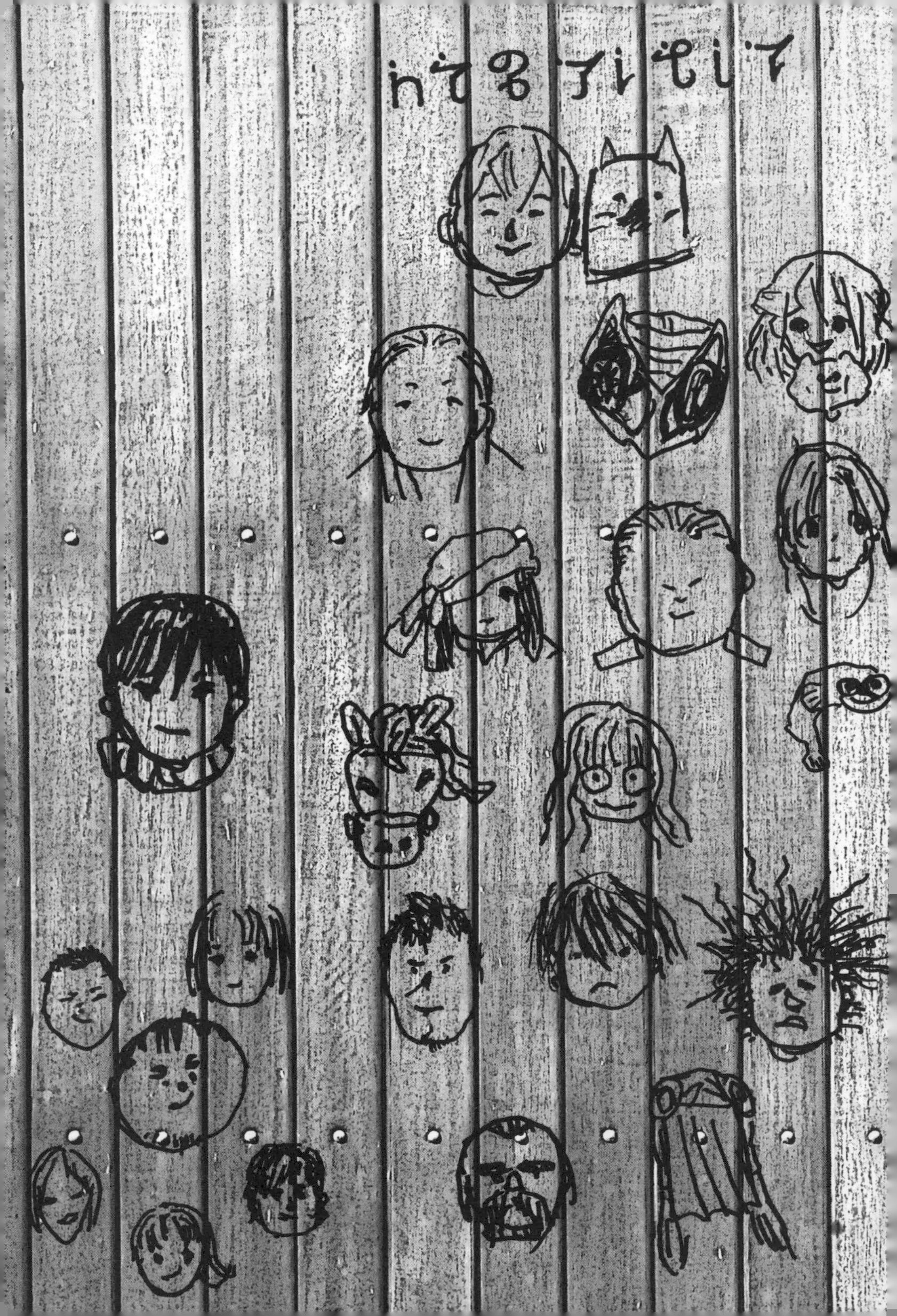

A Kodansha Comics Trade Paperback Original
To Your Eternity 15 copyright © 2021 Yoshitoki Oima
English translation copyright © 2021 Yoshitoki Oima

Published in the United States by Kodansha Comics, an imprint of Kodansha USA Publishing, LLC, New York.

Publication rights for this English edition arranged through Kodansha Ltd., Tokyo.

First published in Japan in 2021 by Kodansha Ltd., Tokyo as *Fumetsu no Anata e*, volume 15.

ISBN 978-1-64651-227-0

Cover Design: Tadashi Hisamochi (hive&co., Ltd.)
Title Logo Design: Shinobu Ohashi

Printed in the United States of America.

www.kodansha.us

1st Printing
Translation: Steven LeCroy
Lettering: Darren Smith
Editing: Haruko Hashimoto, Alexandra Swanson
Editorial Assistance: YKS Services LLC/SKY Japan, INC.
Kodansha Comics Edition Cover Design: Phil Balsman

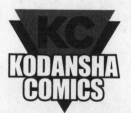

D0064042

Publisher: Kiichiro Sugawara

Director of publishing services: Ben Applegate
Associate director of operations: Stephen Pakula
Publishing services managing editors: Alanna Ruse, Madison Salters
Production managers: Emi Lotto, Angela Zurlo

NOV - - 2021